ALAN SUGAR

ALAN SUGAR

THE AMSTRAD STORY

DAVID THOMAS

CENTURY

LONDON SYDNEY AUCKLAND JOHANNESBURG

Published in Great Britain in 1990 by Century
An imprint of Random Century Ltd
20 Vauxhall Bridge Road, London SW1V 2SA

Century Hutchinson Australia (Pty) Ltd
20 Alfred Street, Milsons Point, Sydney, NSW 2061, Australia

Century Hutchinson New Zealand Ltd
PO Box 40-086, 32–34 View Road, Glenfield, Auckland 10, New Zealand

Century Hutchinson South Africa (Pty) Ltd
PO Box 337, Bergvlei 2012, South Africa

David Thomas's right to be identified as the author of this
work has been asserted by him in accordance with the Copyright,
Designs and Patents Act, 1988.

Set in Linotron Baskerville
Printed and bound in Great Britain by
Mackays of Chatham, Chatham, Kent

British Library Cataloguing in Publication data
Thomas, David
Alan Sugar: the Amstrad story.
1. Great Britain. Microcomputer industries. Sugar, Alan
I. Title
338.76100416092

ISBN 0-7126-3518-1

Contents

Preface

I became interested in Alan Sugar and Amstrad between 1986 and 1988, when I wrote about the electronics industry for the *Financial Times*. But it was only after I switched jobs within the *FT* that I approached him with the idea of a book.

At first he was reluctant. Asked by many writers and publishers to tell the story of how he had spearheaded Amstrad's startling rise to prominence in the 1980s, his indifference to personal publicity had always prompted him to refuse.

My first thanks must therefore go to Alan Sugar himself for finally agreeing to cooperate with the writing of this book. Not only did he allow me full access to Amstrad's staff; he also gave me introductions to members of his family, including his mother, sister and brother, and to friends and early business associates who knew him long before he became a figure on the national scene. Another journalist once asked Sugar what he did at weekends: 'Avoid journalists and photographers' was his prompt, heartfelt answer. I realize how much it must have gone against the grain for him to be interviewed for this book at length, in his home and at the weekend.

My next debt is to Amstrad's directors and employees who willingly agreed to be interviewed for this project. The company has a reputation for hostility towards journalists, but this was not something which I experienced. I must single out for special thanks Nick Hewer of Michael Joyce Consultants, Amstrad's public relations adviser, who has a deep understanding of the affairs of his client: only fellow journalists will realize how rare this is in his profession.

I showed Alan Sugar a draft of the book because I was keen to remove the inevitable inaccuracies that creep into a story of this kind. After receiving his comments, I made some changes to the draft. But it was clear to everyone before I started the project that it was to be an independent account of the Amstrad chairman and his company. I am therefore entirely responsible for the book's contents and conclusions.

I am very grateful to the many people who gave up their time to be interviewed for the book. They include Richard Altwasser, Ken Ashcroft, Paul Bailey, Matthew Bullock, Richard Clayton, Malcolm Cross, Maureen Cross, Greg Delaney, José Luis Dominguez, Gerry Eriera, Norma Eriera, David Gibbons, David Goldman, Guy Gordon, John Grant, Graham Grist, Chris Hall, Peter Henson, Tim Holland-Bosworth, Peter Hobson, Michael Hollingbery, Peter Horrell, Patrick Isherwood, David Johnson, Mark-Eric Jones, Stanley Kalms, Diana Kieve, Jeffrey Kieve, Gulu Lalvani, Robert Lawrence, Barney Lazarus, Myrna Lazarus, Colin Lewin, Nick Lightowler, Ronnie Marks, Gerry Mason, Ted Merrette, Malcolm Miller, Greg Morgan, Ashley Morris, Margaret Mountford, Rupert Murdoch, Howard Myles, Ron Nixon, Swraj Paul, Roland Perry, Martin Pluck, William Poel, Vic Pollard, Thomas Power, Stan Randall, Jim Rice, Bernhard Schneider, Sir Clive Sinclair, Peter Smith, Callen So, Fay Sugar, Jimmy Tarbuck, David Thomson, Eric Tracey, Marion Vannier, Bob Watkins, Lord Weinstock, Arnold Wesker, Terry Wilding, Paul Williams, Keith Woolcock, Barry Young and Lord Young. There were others who agreed to be interviewed on condition that they were not named.

Some colleagues from the trade press discussed with me aspects of Amstrad and the various markets in which it has operated. I am particularly grateful to Guy Kewney of *PC Dealer*, John Lettice of *Microscope* and Arthur Ord-Hume of *Independent Electrical Retailer*. Several magazines allowed me to look through their libraries or back copies including *Campaign*, *Electrical Retailer and Trader*, *Hi-Fi*

News, Microscope, PC Dealer, PC User, Personal Computer World and *Which Computer?*. Brigitte Morel in Dataquest's Paris office shared with me her knowledge of personal computer markets in Continental Europe, as did Richard Hyman of Verdict his understanding of electrical goods retailers in Britain.

I could not have wished for a better agent than Arthur Goodhart, who helped me in ways too numerous to detail. I am grateful to Mark Booth, my editor at Century Hutchinson, for his civilized approach to his task. My friends Paul Abrahams, Daniel Green, Richard Lapper and Raymond Snoddy commented helpfully on drafts of some chapters.

Finally, I would like to thank for everything the two Jennys – Jenny Rossiter and Jenny Somerville Thomas – to whom this book is dedicated with gratitude, love and affection.

· 1 ·

Sugar Goes Public

Pip Greenwell became more and more restless as his chauffeur inched his way through the traffic. They had left the City behind and swept through what seemed to Greenwell's moneyed eye the wastelands of Hackney. Yet as they pushed further north out of the centre of London, they had suddenly ploughed into a dense line of cars.

Greenwell was on his way to meet a man called Alan Sugar, who was thinking of selling some shares in his audio company, Amstrad. It was not likely to be the largest business deal ever handled by the senior partner of W. Greenwell, one of the City's most prosperous stockbrokers. But Greenwell, a product of Winchester, was a gentleman of the old school. He was punctual to a fault and, at this rate, he reckoned they would never reach Tottenham on time. He told his chauffeur to get a move on.

The stockbroker was much relieved when the car finally turned into the road housing Amstrad's headquarters, even though the sight which greeted him was not one to lift the spirit. Squashed between a railway line and a patch of derelict ground, Garman Road was completely made over to nondescript medium-sized factories and warehouses. Their proprietors were clearly too busy to worry about a lick of paint or any other decoration.

Matters did not improve when Greenwell was ushered through a hallway strewn with cardboard boxes into Alan Sugar's presence. At 32, Sugar seemed too young to be running a company which was thinking of going public. As if to underline his youth, the Amstrad chairman had parked the knot of his tie a couple of inches below the unbuttoned collar of his shirt. He was sporting a stubbly beard at a time when a clean-shaven face was part of the City's uniform.

This stocky, bearded youth appeared none too welcoming, as he stood there tense and with a scowl on his face. Greenwell wondered whether Sugar shared his distaste for being late, and thought it politic to ask forgiveness for this sin. 'I'm so terribly sorry we're late, but the fucking traffic was awful.'

The swear-word sounded odd when uttered in Greenwell's cultured voice. There was a moment of silence as it hung in the air between the stockbroker and the entrepreneur. Then the tension flowed out of Sugar's body and he broke into a grin. 'Thank God someone in the City speaks my sort of language,' he said as he stepped forward to shake Greenwell's hand.

*

New money was meeting old that day in the summer of 1979 when Alan Sugar shook Pip Greenwell's hand. It was little more than ten years since Sugar had emerged from those same poor Hackney streets through which Greenwell had been driven to launch a one-man business selling car aerials and other electrical goods from the back of a van. He had spent the 1970s criss-crossing Britain and the Far East, hunting out ways to undercut his competitors at the low end of the audio market. As the decade drew to a close, Sugar was about to be rewarded for this period of relentless activity.

The group of the City's best and brightest – who set to work on Amstrad's flotation soon after Greenwell's meeting with Sugar – had little reason to realize they were dealing with anything out of the ordinary. The most optimistic among them hoped that Amstrad would consolidate its position in the audio market and grow at a respectable but not earth-shattering rate – perhaps 20–30 per cent a year. Alan Sugar would then be able to rest on his laurels, joining the ranks of quietly successful businessmen who are occasionally profiled in the duller reaches of the financial press.

This was not to be. During the next decade, Sugar was to become one of the best known businessmen in Britain. Amstrad's phenomenal success in the early and mid-1980s, when profits regularly doubled each year, sent the value of Sugar's own holding in the company into the stratosphere, and by August 1988 his fortune stood at £597 million. A few months earlier, he had been named by the *Sunday Times* as the fifteenth wealthiest person in Britain.

The manner in which Sugar led Amstrad was as distinctive as the success itself. Amstrad demonstrated a flexibility and a swiftness of foot which was quite out of keeping with the staid and stodgy traditions of British business. Just when its potential for continuing hyper-growth in the audio market was coming to an end, the company switched tack and launched into personal computers, a graveyard for a whole generation of British entrepreneurs.

Shrugging off a barrage of warnings from City and media pundits that he had chosen the worst possible moment to enter the computer industry, Sugar spearheaded the formation of the first truly mass market for computers in Britain. In the process, he affronted received wisdom in the industry by refusing to think of computers as pieces of techno-wizardry designed by boffins for boffins. Making a reliable computer that was cheap enough for the great majority of people to buy and simple enough for them to use: that was Sugar's goal.

This almost banal philosophy succeeded where more sophisticated attitudes had failed. Amstrad moved computing out of the data processing departments into the studies and spare bedrooms of Britain, helping to stimulate a revolution in the working habits of a whole generation of small business people and other professionals.

In the process, an Amstrad philosophy became discernible, elements of which ran through the company's successes in all its areas of activity from personal computing, through word processing, video recorders, music centres, amplifiers and car radios to

Citizen Band radios and more besides. Amstrad designs cheap and simple products by cutting out features which consumers do not really want; undercuts its competitors by manufacturing its products wherever it finds the best prices; retains the flexibility to switch its source of supply whenever a cheaper one emerges; drives prices down still further by manufacturing in large volumes for a mass market; stimulates that market through massive advertising campaigns; and transforms markets by encouraging a whole new segment of consumers to start using its simple, inexpensive products.

As the 1980s progressed, much ink was spilt debating this formula. Some people argued that it offered little in the way of general lessons for British or European business. Although transparently simple, the Amstrad formula also appeared to be inimitable; it worked on condition that none of the company's competitors went down the same route. There was room for only one Amstrad in any market, for its philosophy of price cutting required it to crowd out its competitors. Indeed, Amstrad often began to prepare to quit a market as soon as its competitors tried to follow its lead. And, the company's detractors argued, it brought little real wealth into Britain because most of its goods were made in the Far East.

Others contended that Sugar had cracked one of the key failings of modern British business: the inability to make and market consumer products for a mass market. Amstrad's success in France and Spain suggested that the company's formula could be exported. Ambitious business people eager to understand how to compete across Europe in the run-up to the completion of the common European market could learn from this unusual British company.

What became known as 'the Amstrad effect' deeply impressed some of the hardest and most sceptical businessmen in Britain. By the middle of the decade, the General Electric Company – Britain's biggest manufacturing group – was considering hiving off its consumer division to Amstrad. There was even talk of Alan Sugar as a possible successor to Lord Weinstock, G.E.C.'s long-serving managing director – a stunning compliment for a company and a man almost unknown a few years earlier.

Alan Sugar's success began to take on still wider significance. He was seen as an archetypal representative of the Thatcher decade. Through its deification of competition, Mrs Thatcher's Government was shattering institutions long considered to be pillars of the British economy: not just those associated with the Conservative Party's political opponents, such as the trade unions and state-owned industries, but also citadels of British business which had failed to adapt quickly enough to the cutting wind of international competition. What had appeared to be permanent fixtures of the City itself, including W. Greenwell, were to disappear into financial conglomerates under the pressures of the 'Big Bang'.

A creative destabilizer of markets like Alan Sugar seemed to embody the positive message of Mrs Thatcher's economic philosophy, the other side of the coin to Thatcherism's rooting out of dead wood from the undergrowths of the British economy. Britain's established electronics companies had become fat and lazy on easy profits made by selling over-engineered products to the Ministry of Defence and British Telecom, two giant monopoly customers. Amstrad chose the harder route of competing head-on with the Japanese in the cut-throat arena of Britain's high streets, where Sugar was vying for the favour of millions of people who had been made affluent by the Thatcher decade – people, in fact, just like himself, even though his affluence was on a vastly different scale. Alan Sugar and Amstrad were the high priests of Britain's new religion, the religion of consumption.

Sugar seemed to confirm Thatcherism's social vision too. Born with no advantages whatsoever, brought up on one of the poorest estates in East London, this Cockney entrepreneur now only just into his forties had amassed almost unimaginable wealth in barely more than a decade. The message rang out from the Amstrad story that anyone could make it in Britain's new land of opportunity if they were prepared to try their arm and work hard. The work ethic Sugar embodied and engendered among Amstrad's employees – he joked that he threw a sandwich at them for lunch as they sat at their desks, if they were lucky – chimed perfectly with the Government's message that British workers had to stop clock-watching and get on with the job.

Yet although Sugar drove his workers hard, he also generated tremendous loyalty among those who lasted the pace. This loyalty was won partly by his distribution of generous share options to many of Amstrad's staff, allowing them to share in the company's success. More fundamentally, it stemmed from the buzz which people experienced when they worked with him – the surge of adrenalin which flowed from the feeling that this was a man rewriting the rules of the market-place.

Sugar symbolized the 1980s by refusing to be assimilated into the establishment once he had arrived. You would not find him in one of London's gentlemen's clubs. He had no time to waste trying to shine among the ranks of business leaders in lobbies like the Confederation of British Industry. As chairman of one of Britain's fastest growing public companies, he continued to speak in exactly the same way as when he first left the East End. Funny, aggressive and peppered with swear-words, his language stood out from the reams of public relations pap uttered by most leaders of corporate Britain.

The Amstrad boss was an icon for popular capitalism, the conscious attempt by the Government to teach the mass of British people to identify with business in the way that is second nature to their American cousins. The use of the privatization programme to spread share ownership meant that companies like British Telecom became the flagships of popular capitalism. But most British people cannot identify with the Oxbridge-educated bureaucrats who tend to run these monoliths. By comparison, Sugar was a perfect role model, as the Government acknowledged when it asked him to spearhead its 1992 awareness campaign. He could speak directly to ordinary British people in words they understood.

Sugar did not alter his lifestyle as he entered the ranks of Britain's super-rich; he did not use his position to seek out the friendship of the rich and famous. His tastes remained the same as those hundreds of thousands of nameless consumers who bought his products. Many of his closest friends had similar upbringings to his own. Sugar shared with them a common journey out of the East End of London into the north-east outskirts of the capital, differing only in the size of the house he could afford. Like many of the most prominent successes of the Thatcher decade – including the Prime Minister herself – he was both part of and curiously outside the new order.

Sugar's dislikes remained those of the outsider and with characteristic vigour he attacked a broad list of hate figures. The City, journalists, boffins, corporate wimps, the established electronics companies in Britain and Europe, Americans, the European Commission – all were to feel the lash of his tongue. Suspicious of people who owe their position to privilege rather than to hard work, he is instinctively against anyone whose talents lie simply in working the system. He reserves a special contempt for bureaucrats, producers of verbiage or regulations which make it more difficult for people like himself to earn an honest penny by bringing the latest gadget to the masses.

Many of those attacked by Sugar – and the list included people with influence in the corridors of the old Establishment – returned the compliment by waiting for his downfall. The decade was littered with confident assertions that Amstrad was past its peak and with predictions that the company was about to fall flat on its face. And as the 1980s drew to a close, the bleakest prophecies of Sugar's critics seemed to be coming true.

Amstrad stumbled as Sugar grappled with a formidable array of problems. The growing volume of components it consumed made it newly vulnerable to the roller-coaster swings from feast to famine and back again in the worldwide supply of electronic parts. The company was forced to modify its manufacturing philosophy, as trade pressures mounted against the flood of cheap imports from the Far East and workers in countries like Taiwan began to agitate for improved living standards. Amstrad's tradition of running the tightest of ships deprived it of the engineering resources needed for the smooth management of its move into a more complex line of business computers. It had to struggle hard to overcome its cheap-and-cheerful image when promoting higher value computers to large business customers.

Most of Sugar's wealth was tied up in the value of his stake in Amstrad. Since he owned about 250 million Amstrad shares, every 1p change in the share price was worth £2.5 million to him. The company's stock came under severe pressure in the late 1980s, when general stock market nervousness coincided with the emergence of difficulties at Amstrad. By September 1989, the paper value of Sugar's fortune had been slashed by £400 million, reducing him to his last £197 million and making him the largest stock market 'loser' of all time, according to one calculation.

The root question facing Sugar as he prepared Amstrad for the 1990s was this: would he be able to manage the company's transition from its heroic entrepreneurial phase of hyper-growth into a more mature future in which Amstrad would take on the settled features of a large, multinational corporation? Put more simply still: are Sugar and Amstrad destined to be a flash in the pan, like other heroes of British business before them, or are they set to become part of the permanent landscape of the British economy?

Sugar ended the 1980s by showing that he understood he was facing one of the most difficult of business problems. He had to transform the managerial culture at Amstrad from that of a small business to one better suited to its new status as a large corporation – without destroying the entrepreneurial drive which powered its original growth. He strengthened the senior management line-up at Amstrad, built up the company's in-house research and development capacity and moved some of its manufacturing back to Europe. In short, Alan Sugar began to lay the foundations for a new phase in the Amstrad story.

*

The team of professionals put together in 1979 to handle Amstrad's flotation was preoccupied with a pressing set of questions. They needed to overcome the doubts raised by potential investors when they were first told about the company.

What exactly were the big investing institutions, like the insurance companies and pension funds, being asked to buy into? Amstrad had neither assets nor staff to boast about. Its Tottenham headquarters in North London would not raise much if ever it came to the crunch; although the company's main physical asset, it was valued at under £400,000. Amstrad's net tangible assets at the time totalled £3.7 million, significantly less than the £8 million price tag the stock market was being asked to put on the company. Neither could Amstrad point to a great array of talent among its staff: it had just 117 employees and only a handful of senior managers of any calibre in whom investors could have confidence.

The answer to the institutions' question was, in fact, simple. Investors were being asked to back the track record and potential of one man, Alan Sugar. But although to the point, this answer made some investors nervous.

Most basically of all, there was the falling-under-a-bus worry; in 1979, Amstrad lacked anyone to replace Sugar if he suddenly disappeared from the scene. Secondly, there was a question mark about Sugar himself. True, he had already notched up a decade of impeccable results, but he was still only just into his thirties. How could institutional investors be assured that this young man was not about to run out of steam? The flotation committee assembled by Kleinwort Benson – Amstrad's merchant bank and main financial advisers – spent much time discussing how to overcome negative reactions to Sugar's youth.

Third, there was the problem posed by Amstrad's area of operations, the audio industry. The roll-call of established British audio companies which had come to grief was long and ominous. Not only did the audio business demand almost continuous innovation embodied in a never-ending stream of new products, it was also the field of combat chosen by some of Japan's biggest conglomerates. 'It was a very competitive market, dominated by some massive companies, and people just wondered whether there was ever going to be any profit in it over the years,' remembers Tim Holland-Bosworth, a Kleinwort Benson director assigned to the Amstrad flotation.

These concerns were reflected in the smattering of press coverage which Amstrad received before the flotation – the start of a nervy love-hate relationship between Sugar and the media.

The *Financial Times*'s influential Lex column pointed out that 'the history of the U.K. hi-fi industry is littered with still-twitching casualties', though Lex hedged its bets by praising Amstrad's flexibility and profit record. The *Financial Weekly* posed a question which was to recur with monotonous regularity down the years: 'Will it be the same perky animal in two to three years' time when chips are ten a penny?' The *Daily Telegraph* mused delicately about Sugar's health: 'Dynamism in the company springs from Sugar himself, and one wonders what might become of Amstrad should he, for instance, lose interest or be unable to continue for any reason.'

Kleinwort Benson and the rest of the flotation team pointed to Amstrad's record to quell these doubts. Ten years of excellent results had left the company with no debt, a return on capital above 30 per cent in the second half of the 1970s and pre-tax profit margins comfortably above 12 per cent during most of the decade. These results were ample testimony to the character of the man in the driving seat.

After a decade of running all aspects of his own show, what Sugar did not know about the audio market was not worth knowing. He entertained his City advisers by explaining the importance of the 'dark hours', the autumn evenings in the run-up to Christmas when working-class consumers bought car radios, cassette players and all the other items in Amstrad's product line. Sugar was also bubbling with ideas for new products. 'The impression you came away with was of someone who knew exactly what he was speaking about in his own field. He knew what he was doing. The contrast with the average managing director in British industry was quite marked,' recalls Howard Myles, then in Greenwell's corporate finance department.

Most impressive of all from a City perspective was Sugar's attitude to profits. 'He had a major obsession with margins. That was the thing which drove him. When looking at a new product, he always worked back from what he considered an appropriate margin,' Holland-Bosworth says.

Obsessed with profits, Sugar talked the language of business. His concerns were with cost, delivery and reliability. This was talk which the City could understand much more readily than the techno-babble favoured by some electronics entrepreneurs. 'He spoke more familiar language to me than lots of other people in technical areas. We have always been nervous of companies trading in technology that we don't understand,' notes Holland-Bosworth.

Crucially, some important investors agreed with the positive message put out by Amstrad's own advisers. Paul Williams, an investment manager with Clerical Medical & General Life Assurance, was initially worried about the risks inherent in Amstrad's line of business, so he went to an investor presentation given by Sugar and came away impressed by the philosophy of total flexibility articulated by the Amstrad chairman.

'What attracted us to the company at the time of the flotation was that they were very flexible in their sourcing. They would source from the cheapest place in the world, wherever that happened to be, and then undercut the competition,' explains Williams, who persuaded Clerical Medical to become the largest single investor in Amstrad after Sugar himself.

Nevertheless, it was an uphill struggle convincing some institutional investors to overcome their fears. The more conservative institutions were worried by their inability to compare Amstrad's performance with that of another outfit, for as Tim Holland-Bosworth admitted at the time: 'We have failed to find a U.K. company even broadly similar.'

In the event, many of the largest institutions refused to buy Amstrad's shares, leaving individual investors to play a crucial role in securing the eventual success of Amstrad's debut on the Stock Exchange. But the Amstrad boss and his team of advisers had to put in a lot of work before they reached that stage.

Sugar was later to tell some of his best jokes and coin some of his most colourful invective about his first contacts with the City. His account of how he first came across p/e ratios – the ratio between a share's price and its earnings, and one of the City's favourite tools for measuring company performance – entered the Sugar mythology as soon as he related it in a public lecture in 1987:

The first time I came to the City was in 1979 when I met up with Kleinwort Benson. I sat in a large board-room with a lot of people who spoke a strange jargon – cash flow, p/e forecasts etc. The last time I heard the expression p/e, I was at secondary school and it meant physical education.

So my mind drifted, oblivious to this strange mumble of exchange of views from all the so-called advisers around the table. I was suddenly woken with the question, 'Mr Sugar, what p/e do you think you have?'

I replied, 'Twenty press-ups every morning.'

The funny thing is that they weren't shocked and went on to talk about press-ups.

Such remarks have created the impression of a character aggressively hostile to the City and all its works. But the Amstrad chairman made quite a different impression on those City people he worked with during the build-up to the flotation. Huge differences in background and language had to be overcome. Sugar's drafted statements for the prospectus committee read exactly as he spoke: they reproduced his grammar and vocabulary precisely, minus only the swear-words. The City team had the unusual job of translating his rich Cockney diction into language acceptable to the money men. Yet, despite the difference in cultures, Sugar buckled down to this task without any fuss. His advisers found him to be a rigorously practical young businessman when dealing with the issue at hand: screwing the best possible deal out of the City once he had decided to sell a quarter of his company, the minimum allowed under Stock Exchange rules.

This pragmatic professionalism shone through in Sugar's approach to the flotation. Guided to Kleinwort Benson by Michael Hollingbery – chairman of Amstrad's most important customer, the Comet retail group – Sugar accepted Kleinwort's advice to assemble a flotation team consisting of some of the most prestigious of City names. Besides Kleinwort themselves, Amstrad hired W. Greenwell as brokers, Touche Ross as auditors and Herbert Smith for its legal expertise.

The Amstrad boss later explained his choice of this quartet of advisers: 'I'm a great believer in professionals. If someone says to me that these people are experts in financial matters, I believe it. It's as though I'd had a pain in my chest, well, I'd have gone and seen a doctor in Harley Street.'

The City professionals Sugar had to deal with were mostly of a class and background which he had never encountered before. Kleinwort Benson's Tim Holland-Bosworth is the very model of a double-barrelled City gent: favouring the widest of stripes in his pin-striped suits, there is not a hair or a syllable out of place in his carefully combed blond locks or his cut-glass accent. Having clawed his way up from the East End, it would have been only natural for Sugar to have bridled at this epitome of City privilege. But he did not. He had no hang-ups about dealing with people like Holland-Bosworth, whom he retains as a financial adviser to this day.

True, some of those working with Sugar detected in him an apprehensive air at the start of the flotation process, fuelled by a suspicion that the City's whizz-kids might be about to rip him off – not surprisingly, since Amstrad's relatively simple flotation cost a cool £183,000. In private meetings with his advisers, Sugar insisted that the meaning of every syllable of City jargon was spelt out in words he could understand. He was a quick learner, particularly where anything touching the value of money was concerned. 'If we were talking about measuring performance by something called the p/e ratio, he'd find out pretty damn quick how much that meant in his pocket at the end of the day,' Holland-Bosworth recalls.

In public presentations to potential investors, there were times when Sugar compensated for his lack of familiarity with City ways by being a little brash, a little too simple and aggressive in his replies. This manner helped to disguise a certain shyness in public, which only those closest to him detected and which it was to take him years of public exposure to overcome.

But there was no doubt that long meetings in plush City offices were not Sugar's idea of time well spent. He delegated as much of the detailed work as possible to Jim Rice, Amstrad's company secretary, making it plain that he would rather be on the road selling to customers. Where his presence was unavoidable, he held as many meetings as possible on home territory. Sugar made his pitch to Clerical Medical's Paul Williams in a side-room during a break from a trade fair; Williams was used to somewhat more formal settings for investor meetings. Holland-Bosworth often had to take his team on the unfamiliar train journey across Hackney Marshes to Tottenham, timing their travel so as to avoid Tottenham Hotspur fans heading for an evening match. Occasionally their calculations went awry and the well-dressed team from the City spent an uncomfortable journey eyeball-to-eyeball with a trainload of Spurs supporters.

Once they reached the safe haven of Amstrad's Garman Road headquarters, they found a set of offices somewhat more austere than their own. 'It was obvious that Alan was not likely to go in for atriums or Henry Moore sculptures,' Holland-Bosworth remarked with well-bred understatement. When David Thomson, Greenwell's head of corporate finance, casually commented on being served coffee out of a machine in the chairman's office, Sugar put him straight: 'We're not having bloody china in this office.'

The flotation team had more important things to worry about than the quality of the coffee cups. As 1979 turned into 1980, the British economy headed into the deep recession that marked the onset of the economic policies introduced by the first Thatcher Government. This caused considerable nervousness about the implications for Amstrad, a company dependent on consumer prosperity. At the end of January, with the flotation date fast approaching, the team was too busy to give more than a passing glance to news which was later to have considerable implications for Amstrad; Clive Sinclair, the electronics entrepreneur, helped to trigger the home computer revolution in Europe by launching the world's smallest and cheapest computer at an exhibition in Wembley.

In the late 1970s, flotations were less glitzy occasions than they are today. Sugar's advisers did much of the selling of the Amstrad issue over the phone, trading on their contacts. They were confident that one or two institutions like Clerical Medical would take large stakes. A week before the 23 April flotation date, Kleinwort Benson was able to announce that 5,800 applications had been received for a total of 23 million shares – over-subscribing the offer nine times. The only disappointment for investors was that the Amstrad stock did not open at a slightly higher premium: on 23 April 1980, its first day of trading, the share opened at 92p, an 8 per cent premium on the 85p offer price.

This scarcely bothered Sugar. What he cared about was the successful sale of all the 2,330,000 shares on offer in Amstrad. He personally raised almost £2 million by parting with a quarter of his company, while also still holding three-quarters of the shares in a publicly quoted company valued at £8 million. Another East End millionaire had been born.

Alan Sugar banked his cheque and returned to what he loved best: raking up profits by selling audio equipment. But by floating Amstrad on the Stock Exchange, he would never be able to forget the City again. Guy Gordon, who had been Sugar's accountant when he first set out in business, phoned after the flotation to congratulate him and to offer help if he should ever need it again. 'Guy, I've got so many advisers, lawyers, accountants, round me, they're driving me mad. I don't know what half of them do,' was the reply.

This did not stop Sugar from throwing a big party to celebrate Amstrad's debut as a public company at the White Elephant, a favourite night spot with showbiz personalities on the banks of the Thames in central London. Over a hundred people were there, including the flotation team with their partners and Sugar's friends and family. It was one of the few occasions when his two worlds, public and private, ever came together.

Sugar's parents, Fay and Nathan, stood around, simultaneously proud of and bemused by their son's success. Shortly before, he had shown his father evidence of the fruits of the flotation. It was a significant rite of passage, as Sugar explains: 'It wasn't until I physically put a cheque for two million pounds under his nose that he realized it was O.K. for him to stop worrying, because I actually could make a living without working for somebody.'

· 2 ·

An Unexpected Child

No one had expected Alan Sugar. The entire family was surprised when Fay Sugar announced late in the summer of 1946 that she was expecting her fourth child. Eleven years had passed since she had last given birth and, at 38, she had every reason to believe that her child-rearing days were over.

The news was a mixed blessing for the Sugar family. Fay, a bright and warm woman, was naturally delighted at the prospect of an addition to the family. Yet there was no escaping the difficult circumstances into which the baby would be born. Fay and Nathan Sugar were only just picking up the pieces after the war.

Their move to Clapton, in the East London borough of Hackney, had been a step in the right direction. It was one remove from their old home in Stepney, in the heart of the Jewish East End, where families were squashed together in terrace houses lacking the most basic facilities such as bathrooms even on the outbreak of the Second World War. Clapton was no less working class, but the local council had transformed the area shortly before the war by building new blocks of council flats. Just as important, Clapton was one step nearer the respectability of London's northern suburbs.

Yet no sooner were Fay and Nathan installed in their new council flat at the top of a block of flats called Woolmer House on the Northwold estate, than the German bombers began to pound Hackney into the dust. None of the Sugars' three elder children spent all their childhood with their parents; they were dispersed to different corners of England in the evacuation, leaving their father and mother to scurry across the playground beneath their flat to the air-raid shelter to avoid the bombs.

The end of the war did not bring much immediate relief. Basic foodstuffs were still in short supply. Hackney council could not lay its hands on enough slates, cement and plaster board to repair the local devastation. With another child on the way, the Sugars' three-bedroomed flat suddenly did not appear as spacious as when they first arrived.

In the event, the birth was not the easiest and Fay had to spend three weeks in Hackney Hospital, where the doctors insisted on a Caesarean birth in view of her age. It was thus with some difficulty that, on 24 March 1947, Alan Michael Sugar emerged into the world. Remembering the hospital, Fay Sugar – now into her eighties but still sharp – says 'her Alan' showed early signs of his later character. 'Whilst he was there, he always seemed to be like a boss overriding everyone. He made such a lot of noise.'

Yet as he was growing up, Alan Sugar struck people as a quiet, almost solitary child, though there were plenty of other children on the estate if he had wanted to surround himself with playmates. For a start, he had a brother and two sisters: Derek and Daphne, the twins, and Shirley, the eldest of the Sugar children. As a result, Alan had to share a bedroom – sleeping in a narrow bed on the far side of the room – until his sisters left home to get married.

The 23 blocks of flats which make up the Northwold estate were full of families with young children like the Sugars. Northwold was typical London council housing of the era before the capital was disfigured by twenty-storey tower blocks. Most of the blocks on the estate were like Woolmer House, four storeys tall with half-a-dozen flats on each landing divided into two sections by a central staircase. The narrow corridors running along each landing have acted as playgrounds to generations of children, as have the courtyards and patches of grass below.

Yet Derek, Alan's elder brother, cannot remember ever looking over the balcony and seeing him kicking around a football between the flats, as he and his friends had done. Brenda, Derek's future wife, thought Alan was living an unusually dull life for a young boy when she started visiting the Sugars. She once prodded her younger brother into taking Alan out with his pals, but the boy seemed to resent it. As he was growing up, the last thing that Alan Sugar appeared to be was an extrovert or a leader of the pack.

Alan's upbringing was close to that of an only child. The twins, Derek and Daphne, were already aged 12 when he was born and were too old to act as real companions. Diana Kieve, a friend of the Sugars since before the war, remembers Alan as a toddler trying to follow Derek around the estate. A teenager with his own gang of friends, Derek paid scant attention to his young brother; by the time he had done his stint in the Army, he had drifted apart from Alan. The youngest Sugar's brother and sisters seemed to be of another generation: 'It was like having more adults around, growing up in an adult environment really,' he recalls.

It fell to Daphne, the younger sister, to spend most time with the baby of the family. Looking back, she sees early signs of her brother's later restless character in what happened on his first day at school. She took the five-year-old Alan to his new school, Northwold, a severe stone-built primary about a quarter of a mile from Woolmer House. It was with some surprise that she opened the door of their flat at 11 o'clock to find him there, none too pleased to be told he had mistaken the morning break for the end of the school day.

Alan found himself growing up in a family which had always struggled for money. Nathan Sugar was a semi-skilled worker in the garment trade. He tacked up the clothes, preparing them for the master machinists to sew together. The money was not bad, compared with some of the East End trades, when there was work to be had. The trouble lay in the insecurity of the job.

In the inter-war years, tailoring had been badly hit by the depression and the growing mechanization of the small garment factories. Even when the country returned to prosperity in the 1950s, the work remained seasonal and Nathan would be laid off without pay at a moment's notice, sometimes for weeks at a time. In his earliest years, Alan did not fully grasp the pall of insecurity thrown over the whole family by this pattern. 'It was only in later years, when I was 14 or 15, that I saw the type of industry he worked in. They simply told him on Monday morning, "Sorry, there's no work. Don't come in." And he used to take it very badly.'

Nathan did his best to cope. He chopped and changed between the small garment factories, where conditions were little better than in the workshops filled by Jewish immigrants new to London in the closing decades of the last century. He went to evening classes to better himself, studying the art of cutting a garment. He earned a few extra pounds by making children's coats in his spare time. Local women would trail their children up to the Sugars' flat to be measured for coats for bar-mitzvahs and other special occasions.

The insecurity of his trade fed Nathan's natural caution. Alan Sugar, the businessman son whose life has revolved around taking risks, looks back on his late father with a mixture of pride at his underrated intelligence and exasperation at his failure to grasp opportunities. 'He had people rushing after him to make coats for them. But the more people he had rushing after him, the more he got nervous. He could have opened his own shop. He could have made coats. He was a very intelligent man. The problem was he would not take a risk.'

Nathan's responsibilities hung heavily on his shoulders. 'He was a provider and he wanted to make sure everyone was provided for. He worried very much. He was a very big worrier.' Alan Sugar repeats the point, highlighting the facet of Nathan's character noted by many visitors to the Sugars' flat.

Nathan always assumed that if things could go wrong, they would do so in spades. He acted as a brake and a dampener on his children, flying into a panic if they suggested anything out of the ordinary. Nathan struck neighbours like the Kieves as quiet and hard-working, if resigned: a man old before his time. But the father of the family would show another side in the privacy of the Sugars' flat. Nathan had a temper like a slow-burning fuse. Almost anything could make him erupt. In one of these moods it was not unknown for him to pick up a bottle and throw it against a wall.

This moody man formed a close bond with his youngest child and later, when he became one of his son's first employees, Alan readily put up with his father's little eccentricities. Alan was the only one of the children to spend his entire childhood with his parents, the others having all been evacuated during the war. As the elder children left school and the boom years of the 1950s rolled by, the economic pressures on the Sugars lightened a little. His parents were able to give Alan slightly more than the others had received.

Nathan Sugar had few means of escape from his tailor's bench, but he would regularly turn to the sports page in the paper to follow the horses. Even then, however, he was not much of a gambler, betting only in shillings. Much of his time was spent visiting his family. Unusually for that time, his father, a shoe-repairer, had married twice; so too had Nathan's mother. They had a family each and a family together, spawning a clutch of half-brothers and half-sisters dotted around the East End.

The Sugars were like many East Enders in basing their social life on the family, inviting neighbours into their flat sparingly. In this they were typical of most of Northwold's inhabitants, contra-dicting the widely held view that East Enders were for ever visiting each other. 'These flats are a world of their own. You live a whole lifetime here and not know your next-door neighbour,' as a character says in Arnold Wesker's play *Chicken Soup with Barley*, which is set in a flat on the Northwold estate.

The main social occasion in the Sugar household was on a Friday night when they would gather to play the card game, solo. Nathan was an avid card player and Derek would join in, bringing Brenda – his wife-to-be – and friends such as Jeffrey Kieve, who lived across the courtyard in the opposite block of flats and was later to teach Alan. Alan would be there, hanging around the older card-players, but too young to join in the family's activities.

The Sugars were unusual in one respect in that, unlike many Jewish families, they took little interest in their family history. Fay and Nathan never discussed whether it was their parents or an earlier generation who first came to Britain to escape persecution, and their children never thought to ask. The most they knew was that Nathan's family was originally Polish. No one quite knew where their unusual surname came from; one line of thought in the family was that it might have been an English version of Zuckerman. Alan himself later speculated that his Polish ancestors had chosen the name Sugar on arriving in England because they worked in a sugar-beet factory.

Fay's ancestors were thought to be Russian and her maiden name, Apple, also to have been Anglicized. The marriage of an Apple to a Sugar had raised a smile among the two families at the time of the wedding. The Apples and the Sugars lived close together in Stepney where Fay's father, Aaron, had his own horse and cart to carry goods between the network of small workshops in the East End. Fay prides herself on not having worked much after her wedding, a pattern common among even the poorest Jewish families of those times. She is blessed with a natural sense of fun, a trait shining through a photo which has survived from her prime and shows her posing as Mrs Mop to please her children: a small, podgy woman with a broad grin clutching a mop on the balcony outside her flat.

The Sugars' lack of intellectual curiosity did not just mark out their attitude to their family history. Theirs was not a bookish household. They never dreamt of imitating the Kieves' ambition of pushing Jeffrey through university. Neither was Nathan troubled by the political and trade union fervour which gripped many Jews in the garment trade. It is doubtful whether he even bothered to vote.

Their flat could not have been more different from that across the way in Weald Square which housed the young Arnold Wesker. The same age as Derek Sugar and Jeffrey Kieve, Wesker was growing up in a flat full of books, records and friends debating the issues of the day. His parents were Communists and working-class intellectuals of a type more common in the 1930s. Yet it was the Weskers, not the Sugars, who were out of the ordinary, as Wesker realized when he went to school. 'Even my Jewish friends saw me as way out, bohemian and arty,' he remembers.

For the Sugars, as for most families on the Northwold estate, struggling to make do was enough. The only holidays which the people of Clapton could afford were occasional day trips to Southend and, for some, a working break hop-picking in Kent. Northwold was mainly populated by respectable working-class families like the Sugars, eager to make the best of what they had. Yet there was a fringe element mixed up in the darker side of East End life, where fathers were in and out of prison. There were other families who buckled under the pressures of living on the bread-line, piled up on one another: the thin walls between the flats did little to muffle a shouting match or worse between husband and wife.

In this unpromising environment, it was not surprising that Alan failed to pass the 11+ exam which would have given him access to one of the East End's grammar schools. But he did well enough to enter Joseph Priestley, a secondary technical school catering for children thought to have a technical bent. Pupils there were considered a cut above those condemned to secondary modern schools. Many of Alan Sugar's schoolmates were destined for places at Hackney Technical College and apprenticeships in the print, pattern-making and other light industries nestling in small workshops and under railway arches all over the East End.

Set in a crumbling building, Joseph Priestley had an old-fashioned head, Jim Harris. A disciplinarian who terrified staff and pupils alike, Harris would lecture teachers found playing cards in the staff-room for setting a bad example. He modelled his methods on the public schools and traditional grammar schools, taking much of his inspiration from Merchant Taylors', the public school where he sent his own son. He gathered around him enthusiastic, well-qualified teachers who tried to set high standards for the boys from the estates.

During Alan Sugar's first two years at the school, Harris was preoccupied with a delicate matter. He wanted to ensure that he and Joseph Priestley were in the driving seat after the school merged with Mount Pleasant, a secondary modern, to form one of the new wave of comprehensives. Most of Joseph Priestley's staff favoured the then novel concept of comprehensives catering for children of all abilities, yet the prospect of having to link up with a secondary modern still sent shudders through the staff-room.

Jim Harris was determined that they would show the Mount Pleasant lot how to run things.

And so they did. Harris assumed the headship of the merged school – named Brookhouse and given a new building a short walk down the Upper Clapton Road from the Northwold estate – and imposed his well-tested system of prefects and house captains. He was so keen for Brookhouse to establish its reputation that he even insisted on the staff and prefects wearing gowns. A gesture which would be unthinkable in Hackney's schools today, it was calculated to appeal to the respect for tradition and ceremony among the local people, particularly within the borough's large Jewish population.

Alan Sugar has glowing memories of Brookhouse. The school's facilities opened up possibilities which he had never dreamt of: he learned to work a lathe, he built a brick wall and he acted in *Twelfth Night*. 'I could still to this day build a brick wall if I had to. And I can still recite parts of Shakespeare. I can turn a lathe and read or draw a technical drawing. It was an amazing school. It's died off, that kind of school.'

Yet at this point one of the paradoxes of Sugar's early years begins to take shape. No one who came across him as a child claims to have noticed anything out of the ordinary in the boy from the Northwold estate, not even when they look back with the benefit of knowing the shape of his later career. 'If anyone had asked who was going to beat the world, I doubt whether anybody would have picked Alan Sugar,' says Jeffrey Kieve, who was surprised to see Alan when he was ushered in to teach the first year in Joseph Priestley as a new teacher fresh from the London School of Economics.

Alan struck Kieve as a determined lad, who conscientiously took away his homework in the brown satchel over his shoulders and just as conscientiously brought it back the next day. The young boy was obviously no fool; he could hold his own. Yet he was not one of the adventurous spirits who tested the rules of conduct laid down by Jim Harris. Alan chose the science and engineering stream, preferring that to commerce as he progressed through the school. He enjoyed metalwork, technical drawing and the labs, yet was not the type of boy who devoted endless hours to pulling radios apart. In class, he was neither top nor bottom of the form. In short, he was relentlessly average – precisely the kind of child overlooked by teachers.

Vic Pollard, who taught Alan science in the third form and now runs an Outward Bound centre, agrees: 'This is one of the strange things. Looking back, it just amazes me that this lad has achieved so much. He didn't stand out in any way at all.'

If anything Alan was on the quiet side, a boy who steered clear of the school's clubs and other activities. At home, he opted for solitary hobbies such as photography and even cookery, making cakes and pickling onions. Vic Pollard wondered whether his size played its part. Sugar was slight as a boy, a not unimportant trait for a lad growing up in a tough area like Hackney. Also he seemed a bit of a loner to his teachers, not the type to hang out in a gang. 'I can't remember Alan letting loose that outer shell,' Kieve says.

Yet the personality of the man who was to become an emblem of British business twenty years later was, in fact, taking shape under their eyes. Alan began to develop an unusually intense interest in business and money. His mother chuckles now over her memories of some of the first signs: 'When he was at Brookhouse, he wanted to make a school magazine and he wanted a printing machine. But he didn't have the money and, do you know what, he went to the headmaster and said, "Will you loan me the money?"'

This early transaction still ranks as one of Sugar's boldest in the eyes of someone as unassuming as his mother, not least because it worked. Jim Harris, who was later to tell Fay that her son would be capable of selling anything from a matchstick to a car, answered the budding entrepreneur, 'With your cheek, I will.'

Alan Sugar's interest in money even predated his days at Brookhouse. As a small child, he had made a point of going around the flats to ask people if he could take their pop bottles back to the shop. The young boy could not understand why adults would not make the effort to reclaim the deposits on the bottles themselves: 'I'd take twelve bottles back to the sweet-shop down-stairs and get a shilling for them. I used to think to myself, "These people must be mad." All I had to do was walk down the stairs with the bottles.'

Alan later graduated to making pop and selling it to his classmates, after a relative had given him a ginger-beer plant. Still only 13, he saw it as an opportunity to undercut the price of a bottle of Coca Cola or Tizer, which the children from the estate could ill afford. He can still recall how to make a gallon of ginger beer by feeding the plant every day with two teaspoonsfuls of ginger and two of sugar, adding lemon juice and a gallon of water, siphoning off the concoction and bottling it up.

Later in his teens, he would rise at 6 am on Saturdays to boil raw beetroot for the local greengrocer. He helped out a family friend on his market stall, selling linens and fabrics. Then, for a while, he tried selling household goods like washing-up liquids from a stall he ran with some other lads on a Saturday.

Alan even turned a penny from his photography hobby. Old friends now in their forties still have black and white snaps of family occasions with 'Alan Sugar, Photographer' printed neatly on the back and developed in Alan's bedroom-cum-darkroom. From a distance of thirty years, he happily admits that his photography sideline owed nothing to the technical excellence of the shots, but flourished thanks to his instinct for selling. 'People want pictures of their kids, always, and grandparents want pictures of their grandkids more than anything else. So I went straight to the grandparents and said to them, "I'll photograph your grandchildren for half a crown." And the answer was always, "Yes, yes, yes, yes." They could never have enough pictures of their grandchildren.'

Alan showed an unusual talent for selling in his many Saturday jobs. Fay Sugar remembers a department store in Hackney being so impressed with the schoolboy's prowess in selling shoes that they offered him a permanent position on the spot.

These Saturday jobs were taken on Alan's own initiative; so too was his careful husbanding of the money he earned, which he kept at home largely unspent. 'I was quite a good saver as a kid. It was always indoctrinated into me from my family that you had to save your money,' he recalls.

Some of this might be dismissed as the rose-tinted memories of proud relatives were it not that Alan also acquired a reputation with his teachers. Vic Pollard heard on the school grapevine that Alan was involved in all kinds of little deals; he became known in school as the boy who could *get* things for people. This reputation was illustrated by the little routine which Alan and Jim Harris, the head teacher, would go into whenever they bumped into each other.

'Ah, Sugar, yes, hmm, commerce section, aren't you?' the head would say, eyeing Alan from a great height.

'No, no, sir, science and engineering I'm in,' Alan would reply.

'No, you're not, Sugar, I know you, you're in commerce,' Brookhouse's head would insist. The exchange would end only when Alan brought out his school card to prove he was in science and engineering.

The East End has long been famous for its traders. Street markets like those in Brick Lane and Ridley Road, the flow of goods from the London docks, the myriad small workshops – all these contributed to the area's reputation as a place where deals were done. Nowadays the head teacher at Homerton House – the school which later absorbed Brookhouse – complains that there is little contact between his school and business. But in the Hackney of the 1960s it was not uncommon for the boys, particularly the Jewish lads, to go straight into the family firm.

Unlike many of his schoolmates, however, there was no relative to shape or encourage Alan Sugar's earliest interest in selling and trading. Going out to work for someone else was all the family understood. 'We were very working-class people,' Daphne explains, without the slightest hint of affectation.

The nearest the family could offer to an entrepreneur was one of Fay's brothers, John, who ran a hardware shop in Victoria. The shop was known locally for the captions, puns and slogans he used to pin to the merchandise; a journalist on a national paper found it sufficiently amusing to write an article about his advertising techniques. It would make a good story to report that Uncle John had held the infant Alan Sugar on his knee while teaching him the mysteries of business – a good story, but untrue: Uncle John was no closer than any other relative. Alan Sugar learnt the tricks of his trade by himself.

So Alan already had one step in the world of work as he came to the end of his schooling. Ten years earlier, his brother Derek had been forced by Nathan to leave school as soon as he was 14. Derek had a good head for figures and the backing of his headmaster in his wish to stay on at school, with the hope of eventually studying book-keeping. But Nathan would have none of it, insisting that Derek had to bring in a wage immediately by following him into the rag trade as a machinist. An intelligent man, Derek quickly grew to loathe the work, drifting after a spell of National Service into cab-driving.

The pattern repeated itself with Alan, who wanted to stay on at Brookhouse. The financial pressures on the Sugars had eased by the early 1960s, the end of Harold Macmillan's 'never had it so good' era, and Nathan felt torn. His gut instinct was for Alan to start earning as soon as possible, just like his other children; but he also understood that staying on at school might help Alan into a better job, maybe even to enter the mysterious world of the white-collar professional. 'But apart from my father being very nervous, he was also a very sceptical kind of person. He didn't have much confidence that anyone from his family would end up in anything like university,' explains Sugar.

An uneasy compromise was reached, Alan staying on beyond the minimum school-leaving age to start an A-level science course. But in the end Nathan's instinct prevailed. A family member recalls a row at one of the family's Friday evening gatherings, and that was that. Alan Sugar, aged almost 17 and with a few O-levels to his name, abandoned any thought of furthering his education. When he left school, he was already earning more from his various sidelines than his father.

*

The Sugar family's Jewish background reinforced a sense of security and solidity in a way which it is difficult for non-Jewish people to understand, for they were never meticulous in their religious observance. Fay's and Nathan's children were not brought up to be particularly religious. Only the photos of the children's bar-mitzvahs on the walls tell visitors who enter Alan Sugar's home today that they are in a Jewish household.

But it would be easy for outsiders to misinterpret this secular attitude as evidence that Alan Sugar has not been deeply touched by his Jewish background. Easy and wrong: it has played a part in most of the main milestones in his life, outside the realm of business. For one thing, all the rites of passage in Sugar's life have been carried out according to Jewish custom, from his bar-mitzvah in a small synagogue in the Upper Clapton Road to his marriage in the Great Portland Street synagogue. Although his friends have tended to share his cool attitude to religion, nearly all have been Jewish. In his adolescence Sugar made friends with other young Jews who gathered around the Jewish youth clubs of Stamford Hill, and it was through this network that he first met Ann, his future wife. His brother and sisters, and all his friends, also married Jewish partners; it would have been 'quite upsetting to do otherwise', says his sister Daphne.

Fay's and Nathan's original move from Stepney to Clapton was on the well-trodden route of Jewish emigration out of the traditional East End. In the days before widespread car ownership, it was dictated by the path of the 653 trolleybus, which ran from Stepney to Hackney and Clapton and then on to Stamford Hill. By settling along the trolleybus's route, Jewish families could keep in touch with relatives and friends in different stages of the exodus – a particularly important requirement in the 1930s, when anti-semitic agitation by the British Union of Fascists was strong in the East End. Alan Sugar moved to Redbridge, on the north-east outskirts of London, as a newlywed in the 1960s, the decade when Jewish immigration into Redbridge was at its peak. He made his first home in Clayhall, the area with the densest concentration of Jews. Local Jewish charities were among the main recipients of donations from him once he had made his fortune.

Alan Sugar mixes easily with non-Jews, yet his upbringing in a self-consciously Jewish (albeit largely secular) family was an important factor in forging his identity. He was named Alan as an Anglicized version of Fay's father's name, Aaron; similarly, he named his own eldest son Simon after Nathan's father. Sugar drew from his childhood the traditional Jewish emphasis on the family, as well as a desire to improve himself. In other circumstances, that might have been reflected in his going to university and entering one of the professions. Indeed, associates in later life reckoned that at times Sugar regretted his inability to pursue his education further. Given his milieu, business was the alternative escape route.

Sugar himself is typically unpretentious in trying to explain his drive to sell, citing his wish to leave behind the poverty of his upbringing: 'My self-reliance really all revolved around finance. There was never any question of anything being done for me or put on a plate for me. It was quite clear that whatever you did and got and achieved, you had to go and do for yourself.'

Yet many other children shared such an upbringing without turning into tycoons. By the time he left school, Sugar had already discovered an urge to trade and sell that ran deeper than a simple wish for money. He was later to compare this instinct with other people's gift for music. 'I seriously believe I've got an inborn talent,' he explained. 'I've got an inbuilt aptitude for trading and dealing and scenting the way the wind is blowing.'

However, the young Sugar had to put his entrepreneurial instinct on ice as he emerged into the adult world.

*

It is difficult to imagine anyone more unsuited to the daily life of the Civil Service than Alan Sugar. The cautiousness, the anonymity, the respect for established procedures and patterns of thought, the routine meetings – everything that marks out the civil servant is anathema to him. Yet it was to the statistics department of the Ministry of Education and Science, one of the most bureaucratic of all the Whitehall departments, that he headed for his first job.

Unsurprisingly, Nathan Sugar encouraged his son in this move, seeing an office job in Whitehall as a step up the ladder into a professional career. For Nathan, keeping his youngest child at school beyond the school-leaving age had been both a sacrifice and an investment. 'If I had stayed at school longer than I needed and then ended up working as a salesman in a shoe-shop or a men's-wear shop, it would have seemed a total waste to him,' Sugar explains.

Knowing no better himself, Sugar went along with his father's wishes. In any case, working on statistics in the Ministry responsible for science appealed to the young Alan. He had been so pleased to get his first job that he had not enquired too closely into the nature of the work. 'Science – this was something I had always been interested in. Statistics, maths – I wasn't too bad at that. So I thought I'd go for it.'

Sugar was in for a shock. Far from being scalded by the white heat of the technological revolution, which Harold Wilson had just sold to an expectant nation during the 1964 general election campaign, he found himself shuffling paper. The most intellectually challenging work was coding research for the Plowden Inquiry into primary education: how many children drank milk in the morning – and how many did not? 'When I got there, I found it was the most unbelievable bore going,' Sugar says.

People dealing with him in later years were invariably struck by two interrelated facets of his intelligence: the speed with which he digests complicated proposals and his tendency to become bored very quickly. Already an impatient man, he found the Ministry a nightmare and still sounds angry when he remembers it. 'You literally had to watch the clock. It was total agony waiting for that clock to tick to five o'clock.'

During his brief sojourn in Whitehall, much of Sugar's energy went into his after-hours activities. He was probably alone among his new colleagues at the Ministry in holding down a Saturday job, first in a men's-wear shop in Tottenham Court Road, then in a chemist's near Walthamstow market.

Sidelines like these Saturday jobs brought in extra cash and helped to satisfy Sugar's drive to sell, but they were not enough to compensate him for the boredom and lack of prospects at the Ministry. 'He didn't like it because it was a sitting-down job,' is his mother's wry comment on this interlude.

It took Sugar less than a year to realize that he would always be a square peg in the world of committees. Yet when he decided to leave, he was persuaded by his father's anxious vision of a respectable white-collar future to try something similar. He entered the statistics department of Richard Thomas & Baldwin, a steel company central to Britain's heavy industry-dominated economy of the time, but long since a victim of rationalization.

The tedium of the work, which he soon found as dull as anything at the Ministry, was relieved by the office crowd who took a liking to the young East Ender. They joked a lot, and shared with Sugar their worldly wisdom. Already too tied down by wives and mortgages to think of quitting themselves, they reckoned he still had a chance and were sure he was in the wrong job. They told him that selling was where money was to be made: 'Get out there and get into sales.'

Telling Sugar to sell was like telling Rudolf Nureyev to dance. In the lunch-breaks from his Saturday job in the chemist's shop in Walthamstow, Sugar used to meet a friend called Malcolm Cross who worked locally as a television engineer. He had got to know Cross – like himself from the poorest of East End families – a couple of years earlier in one of the Jewish youth clubs in Stamford Hill. They were part of a shifting gang of Jewish teenagers from Hackney, who made occasional forays to the coffee bars and ten-pin-bowling alleys of the West End.

Between them, Cross and Sugar hatched a scheme which can lay claim to being Alan Sugar's first commercial enterprise as an adult. The idea was to combine Cross's skills as a television engineer with Sugar's already evident talents for selling. The pair of them would buy run-down, second-hand TV sets in two-dozen batches; Cross would do them up; and Sugar would sell them.

By the mid-1960s, TV had become a necessity for even the poorest Hackney home, yet the sets on offer then were unreliable, forever breaking down. The *Hackney Gazette* had a regular slot for adverts from friendly, local TV repair men, and also advertised reconditioned TV sets from as little as £5.

Sugar added a little twist to this well-established part of Hackney life, advertising Cross's reconditioned TVs as presents given to the Sugar family which they did not happen to need. 'He used to sell them in his bedroom, pretending they were a one-off, unwanted gift. As he sold one, we used to put another in the bedroom,' explains Cross.

Pretty soon, the whole family was aware of Sugar's new sideline. Derek, Sugar's brother, stopped his cab one day at a coffee stall in Stoke Newington. 'I saw a little advert pinned on it, "TV for sale", and I did a double take because it was my mother's phone number.'

Daphne became used to the procession of odd people climbing the stairs of Woolmer House to look at the 'old monstrosities', as she referred to the TVs. At times Fay had to field the complaints of the not inconsiderable flow of dissatisfied customers: 'They used to come and say, "Television's not working," so I'd say, "Well, here's the money back."'

Sugar and Cross took their fledgling business seriously, christening it 'Maurann', an amalgam of the names of Cross's wife Maureen and Sugar's girl-friend, Ann. Sugar arranged headed notepaper for Maurann and the partners hired a room where they stashed their TVs. The enterprise lasted a year at most, but it represented a bridge between Sugar's brief days as a salaried employee and his life as an entrepreneur.

Selling fitted Sugar's natural temperament better than life in an office ever could, but his eventual decision to quit Richard Thomas & Baldwin was characteristically dictated by something much more immediate: 'What I was really after was wheels.'

He had had plenty of time to contemplate the freedom offered by a car as he looked out from the Northwold estate on to the busy Upper Clapton Road, scything its way through Hackney. A car had always been way off the map for the Sugar family. 'A car was considered to be an absolute luxury. Rich people had cars – that's how you viewed it,' Sugar says.

The earliest ambition that Sugar can remember was for his own car. And since neither he nor his family could afford one, the only way of realizing this ambition was to find a job which came with 'wheels'.

Sugar answered an advert placed by Robuk Electrical, then a well-known tape recorder dealer based in the Holloway Road in North London. Robuk was adding to its firm's sales force throughout the country and Sugar was given the job of covering London, selling its tape recorders to retailers all over the capital. Nathan was less than impressed by his son's move. 'My old man was going mad. I'd had three jobs in about nine months, while he tried to stick with one job for 15 years,' recalls Sugar.

In fact, the job was perfect for him. It allowed him to roam London by himself, getting to know the myriad outlets for electrical goods; it gave full vent to his selling instincts; and, crucially, it gave him the use of a van.

Throwing himself into the work, Sugar was delighted to hear one day that Robuk had done a deal with Currys, the electrical goods chain, which would allow him to sell tape recorders direct to each Currys store. Currys's shop managers had previously lacked the authority to order tape recorders without contacting head office. Suddenly they were set free, an event which Sugar still remembers as a tremendous coup: 'Well, to me that was like a licence to print money.'

Sugar talked every Currys store in London into buying Robuk's tape recorders, but come pay day, he found that his commission was about a quarter of what he had been expecting. None too pleased, he demanded an explanation from Robuk and was told that because the Currys business represented a bulk deal, the commission was correspondingly less. There was a row and, right or wrong, Sugar waved goodbye to Robuk.

His next port of call was R. Henson Ltd, an electrical wholesaler in Finchley. Hensons handled the products which were pouring into London from importers and manufacturers to fuel the mid-1960s boom in electrical goods: transistor radios, car aerials, car radios, clock radios, walkie-talkies. Sugar's job was to take samples to Hensons's retail customers, strike a deal, then deliver the order and collect the payment.

Driving around in the Hensons van, Sugar rapidly boosted his knowledge of the hundreds of independent outlets and shifting product ranges that made up the electricals business. But respect for his new employer did not develop in equal measure.

'Hensons was really an eye-opener. I thought they were a stingy load of sods, I did. I used to sell the stuff for them, then deliver the bloody stuff, then collect the money for them. And you never got a pat on the back for doing anything right,' he says.

The final straw came when Sugar located a stock of surplus records, a line which had sold well for Hensons in the past. He told them he could buy these cheaply and already knew someone who would take the records off their hands at a tidy profit. Hensons gave him the go-ahead and the cash to cover the deal. Sugar duly returned with a couple of hundred pounds to show from a day's work.

'If Hensons had been clever at that stage, they would have made me a partner of the firm, and it might have been Hensons-cum-Amstrad by now,' Sugar says.

Instead, they criticized him for not making an even bigger profit and, adding injury to insult, refused to give him an extra bonus on the deal. 'That naffed me a little bit,' Sugar adds with feeling even twenty years later. Peter Henson, who now runs the family firm, does not remember this incident, but Sugar continued to trade with Hensons after he set up his own business, suggesting that relations were soon restored.

This episode crystallized the suspicion which had been forming in Sugar's mind that he could do better on his own. He used to pick up goods for Hensons from one of its main suppliers, Binatone, a company which had been importing anything which would sell from the Far East since the late 1950s. With the other drivers, he would queue at the loading bay at Binatone's main premises in Finsbury Square, just north of the City.

During his enforced waits by the loading bay, Sugar fell to chatting with Gulu Lalvani, one of the two brothers who runs Binatone. Although only a few years older than Sugar, Lalvani was already a suave and successful businessman, an obvious role model for the ambitious East Ender. A tall, elegant man who set up Binatone in 1958 after coming to Britain from Bombay, Lalvani remains one of Sugar's closest friends. He remembers Sugar's acumen and will to succeed marking him out from the other drivers.

It had not taken Sugar long to understand the fundamentals of the business. He knew the credit terms Binatone gave Hensons; he knew what Hensons paid for Binatone's goods; he knew Hensons's outlets and the prices they paid. In short, he grasped that Hensons was getting goods on credit and selling them for cash: 'In the end, I realized that's all they were – a glorified buying and selling agency.'

Sugar was earning about £20 a week with Hensons, and he reckoned he could make that in a day on his own. He spent £80, the bare minimum, on a second hand Mini-van and went to Lalvani with a proposition. He was going to quit Hensons, so if he gave Lalvani a seven days' post-dated cheque for a couple of hundred pounds, would Lalvani give him goods to that value?

Lalvani hesitated. In those days John Henson was one of his best friends and the Binatone chairman was loath to be seen to be encouraging one of Hensons's workers to strike out in competition with him. 'Look, I'm going to quit, whether you help me or not,' Sugar said.

To satisfy his conscience, Lalvani suggested as a compromise that Sugar should go away for a couple of weeks' holiday before launching out on his own, so that it did not look as though Lalvani had directly encouraged him to make the break. Sugar agreed.

When the two weeks were up, Sugar duly presented Binatone with the post-dated cheque and collected his goods. Lalvani was surprised to see Sugar's van rolling into Binatone's premises that same evening: 'Give me the cheque back. Here's the cash,' Sugar said, handing over the money.

Sugar had managed to sell the week's deliveries in a day. He was back at Binatone bright and early the next day for another consignment. Sugar earned a profit of 20–25 per cent on everything he sold. It was 1966 and Sugar was a 19-year-old entrepreneur. He knew at once that he had made the right move.

That was not how it appeared to Nathan, the ever-cautious father who had spent his whole life working for other people. When Sugar told Nathan that he was quitting Hensons to work for himself, his father asked anxiously, 'But who's going to pay your wages?'

· 3 ·

Starting Out

The year 1968 has gone down in the history of the twentieth century as a year of pseudo-revolution. Students revolted in Paris, occupied university buildings in London and held love-ins in San Francisco. For a brief moment, the foundations of Western society seemed to be cracking as the children of the privileged attacked authority in the name of the working classes.

The year also saw momentous changes for Alan Sugar, but for the young East Ender the upheaval was a private matter. A product of the working class himself, Sugar had no time for the romantic myths of his middle-class contemporaries. He knew that changes in his life would flow from his own efforts. And in 1968 the changes to Alan Sugar came thick and fast: he married, he left Hackney and he founded Amstrad.

Sugar had met Ann Simons through the network of friends which congregated around the Stamford Hill youth clubs. A shy girl a couple of years younger than Alan, Ann soon formed a strong attachment to her rough diamond boy-friend. Sometimes when she had a day off from her job as a hairdresser, she would accompany him on his deliveries, quietly reading a book in the front of the van while he loaded or unloaded a consignment of aerials or radios.

The budding romance was not greeted with universal approval. At first the Simons family did not think much of Ann's choice. What could Sugar offer her? He had already gone through a string of jobs and was now running a one-man business from the back of a clapped-out van. He was not much of a catch for a daughter who might have hoped to marry a lawyer, an accountant or a doctor – someone with a future.

Not only did Sugar have nothing to his name, he even came from the wrong part of town. Living in Redbridge – the London borough to the north-east of Hackney where many Jews moved once they were prosperous enough to leave the East End – the Simonses had no wish to be linked with a family still stuck in Hackney. Johnny Simons tried to impress his views on his daughter, but to no avail.

Sugar was already acutely aware that he came from the wrong side of the tracks. As a teenager, he had begun to make friends outside his immediate social circle, partly through the Jewish youth clubs in Stamford Hill – an area one step further away from the East End than Clapton and visibly more affluent. He socialized with people of his own age from Stamford Hill or even, like Ann, from Redbridge. 'I met a different class of person. Some of their parents were in business and I saw a little bit of a different way of life,' Sugar recalls.

He was not the only member of the gang to come from the poor parts of Hackney; Malcolm Cross, his partner in the television venture, shared this background. But Maureen, Cross's future wife and also part of the crowd, distinctly remembers: 'Alan was the poorest out of all the boys. He really was. Few of us had anything, but he had less than all of us.'

Some of his new friends lived in houses which seemed way beyond the dreams of the Sugar family. This disparity fed his drive to leave behind the poverty of Hackney, which had been growing more intense in the young Sugar:

As I began to mix with this different circle of friends that came from better-off families, it was evident there was no point asking my father if he could buy me some nicer clothes, a car and things like that. It was not that he didn't want to, he couldn't. So it was clear that if I ever wanted anything, I had to do it for myself, simply to improve my lifestyle. So that's what I did.

The idea of dropping Ann because he was too poor cut right across the grain of Sugar's sensitivities. Disapproval from his girl-friend's family only reinforced his determination to make a go of his one-man business. Associates of the time, like Binatone's Gulu Lalvani, noticed the impact on Sugar: 'It motivated him even more. He wanted to prove to his girl-friend's father that, O.K., he might not be a doctor or an accountant or a lawyer, but he could be a successful businessman,' Lalvani recalls.

In the end, the family opposition proved futile and the young couple were married in 1968, when Sugar was 21. The families put on a good show at the wedding, a clear signal that the Simons side was reconciled to Ann's choice. The service in the Great Portland Street synagogue was followed by a reception in the West End.

Alan and Ann Sugar bought a house in Marlands Road, Clayhall, an area of Redbridge not far from where Ann's parents lived, reflecting the fact that Sugar's business was already showing signs of success. Clayhall is full of neat semi-detached houses newly clad in stone chippings. The classier of the dwellings sport mock-Tudor exteriors, with black and white panelling and opaque diamond window-panes – or even Greek frontages, with fake Doric columns supporting the porchways.

The young couple could not yet manage anything quite like that, but they moved into a quiet street of handsome semis with wide bay windows. In any case, it was enough that they were in Clayhall at all; they were on the first rung of the ladder.

*

It was not all plain sailing for the young businessman, however. Sugar had had to struggle with his Mini-van from his earliest days working for himself. It had been the cheapest which he could find and as a result was for ever breaking down: 'Because it was always in the bloody workshop, I couldn't go out and sell. We needed a more reliable vehicle because that was the lifeblood,' Sugar explains.

Under normal circumstances, the solution would have been simple: Sugar would have bought a new van, using hire-purchase. But when he first went into business, he was too young to sign a hire-purchase agreement. So he turned to his parents for help, but in doing so once more ran up against his father's ultra-cautious instincts.

Sugar's idea was that he would put down a £100 deposit – the most he could manage – towards a Vauxhall Viva costing about £500. Nathan would sign the hire-purchase agreement and Sugar would then take care of the weekly payments. But Nathan felt anxious about the prospect of his son being in hock to a hire-purchase outfit, so instead he came up with the balance of the money from his own savings and Alan paid off a weekly amount to his father. Sugar recalls: 'It was the typical mentality of my father. He couldn't understand that I'd ever be able to pay the money back.'

Robbery was the next hurdle Sugar had to confront. At the time, he was keeping his stock in a lean-to built for the purpose on the back of the Sugars' new house in Marlands Road. Describing the setback to his fledgling business, he says: 'I'd built the business up and was making a good salary and had about £1,500 worth of stock. And one day someone broke into the back of the house and nicked it all. It was bloody stupid when you think about it.'

Luckily for Sugar, the robbery was not fatal to his business because a lot of his assets were in the form of money owed to him by customers. But he quickly learned his lesson: 'I wasn't completely flattened, but I decided then that I needed some premises, a burglar alarm and proper insurance, so that it could never occur again.'

Sugar found his first business premises in a house in St John Street, just down from Islington High Street in North London and almost opposite the Sadler's Wells opera house. St John Street marks the point where Islington's bistros and antique shops give way to an area of dingy small businesses and workshops. His headquarters was in a tall, austere terrace of houses which would have made fine homes if they had been tucked into an Islington back street. But since the terrace was on the main road to the City and Fleet Street, it was in fact made over almost exclusively to small businesses. Yet the aesthetics of the building were Sugar's least concern; what mattered to him was that the larger premises allowed him to build up bigger stocks and a wider range of products.

Through a cousin of Ann's, Sugar found his first accountant – Guy Gordon, a podgy, avuncular man who was a partner in a firm specializing in small- and medium-sized companies. Gordon told Sugar what records to keep and, just as crucially, initiated the young businessman into the mysteries of limited liability. Shortly after Sugar moved into Marlands Road, Gordon advised him to form a proper company so as to guard himself against bad debt problems, a perennial risk in his line of territory. By doing so, Sugar would limit his personal liability if his company ran into difficulties and so prevent his house – his one personal asset of any value – becoming vulnerable to creditors.

And so in 1968, on the first day of November, A.M.S. Trading Company (General Importers) was registered as a limited company. The name is instructive for two reasons. First, Sugar's initials are spelt out in the title, showing it to be a half-way stage on the road to 'Amstrad', the brand which was to become a household name almost two decades later.

Second, the use of the term 'trading' – and even more so of the description 'general importers' – reveals how Sugar envisaged his business at this stage. It was to be a buying and selling operation: manufacturing was not part of the equation. And since he was mainly buying and selling electrical goods, much of his merchandise would inevitably be imported.

Sugar slipped into using 'Amstrad' not long after the registration of his company, certainly well before he formally changed the name of the operation to A.M.S. Trading (Amstrad) in November 1972. As he began to take a regular flow of goods from particular importers, it occurred to him that he would create a more substantial image among his retail customers if he had his own brand name. 'It just seemed that if I had my own brand name on a product, it gave it more credibility, rather than it being simply something passed on by a wholesaler,' he explains.

Cigarette lighters and intercoms for connecting different rooms in an office were the first products to bear the Amstrad name. Sugar did not manufacture these: they were goods which he bought from importers and then badged. Amstrad – a name which is so catchy that it deserves to have been invented by a team of image consultants – simply evolved as a shortened version of A.M.S. Trading: 'It sounded right, but it was more luck than judgment. A lot of the other brand names of people we were dealing with in those days were also anagrams of their trading titles,' Sugar recalls.

Sugar was just 21 when he registered his company. That same year, a man seven years his senior and destined to play a considerable role in the Amstrad story was making *his* first big splash. Clive Sinclair caused a considerable stir by placing a four-page colour ad for an expensive amplifier in *Hi-Fi News*, the normally black-and-white journal of the audio hobbyists. Sinclair was becoming an exciting name in the world which Sugar would soon enter himself.

The next couple of years were punishing ones for Sugar. He spent the time remorselessly extending his contacts with the multitude of small independent outlets which dominated the electrical goods and audio businesses at the time. That meant buying from whichever wholesalers were prepared to shave a few pence off their cost, and selling to whichever outlet offered the best price. He had to make countless journeys in his van, not just all over London but also to towns like Cambridge and Portsmouth – wherever, in fact, the best deal could be done.

One of the first people he came across after moving into St John Street was Colin Lewin, who had a shop trading in electrical goods in Gray's Inn Road, just down from Sugar's premises. A few years older than Sugar, Lewin had the same short, stocky, bustling physique as the younger man and shared something of his background too. Brought up in a poor family, although on the other side of London in Battersea, Lewin had originally worked as a telephone engineer for the Post Office in the West End, but this left him with so much time on his hands that he started selling transistor radios while waiting to be called out to repair a customer's telephone.

Lewin and Sugar were in the same line of business, selling

amplifiers, tuners, turntables, car radios, aerials, speakers, transistor radios . . . in fact, pretty much anything they could get their hands on. Both young and ambitious, they soon started trading with each other – swapping bits and pieces they had picked up, sometimes in batches of a hundred, sometimes in one-offs.

The two became friends and Sugar often stopped off at the café next to Lewin's shop for a cup of tea – provided, that is, that he could carve out the time, for his first priority was always doing a deal. 'Alan certainly put in a good six-day week. He'd sell anything, anywhere,' Lewin remembers.

Sugar took more and more of the radios, tape recorders and car aerials imported from the Far East by Gulu Lalvani for Binatone, impressing him with his ability to spot the slightest opportunity. One day, for instance, Lalvani happened to mention that Binatone had imported a batch of radios with a slight fault; although the repair would be easy to do, his engineers were preoccupied with other work, so the radios would have to lie around in the warehouse for a few months.

'Give me batches of 100 to 200 a time and I'll get them done for you,' was Sugar's immediate reaction to the news. So he started taking batches of these radios home overnight and bringing them back adjusted the next day. It was pretty clear to Lalvani that Sugar and his wife were doing the work themselves; this was the kind of initiative that he was beginning to expect.

At the end of the 1960s Tottenham Court Road, in London's West End, boasted the greatest concentration of independent audio and hi-fi shops in the capital, just as it does now. Twenty years ago, there were few more important people in this business microcosm than Ronnie Marks, boss of Premier Radio which had started as a wholesaler and then became one of the first outfits to open an audio shop on Tottenham Court Road. Marks was working in the back of his wholesale operation one day when the chap on the counter came in and said, 'I've got a new face out front. He says he needs some credit.'

Marks went out to see this new face and found a brash youngster who said his name was Alan Sugar, he had just started up on his own and he needed some credit to get going. Marks was cautious:

'Credit is difficult. We don't know you or what you're like.' Sugar was adamant: 'If I don't have credit, I can't get business.'

After a bit more sparring, Marks agreed a 'one-over-one' arrangement, the most basic type of credit. Sugar could have a load of goods from Premier, but he had to pay for them when he came back for another consignment. It was take-and-pay and Sugar started coming into Premier every Friday, increasing his take week by week. After a few months testing him out on this tight leash, Marks agreed to loosen the terms and gave Sugar a month to pay for each batch of Premier's goods. 'He always, always honoured his obligation,' Marks recalls.

Credit from established wholesalers like Binatone and Premier Radio helped Sugar to generate credibility with other suppliers, who would ring up Lalvani or Marks to check out his record before giving him credit themselves. Sugar was learning how to balance his sources of credit and cash, allowing him to finance his growing business by building up a range of credit sources. By selling quickly, he was taking in money on goods he had not yet paid for himself.

Still only just into his twenties, Sugar was rapidly forging a reputation as one of the most promising young middle men in the business – a reliable conduit of goods from the wholesalers to the independent retailers. Unknown to either group, however, he was also hedging his bets by taking a stake in a retail operation himself.

*

Home in Clayhall, Alan Sugar had struck up a friendship with a man of his own age called Ashley Morris. The Sugars were linked to Morris through one of those family chains typical of the Redbridge Jewish community: the first cousin of Morris's then wife was married to Sugar's sister Daphne.

The friendship blossomed in 1969 when the birth of the Sugars' first son, Simon, coincided with that of Morris's daughter. The two wives, having gone through ante-natal clinic together, started dropping in on each other during the day and it was not long before the couples were going out as a foursome in the evenings.

The two men took to discussing business over dinner and Sugar explained that one of his old friends, Malcolm Cross, had opened a discount hi-fi shop in Stamford Hill, called Audio Supplies. Customers would travel from all over London in the hunt for bargains on the latest amplifier, tuner or other hi-fi item. Cross and his partner were also running a mail order operation by advertising lists of products in the hi-fi magazines. Sugar told Morris that he would be amazed at the amount of money which was changing hands in Cross's shop.

Morris worked in the fashion business in those days, but Sugar persuaded him to cast an eye over Audio Supplies one Saturday morning. He introduced Morris as his cousin because he did not want Cross to realize they were there to take a look at the business. Sugar and Morris made some small talk and saw that, sure enough, people were coming in every five minutes and buying £100, £150, £200 worth of equipment – money to be reckoned with at the end of the 1960s.

Back home, Morris agreed to Sugar's suggestion that they should open a similar operation themselves. They took premises in Pentonville Road, not far from St John Street, called their business Global Audio and drew up adverts for the hi-fi magazines modelled on Malcolm Cross's efforts. Morris explains: 'We decided to set up a business which was really copying Audio Supplies completely, except we slashed the prices as much as we could, while still making a margin to live on.'

Sugar and Morris put in £2,000 each to launch Global Audio, but the business got off to a bad start when a company from which Sugar had ordered £1,700 of record decks went into liquidation just before making the delivery. That wiped out almost half of Global Audio's initial capital. Sugar retrieved the situation by arranging a line of credit from one of his many contacts in the business, Dallas Electrical, an outfit based in the City which sold hi-fi gear and musical instruments.

The two partners were listed as directors of Global Audio, but Sugar wanted his involvement in the shop kept quiet. He feared that other retailers would resent it if they realized that Sugar – whose prime job was to sell to them – also had a retailing operation: they would suspect that he was selling equipment to

Global at discount prices. Manufacturers might also take a dim view of Sugar's move; in those days they tended to deal only with wholesalers, not with retailers, so they might accuse him of confusing the market by dabbling in both sides of the business. He was just becoming established in the close-knit London audio world and could not afford to put his hard-won position at risk by being seen to ride two horses at once.

Sugar would drop into Global Audio on a Saturday, chat to the kids in the stock-room, serve a customer or two and pick up his cut of the week's takings. His position in the company was never broadcast, although plenty in the trade knew about it. Colin Lewin, for one, would wander up from his shop in Gray's Inn Road to Global Audio on a Saturday and find Sugar serving behind the counter: 'Alan was like me. He couldn't just sit there and watch people being served.'

But Sugar did not like having to keep his stake in Global Audio perpetually hidden. He told Morris: 'Look, I can't stay involved in this much longer. I want to go places in the hi-fi world. So you can buy me out.' He put a take-it-or-leave-it offer on the table, which Morris took.

By then, Sugar had another reason for wanting out of Global: he had launched the first Amstrad product and it was beginning to take off.

*

By 1970, when his company was almost two years old and Sugar was 23, he was already becoming aware of the limitations of his chosen field of operations:

> I rapidly started realizing that I was just going to be a dealer for the rest of my life. It wasn't really exciting because there was no big money to be made. Everything I was selling was commodity stuff. There were no big coups to be had, because everybody knew the prices.

Casting around for something to drag him out of the one-man-and-a-van rut, Sugar concluded that he could move his business on to a new level if he could find a product which he could manufacture more cheaply than anyone else. The problem was: what?

In the early days of hi-fi, it was standard practice to buy all the parts that made up a hi-fi system separately. Customers would often purchase a record player in one place, amplifiers elsewhere, turn to yet a third brand for speakers and then assemble the components into one system. Hi-fi enthusiasts would also have to acquire some distinctly unglamorous, low tech parts before they could unveil their system to an admiring world: one was the wooden base on which a record player sat, known in the trade as a plinth; the other was a plastic cover to keep dust off the turntable.

Sugar noticed that the cost of the plastic dust covers being sold at the time appeared inordinately high. He decided to find out why and soon learned that the covers were made by a process known as vacuum forming. A sheet of acrylic – or perspex, as it would be called today – was sucked into a warm mould, shaped and then trimmed off. The trouble with this process was that it used a lot of acrylic, a relatively high-cost raw material.

The young businessman reckoned that there must be a better way of doing it, so he picked up the phone book and started ringing any organization he could find with the word 'plastic' in its title. He discovered that it would be possible to make the covers differently, using a technique called injection moulding. This would require a large initial investment in an injection moulding tool, but would yield big savings on the material costs.

After another burst of phone calls, Sugar found a tool-maker who could produce the injection moulding tool for him. He invested £1,805 in the tool, which was a fortune to him at the time, but that proved the easy part: 'I took the cheapest bloke going. There was heartache and aggravation there, because he was supposed to make the tool in three months and it took about five months. And when he made the first moulds, they broke. He moulded them at the wrong temperatures.'

But Sugar persevered and soon he was making plastic dust covers more cheaply than anyone else in the business, buying in a set of plinths and sticking them together. Plinths and covers were the first articles which he manufactured himself. They were products which everybody wanted. He shifted his plinths and covers in large quantities, cashing in on the contacts he had made and the reputation he had built for always honouring deals during his van delivery days.

Sugar sold his plinths and covers to the cluster of Tottenham Court Road hi-fi specialists like Premier Radio and Lasky's. He sold them to manufacturers such as BSR, who incorporated them into their ranges. He sold them to Ashley Morris at Global Audio, who advertised them at £2.95 each. He sold them at a slight discount to other old pals, like Colin Lewin who at one stage was taking 1,000 a time from Sugar and passing them on to his dealers in bundles of a hundred. With everybody screaming for his covers, the injection machine at the moulder's plant could not pump them out fast enough to keep up with demand.

With the benefit of a large amount of hindsight, Sugar's plastic dust covers already exhibited many of the features which were to become Amstrad hallmarks. The product might not itself be innovative, but Sugar had broken new ground by radically reducing the cost of its production. This allowed him to carry off his three-card trick: high volumes, low prices and large margins. He could offer his customers so keen a price that it was bound to undercut his competitors, *and* he could simultaneously generate high profit margins for himself.

Of course, this was not how it appeared to Sugar back in 1970, but he was fully aware that his business was set on a new trajectory: 'We came out of the era where I was just distributing all those wholesale imports into an era of becoming a manufacturer.'

*

One evening, the Sugars and the Morrises went to a smart West End restaurant, where over dinner the two men fell to chatting about their favourite subject. Ashley Morris opened up: 'I don't care what you say, Alan, success in business is 50 per cent hard work and 50 per cent luck. You have to have the luck running

with you, otherwise you get nowhere.' Sugar's reply was immediate: 'No, mate, it's hard work. It's all hard work.'

In his early twenties, Sugar had reason to be pleased with the
progress of his business. He had disproved all the sceptical
forebodings of his father by showing that he could live off his wits;
he had left Hackney behind, moving into an area inhabited by the
most affluent of his teenage friends; he was earning enough to keep
him and his young wife – in fact, more than enough, since they
were beginning to be able to afford the occasional extravagance,
like a night out at an expensive restaurant or discotheque.

Yet Sugar displayed no sign of throttling back or of taking it
easy. On the contrary, friends of his from that time describe an
intense man, preoccupied with succeeding in his business to the
exclusion of everything else. He confided in one friend that the
demands of running his business on his own used to keep him
awake at night. He had a compulsion to win which was quite out
of the ordinary, as one old friend relates: 'If you sat down and
played a game with him, if he wasn't winning, he played till two
or three o'clock in the morning till he *was* winning. He was like a
bear with a sore head if he didn't win. He wanted to prove
something all the time to everybody.'

True, Sugar liked few things better than going out with his
friends for a meal in the evening, an event which would have
seemed an unimaginable luxury for him only a few years earlier.
But even on these occasions he found it difficult to throw off the
cares of his work and became really animated with his friends only
when he was discussing business. 'I can't remember him relaxing,
to tell you the truth. I can't visualize it,' says one old friend.
Another adds: 'He never seemed as if he was listening to you. His
mind was always ticking over on something else.'

The fact is that with his growing business to manage, and the
responsibility for a young family, at this stage of his life Alan
Sugar had no time left over for demanding hobbies or interests.
Daphne, his sister, remembers from this time: 'Once he started in
business, that was his hobby.'

Daphne was close to the Sugars while they lived in Marlands
Road. Although she did not realize how well Alan Sugar was

doing in his business, it was impossible for her to be unaware of the streak of intense ambition running through her young brother. In a moment of prescient candour, he once confided in her: 'I won't be satisfied until I come home and land at Heathrow and there's a big board with the Amstrad name on it. I want the Amstrad name to be as well known as Hoover.'

· 4 ·

The Truck Driver and His Wife

Alan Sugar was scratching his brain about how to get Amstrad into Comet. There could be no more important breakthrough for his business in the early 1970s than to have his goods on the shelves of Comet's stores. By then he had launched a string of products for the fast-growing audio industry – parts like amplifiers and tuners which went to make up a hi-fi system – and he knew that Amstrad and Comet were made for each other.

In its time Comet was one of the true retailing revolutionaries. It had the same transforming effect on the sale of audio and hi-fi equipment as Habitat later had on household furnishings and Next on men's clothes. Like all retailing pioneers, Comet's success flowed from its recognition that the aspirations of a new group of consumers were not being met. And it so happened that Comet's and Amstrad's natural constituencies were identical.

Comet's roots lie in a small family business in Hull. Michael Hollingbery, who led the company's discounting revolution, inherited just one shop from his father. His key decision was made in 1968 when he began to offer electrical goods for sale below the prices recommended by the manufacturers. The manufacturers loathed the idea of discounting, but they could do nothing about it thanks to the Government's abolition in 1964 of the rigid set of pricing rules known as retail price maintenance.

A whole new philosophy of selling audio equipment accompanied Comet's decision to discount. Comet opened large stores on the edge of town which were notable for their absence of frills, and carried this spartan philosophy into its advertising. A Comet advert was little more than a list of the equipment that it held in stock, identified by the manufacturers' names and product descriptions, together with the discounted prices. A customer could buy the goods either through mail order or by visiting a Comet store.

Before the emergence of Comet, the audio market had been dominated by small independent outlets, made for hi-fi buffs to linger lovingly over the latest breakthrough in high quality sound. Comet and Hollingbery were angling for an entirely different market: newly affluent young consumers, who wanted their own hi-fi set because they had been reared on pop music but did not want to bother about the technical details of the equipment. They wanted something which worked, looked good, gave value for money and could be bought with the minimum of fuss. 'The truck driver and his wife' – this was how Sugar was later to sum up this market. It was precisely the market which he coveted for himself.

But there was a problem: how could Amstrad make the initial breakthrough? Comet's stores had spread rapidly in the north during the late 1960s and were beginning to colonize the south by the early 1970s. Already keenly aware of its market power, Comet knew it could make or break a budding young manufacturer like Sugar. With plenty of other fish in the water, there was no reason for it to favour Amstrad.

Sugar fretted long and hard about Comet. The Sugars spent a restless holiday in Majorca with the Amstrad boss brooding by the poolside about this dilemma. He knew that the first step was to secure a face-to-face interview with Gerry Mason, Comet's marketing director.

Mason was a volatile Yorkshireman who made most of Comet's key purchasing decisions. Years later he was to affect the life of a country squire, ensconced in a newly built 'manor' on top of a hill south of Harrogate, with half a dozen retrievers, as many cats, stables, a younger wife and a huge leather-topped desk in the middle of a study that looked totally unused. Short and stocky, his shirt open at the neck to reveal a tuft of white hair and a gold medallion, with gold sovereign rings on his fingers and green wellies on his feet, there hung about Mason even in his retirement echoes of the hard-living and hard-swearing reputation which had been a legend in the industry.

Sugar started phoning Mason to pester him for a meeting, at first to no effect. 'Eventually, one day I got an interview with him. It was about as easy as getting an interview with the Queen,' Sugar recalls.

Mason made it plain that he was not interested in Amstrad's new line of amplifiers, precisely the goods which Sugar wanted Comet to take. Instead, Mason wanted Sugar's help in getting hold of record players sold by Garrard, a leading British audio manufacturer of the time.

Garrard had an odd pricing policy for its record players, which it sold as chassis without plinths and covers. It set one price for a retail outlet which planned to sell them direct to the general public and a lower price for a manufacturer like Amstrad intending to incorporate them into its own products to sell as completed units.

This two-handed pricing policy was almost calculated to open up a secondary market, known in the trade as a 'grey' market. A canny manufacturer like Amstrad could buy Garrard's record players at the cheaper price and then sell them straight on to a retailer, allowing Amstrad and the retailer to split the saving they had made at Garrard's expense. Sugar explains: 'There was a good grey market business going on there. We were a manufacturer, so Garrard would sell us the record players at the cheaper price. We could then fit them into our plinths and covers and ship them on to the likes of Comet who could sell them as fully made up record players.'

Sugar travelled up to Comet's Hull office to see Mason on the understanding that he was going to sell Mason lots of Garrard record players at the grey market price. Once safely over the threshold of Mason's office, he quickly agreed to the Garrard deal – but on one condition: 'I'm only going to do it on the basis of you taking some of my amplifiers,' he told the Yorkshireman.

Mason was reluctant because Comet had no need of another line of amplifiers, but in the end the two reached a compromise.

Mason would not buy any of Amstrad's amplifiers, but he *would* include them in the Comet listings. Then if anybody asked for the amplifiers, Comet would order them ad hoc.

Sugar returned from Hull well pleased with the day's business. True, Comet had not actually bought any of his gear, but featuring the Amstrad name in Comet's listings was the next best thing. On the journey back to London, Sugar was already turning over in his mind how he could transform this opening into hard orders.

As soon as Comet published the advertisements with Amstrad's equipment in its listings, Sugar moved into action. Mobilizing half a dozen relatives, friends and colleagues to write to Comet with an order for an Amstrad amplifier, he was careful to ensure a geographical spread. Johnny Simons, his father-in-law, wrote in from Redbridge, in north-east London. George Chinchen, who had designed Amstrad's first amplifier, ordered one from Croydon, to the south of the capital.

Sugar sat back and waited. A week or so later, a clerk phoned Amstrad from Comet's head office: 'It appears we've received seven orders for your new amplifier. Just to be on the safe side, we've decided to take ten.'

Sugar immediately went into his angry act: 'Don't be so bloody stupid. You're supposed to be Comet. I'm not selling you ten of anything. You've got to take at least 100 or it's ridiculous. That's it,' he shouted down the mouthpiece and hung up.

Then he waited by the phone, wondering if he had overplayed his hand. To his relief, the phone rang again a few minutes later. 'All right. Send us 100,' said the man from Comet.

The relationship between Amstrad and Comet quickly flourished. 'We've never looked back. We've done mega-millions of pounds of business with them. But that's how it all started. That's how I broke into Comet. I conned them into it really,' Sugar says, and grins.

*

Alan Sugar had started making amplifiers in 1970, a couple of years before his breakthrough into Comet. He realized that the big manufacturers would sooner or later catch up with his production methods for the plastic dust covers, wiping out his price advantage in the process. It was imperative for him to launch a new line of products before that happened.

Early in his back-of-the-van days, Sugar had met an engineer called George Chinchen, who hailed from the West Country. He helped Sugar out by repairing the dozens of dud radios that the latter acquired in his buying and selling operations. Every week, Chinchen would come round to Amstrad's St John Street premises, pick up a few radios, fix them for half-a-crown (12½p) a set and then Sugar would re-sell them.

His success with the plinths and covers set Sugar thinking about the other bits which went to make up a hi-fi set. He had been impressed by Chinchen's claims to understand the insides of audio equipment, so he put two-and-two together and made him a proposal: 'O.K., George, how about making an amplifier? I'll finance it and we'll go into production.'

It was not long before Sugar was hawking Amstrad's first electrical product, the Amstrad 8000 stereo amplifier. St John Street was not big enough for a full production line, so he looked around for larger premises. In 1971 Amstrad moved into an area of small warehouses and workshops at the back of Fleet Street and within a few hundred yards of St Paul's Cathedral. His new premises in a four-storey, wide-fronted building in Great Sutton Street offered Sugar more space than his first headquarters, and he was able to install his first small production line with the help of some associates of George Chinchen. Amstrad was soon employing a couple of dozen people, mainly women assembling bought-in components to make the Amstrad equipment.

Looking back, Sugar has no illusions about what he was selling at first: 'It was the biggest load of rubbish I've ever seen in my life. Absolute garbage, it was. I didn't know any better.' No sooner was the 8000 amplifier on the streets than he began to think about an improved version. 'It was trial and error, because I didn't know anything about amplifiers or hi-fi. I used to read the magazines, trying to understand what people wanted. I read about watts and frequency response, and all that sort of stuff.'

Sugar would discuss with Chinchen proposals for an improved

model, quizzing the other man on how well a prototype amplified a musical note: 'Is that good frequency response, George?' Chinchen would invariably reply: 'Well, not really, you'll have to spend more money on it.'

So Sugar duly launched the Amstrad Mark II stereo amplifier in 1971. Its great improvement over the earlier version was a filter to reduce noises from scratches on a record – designed 'to further enhance its remarkable and outstanding performance' as Amstrad's adverts put it at the time; or 'another marketing ploy' as Sugar describes it now.

Sugar's homework among the hi-fi magazines shines through his adverts for the Amstrad 8000 Mark II. The readers of *Hi-Fi News*, a leading journal for the buffs, were told in a December 1971 advert that soundings 'on our test bench' had demonstrated 'the rich harmonics and good transient and frequency response so necessary for reproduction'.

That was not quite how retailers perceived Amstrad's early efforts in audio. Malcolm Cross was one of the first to sell the amplifiers from his shop in Hackney: 'As many as we used to sell, we used to send back. The cabinets were always breaking. We would take a whole van-load of repairs to him and he was set up to receive them. He'd have them repaired and brought back the next day. He had to do it like that, because so many went wrong.'

But Amstrad's earliest amplifiers had an overwhelming advantage which more than compensated for the initial quality problems: price. The Amstrad 8000 cost just £17.70. Even the Mark II, with its 'exceptional flexible facilities', sold for only £27.95, undercutting almost everything else on the market.

Malcolm Cross soon found that he needed only minimal effort to sell Amstrad's amplifiers. Youngsters would travel for miles to buy Sugar's equipment. They were ordinary working-class lads who wanted a sound system in their bedrooms, but could not afford an up-market stereo system. Cross began to sell Amstrad equipment by mail order and money flooded in from around the country.

When Cross had a spare moment in his shop, he would compare the sound quality of the expensive machines with that of

Amstrad's: it was as though they were from different planets. But this did not bother the teenagers in their anoraks who carted away Amstrad's amplifiers. As Sugar explains: 'There was the snooty area of the public that would never buy an Amstrad hi-fi and they went out and bought Pioneer or whatever, and they're 5 per cent of the market. The other 95 per cent of the market wants something that makes a noise and looks good. And they bought our stuff.'

Meanwhile, Ashley Morris had been going from strength to strength with Global Audio. When Sugar sold his stake in the firm, Morris agreed to give special prominence to Amstrad's equipment in return for a discount. This understanding continued as Global expanded into a chain of ten shops. Global always featured Amstrad's line when advertising in the hi-fi and music press. 'Global Audio Present Their Velvet Sound of 1973' was the headline of one typical ad introducing a splurge of equipment, nearly all of it from Amstrad.

Doing an old friend a favour was the least of the reasons why Morris kept to the arrangement. Like Cross, he found that Amstrad's line sold in large volumes – and it was not difficult to understand why.

All the names in hi-fi, the Quads and the Pioneers of the world, would beat their way to the door of Morris's flagship showroom in Notting Hill Gate, one of the trendiest hang-outs for the post-hippy rock generation in the early 1970s. Their reps would come in with wonderful-looking machines and launch into the patter: 'This one's got 5DB distortion level, and it's got this twinkler switch, and this star-gazer switch . . .' They would carry on for five minutes in a lingo that only a hi-fi enthusiast would understand, until it came to the bottom line. How much would it cost? Typically £50, or £70, or even £100, just for an amplifier.

Amstrad's approach was somewhat different. Sugar himself – never a rep – would turn up with a new product, dump it on Morris's desk and say, 'Get a load of that.' He did not need to say much about it, because the bottom line spoke for itself: £20, £30, £40, whatever it was, Morris knew immediately that there was nothing which could begin to touch it for price.

The established hi-fi manufacturers were hung up on producing

Aston Martins or Rolls Royces of sound, but Sugar understood that the era of mass consumption demanded a Mini. Newly affluent workers, taking a music machine into their homes for the first time, wanted a box that would do the job, looked attractive to them and could be made to work without messing around with endless wires. 'No one, but no one ever gave Sugar a run for his money. He was the only guy who had a little bit of marketing foresight to produce crap,' Morris says.

Except that Amstrad's equipment was not really that bad, once Sugar had begun to improve on the unreliability of the earliest versions. Above all, the Amstrad line offered excellent value for money, as Morris acknowledges: 'Not one person came along in the whole time I was in retail and said this one is more reliable than Alan Sugar's, it's much more attractive and it's approximately the same price or a pound more.'

The Great Sutton Street premises soon proved too small for Sugar. The success of his fledgling manufacturing operation meant he needed to hire more assemblers, testers and packers. In 1972, he took a couple of floors in 89 Ridley Road, a large building which extends for fifty yards down a side road leading into the heart of one of the East End's liveliest street markets. Ridley Road market caters for all the racial groups that make up the East End working class: white, Asian, Afro-Caribbean and Jewish. Halal butchers jostle with sellers of yams, sweet potatoes, bagels, pigs' tails, jellied eels and cockles.

No. 89, almost exactly in the middle of the market, is by far the most imposing building in the neighbourhood. Stars of David on its parapets and on the railings outside suggest past links with Hackney's Jewish community. For Sugar, it was like coming home. Ridley Road is only a mile or so south of the Northwold estate; his mother used to do her shopping there as he was growing up, and was occasionally seen about the market by old friends until a few years ago.

Fay Sugar says she first began to realize her son was becoming successful 'when he took that place in Ridley'. The family found it difficult to grasp that one of their own was employing dozens of people in the same streets which their relatives had recently pounded looking for work. Fay, with daughter Daphne sometimes in tow, would hesitate before mounting the stairs to Sugar's new offices-cum-factory: 'We used to be amazed, because we used to go out shopping, and we would walk in, and we couldn't believe it. This was Alan's factory, and he had all these people working for him,' Daphne remembers.

Sugar's progress registered with the trade too. Ronnie Marks of Premier Radio first appreciated that Amstrad was beginning to rise above the pack of small manufacturers scrabbling around the edges of the audio market when Sugar became established in Ridley Road. Yet no sooner had he filled every corner of his new premises with women working on his audio equipment than he began to change tack. Amstrad, the budding manufacturer, gradually turned itself into Amstrad, the highly efficient sub-contracting and importing organization, sowing the seeds for the flexibility towards sources of supply which was to become a hallmark of the Amstrad philosophy in the 1980s.

*

Many of Amstrad's adverts in the 1970s carried the proud words 'British made' wrapped round a Union Jack. No doubt this was largely a marketing ploy at a time when it was fashionable for ads to feature these patriotic tags, but it also at first reflected Sugar's perception of what he was doing: making British amplifiers, tuners and other audio equipment out of British components in the heart of London. His attitude changed when he began to notice where the components came from.

'We prided ourselves on being British manufacturers. And we used to buy components from Plessey, Mullard, IT&T – all the main British suppliers,' Sugar recalls.

But the words 'Made in Japan' on the boxes in which the components arrived stuck out like a sore thumb. Sugar quickly concluded he could do without the electronics giants as middle men: 'We don't need you, mate, thank you very much, to act as an agent for us,' he thought to himself.

Sugar found an agent in Japan to buy the components direct for Amstrad. Not possessing even a telex then, he communicated by telegram with his new Japanese agent, Shomei Trading. But the effort paid off, as Sugar explains: 'We were able to buy components at much lower prices than we were buying from the likes of Plessey, who were just importing the things and sticking their name on them.'

The time came when Sugar decided he ought to visit the Far East himself. The volume of components he was importing from Japan was such that he wanted to discuss future plans face to face. Sugar and his agent met at Tokyo airport, but there was a moment of embarrassment when the agent asked whether Sugar had come with his father. Age and seniority count for much in Japan and the Japanese businessman had never met such a youthful entrepreneur. 'He couldn't get to grips with a businessman in his mid-20s,' Sugar notes.

Unknown to the venerable Japanese businessman, however, the young man from London spent much of the visit fulfilling a lucrative series of orders which more than paid for his first journey to Japan. These orders had come Amstrad's way in a rather unusual fashion.

A couple of months before the Japanese trip, a man had phoned Sugar to arrange an appointment in Ridley Road. He worked for the United Africa Company (UAC), a subsidiary of Unilever, the giant Anglo-Dutch corporation which had extensive links with Nigeria. It so happened, he told Sugar, that Nigerian civil servants had recently received large amounts of back pay and were keen to spend their new-found wealth on hi-fi equipment. The UAC would like to buy Amstrad equipment for sale in Nigeria.

It sounded as though a very large order was in the offing, so Amstrad's boss was more than disappointed when an order arrived for six amplifiers and six loudspeakers. To make matters worse, it was accompanied by elaborate instructions on how the equipment should be packed for its journey to Nigeria. Sugar took one look at these instructions and threw the order in the bin.

The Amstrad chairman had almost forgotten about the episode when the UAC rep phoned up. 'I'm sorry but I made a big mistake with the quantities. I've had a word with my superiors and we need 2,000 amplifiers and speakers. But we need them in a hurry. We want as many as possible this week.'

In those days Unilever meant nothing to Sugar, who had no particular reason to trust the UAC man. Sugar reflected that he was being asked to supply at short notice equipment worth almost £200,000. 'This is it,' he thought. 'This is the big sting. I'll hand over my amplifiers and never see the money.'

Sugar made his reservations plain and the UAC rep said he would put the money into Amstrad's bank account the next day by telegraphic transfer. Sugar had not heard of telegraphic transfer, but the following day his bank rang up to say that the money had indeed been deposited.

When the UAC rep heard that Sugar was about to go to Japan, he asked him to keep his eye out for goods that might interest the Nigerians. Sugar thought little of this until he arrived in his hotel room in Tokyo to find a message from the UAC asking him to arrange the urgent shipment of 5,000 radio cassette recorders to Nigeria.

Amstrad's chairman turned to his agent at Shomei Trading to find the cassette recorders, but he felt obliged to keep secret the price he was charging the UAC. 'The point was that I was adding a 50 per cent mark-up to the price I was paying for the goods in Japan. It was unbelievable. But it would have been embarrassing if my agent had realized how much I was making out of the business.'

Sugar found freight forwarders in Japan who shipped the cassette recorders to Gatwick for transit on to Nigeria. No sooner had he despatched them than another message came through from London asking for thousands more pieces of equipment.

The Nigerian gravy train continued to run a little while after Sugar had returned to Britain, helped by the fact that the UAC man was innocent of the audio world. Only after the Amstrad batches of amplifiers and speakers reached Nigeria did he realize that the Nigerians would also need record players. 'He really hadn't the faintest idea of what he was buying,' Sugar says.

But the Nigerian civil servants' wealth dried up, and with it Amstrad's business in that part of Africa. Shortly afterwards, Gulu

Lalvani returned from a trip trying to sell his Binatone equipment to Nigeria. He had been amazed to find Lagos, the Nigerian capital, swamped with Amstrad amplifiers even though Sugar had never set foot in the place.

Sugar's visit to Japan was to be the first of dozens of trips to the Far East. Negotiations over the import of components were the main reason at first, to be followed later by visits to sub-contractors, as he began to have some of his machines made in Japan, Taiwan and Korea. But right from the start there was another motive: to take a look at the latest equipment pouring out of Japanese factories. Sugar would spend a profitable hour or two wandering around Akihabara, the district where Tokyo's consumer electronics shops are clustered, noting the trends in audio equipment, picking up hints about how to style his machines, imagining to himself how he could improve on what he saw there.

Japan also houses an array of companies specializing in making audio equipment for export to the West, to be sold under the name of a European or U.S. company. Western companies typically make smaller profit margins on these badging operations, known as OEM (original equipment manufacturing) in the trade, than on equipment made in their own factories. Yet OEM business has two important advantages for the Western company whose name ends up on the equipment: it generates profits without the hassle of having to manufacture the equipment, and the OEM factories can supply goods which complement those made in-house – a turntable to go with an amplifier, for example.

Sugar grasped the potential of these arrangements and, through introductions arranged by his agent, he struck up a relationship with a Japanese OEM company called Orion which was destined to become one of Amstrad's most important suppliers. Wanting to sell cassette tape decks to expand his audio range, Sugar turned to Orion to supply them. As a result, in 1974 he was able to unveil his 6000 stereo cassette deck. This was quickly followed by the 7000 series which boasted a Dolby noise reduction facility and had been 'designed to provide all the necessary features to line up with your high fidelity set-up', as the ads put it. The deck was made in its entirety by Orion, but carried the Amstrad name. Nick

Lightowler, Gerry Mason's right-hand man at Comet, remembers the episode. 'He imported two tape recorders which were pig-ugly, but dirt cheap. They were phenomenally successful, because they were phenomenally cheap.'

This experience set Sugar thinking about what he was doing in Ridley Road: 'It opened my eyes again. There I was knocking my brains out with dozens of people working in Ridley Road, soldering and assembling, and I realized that we were making a profit on these cassette decks coming through and not really doing anything at all. I was just opening a letter of credit and importing the things.'

The answer, of course, was not to transform Amstrad totally into a badging operation, because that would have deprived the company of the greater profits to be won from controlling the design and manufacturing of the bulk of its equipment. But Sugar reckoned there was an easier way to make money than spending his life supervising the women in Ridley Road. 'I'm not going to knock myself out. I'd rather sub-contract things out,' he concluded.

Not long before Sugar reached this conclusion, Ron Nixon bought a chalk-pit just off the A2 between Maidstone and Rochester, in the middle of the North Kent belt of light engineering factories. He and his partner, Len Lawrence, were set on expanding their business, L. & N., which had flourished in the 1960s assembling toys and bits of audio equipment. Now Nixon intended to build a new factory on the site of the chalk-pit.

He struck a deal with Fidelity Radio, then a force to be reckoned with in Britain's high streets, whereby L. & N. would make a range of Fidelity hi-fis and televisions. But the factory for the Fidelity contract would occupy only about half L. & N.'s new site. Nixon began casting around for another customer. A close observer of the audio market, he had become aware of this newcomer, Amstrad, in the previous couple of years. So he tried a direct approach.

Nixon's call to Sugar could hardly have been better timed and the two agreed that Amstrad would sub-contract to L. & N. the job of making most of its audio equipment. With this deal in his pocket, L. & N. built a second facility on the chalk-pit dedicated to Amstrad work. The foundations of the Amstrad plant were laid just as L. & N. was opening its Fidelity factory.

From 1974 for the rest of the decade, most of Amstrad's equipment that was not imported in finished form from the Far East flowed through L. & N. At its height the factory had about 120 people working full-time on Amstrad's requirements. Amplifiers, tuners, tape decks, compact music centres – the expanding range of Amstrad equipment all emanated from L. & N.'s plant. Ironically, the official description of Amstrad in its annual report and accounts changed from 'wholesaler' to 'manufacturer of electronic equipment' in 1973, just as Sugar was preparing to subcontract out most of his manufacturing activities. This was not to be the last time that Amstrad's self-image was slow to catch up with the company's fast changing character.

Sugar settled into a pattern with L. & N. during his frequent visits to their factory. Early on in the year, he would bring down prototypes of the new models for the coming Christmas season. He controlled not just the designs, but also component purchasing. It was L. & N.'s job to place the components into the printed circuit boards, assemble all the parts into the finished products, test them, box them with the Union Jack clearly displayed and send them off to Ridley Road for final testing and packaging. L. & N. began production of the season's models early in the year, building up to a climax in the second half as the exact pattern of Christmas demand emerged.

Ron Nixon soon learned to understand – and appreciate – the way Sugar operated. 'He was in bold all the time. He'd go round and rave and rant at anything that wasn't right,' remembers Nixon, a heavy-set, slow-speaking man now into his seventies who in his day was not beyond a bit of ranting himself. 'We used to have some real old slanging matches.'

Throughout the 1970s, L. & N. grappled with a chronic shortage of skilled workers – one of a gamut of problems which eventually persuaded Sugar to switch even more of Amstrad's manufacturing to the Far East. Ron Nixon explains its impact: 'We gave him problems, because there was a tremendous shortage of people in those days. You couldn't find anybody who knew a resistor from a capacitor if you walked from here to Russia. So we gave him certain aggravation, because we couldn't get the people to do as much as he wanted or to maintain the quality that he wanted.'

Sugar's visits were always conducted at whirlwind speed, as Nixon recalls: 'He wouldn't stay long. He wasn't the sort of man to say, "Let's go out for some lunch." Or if he was here over lunch, it would be a sandwich in a pub. Then he would rush off. He would never waste time.'

The Amstrad boss was always pressing L. & N. to turn out his machines more quickly and in greater quantities, but beyond these overriding preoccupations Sugar invariably focused on one factor. 'He was mainly interested in the finish of the thing. Amstrad was more fussy cosmetically about how the thing looked than Fidelity,' Nixon learned, although Sugar was totally unconcerned about technical details: 'I don't think he cared tuppence *how* it was made, as long as it was made.'

Sugar could not always control the appearance of equipment which he imported from the Far East simply to badge, but from his earliest days as a manufacturer of audio equipment, he had insisted that equipment designed by Amstrad should look good. His advert for the 8000 Mark II amplifier, his second audio product, proclaimed: 'All this electronic technology is housed in an elegant low-line, decor-styled satin teak finished enclosure with matt black facia with silver trim and brushed aluminium controls.'

Right from the start too, although uninterested in technical details, Sugar seized on one measure which he believed would sum up the power of his machines in the eyes of his customers – the watts they were capable of delivering. Believing technical ignorance to be the norm, he reckoned that most people going into a shop would latch on to one measure of up-to-dateness: they would ask about the amplifier's wattage. What mattered was for Amstrad to match the industry leaders on this one measure. It was a lesson he would apply later to computers.

For the fact was that while Amstrad equipment might have seemed cheap and even vulgar to hi-fi experts, Sugar was not trying to sell to the connoisseur. He knew that people like the truck driver and his wife who bought Amstrad's machines did not need to hear the second violins in an orchestra. He also knew that an expensive-looking finish was one of the main features that would attract the working-class and lower-middle-class purchasers of his equipment. He did not need to rely on market research, consultants or a textbook to tell him this; he understood their needs and their aspirations because he was one of them.

*

The full glare of publicity was turned on Amstrad's years of spectacular growth in the 1980s, when the company launched into computers and word processors. Yet Alan Sugar had been there before.

In the 1970s, he had to cope with rates of growth that ranked with anything he experienced a decade later, though obviously from a much lower base. In 1971, when the first line of amplifiers began to take off and he was still making the plastic dust covers, sales more than doubled to £207,534 and profits rocketed eleven-fold to £24,242. The next year saw a further tripling of sales and profits. In 1973, when Amstrad began to export to France, the figures doubled again, with the company notching up profits of £194,063 on sales of £1,327,366.

Coping with that growth meant he had to start hiring managers to whom he could delegate some of the work. Sugar signed up an engineer and a draughtsman to help design the audio equipment, a sales manager to link with his customers and a purchasing manager to deal with suppliers. Amstrad was no longer quite a one-man band, although all the company's activities still revolved around that one man.

Sugar's relations with his early customers, the dozens of independent audio retailers, began to take on a new light. The Amstrad boss had always been straightforward to the point of bluntness with his customers. Secure in the increasing volumes of his goods that were passing through Comet, he could now choose more carefully among the small independent retailers who as a group still dominated audio retailing. He could afford to drop those who took a long time to pay, who ordered two pieces of equipment and sent back one, the incompetent or fickle dealers who were destined to stay in the small league.

Selling through the independents meant dealing with hundreds of outlets stuck in crowded streets in the centre of towns. By contrast, Comet offered Sugar economies of scale that pushed Amstrad's profits into a new league. Comet was in the business of shifting boxes in very great numbers and Amstrad was able to drop off large deliveries at the back of each Comet store, perfectly located near fast out-of-town roads.

Amstrad's links with Comet became closer throughout the 1970s when Sugar was a frequent visitor to the offices of Gerry Mason and Nick Lightowler. He would make the trek to Leeds or Hull, where Comet's operations were based, about half a dozen times a year. Sometimes Sugar would be there to negotiate what he called a 'blow your brains out' operation, when he wanted to clear out a couple of thousand pieces of an old line in a hurry by slashing prices. His most important visits were made in the late spring and early summer, the period of peak preparation for the Christmas season, when he would discuss with Comet what he was planning for the season and agree with Mason or Lightowler the terms of the deliveries.

Mason had come across many brash young entrepreneurs like Sugar trying to make their way in the fast-growing audio world. While some showed early promise, in the end most fell down in some respect: the quality of their equipment was too poor, or the price was not right, or they simply could not deliver when the goods were needed. 'When it was quiet, you'd get all the supplies you needed at the right price, but when it was busy, you wouldn't see them,' Mason says.

Not so with Amstrad. Comet found that Sugar kept to delivery dates, a quality particularly unusual at the lower end of the market which was heavily dependent on the often unreliable flows of imports from the Far East. Sugar built up an enviable reputation with Comet for keen pricing within his segment of the market, as Mason notes: 'If Alan was selling it, you wouldn't buy it cheaper from anyone else.'

Mason was the first executive in a large company to experience what at first sight seems a surprising side of Sugar's character. He found Sugar *easy* to deal with. Easy, it must be stressed, does not mean weak or soft. On the contrary, negotiations between Amstrad and Comet were often fierce on detail and aggressive in style. Mason met Sugar head on: 'Alan used to curse like an old trooper. But then I would curse back at him too.'

When Mason says Sugar was easy to deal with – and it is a comment echoed by many, if not all, of Sugar's later business associates – he means that negotiating with him was straightforward, that Mason knew where he stood. The Amstrad boss would set out his stall, telling Comet precisely what products he could deliver over what period, together with the prices he would charge and the credit arrangements he would give Comet. Sugar would then listen to any alternative ideas that Comet had, show surprising flexibility in amending his initial plans where he could and make it perfectly clear where he would not meet Comet's counter-proposals.

Relations between suppliers and retailers in cut-throat areas of the high street are fraught with possibilities of two-timing. A supplier will swear blind to a particular retailer that he is getting better terms than any of his competitors, and promptly say the same thing to the next retailer. Mason was used to dealing with sweet-talking manufacturers and then finding out through the grapevine that they had been economical with the truth. But he says of Sugar: 'When Alan told me that Comet was getting the best price from Amstrad, I never found him out in a lie. And he never welshed on a deal.'

Nick Lightowler, who continued to have an important role in Amstrad's fortunes in the 1980s when he became purchasing director of Currys in the Dixons group, was impressed by Sugar's reaction to any new proposals from Comet. Sugar's first response would usually be: 'Naw, it can't be done.' Then invariably he would phone Lightowler a few days later: 'You know that thing we were talking about, well, I've been thinking about it and this is what I've come up with . . .' From such incidents, Lightowler formed a lasting impression of Sugar as 'a guy who would work on how it could be done, rather than on why it couldn't'.

There was another major advantage about negotiating with Sugar. As far as Comet was concerned, Sugar was chairman, managing director, sales director, finance chief, distribution manager, technical supremo and sales representative all rolled into one: no one else in Amstrad ever got near the Comet deals. Mason found dealing with other companies 'more of a long negotiating job'. The pattern with Japanese groups, with Philips or even with most of the British audio companies was for Comet to discuss business regularly with one contact point, typically the sales or area manager, and then to negotiate a main contract with the chairman or managing director once a year. This meant that Comet's regular contact had to refer back most decisions during the year to head office. Sugar, by contrast, was able to make instant decisions about any aspect of his business, a freedom perfectly suited to his temperament.

As Amstrad grew hand-in-hand with Comet during the 1970s, Sugar and Mason often found themselves in each other's company during visits to American audio fairs in Chicago or Las Vegas, where they would scour the exhibits for ideas as to what might catch on in Britain. On these trips away from the minute-by-minute pressures of running the business, Sugar unwound: 'He was always one of the boys. If we were going out on the booze, Alan would come along with us. If there was a trip to the Grand Canyon, he was always there,' Mason recalls.

Yet the process of relaxation went only so far; when the Comet director and the Amstrad boss found themselves in some bar or restaurant thousands of miles from home, their conversation usually turned to business: 'We never stopped talking about business in those days. It was all we used to talk about. We both loved what we were doing,' says Mason.

Both then and since, Sugar's associates have always found his focus intense when he turns his mind to something. But he never bothered to focus on the keepers of conventional wisdom in the established hi-fi industry as epitomized by the trade press. His tactic was to ignore them and, if that became impossible, to treat them with disdain. 'What we were doing was making money, while what the others were doing was getting rave reviews in magazines that only a tiny percentage of the market was buying,' Sugar explains.

Hi-fi specialists repaid Sugar's contempt – at first by indifference, then through hostility to Amstrad. Arthur Ord-Hume, a leading audio journalist for twenty years and later editor of *Independent Electrical Retailer* magazine, recalls the complex of prejudices which greeted Sugar:

> His operation was quite frankly rather looked down upon by the serious side of the industry. He had all the appearance and the trappings of the back-street marketeer, while the attitude of the trade press was to support the activities of those who were thought of as 'legitimate' traders. Beards weren't very popular in those days and he always looked slightly dishevelled. He was emerging at the time of the aspiring youngster and it was difficult for the industry's establishment to understand or accept this.

The first reviewer in *Hi-Fi News* to cast his eye over a piece of Amstrad equipment – the IC2000 amplifier reviewed in April 1972 – ran through a string of grouses about the tone control and the filters and then exploded with the complaint: 'I cannot help feeling that Amstrad set out to provide too many functions for too little cost'. (This must rank as the earliest definition in print of a core component of the Amstrad philosophy.) Dimly aware that maybe he was missing the point, the reviewer rounded off with this declaration: 'Admittedly, manufacturers have to design with the market requirements in mind, but we don't have to review in that vein!'

This tone of aggrieved incomprehension was to recur in the very few reviews of Amstrad equipment which crept into the pages of *Hi-Fi News* in the 1970s. In a comparison of the Amstrad 5050 receiver with competitive offerings from JVC and Toshiba in June 1977, the reviewer surpassed himself by declaring: 'The Amstrad is not bad looking by any means; but detailed exploration of its nooks and crannies leaves one feeling a trifle sad' – a cry from the heart which no doubt kept Alan Sugar awake at night.

Yet between 1972 and 1977, when these two reviews were published, many of the industry's pundits had been forced to revise their opinion of Amstrad, as Arthur Ord-Hume describes:

> Suddenly, we were aware of the fact that this back-street trader was one of the most significant people in the industry. Once he began to get distribution in places like Comet and Rumbelows, he began to make inroads into the markets of the 'legitimate' suppliers. When we began to find Amstrad equipment alongside that of Philips and Sony, we had to sit up and take notice.

Some specialists understood that Amstrad was about value for money. A reviewer in *Hi-Fi News* of Amstrad's 3000 Mark II tuner in February 1976 – having noted that it was difficult to find a competitor's product for less than £100 – confessed that he found it almost difficult to believe that the Amstrad price tag of £60 included 25 per cent VAT. Even the journalist who was overcome by melancholia when exploring the nooks and crannies of the Amstrad receiver acknowledged that, compared with the Toshiba and JVC machines, 'It is the least costly of the three and sports the most features.'

There were some commentators in the mid-1970s who also recognized that the quality of Amstrad's equipment was not at all bad – for its price range. Some of Amstrad's earliest amplifiers had been of poor quality, assembled out of the barest number of the cheapest quality components available. If one component failed, it was often less hassle to throw away the piece of equipment than to try to repair it. But as Sugar gained experience of the business, he steadily improved the reliability of his machines.

True, Amstrad was not beyond the odd trick. Robert Lawrence, son of one of the partners in L. & N., was a young man working on the production line when Amstrad sent down the specifications for its EX range of tuners in 1976. He noticed that when he pressed a switch designed to measure the quality of the sound, the needle always moved to the dead centre, indicating perfect sound.

An examination of the machine's workings showed them to be arranged so that the needle would automatically do this. 'When you pressed the switch, it cut off the meter, so that the needle automatically fell in the middle. It just got completely switched out of the circuit,' Lawrence recalls with a laugh.

Later, when Amstrad started doing business with Rumbelows, the chain's service department opened up an Amstrad speaker and found that one of the three cones in the speaker boxes was not connected; it seemed to be there just for show. Sugar continued to insist in the face of some scepticism that the cone had a purpose in modifying the sound; but the incident quickly entered the Amstrad mythology, and everyone in the know at Rumbelows joked about it for months.

Yet such tales disguised the more mundane story of steady quality improvement. Ron Nixon at L. & N. was able to compare Amstrad's attitude to quality with that of Fidelity, then a better-known brand. He says Sugar was the more obsessive of the two about reliability. He did not care what was inside the machines, but he wanted them to work and to look good.

As Amstrad's biggest customer by far, Comet was in an excellent position to assess the quality of Amstrad's products. Both Mason and Lightowler insist that Amstrad's fault rate was not out of line with other equipment in the same price range, a view shared by David Johnson, then managing director of Rumbelows. Mason explains: 'He wanted to make cheap and cheerful, but not cheap and nasty. In its bracket, it was as good as anything you could buy.'

Three factors conspired to convey the opposite impression, however. First, memories of the poor quality of Amstrad's earliest machines lingered. Second, opinion formers in the industry, the hi-fi pundits, would not have dreamt of having a low end machine like an Amstrad in their own homes, and so failed to appreciate that Amstrad's equipment performed adequately *for its price range*. Third, because Amstrad sold more machines than its rivals, the *absolute* number of Amstrad boxes returned for repair was higher, even though the *relative* number was typically the same or lower: many shop assistants did not appreciate this distinction and by word-of-mouth fed Amstrad's reputation for unreliability.

This reputation still stuck to the company much later when it entered the computer business. It was to be many years before most Amstrad products were generally recognized as being excellent value for their niche in the market.

By shunning the trade press and the rest of the industry establishment, Sugar was following a sound commercial instinct. He had nothing to gain and arguably much to lose by trying to compete on the same basis as up-market hi-fi equipment. Yet by refusing to submit to the industry's judgement he was also fulfilling a more basic need. As a man who in his mid-twenties had forced himself without help or favours into the heart of a tightly meshed industry, the one thing Sugar loathed was to be underestimated.

Sugar's aggressive reputation among suppliers and customers not only reflected his natural character, but also acted as a defence against what to him seemed the ever-present danger of being patronized. In a passing conversation about a particular parts supplier, he once confessed to Ronnie Marks of Premier Radio, 'I can't stand doing business with him because he treats me like a little schoolboy. He always calls me "son". I'd rather talk to his storeman.'

*

As the 1970s progressed, Amstrad's success was flowing through into Sugar's standard of living and he was beginning to live the life of a successful small businessman. In 1972 the Sugars moved to a house in Chigwell Rise, a long road on the borders between Essex and Redbridge which is home to many former East Enders who have made it. Many of the driveways of the detached houses in Chigwell Rise boast a Jaguar or Mercedes. Although the Sugars' new home was by no means the most opulent in the road, the fact that they could live there at all spoke volumes about Sugar's progress.

Bit by bit, he was acquiring the trappings of wealth. By the end of the 1970s Amstrad had provided him with a Rolls Royce as a company car, a fitting accolade for someone whose prime goal ten years previously had been 'wheels'. Sugar took flying lessons at a local airport, pitching himself into his hobby with typical single-mindedness. He passed advanced all-weather tests as well as his ordinary pilot's licence.

In 1975 Amstrad duly bought a plane for £7,500, allowing Sugar to make the trips down to L. & N. by plane. He cut two hours off the journey by landing his small aircraft on the grass runway at Rochester airport. He also flew to his meetings with Comet in Hull – dodging around the large chimney at the end of the runway at Brough airport as he came down out of the bank of mist lying low over the Humber.

One day Sugar had a lucky escape when flying his single-engined aircraft back from France. He had noticed something a bit odd with the machine when it was over the Channel, but landed as normal at Southend airport to clear customs. After taking off from Southend, the real problem started, as he recalls: 'The engine crocked when I was hovering over Southend town. So the only way out was to turn right towards some fields and put the thing down there.'

The shattered cylinder which caused the problem still sits in Sugar's office as a memento. He decided that prudence required his next aircraft to be twin-engined, but twin-engined planes bored him: 'It really took the fun out of flying. The single-engined plane had been simple: I just got in it, took it up, went round in circles and looked out the windows. A twin was too serious a form of flying. It's not for just flipping around in.'

So Sugar went back to a single-engined machine, much against the advice of his wife, Ann, whose initial nervousness about her husband's new hobby was reinforced by the Southend crash. In the early 1980s, reckoning that he had an additional responsibility as the chairman of a public company, Sugar bowed to Ann's pleas to quit flying. By then, he had discovered a new hobby into which he could channel his energy: tennis.

Flying became available to Sugar as a hobby thanks to the wealth flowing to him from Amstrad's success, yet in a more important sense he was little changed by this success. True, he lost touch with some of his old friends after he moved to Chigwell Rise; but the new friends he made were of the same background and with the same tastes. Neither in the 1970s nor in the 1980s, when he could have chosen to move among the wealthiest and most successful in the land, did he fundamentally alter his way of life. Indeed, many of the friends he made in the early 1970s who have remained close to him were part of the extended Sugar-Simons family.

Shortly after establishing themselves in Chigwell Rise, Alan and Ann Sugar took to visiting Gerry and Norma Eriera, who lived in an even smarter house just down the road. Norma was Ann's first cousin, but the Erieras were 8–10 years older than the Sugars, an age gap which had kept them apart until they became near neighbours.

Naturally more extrovert than the Sugars, the Erieras are a friendly couple who laugh a lot and know how to enjoy themselves on an evening out. Alan Sugar found that he could unwind in their company, and pretty soon the two families were arranging to spend their holidays together.

Early on Sugar acquired a taste for relaxing through expensive holidays. For instance, the Sugars, Crosses and a group of other friends spent New Year's Eve 1972 at the Paris Hilton, having to abandon their first-class plane tickets and return by hovercraft when Paris became fogbound. Over the next decade, outings like that were to become a regular part of life for the Sugars and the Erieras.

Alan Sugar put his business skills at the service of his new friend. A businessman who has spent all his life in the ladies' garment trade, Eriera had never tapped the rich seam of clothes made in the Far East before meeting Sugar. He accompanied Sugar on one of his trips to Hong Kong and South Korea, where the latter showed an unsuspected talent for the garment business. Eriera sat quietly next to Sugar in a raincoat factory while the Amstrad chairman bartered over raincoats as though they were amplifiers.

Sugar turned to Eriera and asked, 'Well, how many could you sell?'

Eriera replied that he was not sure. After some more haggling, Sugar said, 'We'll get a good price if we buy 15,000.'

So Sugar duly bought 15,000 raincoats on behalf of his friend and also put some money into Eriera's business, allowing him to build up his trade with the Far East. Back in Britain, he would fly Eriera over to Le Touquet for lunch on a Saturday. Twice a year, the Sugars and the Erieras would spend a couple of weeks on holiday together. The Grand Hotel at Rimini was the venue of their first family holiday, followed by jaunts to Hawaii, San Francisco, Bermuda, Fort Lauderdale and a dozen other far-flung places. The Erieras introduced the Sugars to Los Monteros, a hotel which boasts ten tennis courts, its own golf course, a riding club and a private beach, and where suites can cost more than £300 a day. The hotel in Marbella, one of the main haunts of Europe's super-rich, quickly became a favourite with the Sugars, who still regularly spend a fortnight there.

Alan Sugar was able to forget the pressures of his business totally while on holiday with the Erieras. He could indulge his growing enthusiasm for tennis and his passion for flying. Staying in the Catskill Mountains, he flew with an instructor to Albany airport for the afternoon to pick up his American pilot's licence. Another time in Hawaii, when the Erieras were on the golf course Sugar amused himself by flying over the island and buzzing their hotel.

These pastimes and holidays were way beyond the reach of the vast majority of British people. Yet it was possible to say without affectation, as Sugar did in 1980 at the time of Amstrad's flotation, that at heart he was still one of them. Asked what he spent his money on, he answered: 'Oh, clothes and gadgets and trinkets and toys, video cameras, calculators that sing songs, spelling machines for the kids.'

Despite Amstrad's growing success, Alan Sugar still went to the office every day at 8.30 am, came home at 6.00 pm, watched television, read three books a year, played tennis at weekends, spent as much time as he could with his family and saw the same friends he had always seen. 'I know where my roots are,' he explained. 'My family are still working-class people.' In the 1980s, Sugar was to become one of that rare breed: a working class multi-millionaire.

A Mug's Eyeful

Alan Sugar came back from a trip to the Far East in 1978 with the germ of an idea which turned into the first blockbuster Amstrad product. In the second half of the 1970s, Japanese audio companies had begun to group the separate elements of a hi-fi system – the amplifier, cassette deck, tuner and record player – into one rack. Sugar was among the first in the British industry to appreciate the significance of the move: it allowed a manufacturer to sell all the hi-fi pieces to a customer at the same time. But it was his own trick to go one step further.

The Amstrad chairman pondered what the racking development meant to consumers. They benefited by being able to buy all the hi-fi pieces in a common design in one place; yet once they had taken the parts home, they still had to go through the tedious process of linking them together, which meant grappling with a whole mess of wiring before they could use their system. A typical hi-fi system looked as though it had a fistful of spaghetti hanging out of its back, and it might also have up to four or five plugs. Sugar realized this made little sense.

'The wallies that ended up buying this stuff didn't know what they were buying anyway. Once they had fitted them all up in their houses, connected all the wires from the tuners to the amplifiers and the cassette deck, and put the record player on, the thing never got moved ever again,' he comments.

Nor did this make sense from a manufacturing point of view.

The separate pieces in a rack system all had to have their own components. Thus there were power supplies, transformers and an array of other electronics in each part. Sugar's instinct for cutting out duplication, one of the most powerful in his make-up, was roused. 'It was obvious to me that a lot of this was a waste of time,' he recalls.

His solution was simplicity itself. He made a front panel to look as though it were three separate units – amplifier, tuner and cassette deck – but in fact it was a single box. Sugar christened his idea the Tower System. His one-plug hi-fi was a breakthrough for people who had no taste for the wiring gymnastics demanded by conventional hi-fi units. By eliminating duplicated components, it also allowed a significant advance in cost reduction. Anyone opening up a Tower System would have been amazed to find very little there – one set of electronics and a hole.

Sugar was careful not to stint on the appearance of the front panel. Make a cheap product look expensive: this cardinal principle of the Amstrad philosophy had already served him well. The silver-coated front of the Tower System was festooned with flashing lights, knobs and buttons. It passed the Amstrad test: it was, Sugar declared, 'a mug's eyeful'.

By 1979, Sugar knew that he was sitting on a winner with his Tower System and realized that it was the first Amstrad product likely to sell in large volumes in the high street. Although he had sold some amplifiers and other lines through chains like Rumbelows, few of Amstrad's previous products were of a kind to take the high street by storm. The Tower System changed that.

Breaking into this area of the market in a big way offered Sugar not only larger volumes, but also the chance to reduce his dependence on Comet. By the end of the 1970s, Comet was accounting for over a quarter of Amstrad's sales, leaving Sugar exposed to any downturn in Comet's fortunes. He showed the Tower System to Woolworths, who were eager to buy it.

First the Amstrad boss had to broach his plans with Gerry Mason at Comet. The firm was naturally suspicious of a move by Amstrad into the high street. If Amstrad built up other customers to rank with Comet in importance, then Comet's bargaining power with Sugar would be correspondingly reduced. More important still, Sugar would inevitably become more reluctant to allow Comet to discount Amstrad's goods for fear of offending the high street chains. 'Over my dead body' was how Mason responded when he heard about the plans. It was not a threat which worried Sugar.

The Tower System was set to become Amstrad's most important product as the 1970s came to an end. Rumbelows and Currys bought the machines once Woolworths had taken the plunge by becoming the first high street chain to stock them. Comet also sold them, after Mason realized he could not hold Sugar back. David Johnson, then managing director of Rumbelows, was at one stage selling up to 1,000 a week from his chain alone. In the early 1980s, after Amstrad's flotation, the Tower System became the first Amstrad product whose sales were measured in the hundreds of thousands. 'That was when it really started booming, when we began to understand what orders were all about. People like Woolworths were banging in orders for 5,000 at a time. They sold for £199 in the shops, which meant £130 each for us – that was a lot of money,' says Sugar.

One group unimpressed by the Tower System were the hi-fi buffs, the protectors of the industry's virtue. 'Anyone who thought from the technical point of view frowned upon it. They thought what we had done was disgusting. To them, the idea of hi-fi was that you had to separate all the parts,' Sugar notes.

Their reservations cut little ice with him. 'We were attracting the truck driver and his wife. They saw this bloody big mug's eyeful in this cabinet. This whacking great big cabinet, with a beautiful front panel with knobs on it. It was a very uncomplicated product. Plug it in the wall and away you go.'

*

Early in 1979 Alan Sugar was approached with a proposition. Would he sell Amstrad? The unexpected proposal was made by Audiotronic Holdings, a quoted company which had swallowed up two of the most successful independent hi-fi retailers, Lasky's and G. W. Smith. A man called Geoffrey Rose, who enjoyed a brief reputation as a company doctor at the end of the 1970s, had been brought into Audiotronic in 1978 to revive its flagging fortunes. Rose reckoned that one way to turn Audiotronic around would be through acquisitions and his eye lit on Amstrad, by then a force in the audio industry.

The deal Rose had in mind was to pay Sugar about £2 million for 75 per cent of Amstrad, leaving him with a 25 per cent stake. Sugar would continue to work for Amstrad/Audiotronic on a service contract.

Sugar did not turn down the proposition immediately, but met the people at Audiotronic to discuss what they had in mind. He also talked to friends whose business judgement he trusted. One Sunday he rang Gulu Lalvani of Binatone and explained the proposal. 'I'm seriously considering it. What do you think?' he asked.

Selling out had not occurred to Sugar before the Audiotronic approach; insofar as he thought about the future, he simply envisaged a bigger and bigger Amstrad. But the prospect of being able to bank a £2 million cheque made him ponder his options, as he recalls: 'I wasn't really thinking of cashing in on the thing. But I suppose something sparks off in your mind a deal, and you start to think maybe the time has come for me to secure myself. It could have provided a stepping stone where I wouldn't have had to worry about my own personal security.'

The Audiotronic offer forced Sugar to look at Amstrad from a new angle. He had been working his guts out for a decade – and for what? True, he now had a more than comfortable lifestyle. Amstrad's continuing growth – with profits reaching £649,749 on sales of £4,469,396 in the year to June 1978 – ensured that. But still he did not have a pile of money in the bank. The Amstrad chairman talked through his future with Nick Lightowler at Comet: 'Why am I doing this? If I die now, my wife's got nothing,' he said.

The breakthrough came when Sugar discussed Audiotronic's offer with Michael Hollingbery, Comet's chairman. He explained that he was interested in selling some of Amstrad, but was not sure whether Audiotronic were the right partners. Sugar's caution proved to be amply justified as a succession of disasters struck Audiotronic over the following two years: first the Lasky family quit the company, then it declared a heavy loss, prompting a sale of the Laskys stores to Ladbroke, and finally Rose departed abruptly from the scene.

Sugar told Hollingbery that he was much keener on a partnership with Comet: 'I wouldn't mind a deal with you, if you offered me the same terms.'

The Comet chairman was wiser in the ways of the financial world than Sugar in 1979. Hollingbery was already a millionaire, thanks to the flotation of Comet in 1972, and was to become one of Britain's seriously rich businessmen as he sold more of the company's stock over the years, culminating in the takeover of Comet by Woolworths in 1984.

With the experience of Comet's own share issue behind him, Hollingbery thought there was a better alternative for Sugar. 'Why don't you go public?' he asked.

'Go what?' Sugar replied in his best East End manner, but he soon grasped the potential when Hollingbery explained how it was possible to tap the stock market for cash. Then Hollingbery went one better and introduced Sugar to Tim Holland-Bosworth at Kleinwort Benson, the merchant bank which had handled Comet's share issue. Thus was Sugar launched on the road to Amstrad's flotation.

*

A snapshot of Amstrad in 1979, as Sugar prepared to go public, would have showed how far the company had moved since 1970 when he sold his first amplifier. It would also have highlighted the characteristic which more than any other marks out Sugar – his ability to change both product lines and production sources rapidly when fashions change among the thousands of individuals who make up his ultimate customers.

Sugar had introduced more and more products into Amstrad's line-up as the 1970s wore on. 'Every year, he produced something better and then usually upgraded it, but still aimed it at the same sort of customer. It was nothing for Alan to produce a radio that was an absolute winner for a season, but for it then to disappear from his offering as fashions changed,' recalls David Johnson, then managing director of Rumbelows.

An important addition to Amstrad's product line had occurred in 1975 when it began to import car radios, cassette players and speakers from the Far East. Sugar entered the market just as demand for in-car music took off. Sales of radio-cassettes for cars rose from 276,000 in 1976 to 418,000 in 1977, to 588,000 in 1978, and touched a million in 1979.

Sugar did not just ride the crest of this wave but carried off the Amstrad trick of helping to transform the market. He foresaw an explosion for low-priced car music systems, an explosion which would be ignited by the move towards do-it-yourself installation by motorists. Until then, a garage or fitting specialist had charged as much as £150 just to install a music system in a car. Sugar realized that he could both undercut the competition and create a mass market by bypassing the need for fitting charges. Along with companies such as Binatone and Sharp, Amstrad was among the first wave to market D.I.Y. packages of radio-cassettes, loudspeakers and parts for fitting. He also had the sense to sell these packages through his normal outlets, like Comet, rather than through specialist motoring stores.

Amstrad had to contend with a setback to its in-car business when it was forced by Pioneer – one of the leading Japanese companies in the sector – to destroy a batch of speakers which it had bought from a factory in the Far East without realizing they were directly based on a Pioneer design. This was an incident which coloured Sugar's behaviour when he entered the computer business: he was extremely careful to ensure that his designs did not infringe other people's patents.

By the end of the 1970s, Amstrad was claiming about 30 per cent of the U.K. in-car music market by volume – its market share would have been perhaps half that by value, because it concentrated on the inexpensive end. Sugar's ability to spot, transform and dominate this business underpinned Amstrad's growth in the run-up to flotation. By the time the City heard about Amstrad,

Sugar was doing more business from in-car entertainment systems than from his traditional audio sales, representing yet another metamorphosis in the company's many different lives.

In 1977, Sugar turned his mind to selling portable small-screen television sets made in South Korea, but the venture was thwarted initially by one of the periodic bouts of trade friction between Korea and the West. Not to be put off, he returned to the idea the following year, also adding clock radios to his new line in portable TVs.

A breakdown of the £4,796,000 of sales notched up by Amstrad in the second half of 1979 gives some idea of the range of products Sugar was then selling: in-car entertainment systems represented 30 per cent, the biggest slice, followed by amplifiers, receivers, tuners and turntables (19 per cent), clock radios (12 per cent), speakers (12 per cent), the new Tower Systems which by then had not fully taken off (8 per cent), televisions (7 per cent), cassette decks (6 per cent), leaving an assorted mixture of goods to account for the final 6 per cent. Not content with that spread, Sugar was toying with the idea of making a radio receiver for boats in what would have been a concerted Amstrad attack on the high-cost marine electronics suppliers – one of the many ventures considered, but then dropped in Amstrad's offices down the years as Sugar restlessly sought new openings.

Perhaps even more impressive was Amstrad's range of suppliers, which by the second half of 1979 fell into three broad groups. First, 49 per cent of its goods came from eight suppliers in Japan, Hong Kong, South Korea and Taiwan; factories in the Far East were making car music systems, clock radios and televisions for the company. Second, 39 per cent of Amstrad's products were put together by six U.K. sub-contractors, with L. & N. the largest; amplifiers, receivers, tuners, turntables and the Tower Systems were among the products assembled in this way. The remaining 12 per cent of Amstrad's turnover came from speakers which it assembled in a factory in Southend. Sugar had bought the Southend lease in 1978, thus launching a long Amstrad association with Southend and the neighbouring town of Shoeburyness.

Such a wide spread of suppliers meant that Amstrad was not

over-dependent on any one. Sugar had no long-term contracts with any supplier or sub-contractor and was confident of being able to find many alternative sources if he fell out with an existing supplier.

In most other respects, however, Sugar's advisers found Amstrad to be an admirably simple company as they prepared it for flotation. Financial arrangements had remained essentially unchanged from its earliest days. Strong growth coupled with the lack of a need for substantial capital investment allowed Sugar to finance company activities out of cash flow. An overdraft to tide Amstrad over the gap between delivering goods to its customers and receipt of their payments was the only external financial help he needed: for example, he would be paid by Comet in December for Christmas stock delivered in July or August. In 1974, Sugar had agreed overdraft facilities with Lloyds Bank, giving them a claim on Amstrad's properties in the event of the company running into financial problems – arrangements which stayed in place for the rest of the 1970s. Lloyds extended these credit facilities in early 1980 just before the flotation, allowing Amstrad a maximum overdraft of £2 million (with interest at 1½ per cent above base rate), as well as a £1 million facility to cover letters of credit.

Amstrad had had to change in other respects as it grew from being a one-man band to a medium-sized business. The company's chronic tendency to outgrow its premises forced another move on Sugar in 1977, when he bought premises in Garman Road, Tottenham for just over £300,000. This time, the move was motivated mainly by Amstrad's desperate need for more storage space: Garman Road was little more than a large warehouse fronted by a small, two-storey set of offices.

Sugar also had to take on more managers as Amstrad increased in size. Like many a small businessman, his first inclination had been to surround himself with family and friends. Back in 1968, the documents establishing the company listed three directors: Alan Sugar, Ann Sugar and Sugar's brother-in-law Harold, a cheerful fellow without any of Sugar's drive who severed his links with the company just two months later. Ann Sugar remained one of the two Amstrad directors throughout the 1970s, although this was essentially for tax reasons, since the arrangement allowed her to be paid a salary and to be furnished with a Jaguar car. She did not play an active role in the company.

One of Alan Sugar's first employees had been his father, Nathan. Sugar saw his own business as a way of freeing Nathan from the need to work in the East End garment trade:

> He worked for me because I wanted to stop him working for the old sweatshops. He was earning something like £20 a week in the garment business, and the way I was doing business, twenty quid a week was nothing. So he might as well come and work for me and answer my telephones and wrap a few parcels up. He was much happier doing that than being under the constant threat of having no work in the sweatshops.

Nathan never quite adjusted to his son's success; he acted as though it were built on sand and might come crashing down at any moment. When Amstrad was in Ridley Road, he would wander the nearby market picking up pieces of string and tying them together for Amstrad's parcels. Nathan would sit in the office steaming off unfranked stamps to put them on envelopes that might contain invoices going out to customers like Comet for tens of thousands of pounds. Alan Sugar would battle with his father – 'Dad, do me a favour – we can afford stamps' – but had no hope of changing him. Many a time, Nathan interrupted a meeting his son was holding to show him a bargain he had picked up in the market: 'Look Alan, look at these lovely oranges – I got you them cheap.'

Derek, Alan Sugar's brother, also started working for Amstrad in 1973, supervising the stock in Ridley Road. The plan was that if he stuck it for a year, he would move to a more senior position and get 5 per cent of the business. However Derek lasted only a month with Amstrad before returning to taxi-driving, although at the end of the 1980s he helped his brother by managing some properties into which Alan had sunk some of his private wealth.

But Sugar could not rely on his family to staff the whole of

Amstrad and one of the first people he hired was Stan Randall, a friend of George Chinchen. Randall helped to shape the company's later history by opening Amstrad's first overseas subsidiary in Hong Kong in 1981. An open, friendly man, he is a workaholic who lives for Amstrad: in Hong Kong in the late 1980s, his constant companion was his portable phone in case Alan Sugar, or anyone else from Amstrad headquarters, was after him.

Randall had a small electronics assembly plant in Suffolk when he was introduced to Sugar by Chinchen. He was one of the first sub-contractors to work on Amstrad's earliest line of audio equipment launched from Sugar's base in St John Street, Islington. When Sugar decided that Amstrad would have to start manufacturing, he turned naturally to Randall. Sugar met Randall and his then partner over dinner and offered to take them over, which would have given Amstrad ready-made manufacturing capacity. Randall's partner declined, but Randall had been sufficiently impressed by the young East Ender to decide to throw in his lot with Sugar. The 32-year-old Randall started working for Sugar in 1971 on the day that Amstrad moved from St John Street to Great Sutton Street. By then Amstrad had about a dozen employees, most of them recently recruited to run its first manufacturing operation.

Stan Randall's first job was to oversee the new manufacturing line in Great Sutton Street, but he quickly established himself as the company's chief component buyer – chief, that is, after Sugar, who was chief everything at Amstrad. Randall's previous experience of buying electronic components from the Far East came in particularly useful when Amstrad first began to buy large volumes of parts from that region.

Another early Amstrad employee who was to play a key role in the company's future was Bob Watkins, a large, engaging man from Essex with an accent as broad as Alan Sugar's own and a habit of speaking his mind second only to that of the Amstrad chairman. In 1975, Watkins was becoming increasingly disillusioned with his work as a draughtsman for the Ministry of Defence. 'I'd been very pleased to get work for the M.O.D. because they had such a strong technical reputation. But I couldn't believe what a bunch of wasters they were. They didn't use their brains. Everything I was doing was being repeated and duplicated by other departments. Everything took longer than it should have,' he recalls.

Watkins reacted to the Ministry of Defence in much the same way as Sugar had to the Department of Education and Science, so he looked around for another job and spotted an advert from Amstrad, a name which meant nothing to him. 'I did a bit of research and found out that Amstrad was at the rubbish end of the market, but I joined just the same,' Watkins says.

When Watkins started with Amstrad in 1976, there were just four people in its technical department: a chief engineer, an electrical engineer, himself as draughtsman and an assistant. Watkins loathed the place at first, not only because he was earning less than in his previous job but also because of the behaviour of his new boss. Alan Sugar kept wandering into Watkins's office, looking over his shoulder and telling him what to do. This did not please Watkins, who reckoned he knew his job. 'I don't like this guy. This is a wind-up,' he thought.

So he went to Sugar and said he was quitting, but Sugar dissuaded him by awarding him an immediate pay rise and suggesting that he give the place another couple of months. Watkins agreed, but when Sugar started hassling him once more, he threatened to leave again. Yet another pay rise kept him at his drawing board.

This rigmarole might have carried on indefinitely had not something clicked within Watkins: 'After a few months, I suddenly realized this guy was a bit clever. Some of his ideas were daft, O.K., but some of them were better than I could have thought of and I reckoned I was pretty good. My experience of bosses up till then was that they didn't know what they were talking about. But here was a boss who was different.'

Watkins was less inclined to take his initiation into Amstrad personally when he noticed that he was not alone in receiving the Sugar treatment. Sugar was involved in everything that went on in the company, from the accounts, through the warehousing and the manufacturing to the work of the electrical engineers. And, as far as Watkins could tell, most of what Sugar had to say in these very different areas made sense.

Once he had become used to his unusual boss, Watkins found Amstrad's way of operating a great relief after the bureaucracy of the Ministry of Defence. If anyone within Amstrad showed a talent for something, they tended to do it, irrespective of their job title. After a while, he discovered he had a talent he had never suspected: he was rather good at hunting out cheaper sources of supply for the various parts such as metal work and plastics that Amstrad was buying from U.K. manufacturers. Watkins is a street fighter like Sugar, a man who knows where to find the cheapest sources of supply, understands about tough negotiating and can almost instantaneously calculate the likely cost of a new product.

Recognizing Watkins's skill, Sugar began to take him on his expeditions to the Far East where he bought components and negotiated deals with his sub-contractors. Gradually Watkins took over from Randall as Sugar's right-hand man in this key aspect of Amstrad's operations.

Watkins's main responsibility at Amstrad has always been for new products. In the 1970s, Sugar invariably came up with all the new product ideas and would normally have strong views about how they should look. He would use Watkins as a sounding board to discuss these ideas and the two men found that they thought in similar ways. Both wanted to design simple low-cost items. And Sugar impressed on Watkins his philosophy of new products: 'Once we've come up with a product, we have to assume it's old and will have stopped selling next year. It may turn out to have a longer life, but that doesn't matter. We have to assume it's already old-fashioned.'

This was a lesson which Watkins did not forget even after he joined Amstrad's board as the company's technical director in the 1980s: 'Once an Amstrad product has come out, I have absolutely no interest in it,' he says.

As each wave of Amstrad's new products tended to sell in ever larger quantities, Alan Sugar realized that he needed help on the marketing side. In 1977 he began to talk about finding some bright lad who could give him a hand. Malcolm Miller was such a lad.

Miller had just finished a degree in business studies at the Central London Polytechnic, which had included a year working on marketing for Birds Eye – a flagship brand in Unilever, the Anglo-Dutch group which is widely considered one of the world's most professional marketers. Miller heard through a friend of a friend that Sugar wanted to appoint a marketing professional, so he rang up and was interviewed by the Amstrad boss.

Sugar would not offer the salary Miller thought he deserved, so the young graduate took up Birds Eye's offer of a full-time job. He spent the next year and a half learning about product management and marketing on Unilever's training scheme, which has been compared in its intensity with an M.B.A. (Master of Business Administration) in marketing.

After about eighteen months with Birds Eye, Miller decided that the clever thing to do would be to apply the marketing skills he had learnt at Unilever within a small or medium-sized company. He saw a vacancy for a product manager at Amstrad advertised in London's *Evening Standard* newspaper, and this time took the job when it was offered. It was 1979, Miller was 24 and Amstrad had hired its first marketing executive.

In the 1980s, when Miller had joined Amstrad's board as its sales and marketing director, he was often privately described by the company's critics as Sugar's chief clone. Like a handful of other senior Amstrad people, he happens to look like the Amstrad chairman – taller and gaunter, but with the same mop of black curly hair and the same beard. On occasions, he can also affect Sugar's brusque manner. Yet what the clone jibe misses is that Miller brought into Amstrad big-company marketing disciplines which complemented Sugar's gut feeling for what the consumer wants.

When Sugar wrote to Miller offering him a job, he told him that he would have to learn a hell of a lot and no one would have the time to teach him. Miller soon found out what his new boss meant. In his first few months with Amstrad, the young man had to handle the company's advertising, link with its retail customers, telex Far Eastern suppliers about shipments of speaker parts, open letters of credit, write instruction manuals and design gift boxes for promotional launches of Amstrad's products. More mundanely, Miller also had to type his own letters, since Sugar made it clear that a secretary was an unnecessary luxury. It was all rather different from Unilever, where everyone had had their precisely allotted function.

Another big difference from Unilever was that no one outside the confines of the audio industry had ever heard of Amstrad: 'When I phoned up an agency or anyone and I said I was from Amstrad, they'd say: "Who's Amstrad?"'

That was galling enough for an ambitious young man like Miller, but more worrying still was the complete lack of anything approximating to conventional marketing disciplines within Amstrad. The company's entire marketing strategy was locked in Sugar's fertile mind: 'The first thing I said to Alan was: "Look, we don't know who our customers are – what they do, where they live, what papers they read,"' Miller recalls.

An early change suggested by him was to include a questionnaire with Amstrad's guarantee card, so that the company could begin to gather some intelligence on the people who bought its equipment and how they had heard about it. The replies which flooded in soon indicated at least one thing: that the television advertising campaign for the Tower System had been an overwhelming success.

One of Miller's early tasks was to keep an eye on the shooting of a television advert for the Tower System. Sugar had decided that since he wanted a mass market, he ought to use the advertising medium that talked to the great majority of people – television. Amstrad was one of the first companies to advertise a brown goods product like an audio system in such a direct and simple way.

The commercial which Miller saw being shot was pure Sugar. The camera travelled through space, breaking the £500 barrier, the £400 barrier, then £300, coming to rest below the £200 figure. By the end of the advert, no one could have the slightest doubt as to what product was being advertised, where it could be bought and how much it cost. 'When we researched that advert, we found that consumers really appreciated it. Don't forget we were talking to C2s and DEs (working-class consumers). ABs (the professional classes) had bought their Sony and didn't mind paying a high price. C2s and DEs wanted something that looked like hi-fi separates, but cost them £179,' Miller explains.

Simple to the point of being corny, perhaps, but the advert worked. Amstrad received feedback from outlets in the Midlands and the North that whenever it ran on a Saturday afternoon, a surge of customers would come into the shops to buy a Tower System an hour later. The power of advertising – especially large volumes of simple advertising on television – was a lesson that Amstrad would never forget: 'The correlation between advertising and our product offtake is still phenomenal,' Miller says.

As a growing company, Amstrad also began to need more conventional financial controls. In 1977, Sugar asked Nevill Shearman – a partner in Amstrad's auditors, Mordant Latham – to find him a financial controller. The advertisement which Shearman placed in the *Daily Telegraph* attracted Jim Rice, then working with a Swiss cosmetics firm. Rice did not have an accountancy qualification, but he had worked in the financial departments of a range of large companies including A.E.I., the engineering group, and Philips, the electronics giant.

Rice's first task in 1977 was to introduce elementary accounting systems into Amstrad and to help computerize its administrative operations. As is the way with Amstrad, Rice's job soon spread. In the late 1970s and early 1980s, he assumed responsibility for most aspects of Amstrad which were not front-line selling activities, like warehousing and manufacturing. When Amstrad applied to join the stock market, it needed a more conventional board structure, so Rice began to wear yet another hat – that of company secretary and main contact point with the City.

When Rice joined Amstrad, the company's headquarters were still in the centre of Ridley Road market and, like many newcomers to the firm, he took a good six months to adjust to his new surroundings. 'It was a cultural shock after working for someone like Philips. Philips is very well structured – very slow and cumbersome, but very well structured. In Philips, everybody knew their status. If you had two windows in your office, you'd made it.

If you had a window at all in Ridley Road, you were lucky,' recalls Rice.

*

Alan Sugar was beginning to build up a team, many of whom were to play important parts in Amstrad's success in the 1980s. Yet he himself continued to provide the driving force in all aspects of company operations. The memo pad on his desk in Tottenham in 1979 proclaimed: 'From the Boss'. Nowhere was this more true than in relations with Amstrad's main customers, the large chains; Sugar reserved for himself contact on all but the most trivial matters with retailers like Comet and Rumbelows.

David Johnson at Rumbelows says that it was nothing for Sugar to visit his offices two or three times a month to sort out problems. Differing from the heads of other Rumbelows suppliers in never standing on ceremony, the Amstrad chairman would deal with whoever was most appropriate, unlike many rival suppliers who felt their dignity deserved personal contact with managing director Johnson. 'Alan didn't mind who he talked to. If there was a 23-year-old in Rumbelows who was important for a particular line, you'd find Alan stuck in some cubby-hole talking to the lad about how the sales were going, what improvements could be made and so on,' Johnson remembers.

One evening just before Christmas, after most of the staff had gone home, Johnson came down into the lobby to find Sugar sitting beside the reception desk: 'Alan, what on earth are you doing here?' Johnson asked.

'I've come for the cheque,' Sugar replied, explaining that Rumbelows still owed him for the Christmas season. He saw no reason why the money should be sitting in their bank account over Christmas earning interest, when it could be in Amstrad's, and was prepared to wait for as long as it took Rumbelows's finance director to sign the cheque.

Sugar addressed the early preparations for the flotation with that same single-mindedness. When a team from Touche Ross, who became Amstrad's auditors in the run-up to flotation, first visited the Tottenham headquarters, Sugar introduced Malcolm

Miller to them: 'Malcolm's our product manager on the marketing side. He's worked for Unilever and he's a graduate. He came to me about two years ago looking for a job, but I said to him, "No, you could be more valuable to Amstrad if you worked for a big company like Unilever first. Come back after you've had a couple of years experience and then join us."'

Miller had to suppress a smile at this new version of how he had joined Amstrad – a story which quickly became the authorized version for anyone connected with the company's share sale. Sugar also needed publicity material for the flotation process which would show where Amstrad's machines were made. So he travelled down to Ron Nixon's factory in Rochester and, for the photographer's benefit, temporarily replaced the L. & N. sign on the factory with an Amstrad one. Nixon asked Sugar whether the effort in preparing for the flotation was worth it. 'Once we've gone public, I'll have a million quid of me own and so will the missus. Then I'll be able to gamble with someone else's money,' Sugar replied, breaking into one of his grins.

Yet Sugar had no intention of putting his feet up after Amstrad went public, even though it guaranteed his own security and that of his family. As he told the *Evening Standard* when asked how the money would change him: 'I'm not going to book into a suite at the Hilton and take things easy for the rest of my life. Don't forget I've still got the business to run.'

· 6 ·

In the Public Eye

Launching into a recession is not the best start a consumer electronics concern could wish for as a public company. Consumers who feel the cold wind of economic problems blowing around them tend to shelve plans to buy the kind of equipment Amstrad sold back in 1980 – hi-fi units, car radios, small-screen televisions and so on. Yet recession is precisely what Amstrad had to contend with in its first two years as a public company.

Sir Geoffrey Howe unveiled £3 billion of public spending cuts in his second budget as Chancellor of the Exchequer on 26 March 1980, a month before Amstrad's late April flotation. In August, unemployment passed the 2,000,000 mark for the first time since the 1930s and the gloom continued almost unabated for two years: in the first half of 1982, the Confederation of British Industry called for an emergency £3 billion package of government spending to help industry and released one of its most pessimistic surveys of business confidence.

Alan Sugar was prudent enough to bend his plans to the prevailing economic climate. In the summer of 1980 he cut stocks and postponed the launch of a new hi-fi system. Yet more symptomatic of Amstrad's fortunes at the time was the announcement in October 1980 that the firm had beaten the profit forecast made by Sugar before flotation: pre-tax profits for the financial year 1979–80 leapt 50 per cent to £1.36 million on sales up 56 per cent at £8.76 million.

Growth on that scale was to be the pattern for the next few years. The problem Amstrad faced was not one of demand, but rather of increasing its sources of supply. Sugar seemed to be almost semi-permanently engaged in a search for larger warehousing and factory capacity. By October 1982, he was feeling sufficiently confident to observe that the recession had passed the company by. He even wondered why the C.B.I. never consulted Amstrad before producing its gloomy accounts of the economy, furnishing the answer to his own question by observing that perhaps Amstrad was, after all, still too small.

Knowing with hindsight what was in store for Amstrad later in the decade, it is tempting to dismiss the period between 1980 and 1983 as an irrelevant interlude. But that would be wrong: for these years, when Amstrad was fully exposed to the public view for the first time, revealed some of the company's main characteristics. Sugar demonstrated immense agility in the way he moved into and out of markets; he laid important foundations for Amstrad's future growth; and he began to articulate a distinctive Amstrad business philosophy. Moreover, relations with the City were set on the fraught path they have followed ever since.

Sugar's marketing agility was most clearly demonstrated during the early 1980s by the way he coped with Citizen's Band radio. Britain was one of the last countries in Europe to legalize the craze among radio hams for endlessly chatting to each other over the air-waves – a craze which had become a national obsession in the United States. The British Government had been dithering for more than two years over what form of CB system to allow. Amateur radio enthusiasts had lost patience: a million CB radios were thought to be illegally occupying air-wave space.

Interest in the potential CB market was intense by the end of 1981, as it became clear that the Government was finally lumbering up to a decision. About twenty companies including Amstrad were poised to enter the market, mainly with CB sets imported from the Far East. Optimistic projections abounded: one pundit predicted sales of a million sets in the first year, but added that the market would not be saturated for a further five years, when six million CB radios would be sold annually.

Alan Sugar had been keeping half an eye on CB for a long time; before Amstrad's flotation, he had declared his interest in jumping on the band-wagon as soon as the hobby was legalized. But he also made plain his scepticism of the rosiest projections of CB's potential. As he wrote in his chairman's statement accompanying Amstrad's 1980–81 report and accounts:

> It is a market which in other countries has caused several failures, due to the bad quality of products and a poor understanding of the demand, and its recent legalization may incite some over-enthusiasm on behalf of some suppliers in respect of market size and potential. It is therefore our intention to enter the market . . . with a degree of caution in our commitment. We will try to adopt a sensible medium whereby we can react either way to its future.

The statement was dated 6 October 1981, five days after the Government had announced plans to legalize CB.

Sugar suspected that CB would be a one-week wonder. He knew there was a reservoir of pent-up demand from frustrated would-be radio hams, but he also reckoned that there was a distinct limit to the number of Britons who wanted to spend their leisure hours swapping call signs over crackling air-waves. Armed with this intuitive feel for the market, he concluded that the way to make money out of CB was to be there early, in large volumes, but also to be ready to quit the minute the market looked like drying up.

Amstrad was one of the first companies to secure large orders, running into tens of thousands of sets, from chain stores like Argos, Currys and Rumbelows, who were busy stocking up for a Christmas CB boom following the October legalization. Sugar was also the first big player in the market to spot the end of the craze early in 1982; as soon as he realized the CB bubble had burst, he moved quickly to ensure that all the sets which the retailers had ordered from him were safely booked into their warehouses. By contrast, most of Amstrad's main competitors were stuck with large stocks and heavy losses.

Gulu Lalvani, Sugar's old friend from Binatone – which also

went for CB in a big way – says: 'Alan smelt, I mean smelt, that the market was on the point of going down. And his reaction was incredibly sharp.'

A couple of months later, when everyone had realized that CB was fizzling out, Lalvani asked Rumbelows to take some of his remaining stock at discounted prices. 'I was told by Rumbelows: "We can't take another set, because our warehouse is bursting with Amstrad CB radios." That was Alan's sharpness,' Lalvani recalls, with a rueful smile.

Meanwhile, Sugar was shifting his Tower Systems and a host of new audio products in ever-increasing numbers. In retrospect, it is easy to see that Amstrad's product line was ideally placed to benefit – not suffer – from the recession. Consumers feeling the pinch were as likely to opt for value-for-money as to abandon their purchasing plans altogether. They chose a music system a little less expensive than they had originally planned. In February 1982, the *Daily Telegraph* explained Sugar's ability to buck the trend of the recession as 'deliciously simple': Amstrad was producing 'an audio entertainment system that looks like it should cost £400, to sell at between £150 and £200'.

The financial pressure on the working- and lower-middle-class customers who tended to buy Amstrad's equipment was eased a little in 1982 when the Government abolished restrictions on hire purchase. The company was waiting to take their business and Sugar made sure they knew about Amstrad by pouring ever-larger sums of money into advertising. Some £3 million went on television advertising and full-page ads in all the popular daily newspapers in the Christmas season of 1982, for example, as compared with Amstrad's total annual advertising budget of about £100,000 in the late 1970s. Fuelled in part by this television exposure, Sugar was able to claim a third of the 850,000 hi-fi units sold in Britain in 1982 – much more than any competitor, including the Japanese.

Many business people would have been stretched simply to keep up with such a boom in their core business, but Sugar was careful during these early years in the public eye to sow seeds designed to maintain Amstrad's rapid growth. One important area was his continuing struggle to diversify the company's spread of customers, thereby reducing its over-reliance on Comet. The obvious mass market appeal of the Tower System allowed Amstrad to penetrate the mail order business by forging links with mail order leaders such as Grattan. Sugar consolidated his one substantial export market by opening a French subsidiary in 1982. Sales to high street chains like Rumbelows, Woolworths and Currys also flourished, to the point where by 1982 Amstrad's equipment was being sold through 3,000 retail outlets.

Sugar realized that his manufacturing arrangements would have to evolve if he was to sustain Amstrad's growth. He could no longer rely on a clutch of small British sub-contractors, like L. & N. in Rochester, whose output could not always be guaranteed because of their perennial struggle to recruit enough skilled labour. Sugar broke the news to Ron Nixon at L. & N. that Amstrad would no longer be putting work his way. Nixon then experienced – for the first and last time – Sugar's tendency on occasion to stick so rigidly to the letter of an agreement that the person on the receiving end perceives it as ruthlessness: a tactic which he is particularly prone to employ when he has no further business with someone.

While assembling an entire piece of equipment for a customer, a sub-contractor like L. & N. inevitably has to contend with mismatches in the component parts supplied by the customer. L. & N. needed more than 1,000 sets of components to make 1,000 of Amstrad's products, because individual components were lost or damaged during the manufacturing process. When Sugar wound up Amstrad's dealings with Nixon, he charged L. & N. for all the components that could not be accounted for down the years. 'It's normally accepted with everyone else I've worked with that they give you a bundle of stuff now and again to offset component losses,' Nixon says.

Insisting on what was undoubtedly Amstrad's legal rights, Sugar refused to follow suit. 'It chewed away about half the money that they owed us in the end. And it was on that that we came to blows virtually,' recalls Nixon, before adding, 'Mind you, that was the only example where I considered him to be unfair.'

In place of L. & N. and other similar sub-contractors, Sugar relied on two centres of manufacturing. Amstrad's first and most important manufacturing base was in the Far East. In 1981 Sugar strengthened his links with the region by opening a Hong Kong office, the company's first overseas subsidiary. Secondly, he built up his U.K. capacity, initially in 1981 by leasing a 40,000-square-foot factory in Southend near the one he had leased in 1978. When Amstrad outgrew that too, he paid £2.5 million in 1982 for a 133,000-square-foot plant at Shoeburyness, on the Essex coast.

Stan Randall, who had been one of Amstrad's first employees when he joined the company a decade earlier, was going through a separation from his first wife in early 1981 which he describes as 'ugly'. A strong family man, Sugar did what he could to help Randall over a difficult patch and approached him one day in August with a proposal: 'How would you like to go to the Far East for a couple of years to help you get over it? I think I can get you out there fairly soon.'

Sugar explained to Randall that he had been thinking of setting up a Hong Kong office, which would allow Amstrad to cut out its Japanese agent. In future, it would deal directly with all its sub-contractors and suppliers, which would not only save on the agent's mark-up but also give Amstrad greater control over suppliers. Sugar planned to negotiate the main contracts with sub-contractors and suppliers during his frequent visits to the Far East, but Amstrad's Hong Kong office would be in a better position to keep in day-to-day touch with its Far Eastern suppliers, not least because it was in the same time zone. In addition, Randall in Hong Kong would be able to oversee the shipping of Amstrad's goods to Britain.

So keen was Randall to accept Sugar's offer that by October 1981 he had started work as the first employee of Amstrad International (Hong Kong) Limited. Amstrad occupied a small corner of a textile company run by Simon Mak, a Hong Kong Chinese businessman. It was thanks to Gerry Eriera, Sugar's Chigwell friend, and Ann Sugar that Alan had met Mak, the agent through whom Eriera imported materials for his ladies' fashion business in which Ann had taken an interest. Sugar and

Mak hit it off so well that he asked Mak's help when setting up the Hong Kong office. Stan Randall launched Amstrad's Hong Kong operation surrounded by Chinese haggling over cloths: 'I was given a desk and a chair and a very tiny office, with a telephone line, and I was expected to get on with it,' he recalls.

Randall hired a secretary recommended to him by Simon Mak, but she lasted only two weeks because she had worked in Britain and therefore was used to a 9–5 routine. As his new secretary he employed Callen So, a 19-year-old Hong Kong Chinese woman who quickly proved to have the essential Amstrad qualities: an appetite for extremely hard work and the ability to turn her attention to almost any problem. The Hong Kong office's responsibilities expanded steadily. Amstrad began to arrange some of its letters of credit in the Far East, leaving Randall to discuss terms with bankers there. In addition he hired design and engineering staff who often acted as intermediaries between Hong Kong and Amstrad U.K. After Amstrad France was launched in 1982, the Hong Kong office also started to arrange shipments direct to France, saving on the time and money involved in shipping via Britain. In the early years, Callen So often worked in Amstrad's little offices till 9 or 10 in the evening. Her mother began to scold her, saying these hours were not good for a young woman and asking her to quit Amstrad. But she had caught the Amstrad bug and Sugar rewarded her later in the decade first by making her Amstrad's marketing director in the Far East, and then by bringing her to Amstrad headquarters as his special assistant.

As far as manufacturing was concerned, Amstrad Hong Kong's relations with Amstrad U.K. quickly settled into the groove they were to occupy for much of the 1980s. Most Amstrad products were either made by sub-contractors in the Far East or were simply badged goods imported from Far Eastern OEM manufacturers. The Shoeburyness plant acted as a large warehousing centre for the distribution of Amstrad's goods arriving from the Far East. It was also used for putting the finishing touches to goods made there and for assembling into finished form products whose bulk made them uneconomic to import. Amstrad had originally acquired factory space in Southend back in the 1970s to assemble bulky products like loud-speakers. The large-screen televisions which the company started selling in 1983 were one of the first products to be assembled in Shoeburyness.

Alan Sugar also spent the early years of the 1980s restlessly thinking about new products. He constantly unveiled new models for Amstrad's audio line-up, for instance adding a remote control to the Tower System, a feature which in those days tended to be found only in hi-fi systems in the £1,000 bracket. Yet he knew that Amstrad could not realistically expect to take an ever greater share of the U.K. audio market. Moreover, by the end of 1982 he had already dropped two of the main product lines important to Amstrad at the time of its flotation: in-car music systems and a range of small electronic goods such as portable and clock radios.

It was imperative for Amstrad to build up product areas outside audio. Fundamental to Sugar's business philosophy is the maxim of never becoming too dependent on any particular product. The Tower System was a winner for the moment, but he knew that its very success would encourage others to imitate it. The resulting pressure on Amstrad's market share would inevitably force him to cut prices and margins.

Sugar's first two entirely new product offerings in these years proved a dead end, for the time being at least. In 1982, Amstrad began to import badged 14″ and 20″ colour televisions from the Far East. They sold well and the 14″ version was voted joint best buy by *Which?* magazine in February 1983. He decided that Amstrad should go one better and assemble its own 22″ colour TVs. When it opened the Shoeburyness plant in 1983 a line was installed which could produce 900 TVs a day. Sugar also decided to launch into video recorders in 1983, then a relatively new product. He began by importing complete video recorders from Japan, but laid plans to assemble these in Shoeburyness too from mid-1984. Taken together, he realized, colour TVs and video recorders accounted for a very large slice of all consumer electronics sales and were also likely to furnish much of the growth in the market in the immediate future. In October 1983, he talked of winning 10 per cent of the £1 billion annual sales of video recorders and 22″ TVs.

But this was not to be. Very few European companies were managing to make money from colour televisions in the face of the onslaught from Japanese companies, which regarded output of a million sets a year as the minimum necessary to guarantee adequate economies of scale. Towards the end of 1983, the Shoeburyness TV production line also suffered technical problems which occupied much of Bob Watkins's time. With video recorders, Amstrad felt the backlash of an early round of trade friction between the European Commission and Japan: the EC included the kits of video recorder parts, which Amstrad wanted to import, in quota arrangements designed to protect domestic European video recorder producers against the wave of Japanese imports. Sugar bowed to the inevitable, announcing his decision to run down the company's activities in large-screen colour TVs and video recorders in October 1984.

Predicting a market glut in both colour TVs and video recorders, he said in his chairman's statement accompanying the 1983–84 results that Amstrad 'would be more comfortable as an observer rather than a participant in what could become a price war'. He underlined Amstrad's pragmatic attitude to products, adding that his decision might turn out to be temporary: 'We have the flexibility to turn off our supplies when we consider the market is vulnerable.'

In his chairman's statement in October 1984, Sugar justified his withdrawal from the video recorder and large-screen TV market in terms of Amstrad's overwhelming commitment to the bottom line:

I have always tried to emphasize how margin is important to us; we shall only continue in sectors where there are good margins of profit. It may seem surprising that one year we are selling large quantities of VCR and the next we sell none. Quite frankly, when there is no margin in a product, we see no reason to endanger our cash flow simply to impress the compilers of market share statistics.

By the time he made these comments, however, Sugar had launched Amstrad into a product line – personal computers – which was to open a new chapter in the Amstrad story.

*

A curious episode in Amstrad's history – which resulted in two of Britain's most eminent barristers arguing over the company's conduct before the House of Lords – can also be traced back to the early 1980s. As with most complex legal proceedings, the case of Amstrad versus the music industry stretched out over several years and was not finally resolved until 1988. But the issues it raised for the company stemmed from decisions taken before it launched into computers.

Amstrad fell foul of the music industry's determination to stamp on individuals making copies of music cassettes in their homes. This is technically illegal in Britain because it infringes copyright legislation. The music companies claim that their losses through home taping run into millions of pounds each year. Unfortunately for the music business, however, the law cannot be enforced against individuals and in the early 1980s the industry hit upon another tactic: to make an example of an audio manufacturer who brought out a high-speed tape-to-tape copier, then a relatively new high street product.

The British Phonographic Industry, the music industry's trade association, thought it had caught its prey in 1982 when Aiwa, the Japanese audio company, launched a high-speed tape deck which copied tapes at four times the normal speed. But Aiwa agreed not to sell its recorder in Britain when warned that the B.P.I. would make it a test case: like many Japanese companies, it was sensitive about its public profile.

Amstrad was made of sterner stuff. The company's interest in the new tape-to-tape copying market dated from 1980, when it released a double cassette tape recorder which allowed customers to copy from one tape to another and record off the radio or records – all for less than £100. But the music industry really woke up to Amstrad in 1984, when the company issued three new tape-to-tape recording machines which could record at twice normal speed and sold for £150 to £200.

As is its way, Amstrad was not shy about broadcasting the merits of its new machines and launched a big television and popular newspaper advertising campaign. 'You can even make a copy of your favourite cassette,' the ads stressed, just in case anyone was dumb enough not to grasp the point of the machines.

Japanese manufacturers already had recorders on the market which could copy at double speed, but Amstrad's machines were in a different league as Patrick Isherwood, then the B.P.I.'s legal director, explains:

> Amstrad's advertising was totally different to anything that had been seen before. They were spending huge amounts of money on national TV at prime times – 'Coronation Street', 'News at Ten' and so on. The second difference was the size of their market. Amstrad's whole business was geared to large turnover at low price. Before, relatively speaking, the quantities weren't large. The Japanese machines were usually separates designed to go into hi-fi systems. Amstrad took it into the Tower Systems market.

In October 1984 the B.P.I. wrote to Alan Sugar and to eleven of Amstrad's main high street customers, pointing out that home-taping was illegal and that encouraging people to tape at home was potentially illegal in itself. Sugar's response was immediate: he issued a writ against the B.P.I. on the grounds that the trade association had falsely accused Amstrad of behaving illegally. He also sought a declaration from the High Court that it was doing nothing wrong.

The two sides did not meet each other throughout the legal twists and turns of the next four years. Sugar never needed to appear in court. It was a highly professional engagement, with no room for compromise between two fundamentally different objectives. Amstrad wanted the shadow cast over itself and its customers lifted, while the music industry was trying to reduce home taping through a clarification of the law. Indeed, so keen was the music business to have the law clarified that private worries were expressed within the industry about the health of its opponent. At a meeting of the B.P.I.'s governing council in late 1984, one of the assembled music moguls voiced concern about Amstrad's staying power: it was only an insignificant little outfit, so how could they be sure that it would still be around in a few years' time to continue a legal fight against the massed ranks of the world's biggest music conglomerates? Shortly afterwards, Amstrad's sales went through the roof and Sugar emerged as a star of the business scene: by luck the music industry had chosen the perfect company to ensure that its anti-copying case received maximum publicity.

The first round went to the music business when the case reached the High Court in June 1985. Mr Justice Whitford was unimpressed by a note Amstrad stuck on its twin-cassette decks, which read: 'The recording and playback of certain material may only be possible by permission. Please refer to the Copyright Act 1956 and the Performers Protection Acts 1958 and 1972.' Stating that the note was 'barely noticeable or unintelligible to ordinary people', the judge dismissed Amstrad's request for a declaration and found for the music industry on all points.

The music industry was naturally cock-a-hoop; immediately after the judgement the B.P.I.'s Patrick Isherwood said, 'It will be difficult for retailers to sell twin-deck cassette machines after this decision. . . . They will have to show adequate warning notices which will be off-putting to most consumers.'

Sugar cast a different light on the judgement and accused the judge of 'losing his bottle', explaining this unusual aspersion on the English judiciary: 'It seemed to me he was being evasive. He wanted to force us to take the matter to the Court of Appeal, because it is such a fine point.'

He was not planning a retreat. 'What the judge has done is so anti-Amstrad that we have no choice but to appeal. We have no intention of stopping selling the decks,' he said at the time.

At this point the legal process moved with unusual speed. It took only four months for the case to reach the Court of Appeal, where the three judges distinguished themselves by producing a ruling which satisfied neither side. All the findings of the High Court were reversed. Lord Justice Lawton ruled against the B.P.I. on the grounds that Amstrad was not authorizing people to copy tapes simply by advertising the copying ability of a particular machine. This insight – that Amstrad was not itself authorizing home-taping – was to prove fundamental to the rest of the case. A parallel would be this: a gun manufacturer does not authorize people to commit murder simply because his products can be used for this purpose.

Yet still the Court of Appeal would not give Amstrad a declaration that it was doing nothing wrong. On the contrary, the Court found that Amstrad might be committing the criminal offence of inciting people to break copyright law, but that this would have to be settled by a criminal prosecution and not by the civil action then under way.

Amstrad had failed to get its declaration, but the B.P.I. had not squeezed out of the Court the simple statement of the law it was seeking, as Patrick Isherwood recalls: 'The B.P.I. had not gone into this as a way of punishing Amstrad, but in order to get the law clarified. So it was a hollow victory for the B.P.I.'

There the matter might have rested except for the fact that a group of music companies led by C.B.S., the world's largest music group, had launched a parallel action claiming damages from Amstrad for copyright infringement. This had lapsed while Amstrad's request for a declaration was wending its way through the courts, but now that this action had come to a halt the C.B.S. case was revived, eventually reaching the Court of Appeal in February 1987.

The conclusions of the Court of Appeal on this occasion did not differ markedly from those of the same Court two years previously. By a two-to-one majority, the Court found against the music companies, ruling that incitement to infringe copyright is a criminal matter not subject to the civil courts. Lord Justice Nicholls told the music companies that their remedy lay in launching a private prosecution against Amstrad. Sir Denys Buckley – the dissenting judge, who argued that the record companies should be allowed to sue Amstrad – quoted a precedent dating from 1861 when the Emperor of Austria had been allowed to sue individuals who had imported fake bank-notes into Hungary.

This was the first and last time that the Emperor of Austria entered the Amstrad story. It took another fifteen months for the C.B.S. case to move from the Court of Appeal to the House of Lords, the highest court in Britain, where lawyers were treated to the delicious spectacle of two of Britain's foremost QCs – Robert (now Lord) Alexander for Amstrad, and Sydney Kentridge for the music companies – dissecting ever more abstruse points of law. The Law Lords ruled in favour of Amstrad, reaffirming the fundamental point: Amstrad was not guilty of a breach of copyright because it was not authorizing the people who bought its recorders to copy tapes. Within the hi-fi industry, the ruling evoked a sigh of relief – albeit a rather discreet sigh, as leading audio journalist Arthur Ord-Hume recalls: 'Alan Sugar was the only one with the gumption to take on the music companies. The entire industry went into a huddle and toasted him. The ruling was particularly helpful to the Japanese, who had been too cautious to take on the B.P.I. legally.'

Yet the Law Lords coupled their judgement with a ringing denunciation of existing copyright law as unenforceable. Indeed, Lord Templeman became quite lyrical on the point: 'Whatever the reason for home copying, the beat of "Sergeant Pepper" and the soaring sounds of the "Miserere" from unlawful copies are more powerful than law-abiding instincts or twinges of conscience. A law which is treated with such contempt should be amended or repealed.'

Once more, both sides could claim a victory of sorts. Nothing now prevented Amstrad selling its cassette-recorders in precisely the form it had always intended, as Alan Sugar stressed after the result: 'We are not going to be bullied by powerful record and music industry pressure groups into withholding from consumers the advantages of developing technology.'

For their part, the music companies had won a clear statement from Britain's highest court that the existing law on home taping was practically worthless. This statement could hardly have been better timed from their point of view, because it coincided with the passage through Parliament of the Government's attempt at a root-and-branch reform of copyright law in the Copyright Bill.

At that stage the Government was committed to introducing a

levy on blank tapes – in effect, a tax on home taping. The music industry used the Law Lords' comments in the Amstrad case to lobby for similar action against manufacturers who launched recording machines which encouraged copyright infringement. In the end, however, the Government quietly laid to rest the notion of a blank tape levy – and, in effect, any parallel action against recorder manufacturers. Too many Conservative MPs rated the interests of music listeners well above those of the music companies. After almost four years of pursuing Amstrad, the music industry came away empty-handed.

*

Alan Sugar's success with the Tower System, coupled with his swift moves in and out of markets, shone through Amstrad's financial results in the early 1980s. Profits increased by 75 per cent in 1980–81 (Amstrad's financial year ends in June); by 101 per cent in 1981–82; by 69 per cent in 1982–83; and by a relatively modest 13 per cent in 1983–84, when profit margins were squeezed by the venture into large-screen televisions and video recorders, as well as by the fall in the value of the pound which boosted the cost in sterling of Amstrad's imports of equipment and parts. Nevertheless, figures for that year – profits of £9.1 million on turnover of £84.95 million – registered just how quickly the company had grown in the short time since its flotation. In 1984, Amstrad's progress received public recognition when the 37-year-old Sugar was named *Guardian* Young Businessman of the Year.

The stock market was beginning to notice this odd little audio company. Amstrad's shares traded for 178p in October 1981, twice the price at which they had been floated. In February 1982, they touched 205p. By October 1982, when the doubling in profits for 1981–82 was declared, the shares reached 395p, thanks to a 115p surge in one week. People who had held Amstrad stock since its flotation in April 1980 had seen the value of their investment increase four-and-a-half times in thirty months.

So strongly were the shares performing that Amstrad carried out a one-for-one scrip issue in late 1982. This is an accounting device which halves the face value of a share and doubles the number of shares in existence. A scrip issue makes no difference to the value of individual shareholders' stakes: instead of holding 100 shares worth 400p each, for example, they find themselves holding 200 shares worth 200p each. But conventional wisdom in the City is that once the face value of a share becomes too high, some psychological resistance emerges to trading in that share. Amstrad shares resumed their onward march, prompting the company to decide on another sub-division of its shares in late 1983 – on this occasion, by five times.

The upward journey of the Amstrad share price had been closely watched by Alan Sugar – naturally enough, since on flotation he had been left with 75 per cent of the shares. In March 1982, he realized £2 million by selling almost 900,000 shares at 229.5p each, cutting his stake in Amstrad to 65.4 per cent in the process. Almost a year later, in February 1983, he raised another £4.6 million by selling 1.2 million shares at 382p each, leaving him with 58.9 per cent of Amstrad.

Towards the end of 1982 the press began to quote the value of Sugar's remaining stake in Amstrad which, thanks to the share price rise, was pushing him into the league of Britain's super-rich. The *Evening Standard* calculated on 6 October 1982 that Sugar's stake was worth £23 million, including a £3 million increase on the day following the release of Amstrad's 1981–82 results. By the end of January 1983, the value of his stake in Amstrad had more than doubled to £48 million.

Of course, these sums represented nothing more substantial than a paper fortune. Sugar would never be in a position to realize the entire face value of his holding in Amstrad by selling all his shares on the stock market: the very news that he intended to do so would result in a collapse of Amstrad's share price because investors would conclude that he no longer had confidence in the company. Yet by February 1983 he had raised about £8.6 million in total from three sales of tranches of his Amstrad shares. This money – and larger sums which were to follow later – formed the basis of the personal fortune which he held independently of the company. So financially secure was Sugar that he felt able to waive about £1 million of dividend payments due him from his

Amstrad stake between 1981 and 1983: given the then high tax rates on unearned income, it made more sense for him to keep this money within Amstrad to develop the company.

The Sugars moved house again, completing the journey out of the East End which Alan had begun less than twenty years previously. Their new home was in a lane just around the corner from their old house in Chigwell Rise, but in a totally different league from even the detached homes of the small businessmen and professionals who inhabit the Rise. Now they were able to move into a millionaires' row, where half a dozen newly-built mansions cater for some of Britain's wealthiest people. Extensive grounds glimpsed behind the driveways, tennis courts, private gyms and swimming pools – these were the norm among the Sugars' new neighbours. The Sugars bought a handsome, L-shaped house in red brick, nestled round a central courtyard, complete with roof terrace and living rooms opening out on to a large rock garden in the middle of extensive lawns.

The Sugars' house is simpler and more classical than some of its neighbours, which include a sprinkling of mock Tudor mansions, but it was more than enough to stun Alan Sugar's family. Ann tried to prepare Daphne, Alan's sister, by telling her that their new home was big; but when Daphne and husband Harold went out to see it, they had to drive past it a couple of times before they dared to enter: 'We couldn't believe the size of the property. We'd never seen anything like that,' Daphne says.

Fay and Nathan, Sugar's parents, shared this reaction. 'When my mother and father first went to see it, they were totally confused. They couldn't take it in. They just hadn't realized how big Alan had got,' recalls Daphne.

*

City professionals were also slow to wake up to Amstrad, despite the advance in its share price. W. Greenwell, Amstrad's brokers, struggled to convince the many large insurance companies and pension funds which had ignored the flotation to start buying the stock. It was psychologically difficult for institutions which had squandered the opportunity of buying Amstrad shares at 85p to acquire them after they had passed the 150p or 200p mark.

Paul Williams of Clerical Medical and General Life Assurance, the institution which became the biggest shareholder after Sugar at the time of the company's flotation, was keen to encourage a wider interest in the stock in the City: this would tend to accelerate the upward movement of Amstrad's share price, provided the company continued to perform well. But Williams found that institutional doubters cited Amstrad's very success as a reason for staying clear: 'Other institutions were always frightened they might be getting in at the peak. I was often told by brokers that it would be easier to sell Amstrad to clients when it slowed down to 20 per cent growth, because no one could believe that 50 per cent or 100 per cent growth was sustainable.'

Clerical Medical remained impressed by Amstrad's record and gradually bought more shares to the point where by May 1984 it held 12.8 per cent. But it was bothered by the fact that Greenwell was the only stockbrokers whose analysts regularly followed Amstrad immediately after its flotation. This meant that the one source of informed data and analysis on Amstrad was Greenwell, which as Amstrad's brokers was naturally partisan.

In 1980 Greg Morgan had started work as an analyst for Gilbert Eliott, a small firm of stockbrokers later taken over by the Austrian bank, Girozentrale. Morgan phoned Clerical Medical (one of his clients in his previous firm) to ask whether the insurance company would do business with him at Gilbert Eliott. Clerical Medical pondered the matter and returned with a proposition: it would start channelling business Morgan's way provided Morgan began to follow Amstrad.

Morgan knew nothing about Amstrad but, an assiduous man, he put some effort into researching the business: it would do nothing for his reputation if he began to recommend purchase of shares in a company which flopped eighteen months later. He travelled to Hull and lunched in Comet's board-room with Michael Hollingbery, who told him that out of all Comet's suppliers Sugar had about the best feel for the market. Morgan was impressed by Amstrad's line-up of City advisers: 'You would not have associated a Hackney lad with Kleinwort Benson,' he comments.

But the key factor in swinging Morgan around to Amstrad was a visit he paid to Sugar one afternoon in Tottenham. The meeting was scheduled to last ten minutes, but it stretched to 45. Sugar talked and talked – not *to* Morgan, but *at* him – about audio, television, car radios and all the other markets Amstrad was then in. He spun the Amstrad philosophy of flexibility to Morgan and the City analyst came away with an image of a thrusting young businessman who could cut through to the heart of his markets with blinding simplicity. He briefed his salesmen about the stock, and they began to recommend Amstrad to clients; but, like Greenwell, they found it hard work to interest the institutions.

Part of the problem lay with Amstrad. From day one as chairman of a public company, Sugar made it plain that selling Amstrad's products was a better use of his time than selling the company to the City. Amstrad even began to hold its annual general meetings in Tottenham, first in its Garman Road head-quarters and then in a room at the Spurs football ground premises, rather than in a more conventional venue near the City. Greg Morgan used to trail up to these A.G.M.s where analysts and shareholders were regularly outnumbered by the company's board and advisers. It was all part of the Amstrad ethic of satisfying City requirements in the most economical and time-efficient manner possible.

David Thomson, Greenwell's head of corporate finance, tried to persuade Sugar to do the normal round of institutional briefings. 'But he wouldn't come out of his hole in Tottenham,' Thomson recalls. Not only did visiting the City run against Sugar's natural temperament, but it was also in his opinion a waste of time: Amstrad's share price would depend on his making a profit, which meant selling goods, not on being nice to the City.

In Sugar's view, the height of wasted time is the business lunch, including lunches in the City where the square mile's best and brightest can quiz senior figures from industry about their plans and progress: 'They get on my bloody nerves actually. I get very fidgety sitting around at lunch for 2½ hours. There are people who get to the office at 9.30, read the *FT* until 10.30, then they have tea and biscuits, and at 11.00 they do their bit of brilliance for the day. At 11.55 they down their pen and go out to lunch, roll back at 3.30 and have a final bout of brilliance and that's it,' he told a journalist in 1980.

Despairing of ever tempting Sugar into the City, Greenwell began to arrange broker visits to Amstrad's headquarters in Tottenham, where he was visibly more relaxed among the cardboard boxes talking about company products. There appeared to be a pay-off from these briefings for Sugar: Greg Morgan began to detect a pattern in which the visits – which heightened City interest in Amstrad – would be followed a week or so later by Sugar selling a parcel of his stock. But even these share-selling exercises threatened to cause a rift with the City. On one occasion, Amstrad's share price fell sharply between the time when Sugar briefed Greenwell about his plans to sell and the execution of the sale, suggesting that his intentions had been leaked – a classic example of insider trading. Sugar reacted angrily, convinced that the leak came from within Greenwell though the brokers vehemently denied this.

Some years later Sugar was to say on Terry Wogan's television chat show that he may have been naïve in his dealings with the City. As chairman of a new public company, he was warned in the clearest terms by the Stock Exchange not to divulge price-sensitive information selectively. Wanting to play scrupulously by the rules, he made a point of talking to as few people from the City as possible.

Perhaps: but there is no doubt that this line of argument neatly coincided with his natural inclination to regard many City people as overpaid time-wasters. The upshot was that the signals emanating from Amstrad were always sparse and sometimes misleading. Greg Morgan remembers being leaned on by the firm's City advisers not to be too enthusiastic in his profit forecasts: when Amstrad duly reported another set of stunning results, the market reacted to the news that they had greatly exceeded the City forecasts by marking up the share price sharply. After an unusually disappointing Christmas for Amstrad in 1984, by contrast,

Morgan did not receive a hint of this news from the company until the early spring.

Yet Sugar was developing his own form of communication with the outside world, including the City: the chairman's statement he released at the time of Amstrad's annual results. It is a near universal practice for chairmen of public companies to issue statements when releasing their results, but the accompanying figures usually contain the only serious points of interest. The typical chairman's statement is drafted by some bright young executive at corporate headquarters, then put through the sieve of the company's public relations and financial advisers until it emerges with all the excitement of puréed baby-food.

By contrast, Sugar has always put his personal stamp on his chairman's statements. While obviously scrutinized by his advisers, they are written in a language and with a directness that could have emanated only from his own hand. As a result, they provide useful pointers for Amstrad watchers in the City and elsewhere.

As early as October 1981, when Sugar was reporting on Amstrad's results for 1980–81, he penned an account of his strategy which amounts to the first sustained statement of the Amstrad philosophy. Unveiling a 75 per cent increase in profits, 'during a period which has been described by some as a recession', he attributed these results to 'our expertise in marketing and our efficiency in production and management'.

Sugar had seen no need to expand management or clerical staff despite a 61 per cent increase in sales: 'Our administration staff levels have remained constant and have coped with the company's expansion efficiently, and we remain confident that further expansion can be handled equally well.'

Manufacturing flexibility was at the heart of Amstrad's strategy:

The company has always used a flexible approach to production and we still wish to maintain the options of 100 per cent manufacturing or part assembly or indeed, importation and distribution of finished products. It is important to note that the recent dramatic devaluation of the pound would have left the company in a difficult position had we been committed to one way of producing. With our approach, we were able to turn off quickly certain items imported from the Far East and produce them in the U.K. In the past, when the reverse has been applicable, it was just as easy to hive off the making of some items to other countries.

Revealing that Amstrad was working on a stream of new products, Sugar argued that, 'we have become trend-setters in design concepts, similar in a way to the major Japanese companies, but with the important difference of not being committed to any one method of production or area in which to produce.'

The new products to be unveiled in the coming year would, Sugar assured Amstrad's shareholders, be 'in true Amstrad fashion, one step ahead of the market and most definitely the competition'.

· 7 ·

The People's Computer

It was a baking hot day in early August 1983 and Roland Perry was becoming bored with the annual stock-take. He worked for a small company which traded as Ambit International and made its money by running a mail order catalogue for electronic components, a business that financed a range of other activities more to the taste of the electronics buffs who made up the company. They published an electronics magazine and designed electronic gadgets such as calculators. They had even helped Amstrad in the past by putting some finishing touches to its CB radio.

Counting the number of transistors in stock did not rank as one of Perry's most exciting responsibilities. So it was with more than usual interest that he saw Bob Watkins walk into Ambit's high street premises in Brentwood – a small town in the middle of the Essex commuter belt, where the suburban sprawl to the north-east of London begins to give way to countryside. Amstrad's technical director knew the Ambit people from their past work for the company – work which had come Ambit's way because its managing director, William Poel, was a friend of Stan Randall, who by then was running Amstrad Hong Kong.

Watkins was carrying a cardboard box which he placed on a desk in front of Perry. He produced from the box, first a wodge of papers and then a brand-new computer keyboard. Amstrad's name was unmistakable in a corner of the keyboard.

'You know about computers,' Watkins said to Perry. 'Well,

we've got this computer project we're working on and the designers have done a bunk. Do you think you could finish it off for us?'

This opening gambit raised more questions than it answered, so Watkins elaborated on the reason for his journey to Brentwood. Throughout 1982, Alan Sugar had become increasingly impressed by the home computer boom spearheaded in Britain by companies such as Sinclair, Acorn, Commodore and Oric. They were selling tens of thousands of machines, many for £200 or £300 each – dwarfing the money to be made in Amstrad's audio business. Eventually, Sugar decided that home computers offered a market ripe for the Amstrad treatment.

Sugar knew nothing about computer technology so he asked around, quickly learning how different the business was from hi-fi. If Amstrad intended to make a lot of money in computers, then it could not buy off-the-shelf technology as it had for its audio products; it would have to design its own computers from scratch.

Amstrad could handle the exterior of its computer, the way it looked; Sugar already had some innovative ideas on that score. But it would have to rely on others to design the machine's interior – its electronic circuitry and operating software. For this, Sugar turned to a couple of engineers who had worked for Amstrad in the past and who claimed to understand computers.

In the first half of 1983 Sugar and Watkins busied themselves finalizing the look of their computer. Ignorant of just how much effort goes into designing a computer, they naïvely assumed that their two engineers were making similar progress, but by the summer of 1983 they had begun to suspect that the circuitry and software design were seriously awry. These suspicions were confirmed when the software designer cracked under the pressure, broke off contact with Amstrad and disappeared.

Watkins concluded his story: 'I managed to track down where he lived and get access to his place. I found bits of computer strewn all around the house, as well as all the designs for the Amstrad computer,' he said, nodding at the pile of papers in front of Perry. 'I also noticed a letter from Barclays Bank, so I contacted the bank which said that a cheque had been cashed in the Lake

District. I reckon he's disappeared to the Lake District, so at least we know he hasn't killed himself.'

Asking Perry whether Ambit would finish the project for Amstrad, Watkins made only two stipulations. First, Amstrad's plans to enter the computer market had to remain secret: Ambit must tape over the Amstrad name whenever outsiders were shown the keyboard. Second, the project had to be completed fast – incredibly fast, since Amstrad wanted the finished design before the end of January, some five months away.

Roland Perry talked over Amstrad's request with his managing director, William Poel, and they both agreed to work on the project. Their role would be as project managers: they would find the best designers and oversee the operation. Initially, the two Ambit people envisaged having to devote about half their time to Amstrad – a time allocation that in the event proved wildly optimistic.

Short and wiry, Perry is the type of engineer who elevates method into the guiding principle of his work. His first move was to contact the man responsible for the hardware design thus far – the member of the original duo who had *not* disappeared to the Lake District. The meeting, held in a pub, was not promising, as Perry recalls: 'He was an oldish guy, bearded, with a moustache and smoking a pipe. He arrived in the pub with his young son, who was about 13 or 14. As the conversation progressed, it became clear that the son had been doing most of the work on the Amstrad computer.'

Perry was unimpressed with the work of this man-and-boy partnership. Although their computer was able to put a few letters on the screen, the whole design was untidy and inefficient; the colour graphics in particular were a disaster. On leaving the pub, he decided to assemble a new team.

The newly appointed project manager set about tapping a network of contacts dating from his days as an engineering student at Cambridge University. Cambridge is the nearest Britain has to Silicon Valley, that legendary strip of California which has spawned many breakthroughs in computing and electronics; the university's catalytic role in fostering a local high-tech economy was similar to that played by Stanford University in Silicon Valley. From the 1960s onwards, an easy interchange developed between the academics in Cambridge's world-class science and engineering departments and the electronics companies that were starting up all over town. Many key figures who shaped the Cambridge phenomenon divided their time between the University and their entrepreneurial activities. By 1983 computing, biotechnology, lasers, advanced medical equipment and other high-tech industries accounted for almost one in six of the workers in Cambridge and the surrounding region – an area dubbed 'Silicon Fen' by the media. Sinclair Research and Acorn were the acknowledged stars among a host of other companies which shone in the Cambridge firmament.

Perry was at Cambridge in the early 1970s with a group of friends who saw the beginnings of this intellectual and entrepreneurial excitement. Like him, many of his friends had been inspired by the maths and physics teaching at Brentwood School to study engineering or maths at Cambridge. The Brentwood gang merged naturally into a wider circle of like-minded techies at the university. Many went on to work in computing. It was to this circle that Perry now turned.

Perry moved quickly, travelling to Cambridge within days of Watkins's visit to talk to two sets of computer designers. The most pressing problem was to find software designers for the Amstrad computer. It not only needed an operating system – the master program which controls the main activities of a computer – but also a Basic, the most widely used programming language in personal computers. Only when the operating system and Basic were fixed would software houses be able to write games and other programs which could be used on the Amstrad machine.

The most popular version of Basic is that written by Microsoft, the American company which is one of the world's largest software concerns. But Amstrad would have had to pay a large sum for the right to use Microsoft's Basic, so Sugar had decided that his computer would have its own specially written Basic. 'Save money by designing from scratch' was to become a maxim for Amstrad's early approach to computers. The trouble was that the company's original software designer had made virtually no progress before disappearing to the Lake District.

One design firm in Cambridge gave Perry a dusty reception, irritated by his refusal to say anything about his clients other than that they were 'a big high street company'. But he struck lucky with another contact, Howard Fisher, also ex-Brentwood School and Cambridge. Fisher had recently managed a project for Acorn, the Cambridge-based computer company, which involved developing a Basic for a new Acorn small business package. The work had been done by a two-man design team, Chris Hall and Richard Clayton, who had recently formed a partnership named Locomotive Software. Fisher suggested to Perry that he should get in touch with Clayton, who was part of the old Cambridge gang.

Perry rang Clayton the next day, fixed a meeting and drove down to Dorking, a town in stockbroker-belt Surrey, parking outside Clayton's house. Locomotive Software – then barely six months old – operated out of Clayton's back room. Richard Clayton is the nearest British equivalent to the laid-back software wizards of California. Still sporting the long hair of a 1960s hippie, he talks with infectious enthusiasm whenever the conversation turns to software.

Roland Perry sat on a sofa in Clayton's house in August 1983 and showed the Locomotive duo the keyboard with Amstrad's name taped over. The first thing Clayton did was to fetch a screwdriver and open up the keyboard, spotting in a corner of the circuitry an uncovered Amstrad label. But the discovery added little to his knowledge: 'I didn't actually know who Amstrad were, so it didn't mean anything to me,' he recalls.

The fact that Perry's mystery client had already completed the outside of the machine was a plus point with Locomotive: 'The thing that really impressed me was they'd done the plastics. One of the things I'd learnt was it often took 18 months to get the plastics right. These people had already done the box. It was incredible. They were clearly serious,' Clayton says.

However, it was obvious from Perry's account that the software side of the project had stalled. The electronic circuitry also looked ropey, although neither Hall nor Clayton regarded themselves as hardware experts. Clayton told Perry that Mark-Eric Jones, a hardware expert and another member of the Cambridge gang, lived only ten miles away. 'Why don't I give him a call and see if he can come over?' suggested Clayton.

An engineer who chooses his words carefully, Mark-Eric Jones is universally known by his initials, Mej (rhyming with wedge). Mej's father founded and ran a computer company called Data Recall, which employed many of the ex-Cambridge circle in the 1970s and early 1980s, including Richard Clayton. Data Recall's star product was a word processor, the Diamond, which was well regarded in the days when word processors cost about £10,000 each. It was a background which was later to serve Amstrad well.

Mej had set himself up with a friend as an independent electronics designer, going under the name of MEJ Electronics. When the two electronic engineers came over to Clayton's house in Dorking, they needed only one look at the interior of Perry's machine to start poking fun at it: 'Oh, that's interesting, this power supply isn't linked up to half the chips. That's why it doesn't work,' said Mej.

Perry wanted to press the designers into a decision. Top of the agenda was the issue which had been hanging over the talks all afternoon – time. 'How long would it take you to do an operating system and a Basic for a 6502 processor?' he asked the Locomotive pair.

'About eight months,' Clayton replied. 'I reckon we could deliver it by April.'

The answer alarmed Perry, since Amstrad needed prototypes of the machine by December. The essential problem had become clear during the course of the afternoon. Neither Locomotive nor Mej had had much experience with the particular microprocessor which Amstrad envisaged for its machine. Microprocessors are the brains of a personal computer, the chips which control its core operations. Each one – usually known by a number given to it by its manufacturer – has its own particular architecture for executing instructions. Amstrad had chosen the Motorola 6502 because it was a standard processor in many of the computers with which it was likely to compete. Many games and other programs designed for 6502-based machines were already on the market: a computer company needs to be able to point to such a library of end user programs if it is to sell its machine in any numbers.

Clayton added almost as an afterthought: 'If you did it with the Z80, you could have the software much earlier.'

This was what Perry had been waiting to hear, so Clayton developed the point. Locomotive could complete one half of the software job, the Basic, for a Z80 microprocessor more quickly because it had already done one. The Acorn machine whose Basic Clayton and Hall had just written was based on the Z80, so they would be able to adapt their Acorn work. Moreover, Mej also knew the chip back to front, because Data Recall's word processors had been based on Z80 chips.

As afternoon turned into evening, everyone moved from Clayton's house to a local pub for a drink and a meal. It was in the King's Arms, Dorking, that the final design for Amstrad's first computer was hammered out. They would throw away the existing software and hardware design, transform the computer into a Z80-based machine and knock out an operating system and a Basic by the end of January. At the end of the evening, the Dorking engineers remained in the dark about the client's identity. Perry had talked all day about 'a big high street name'. Clayton went home thinking: 'Dixons? What is Dixons doing building a personal computer?'

Shortly afterwards, Perry solved the problem of how to keep his client's name secret. It was pointless to continue taping over the Amstrad name, because someone was bound to remove the tape. Since he had been telling everyone that his client was 'a very well known British electronics company', he called the machine by the codename Arnold, replacing 'Amstrad' on the prototype keyboards with 'Arnold'. Most people assumed that his client was the General Electric Company, Britain's biggest manufacturer which is headed by Lord (Arnold) Weinstock. Perry did nothing to discourage this speculation; only later did he notice that Arnold is also an anagram of his own first name, Roland. The computer was later to acquire the formal name of CPC464 – C(olour) P(ersonal) C(omputer), coupled with 64 as an indication of its memory size.

Locomotive and Mej had waved goodbye to Perry, more than half expecting never to hear of the project again: 'We didn't really give much chance of him coming back to us, because our proposal was so far away from what Roland had turned up wanting,' Clayton says.

But they had not reckoned on Amstrad's wish for speed. Amstrad was impressed with how quickly the Dorking designers promised to deliver the machine if the microprocessor was changed. A few days later, Locomotive and MEJ Electronics received a call giving them directions to go to the mystery client's headquarters in North London.

Chris Hall represented Locomotive, because he alone of the Locomotive pair possessed a suit. Mej was there too, along with William Poel from Ambit and Bob Watkins from Amstrad. Alan Sugar came in late, having just stepped off a plane at Heathrow airport. No one introduced Sugar to Mej, who spent part of the meeting wondering about the identity of the latecomer. Initially he thought that Bob Watkins must be Amstrad's boss, until he noticed that every time the latest arrival spoke everyone else stopped talking.

Sugar explained his vision of Amstrad's entry into the computer market. He was going to produce a computer, he told the assembled electronics buffs, that had 'perceived value for money'. Although he was proposing to launch what was essentially a games machine, it had to look like the computers people saw in offices and airports. That was one reason why Amstrad was planning a machine with a large keyboard and screen. It also partly explained why Amstrad was proposing to do something almost unknown in low end home computers: to produce a machine with a built-in monitor and a built-in cassette recorder for storing programs.

Sugar had devised this plan not long after he took an interest in the computer market. Having bought some of the machines then on sale to teach himself about the technology, he was amazed how difficult it was to use most home computers. Since they did not come complete with their own monitors or cassette recorders, users had to link up the computer with a television set and tape recorder. This messy process caused no end of aggravation as technically illiterate people struggled to connect the different machines. The sound and picture quality which resulted were often atrocious.

In short, the home computer market was crying out for the clarity which Sugar had brought to the audio industry with his Tower System. As he explains:

> Our first computer was a very typical Amstrad concept. We sat down and observed all this computer stuff. And we saw what people were actually buying with computers. They needed lots of cables and cassette decks, and then they had to plug it into a television. There were lots of rejects coming back because of mismatches on products. I decided that the Amstrad philosophy is an all-in-one piece, so we would present our product as complete with a keyboard, cassette mechanism and monitor.

The one-piece solution would end family feuds over access to the television set caused by the home computer craze. Since most parents were reluctant to surrender the family TV for their children's new toy, many home computers were discarded as useless junk once the novelty had worn off. Sugar saw the need for a home computer that did not rely on the family TV: 'It was obvious that you had to keep the computer far away from the main television in the home. And because of all the wires and other gubbins you had to struggle with, many Sinclair computers were ending up thrown under the bed, never to be used,' Sugar recalls, adding, 'Our computer was too big to be thrown under the bed.'

The size of the computer was also central to Sugar's marketing plans:

> It looked like a mug's eyeful for the old man when he walked into Dixons. He looks at this thing, with its whacking great big keyboard and a monitor, and he has visions of a girl at Gatwick airport where he checks himself in for his holidays. And he

thinks, 'That's a real computer, not this pregnant calculator thing over there called a Sinclair.' So that was my marketing concept: the old man, who has got to fork out a couple of hundred quid on kit because the kid is driving him mad for a computer, sees this thing that actually looks like a real computer.

The one-plug, all-in-one computer allowed Amstrad to repeat the component savings achieved with its Tower System. Duplicated power supplies, transformers and so on were cut out. This was fundamental to Sugar's ability to keep the price of his first computer low. Further cost saving was achieved by the canny choice of components. He used television tubes rather than the more specialist computer visual display unit tubes in the CPC464 because they were cheaper. He also came across a supply of 3″ disks and disk drive mechanisms in Japan, which were being sold cheaply because the 3″ format was in the closing stages of an ultimately losing battle against 3½″ disks. Amstrad's computers were to be the last strong-selling line to use 3″ disks.

At the initial meeting with his new designers, Sugar refused to tell them the price he had in mind for the machine. Indeed, he became quite angry when they asked. The most he would disclose was a general indication of the computers he intended to compete against. He was determined to keep his pricing plans secret, but his reticence also reflected his belief that giving the designers a figure would simply encourage them to make the computer that expensive. 'Do it as cheaply as is humanly possible' – this was the message.

Otherwise, the specification given by Amstrad to the designers was about as minimal as can be imagined. The machine had to have colour, sound and a memory capacity of 64k (64,000 pieces of information) for users, as well as 32k of ROM (read only memory, on which the computer's main operating programs were stored). Sugar had identified 64k memory as essential to his machine's success, since this was the maximum amount of memory available in most other home computers. Matching that was as important to him as making sure that the watts potential of his audio equipment was up with the leaders. He thought that computer-illiterate people would seize on size of memory as the one feature to check when they walked into a shop.

Chris Hall and Mej left this initial meeting with mixed feelings. Unlike his friends, Hall had heard of Amstrad. His brother had once bought an Amstrad cassette recorder and they had decided between them never to buy anything with the Amstrad name on it again. But their unease about working for a company serving the low end of the audio market was outweighed by the excitement of the project. After all, what had they to lose? Neither set of designers was so overwhelmed with work that they could pass over the chance to design a personal computer from scratch, an opportunity given to very few of the world's electronic designers. Mej also came away impressed by the sharpness of Sugar's vision: 'He was the exact opposite of some people who just muddle around. He had this immense clarity in his ideas and in what he was trying to achieve.'

Moreover, the designers were attracted by the sheer absurdity of what was being asked of them. When I.B.M. designed its first personal computer, admittedly a more complex machine, it gave 26 in-house engineers, supported by 100 manufacturing technicians and an array of sub-contractors, a year to complete the project – and this went down as a miracle of speed in the annals of the world's biggest computer company. Amstrad was giving half a dozen engineers barely five months to design its first computer. 'It was sufficiently close to impossible to do in that time scale that it was a very exciting challenge,' Mej remembers.

Both Locomotive Software and MEJ Electronics expected a temporary involvement with Amstrad, because neither was optimistic about Amstrad's computer. 'Acorn's B.B.C. machine was going great guns at the time and it seemed to us that we were unlikely in the time scale available to be able to compete on a techie level either with that machine or with the latest Commodore. And Commodore was known to be working on some further machines, so it was difficult for us to see quite how this was going to sell,' Hall explains.

The designers' pessimism coloured their approach to a follow-up meeting with Amstrad to negotiate their fees. Mej agreed a fixed price for his hardware work, preferring that to a royalty payment because of his scepticism about the number of machines that would sell. Locomotive quickly settled on a similar deal for the computer's operating system, but since it wanted to keep the intellectual property rights to its Basic, Chris Hall initially quoted £30,000 a year for the Basic licence to Bob Watkins. Eager for a substantial immediate payment, Locomotive actually offered Amstrad an even better deal – the use of the Basic for the first two years in return for £45,000 cash down. 'And what about the subsequent years?' Watkins asked.

Hall did not think there would be any subsequent years for the machine, so he settled on a figure of £15,000 a year thereafter. Six years later, at the end of the 1980s, the CPC464 was still selling and Locomotive was still receiving a measly £15,000 each year from Amstrad for use of the Basic. 'How naïve we were. Never mind. It seemed a lot of money at the time,' Hall says, laughing weakly.

During these early stages, Mej pressed on Amstrad a change in design that was to have immense significance for its subsequent computer lines. He suggested that they should use gate arrays. Originally developed by Ferranti, gate arrays allow a large number of discrete components to be packed on to a silicon chip. They also allow a chip to be custom-designed so as to meet a manufacturer's precise specifications for a particular piece of equipment. Back in 1983, gate arrays – also known as uncommitted logic arrays – were a relatively new technology for mass market consumer items; not even the mighty I.B.M. had used them in its first personal computer, although they did feature in Sinclair's home computers.

Mej told Sugar that gate arrays had three advantages. First, by packing many components on to a chip, they would cut the component count and cost of his machine. Second, they would allow more features to be built into the computer for the same price. Third, they would reduce the chances of the Amstrad machine being copied, because once the customized gate array has been made its circuitry is effectively hidden. Sugar was initially reluctant to use this novel technology, because he was worried that the designers would need more time to grapple with it. However, he rapidly grasped the potential of gate arrays. He was particularly impressed by their anti-copying properties, since he had seen enough I.B.M. and Apple clones in the Far East to worry that his machine might be copied. Typically, it took Sugar just one meeting to make up his mind: go for gate arrays. After all, they replicated in miniature the Amstrad philosophy of paring cost by cutting out surplus components.

Roland Perry telexed details of the final specification to Bob Watkins for his approval on 18 August 1983. The ROMs embodying the computer's operating system were due to be sent by air to Orion, Amstrad's Japanese sub-contractor, in the third week in January 1984. But the time scale was in reality even tighter than that, because of the importance of having games ready to use on the computer the very day it was launched. It would take some time for software houses to write games tailor-made for the Amstrad machine, so Sugar decided to ask 50 software companies to supply one game apiece. Each of these software houses would need a prototype machine, which meant despatching 50 prototypes by late November.

Mej and his partner stocked up on frozen pizzas to sustain them late at night as they worked on the circuit designs in Mej's spare bedroom. They used pencil, paper and a drawing board: the computer-aided design techniques which were to become standard among electronic designers by the end of the 1980s were then way beyond their financial reach. Locomotive Software expanded to four people and moved into a tiny office in nearby Leatherhead. When the pace approached breaking point, the designers consoled themselves by joking that they could always disappear to the Lake District.

Amstrad left Locomotive and Mej remarkably free from interference. No one at Amstrad could have contributed much to the technical design of a computer at that stage. Bob Watkins, the person most likely to have become involved, was fully stretched during the second half of 1983 with a production problem on the large-screen television line at Amstrad's Shoeburyness factory.

Communications between Amstrad and its project managers in Ambit were not helped by the different cultures to which the two sets of people belonged – an issue which assumed greater importance after Amstrad's successful launch into computers. Amstrad worked rigid 9 am–5.15 pm hours, partly as a reflection of Sugar's abiding belief that efficient time-management allows any amount of work to be crammed into a standard working day, but also because of the constraints imposed by Amstrad's headquarters in Tottenham. Security was of paramount importance at Tottenham, since the offices fronted a large warehouse stacked high with Amstrad products. Every afternoon at 5.05 pm, the security guard would warn the Amstrad staff that he was locking up in five minutes. Everyone from the chairman downwards had to drop their work and clear out of the building, on pain of being locked in for the night.

By contrast, Ambit worked the more relaxed hours of computer buffs: 10 am–1 pm and 3 pm–8 pm. As a result, Perry recalls: 'We found Amstrad incredibly difficult to do business with. In effect, we only had a short period in the afternoon when we could talk to Amstrad, and they tended to be very nervous in the last ten minutes about being locked in.'

Yet Amstrad steered clear of detailed intervention in the design process, even during later computer projects when Sugar and Watkins had a better grasp of the technology and there were no communications constraints. The company believed that its designers had to be trusted to complete the job and that constant changes to the specification served only to slow down a project. MEJ Electronics had more contact with Amstrad than Locomotive Software during most of the projects, partly because MEJ's hardware designs had greater cost implications than Locomotive's software work. Also, with its background in the audio industry, Amstrad had a stronger instinctive feel for components than for software.

In its first flush of enthusiasm for the computer market and in order to save costs, Amstrad had forward ordered components in huge numbers, typically 100,000 each. Mej thus came under pressure to design in these forward-ordered components, even though they were not best suited for his new design. However, Amstrad minimized this problem by swapping components it had ordered for parts which Mej wanted, and by disposing of unneeded parts in the then buoyant component market.

As project manager, Roland Perry was MEJ's and Locomotive's day-to-day contact with Amstrad as they worked on the CPC464. He was the main communications channel, translating Amstrad's concerns into language the designers could understand and vice versa. An electronics engineer himself, Perry appreciated the virtues of the free hand which Amstrad gave its designers: 'Unlike with other companies, we didn't have people ignorant of what they were talking about deciding it should have a big red knob on the side.'

Perry kept Amstrad happy by organizing staged demonstrations during the design phase. After Amstrad's abortive experience with its previous designers, Bob Watkins felt that Sugar might also need some independent reassurance that the new team knew its job. Guy Kewney, a leading computer journalist, was brought to Amstrad's Tottenham headquarters to test one of the first prototypes, on condition that what he saw remained confidential. Everyone's nerves were soothed when Kewney emerged impressed by the machine.

Locomotive met Sugar only once during the development of the CPC464, towards the end of November after they had produced a functioning prototype. Chris Hall put on his suit again and went to Tottenham one Friday to take Sugar through the prototype. Sugar immediately noticed that the on-screen cursor blob could not be moved when the computer was first switched on; the CPC464 had been programmed so that the cursor would move only once a game had been loaded or some text was in the machine for editing.

'But everybody will think the computer's broken because when you press the cursor key nothing happens,' Sugar protested.

'Moving the cursor key at this point has no meaning. There's nothing for it to do,' Hall countered.

'Well, it makes sense to me,' Sugar replied.

The exchange was typical of the different perspectives of

Amstrad and its designers. Sugar was imagining the reactions of a customer walking into a shop not knowing the first thing about computers. Locomotive was thinking of what was logical from a programming viewpoint. This was one of Sugar's very few interventions in the software design for the CPC464; it made the people at Locomotive shake their heads at the irrationality of non-technical people, but it was also obviously justified.

In early December Roland Perry organized the distribution of prototype machines to the software houses which Amstrad hoped would write games for its computer. A feat of small-scale production was needed to satisfy his demand for fifty prototypes. Drawing on Ambit's contacts in the component industry, Perry arranged the manufacture of fifty circuit boards. He oversaw the production of a board with dozens of chips on it to simulate the gate arrays, which were not ready at that point. Perry collected fifty colour televisions from Amstrad which were used as substitutes for the monitors, and arranged for a local company to make fifty power supplies for the machines.

William Poel visited the software companies, persuading them to sign confidentiality agreements committing them not to disclose Amstrad's name and then trying to enthuse them to write games for this company unknown to the computer industry. Bob Watkins sorted out the commercial side, negotiating the rates Amstrad would pay for the games. He found it an uphill task; many of the bigger games houses, in particular, took the attitude: 'We've got plenty of work for Sinclair and Commodore. Who is Amstrad?'

Roland Perry employed a couple of young women, whom he called his 'angels', to drive the prototypes at high speed to games houses round the country. Alan Sugar took to ringing up Ambit regularly to check the exact location of each machine. If negotiations with a particular software house were heading nowhere, then one of Perry's 'angels' would be despatched at a moment's notice to snatch back the prototype.

Meanwhile, the gate arrays were turning into a nightmare. Amstrad had asked various semiconductor companies to quote for the twin task of helping Mej to design the gate arrays and then manufacturing them. The contract went to Ferranti, because its quote was much lower than that of its rivals, but relations between them rapidly deteriorated thanks to what Mej describes as 'a saga of disasters' at the Ferranti end. Ferranti's design work was riddled with errors. Mej had to fly to the north-west of England so regularly to visit Ferranti's chip centre that the taxi-drivers at Manchester airport began to recognize him. In the end, Amstrad was forced to turn its secret weapon on Ferranti – Alan Sugar, who phoned to tell the electronics company in one-syllable Anglo-Saxon words precisely what Amstrad thought of its performance.

The experience did little for Sugar's already low opinion of British manufacturing. Deciding it would need a second source for the gate arrays, in order to protect itself against Ferranti, Amstrad gave the job to SGS, the Italian chip manufacturer later to merge with Thomson of France. Mej added trips to Milan to his regular round of visits to Manchester.

The prototypes were needed not just for the games houses but also to show Orion, Amstrad's Japanese suppliers for whom it was keen to lay on an extensive briefing. The Japanese company had manufactured many products for Amstrad in the past, but this time Orion was being asked to make something completely outside its – and Amstrad's – experience. Amstrad's Japanese partners had to be assured that the British company knew what it was doing.

Mej, Roland Perry and Bob Watkins boarded a plane for Osaka in December 1983, clutching a prototype computer which they carried to Fukui, a town on Japan's northern coast. Like most of Amstrad's subsequent computers, the CPC464 was destined to be made in an Orion plant in South Korea, but Fukui was the base for Orion's manufacturing headquarters and home to its chief engineers. Watkins busied himself with grinding, day-long negotiations over the price Amstrad would pay Orion to make the machine. Mej, for his part, was engaged in the novel experience of explaining a piece of equipment to Japanese engineers.

Mej had to become accustomed to never dealing with a single Japanese engineer at a time. The Japanese operated in teams because they had an engineer specializing in almost every part in the machine. Baffled by his attempt to discuss the whole machine, at first Mej's Japanese counterparts could not take such a generalist engineer seriously. They began to treat Mej and Roland Perry with more respect only after Mej had suggested an improvement to the monitor – which was very much in Orion's area of expertise. Orion's engineers then immersed themselves in the task of discussing modifications to the computer. But on the occasions when the English pair proposed some addition, the Japanese would say in unison 'Cost-up'. It was their way of indicating that the change would add to the machine's price: 'cost-up' entered the language of the Dorking engineers, along with the ever-present possibility of 'disappearing to the Lake District'.

The Amstrad team returned from Japan with an Orion request to change the screen colouring. The Japanese wanted Amstrad to use yellow letters on a blue background, the strongest possible contrast, because they were worried that the previous colour arrangements were indistinct. Amstrad agreed and Locomotive set about adapting the colour codes. The finishing touches to the design went smoothly thereafter, although the Dorking engineers still had to work round the clock. Locomotive's Chris Hall allowed himself Christmas Day off, when he took home the now nearly completed machine for his mother to play with.

Locomotive met its target of shipping the master codes for the computer's operating program on the third Saturday of January, 1984. First thing on the following Monday morning, Richard Clayton discovered a bug. It was not a major bug – it affected a function that would be used only rarely and Locomotive knew how to fix it by the afternoon – but it was a bug all the same. So Clayton rang Amstrad, explained the problem and said: 'This is a trivial thing, we can change the codes because they can't have reached Orion's factory yet.'

But Amstrad refused to ask Orion to change the master codes. The company was not prepared to alter something which had already been shipped in final form to Japan, and decided instead to remove the faulty function in question from the computer manual. This was just one of many examples down the years of Amstrad's determination never to lose face with its Japanese suppliers: to out-Japanese the Japanese at all times.

Alan Sugar saw his first computer essentially as a games-playing machine for the home. But, unusually for that time, he also wanted it to have one foot in the business market. Part of the plan behind making the CPC464 big enough to look like an office computer was so that users would realize its potential for business functions. The CPC's screen was wide enough to take 80 characters, similar to most computers found in the office and twice that normally available for a home computer.

Initially Amstrad had decided against producing a version of the CPC464 with disk drives which could support business programs, but in March it reversed that decision and told its engineers to start work on a disk drive unit which could be added on to the CPC464. Amstrad then searched around for some business programs to run on the machine. Digital Research, one of the best-known software companies in the United States, was a logical place for Amstrad to look: one of its flagship products, the CP/M operating system, had been working on Z80-based machines since the chip was first introduced. Providing a version of CP/M for the CPC464 would allow business applications like spreadsheets and word processing to be carried out on the new computer. Amstrad quickly came across Paul Bailey, then hard at work developing Digital Research's European sales.

Bailey is a sharp, fast-talking salesman who has spent so long peddling the products of the American software industry throughout Europe that he has come to speak exactly like an American software engineer. After spending the early and mid 1980s building up Digital Research in Europe, in 1988 he moved to Lotus, one of Digital's arch rivals, and proceeded to do the same job for them.

Bailey was more than happy to sell Amstrad the CP/M operating system. Digital Research was then engaged in an ultimately losing battle against the rival MS-DOS operating system produced by Microsoft: MS-DOS had the overwhelming advantage that it had been adopted by I.B.M. for its first personal computer. Bailey was in the forefront of that battle, trying to sell CP/M to European computer manufacturers. Unlike Locomotive Software, Digital Research was as professional as Amstrad in commercial negotiations. Amstrad agreed to pay a set price in advance for a given volume of copies of the Digital software: once the deal was struck, Amstrad was committed to paying Digital Research the money no matter how many of its machines were sold.

Bailey describes his CPC464 deal with Amstrad: 'Sugar basically attracted me by agreeing to very large volumes in advance. The drawback was that he insisted on a very keen price. But in the event, we ended up selling over a million copies of CP/M to Amstrad for the CPC and their later word processors. So it certainly wasn't a low runner.'

Amstrad's first computer, the CPC464, was unveiled in April 1984 – a mere eight months after Bob Watkins had walked into Ambit's offices. By then Amstrad had hired public relations advisers, Michael Joyce Consultants, who were to mastermind its increasingly slick product launches. The great hall of Westminster School, a stone's throw from the Houses of Parliament, was hired for the CPC464's launch. Archimedes, Einstein, Monet and William Shakespeare were just some of the celebrities on hand to usher Amstrad's first computer into the world: improbably, Nick Hewer of Michael Joyce had managed to find people living in Britain who were blessed with these names. Monet showed the fifty or so computer pundits the computer's colour capabilities, Shakespeare talked through its word processing facility and so on.

The CPC464 came in three formats: a green on black screen for £229, colour capability version for £329 and a version with the add-on disk drive for £429. It emerged to a generally good reception in the press, with some journalists dubbing it 'the people's computer'. Jack Schofield, computer editor of the *Guardian*, wrote: 'It out-performs the Commodore 64 (the machine's main rival) in virtually every department', adding that it was extremely cheap, costing £80 less than the equivalent Commodore or Atari machine.

Guy Kewney, the computer journalist who had had an advance sight of the CPC464, praised its all-in-one design as a breakthrough which could finally rid the industry of its 'enthusiast' image. His four-page bench-test of Amstrad's computer for *Personal Computer World* concluded: 'The Amstrad is a powerful, fast machine, with plenty of memory, easy to program, and packaged in a way that means it will comfortably outsell the Acorn Electron, and give the Commodore 64 and Sinclair Spectrum a hard run for their money. I expect some 200,000 systems to be sold by the end of the year.'

Not everyone was so optimistic.

*

When Alan Sugar first became interested in the home computer market back in 1982, it seemed ripe for the Amstrad treatment. Home computers were *the* consumer electronics phenomenon of the early 1980s. Dazzling fortunes were made as a clutch of entrepreneurial companies like Sinclair Research and Acorn began to count their sales in hundreds of thousands of units. Amstrad appeared poised to carry through what it was best at doing: learning from the mistakes of the existing players to produce a value-for-money machine which left the competition standing.

Britain's fascination for personal computers followed in the wake of the boom in the United States, where this precocious industry was born. Dating the birth of an industry is an inexact science, but many people would plump for the day in 1977 when Apple Computer launched the Apple II, the first personal computer which users could put to work without the need for assembling or programming. Apple was the brainchild of two men – Steve Wozniak, a self-taught engineer, and Steve Jobs, hippie turned high tech entrepreneur.

Jobs supplied the vision which launched the personal computer revolution; he wanted to dethrone the Big Brother image of computers that was familiar to anyone who watched a science fiction movie in the 1950s and 1960s. Computers were seen as huge cabinets with whirring reels of tape whose mysteries were guarded by a new priest class – data processing managers. Jobs wanted to empower the people by putting a computer on every desk. 'We build a device that gives people the same power over information that large corporations and the government have had over people,' an early Apple video proclaimed.

This message chimed perfectly with the counter-culture ethos of many computer freaks in Apple's native California. More important, it also coincided with what was becoming technologically possible. Electronics is characterized by an innovation curve to be found in no other industry: its products become cheaper and smaller while at the same time becoming more powerful. This unbeatable mix is underpinned by the speed of development in the technology of silicon chips, the heart of any electronics product. Throughout the 1970s and 1980s, it was commonplace for the power of a particular family of chips to double every two to three years. Apple could put on a desk a machine costing $1,500 in the early 1980s which in many respects was as powerful as a mainframe computer of a decade earlier. Apple seized the possibilities opened up by this rate of innovation to transform itself from a two-man partnership operating out of a garage in 1976 to a multinational corporation with sales of more than $2 billion a decade later.

Britain was the first country after the United States to catch the home computing bug; but British manufacturers initially concentrated on simple machines, less sophisticated than Apple's products and mainly suitable for computer games. This market was supplied in North America by companies like Commodore and Atari. Clive Sinclair sparked the craze in Britain by launching in January 1980 the ZX80: priced at £99.95, it was billed as the world's smallest and cheapest computer. Some 20,000 were sold by September 1980, while a year after its launch the company was shipping about 9,000 a month.

The success of each new Sinclair computer seemed to surpass that of its predecessor. More than 250,000 ZX81s had been sold by December 1981, nine months after its launch. At the start of 1983, Clive Sinclair cashed in on his success by selling 10 per cent of his company, Sinclair Research, in a deal which valued the concern at £136 million. In December 1983, Sinclair proudly announced that a million Spectrums had been sold in the twenty months since its launch.

Home computers were the novelty gift for Christmas 1982, and many high street stores sold out of their stock ten days before the start of the Christmas break. It seemed as though every parent of teenage children was being badgered for this latest wonder product, which was cleverly projected as both fun and an essential educational aide. The home computer fever raged more strongly still in Christmas 1983. Acorn boasted of 200,000 orders, while Sinclair Research said it could have sold 50 per cent more than the 300,000 machines it shipped. 'I don't remember a product which has developed so rapidly in such a short time. . . . It was beyond the bounds of all expectations,' gushed Peter Jackson, marketing director of Rumbelows, as he surveyed the Christmas season.

One might suppose that Sugar's decision to enter such a buoyant market would have been applauded, but that was not how his initiative was viewed by many people. Customers like Comet, Amstrad followers in the City and commentators in the press – all queried Sugar's judgement in attacking an extremely competitive market which appeared to be dominated by a clutch of nimble companies. Before the CPC464 was launched, Comet's Nick Lightowler and Sugar talked over Amstrad's plans on the phone: 'It was a bloody great worry for me at the time,' Lightowler recalls.

The City registered its nervousness by responding badly to a rights issue by Amstrad in May 1984, a month after the launch of the CPC464. A rights issue is a means of raising fresh capital for a company by giving existing shareholders the right to buy new shares. If, as often happens, many existing shareholders forgo their rights, then the new shares can be sold on the open market. Amstrad wanted to raise £12.9 million by issuing one new share for every six in existence to finance the development costs of the CPC464 and an extension to the Shoeburyness factory. Sugar passed up his entitlement to buy his slice of the new shares, which resulted in his stake in Amstrad falling from 58.9 to 50.5 per cent. Even though the new shares were offered at 85p each, 17p less than the closing price on the day when the issue was announced, only 83.3 per cent of them were bought – a snub from the City for Amstrad.

In the event, the City was right to be nervous about the immediate prospects of Amstrad's foray into computers – but for the wrong reasons. Amstrad's first taste of the computer business was characterized not by strong competitors but by a collapsing market. In the opening months of 1984 few people realized that Christmas 1983 had been the high watermark of the home computer craze in Britain. True, a cloud had appeared on the horizon in the summer of 1983 when an abrupt end to the personal computer boom in the United States triggered a round of price-cutting there, but the computer industry in Britain ignored this warning signal. The change of mood became apparent in Britain shortly after Amstrad launched its computer.

A few auguries of the problems to come emerged in the run-up to Christmas 1984. The summer had seen the disappearance of two smaller computer companies, Dragon and Torch, the latter taken over by Acorn. In October, Acorn cut its prices and began to issue advertisements attacking Sinclair – a turn of events which led to a well-publicized exchange of blows in a Cambridge pub during a pre-Christmas drinks session between Sir Clive Sinclair and Chris Curry, Acorn's managing director. 'We party a lot in Cambridge,' a Cambridge high tech entrepreneur wryly confessed to the *Wall Street Journal*, while Amstrad reacted with a tongue-in-cheek announcement of a new computer game called 'This Business Is War'. The game featured a bespectacled Sinclair-character throwing computers at a Curry-figure. 'We're indebted to Sir Clive and Mr Curry for offering this wonderful chance to extend our software range,' Amstrad told the *Daily Mail*.

Christmas 1984 turned into a disaster. Retailers had tried to avoid the problems of the two previous Christmases (when demand heavily outstripped the supply of computers) by placing large orders with all the main manufacturers. Most of the 200,000 Amstrad CPC464s sold in 1984 were snapped up during the Christmas run-up. In the event, demand was weak amid much talk about the home computer market in Britain having reached saturation point. Manufacturers churned out 1.7 million home computers during 1984, but the public bought just 1.35 million. Retailers were left with substantial stocks after Christmas, which meant that orders in the opening months of 1985 dried up.

It soon became plain that the British home computer industry was heading for a shake-out. 'There are too many manufacturers with too many machines chasing too small a market, and they are probably not the products people want,' warned John Rowland, computer buyer at W. H. Smith, in February 1985. Some manufacturers agreed: 'The popular games-playing market has become a very uncomfortable place to be. Price competition will be horrific. It is not a market we want to be in for very long,' said Acorn's Chris Curry.

The bad news piled up as 1985 unfolded and personal computer companies faced the financial headache of having to nurse huge stocks. Prism, a large Sinclair distributor, went into receivership, followed by Oric, a second-string home computer manufacturer; Acorn's shares were suspended while the company worked on a reorganization plan; Sinclair Research postponed long-standing plans for a flotation. These setbacks all struck the industry in the first two weeks of February. Within the next three months, Acorn was rescued by Olivetti, the Italian office products group, while Clive Sinclair began his long search for a capital injection which was to culminate in Amstrad's intervention in 1986.

Computer companies had been the darling of the City during the home computer boom and their fall from grace was sudden and violent. Amstrad suffered by association with the troubles of its competitors and its share price – in the doldrums since the badly received rights issue – was dragged down by the computer industry débâcle to a low of 64p. Alan Sugar tried to reassure the stock market: 'Some companies may have had great ideas during the boom, but lacked the business expertise to manage properly when it faded. We don't have any stocks at this time of year. In the summer, we'll be getting brown in our deck-chairs, not counting up all the computers in our warehouse,' he told the *Financial Times* in June 1985.

The stock market's confidence in Amstrad began to recover only after August 1985, when Sugar unveiled his first word processor and the share price moved back above 85p. Faith was finally restored in October, when he announced results for the 1984–85 financial year ending in June 1985. Profits jumped by 121 per cent to £20.2 million, on a 60 per cent increase in turnover to £136.1

million. These figures were enough to convince the most hardened sceptic that Amstrad had indeed avoided the bloodbath among its competitors: the company's shares were marked up 16p to 134p on the day of the announcement.

Most remarkable of all was the transformation within the Amstrad business which these global figures concealed. In 1983–84 audio, colour televisions and video recorders accounted for 96 per cent of Amstrad's sales; the following year, these lines represented only a third of the company's turnover. In 1983–84, exports made up 13 per cent of sales; the following year, they accounted for 53 per cent of turnover. A new Amstrad had been created by its launch in 1984 – not just into computers but also into some key Continental markets.

Two points had escaped the pundits who bracketed Amstrad with the Sinclairs and Acorns of the world. First, the greatest pain was felt by home computer companies at the bottom end of the market. The buying public had become bored with computers which were no more than games machines. As British consumers became more sophisticated about computers, so they began to demand machines which offered business applications like accounting and word processing. By giving the CPC464 one foot in the business market, Amstrad was ideally placed to benefit from this flight to quality. Sugar welcomed the greater clarity in the home computing market, as he made clear towards the end of 1985: 'We've come to the end of an era. By March all these cheap flog-off lines will have gone. They can't be made any more at those prices and I will be glad to see the garbage and junk out of the market.'

The second factor buoying up Amstrad was its growing overseas success. Sugar had been building up foreign sales of the CPC464, particularly in France, Spain and West Germany. The Amstrad chairman had made no secret of this, emphasizing to the *Financial Times* in February 1985 that the company was exporting many computers: 'The only country we are concerned about is the U.K. because the doom and gloom is making the dealers nervous. Computers are not like CB radio, a market which stopped as if someone had turned off a light switch.'

But the British computer industry and its camp-followers were insular. At that time, few of the industry's leaders like ICL, Acorn or Apricot had significant overseas sales. In consequence, few people were able to judge Sugar's claims of overseas conquests. The truth emerged only later: while the British market was in the doldrums in 1985, Sugar had been selling thousands of his computers on the Continent. This left him in a unique position later in the year to resist the demands from British retailers for price cuts.

Alan Sugar gives a vivid account of this period:

The usual array of predators, such as Dixons, W. H. Smith and Boots, were hovering around like the praying mantis, saying, 'Ha, ha, you've got too many computers, haven't you? We're going to jump on you and steal them off you and rape you when you need money badly, just like Uncle Clive.' And we said, 'We haven't got any.' They didn't believe us, until such time as they had purged their stocks and finished raping Clive Sinclair and Acorn, and realized they had nothing left to sell. So they turned to us again in November of 1985 and said, 'What about a few of your computers at cheaper prices?' We stuck the proverbial two fingers in the air, and that's how we got price stability back into the market. They thought we were sitting on stockpiles and they were doing us a big favour. But we had no inventory. It had gone to France and Spain.

· 8 ·

Birth Pangs in Europe

'Alan, I have to tell you something. I am waiting for a baby. And I must tell you the truth, it will be a very difficult job for me to get this baby.'

This was not the best news that Alan Sugar had ever received. Amstrad's first and only employee on the Continent had telephoned him from Paris to say in her best English that she was pregnant. As though that were not bad enough from his viewpoint, the new 32-year-old managing director of Amstrad France would have to spend about three months in hospital because her doctors were predicting a difficult birth.

Marion Vannier still remembers vividly the call she had to make to Sugar back in 1982. A thin, elegant woman with short red hair and quick movements, she darts round her office answering phones while telling her story. Even now she breathes hard, pausing between each word, as she recalls summoning up the nerve to give Sugar the news. 'You cannot imagine how I felt. I could not tell him. I couldn't. Each time I thought about telling him, I was crying. It was impossible to tell him.'

Only a few months had passed since Sugar had phoned her with the proposal: 'Marion, how would you like to form a French company for me?'

The offer could not have been better timed because Vannier's employer was folding up. She had spent the past ten years working for Cogel, a concern which distributed electrical goods in France.

She had made the most of that decade, joining as a junior assistant and rising to become commercial director after three years. But in 1980 her bosses sold out to a foreign company; the relationship never gelled and early in 1982 the new owners announced that they were liquidating their recently acquired French operation.

So there was no reason for Vannier to hesitate when she heard Sugar's proposition. After all, she had been selling Amstrad's audio equipment in France since the early 1970s; she knew Sugar well and understood the French market. Exports had been important to Amstrad throughout the 1970s. Overseas sales had accounted for between 10 and 25 per cent of turnover since 1973, after Vannier's company started pushing Amstrad's equipment in France.

Yet Sugar had had to expend virtually no effort on his French exports, only visiting the country perhaps once a year to exhibit at the main French audio fair. He was able to leave the hassle and expense of distributing Amstrad's equipment in France to Cogel, a pattern he was to repeat in his early forays into Spain, West Germany and the U.S. That he broke this pattern as early as 1982 in France by setting up his own subsidiary is easily explained. He had come to trust Vannier's business judgement and did not want to lose her. But clearly she lacked the capital to set up as an agent on her own, so he decided to establish his own subsidiary with Vannier as its boss.

The Amstrad business had been relatively small beer throughout the 1970s for Vannier, representing just one of the many lines which her company distributed. She had needed to visit Britain only twice a year to look at Sugar's latest goods and to check out the trade fairs to see what other manufacturers were producing. Indeed, it was at one such fair in 1972 that she had first met Sugar, hawking an early line of Amstrad amplifiers. An agreement to be Amstrad's exclusive agent in France followed shortly afterwards.

Wanting a breathing space from the traumas of helping to wind down Cogel, Vannier did not expect radical changes in her life when she accepted Sugar's proposal to set up an Amstrad subsidiary in France in March 1982. In June she launched Amstrad's

French operation from a one-person office above a boulangerie on the main road through Sèvres, a little town on the outskirts of Paris. The first headquarters of Amstrad France boasted a telephone, a telex and not much else. Alan Sugar had given her a cheque for 50,000 francs (about £4,500) and a free hand, expecting her to get on with it. By then, however, she was well and truly pregnant.

Over the next year, Marion Vannier would have to draw on all the reserves of strength she had built up since her first marriage collapsed in 1971. She had enjoyed a comfortable upbringing in Charentes, a deeply traditional part of south-west France dotted with small towns and the châteaux of cognac producers. Her father was a director of a brandy company; her mother, it goes almost without saying, did not work and Marion was educated in a convent to expect a similar existence. True, there were signs of spirit in the young girl as she grew up: she had a habit of choosing the most headstrong horses to ride through the lush Charentes countryside and she was good enough at gymnastics to compete in the French championships. But everything seemed to be going according to pattern when she became an 18-year-old bride in 1968. She had every reason to anticipate a lifetime of playing tennis and bridge and bringing up her children – a way of life shared by hundreds of thousands of other French middle-class women.

In fact, she had traded the straitjacket of rural French life for a set of equally claustrophobic, almost feudal obligations by marrying the heir to a cognac fortune and moving into his château. She had to attend mass regularly, gloved and with a silk scarf covering her hair. 'I had a beautiful garden, I rode and I played tennis, yet I could not fill my days,' she remembers.

Three years later, aged 21, she cut through her increasing boredom by taking a train to Paris. 'I left my bags with a friend of my father. Forty-eight hours later, I found a job as a switchboard operator in a bank near the Champs-Elysées. I earned 850 francs a month and paid 400 francs for my room. But I was free.'

Vannier was having to earn her living with no obvious qualifications for doing so. After a string of short-lived jobs, she answered an advert from the electrical distributor, Cogel, with whom she was to spend the next ten years. It said that the company was looking for an assistant who spoke English. She had all but forgotten the smatterings of English learnt at school, but she went along in any case.

As she entered Cogel's premises, she was greeted by a man who started speaking to her in English, and she laughs now as she describes her struggle to reply. 'Then he mentioned the VAT problem. How do you calculate the VAT on top of . . . ooh?' she rolls her eyes as she recalls the impossibility of the question.

Vannier's reply was simple and to the point: 'Really, the truth is I don't know about your VAT thing, but if you explain it to me, then in three minutes' time: no problem.' And so it proved. She quickly made herself indispensable. After three years she replaced the commercial director, who had been traumatized by her greed for work.

But in 1982 Vannier was well aware that the combination of giving birth to her third child and to Amstrad France would dwarf the challenges she had faced in the 1970s. She had spent three months in hospital delivering her second child and her doctors warned her to expect a repeat performance. A simple calculation revealed that she would be flat on her back from October, during the build-up to the Christmas season – the most important part of the year for selling Amstrad equipment.

Vannier decided that the only answer was to move her office into the hospital, have a telex installed by her bed and give all her main customers her telephone number there. She conducted Amstrad's business from her hospital bed night and day. To help her she employed as a secretary a man who had worked at her previous company. One of his main jobs was to prepare cheques for her to sign, but he had another role which transcended the normal bounds of a secretary's relationship with a boss, since he happened to share blood groups with Vannier who needed a regular supply of blood. 'This man was coming to the hospital to make me sign the cheques and to give me blood,' she says. It is a moot point as to which vital fluid, cash or blood, was more important to her at the time.

Her doctors had been correct in predicting a difficult delivery and Vannier sketches a large cross over her midriff when she describes the incisions needed to perform the Caesarian birth. It wiped her out. 'I was completely dead when I had the child. When Alan called me in the hospital a couple of days later to talk about business, I could not speak,' she recalls.

But Vannier was back in her proper office in January 1983, where a large picture of her youngest daughter, Djinn, now hangs behind her desk. 'This is my Amstrad kid,' she says, pointing at the picture and smiling.

*

While Marion Vannier was struggling with her new business from a hospital bed in Paris, José Luis Dominguez in Madrid was faced with a problem which, from a commercial point of view at least, was even more fundamental: which business to go into. The wisdom or otherwise of his decision would not only determine whether or not Dominguez would make his fortune. It would also decide whether he was ever to honour a vow made to his dead father.

Like Vannier, Dominguez came from a business background; his father's firm supplied aluminium to construction companies. Also like Vannier, he had to make his own way in the world. For as the youngest of five brothers, he knew from an early age that he could not expect a senior place in the family firm; and to remove any lingering doubt, the family business crashed when Dominguez was 17.

That prompted him to leave school and find work. He had been studying economics and business, more because his father thought it would help him to get a job than out of any natural conviction. But when he left without finishing his studies, the only job he could find was as a door-to-door salesman, touring the big housing estates on the outskirts of Madrid and selling anything that came to hand – encyclopaedias, insurance, English courses.

Unlike Vannier, the young man was not naturally self-confident and had to force himself to knock on the doors. Dominguez is squat and bearded, an Alan Sugar lookalike, but in his case the powerful physique is softened by a diffident half-smile playing permanently on his face. 'This work on the estates was very difficult for me, because I was a shy man,' he recalls.

Dominguez' father urged him to drop this work in favour of something more secure and respectable, like a job in a bank, but he was driven by the suspicion that his father believed him to be incapable of making it on his own. The young Spaniard became obsessed by the need to prove himself. 'I was trying to demonstrate to my father that I could be successful by making money,' he explains.

Slowly Dominguez saved up the commission he earned by door-to-door selling to the point where he reckoned he had enough to impress his father with his diligence. But the day before Dominguez was planning to produce all his hard-won cash for his father to admire, he heard that he had been killed in a car accident. 'On that very day, I swore to myself that I would make a successful business for my father.'

Dominguez had to wait ten years before he was able to carry out that promise, however. In his early twenties he drifted into the insurance business, rising in five years to become commercial director in Spain for Nationale-Nederlanden, the big Dutch insurance group. He was given the job of opening offices all over Spain for his Dutch bosses, which was invaluable experience for his later efforts in setting up a Spanish distribution network for Amstrad. But it was also plain to him that he could not expect to go much further with the Dutch group.

In 1981, by then in his early thirties, Dominguez returned to his earlier dream of striking out on his own and set up a trading company which he named Indescomp. But as he recalls: 'I was wondering what kind of business to get into. I was looking for a business of the future, but this was very difficult for me. Then one day, I read in a magazine about personal computers and their success in America and England.'

Dominguez devoured the latest news about the companies leading the personal computer revolution – Apple and Atari in the United States, Sinclair and Acorn in Britain. Personal computers were then almost unknown in Spain, but it was immediately obvious to him that this state of affairs would change.

Despite speaking only minimal English, Dominguez travelled to a computer show in Britain, at that time by far the most developed personal computer market in Europe. Sinclair's machines, cheap and simple, struck him as ideal for the Spanish market. He went to Cambridge to try to arrange a deal with Sinclair, only to be told that the latter had already signed a distribution agreement for Spain.

Recovering from that disappointment, his eye lit next on Acorn, which was notching up big sales with its B.B.C. micro. He met the person who handled Acorn's international business in London, and quickly won the exclusive franchise to sell the company's machines in Spain.

But Dominguez' first foray into the personal computer business turned into a disaster. He found it impossible to shift the 2,000 Acorns which he had bought, partly because he had no money left for adequate promotion of the machines but also because Spain was not quite ready for the mass introduction of personal computers.

Dominguez changed tack. Let others endure the hassle and risk of launching the personal computer revolution in Spain; he would follow at a safer distance, one step behind. In future, he would supply the gamut of peripheral equipment that the Spanish users of the machines would need – software, manuals and add-ons.

For a year or so, that meant concentrating on the Sinclair market. Sinclair's personal computers took off like wildfire, helping to establish the notion of a personal computer with the Spanish public. Dominguez was a pioneer in persuading big department stores to stock all the bits and pieces needed by Sinclair users. He had his triumphs with writing software too, including one game, Bugaboo, which topped the charts in both Spain and Britain.

Indescomp grew step by step, but still Dominguez hankered after introducing another personal computer to Spain. That was where the big money was to be made and he reckoned he could displace the market leaders, Sinclair and Commodore. He had built up an effective distribution network and he understood the Spanish personal computer market as well as anyone in the business.

In 1983 Dominguez embarked on his travels once more. He went to Hong Kong, to Japan and to the United States in search of his ideal machine, but none that he saw filled him with total confidence and he returned to Spain empty-handed.

Then one day early in 1984 Dominguez read in a computer magazine that a British company, Amstrad, was planning to introduce a computer with a built-in monitor and cassette, and with just one cable. Immediately he was struck by the elegance of this solution to the problems faced by the average Spanish family in connecting up a Sinclair machine. 'In that moment I thought, that is a very good idea. The man who thought that must be an intelligent man. I thought I'd like to meet him.'

This was easier thought than done, however. Dominguez phoned Amstrad's headquarters in London and was put through to Bob Watkins, the technical director. When he explained his ambition to launch Amstrad's new computer on the Spanish market, Watkins was less than encouraging. Amstrad had no spare resources to service sales in Spain; it was fully stretched trying to meet demand in Britain and France. 'We are not interested in the Spanish market,' Watkins concluded. 'Thank you very much and goodbye.'

The only glimmer of hope held out by Watkins was the faint possibility that Amstrad might be ready for Spain in two to three years. In the ever-evolving world of personal computers, that was like promising to do something in a generation's time and was no use to Dominguez.

But the Spaniard kept reading advance news about the launch of Amstrad's first computer and he kept ringing through his interest to Watkins, who continued to fob him off . . . until one day Dominguez happened to mention that Indescomp had had a number one software game, not just in Spain but in Britain too.

Watkins's tone changed. He explained that Amstrad wanted as many good games as possible for its new machine. He was prepared to see Dominguez in London, but only on condition that they talked solely about software and not about distributing the new computer in Spain.

Dominguez was not the first person whose heart sank on first glimpsing Amstrad's headquarters in Garman Road, Tottenham. He had been expecting a large building, replete with the elegant executive suites he was later to favour for Amstrad Spain. In fact, he found cramped offices piled high with boxes, partly in preparation for Amstrad's move to a new base in Brentwood. 'It created a bad image,' Dominguez remembers. But he soon learned that the image of their building was the last thing on earth likely to bother the people at Amstrad.

Watkins told him that Amstrad needed a game from Indescomp in a month flat. When Dominguez asked whether he could take a prototype of the new Amstrad computer (the CPC464) to Madrid to work on, Watkins was reluctant but eventually agreed on the understanding that Dominguez returned in a month with a game. So the Spaniard gingerly carried the prototype back to Madrid.

Dominguez put his employees to work on the software round the clock for a month; instead of writing just one game for the CPC464, they came up with two including a version of Bugaboo tailored to the Amstrad. At the end of the month he phoned Bob Watkins to give him the good news. Watkins told him to send the games to England by courier. 'I then took the most important decision in my professional life,' Dominguez recalls. 'I said to Bob, "No, I want to bring them to you myself."'

When Dominguez reached Amstrad twenty-four hours later, he had one simple request: 'I would like Alan Sugar to come and see the demonstration of my games.'

Watkins hesitated for a second before picking up the phone and urging Sugar to take a look at Dominguez' handiwork. When Sugar bustled in, shirt-sleeves rolled up and not in the best of humour, his manner betrayed his feelings to a fault: 'Who is this man wasting my time?' it said.

This less than fulsome welcome from a man Dominguez had been trying to see for three months reinforced his nervousness. To his horror, his games did not work when they were first loaded into the computer. Sugar stood there scratching his beard.

Eventually, however, the demonstration went smoothly and Sugar seemed impressed. 'O.K. we'll fix up a royalty deal with you.'

Dominguez then made another bold move in his battle for Amstrad acceptance: 'I don't want to sell the games to you. You can have them as a present.'

Nothing in Sugar's business experience had prepared him for presents and his surprise shone through. 'I wanted Amstrad to see that it is possible to do good work in Spain. I know you're not interested in Spain at the moment, but I wanted to make the point,' Dominguez explained.

Sugar immediately softened his attitude and started asking Dominguez about his ideas for launching the Amstrad computer on the Spanish market. Negotiations started there and then over Dominguez becoming Amstrad's agent in Spain.

*

Marion Vannier was building a respectable business for Amstrad in France. She had been able to sell about 20,000 Tower Systems – then Amstrad's flagship audio product – in 1982–83. But it was very much a small-scale enterprise: Amstrad France still employed only two people, Vannier and her secretary.

Sometime late in 1983, Sugar had explained to Vannier about his plans for moving into the computer market. She put this to the back of her mind, assuming that she would handle the business just as she was responsible for Amstrad's audio lines.

One day early in 1984, however, she took a call from Sugar: 'Marion, I have to speak frankly. You are not well enough established to handle this micro business. It's much more complicated than our audio stuff. You will have to translate all the manuals; you will have to have technical people. You are not ready for it.'

Vannier felt confident enough to handle anything. But she did not argue. 'Alan is a difficult man to argue with,' she says.

Sugar was back on the phone a few days later. 'I've been contacted by a French guy who is handling Oric (another computer manufacturer) in France. He's ready to be our agent; he's got forty people already. It's really a better idea for you to handle the audio business and for him to handle the micro business.'

Vannier did not take to this proposal at all and decided to fight back. But all she said to Sugar on the phone was that she would come over to Amstrad headquarters with the Oric man to talk things over. In the late spring of 1984, Vannier and her new rival duly flew to London.

Sugar told his prospective French agent that he would not get any of the new machines until the end of December, because Amstrad was fully booked with British orders. This did not please the Oric man, who insisted he needed some machines for the Christmas season. After much haggling, Sugar gave him 4,000 CPC464s for October and November.

Back in her office in Sèvres, Vannier phoned Sugar: 'Why do you want to give him an exclusive deal? Give me the chance to have the same number of units as him. You gave him 4,000, so give me 4,000 as well. You'll soon see who is the best.'

Sugar saw the sense in this. After all, Vannier was an Amstrad employee – why not see what she could do? When he phoned the Oric man with an alternative proposal for him to handle the CPC464 in France on a non-exclusive basis, the man objected strongly. But Sugar had become convinced that Vannier should handle at least part of the business. However, neither Vannier nor her rival from Oric would give way and in the end the Oric man disappeared from the Amstrad scene.

Sugar decided to give Vannier 8,000 machines – her own quota plus that of her erstwhile rival. In June he phoned her with the news. 'I'm sorry, Marion. It's really only a token quantity, but that's all I can spare.'

Vannier was secretly pleased she was not being allocated any more machines. Her baby was still small and she was looking forward to a summer holiday without worry, so she resolved to sell her batch before going away. In any case, 8,000 personal computers seemed enough to her; she knew nothing about them – not even what a micro-computer looked like – until her consignment of CPC464s arrived from Britain.

Vannier took a sample of the new machines around to show her best customers, the seventeen big department stores who bought the bulk of her audio equipment. But she was in for a shock. None of them had yet moved into the personal computer market. They all ordered a token quantity, five at most, more to maintain good relations with her than because they really wanted these novel machines. 'Seventeen multiplied by five. You can imagine how I felt. It was a horrible disaster,' Vannier says.

So she did not spend a worry-free vacation after all. She had quickly realized that for the CPC464 she would need to employ a completely different form of distribution from that which she had perfected for Amstrad's audio equipment. Most of the personal computers sold in France at that time were channelled through small specialist retailers but Vannier – still virtually a one-woman band – could not conceivably trek round these myriad outlets herself.

Once back from holiday, she advertised the CPC464 in the French computer press, listing her seventeen main outlets as places where the machines could be bought. But, worried that the seventeen were concentrated in Paris, she also used the advert to urge the public to ask any computer retailer for the machine – a bold stroke considering that no computer retailer in France then stocked the CPC464.

The French public followed the British in liking the CPC464. Taking her cue from the way in which the machine had been promoted in Britain, she advertised it in France as 'The Anti-Crisis Home Computer', stressing the convenience of not having to unplug the computer so that the rest of the family could watch television. Free from the need to charge a distributor's mark-up – typically around 30 per cent – the Amstrad machine sold in France for the same price as in Britain.

Computer shops all over France received orders for the CPC464. Never having heard of Amstrad, the retailers offered customers Sinclair, Oric, Commodore, virtually anything else instead. But the customers stuck to their guns and orders flowed into Sèvres from small shops all over France. Amstrad U.K. even managed to find its French subsidiary a few thousand extra machines to help satisfy Vannier's pre-Christmas rush.

The Frenchwoman did not know whether to laugh or cry. She had been used to handling seventeen large customers, each of whom would take a van-load of goods. Now suddenly she had to handle hundreds of new customers, most of whom ordered in batches of half a dozen. And Amstrad France still consisted of three people: Vannier, her secretary and a new technical specialist. 'I had no reps, nobody on the road,' she says.

Marion Vannier remembers the next year as the worst in her life. Day after day, she struggled with the flood of orders with the minimum of office back-up. Night after night, she rushed home, cooked her children dinner and then returned to the office when they were tucked up in bed. Her second husband, an insurance executive, confesses: 'We decided to spend our dinners together, for otherwise we would no longer have seen each other.'

By March 1985 Amstrad France had sold 30,000 computers – the majority during the months after Christmas, traditionally a quiet time for home computers like the CPC464. The company grew fast, expanding to twenty-five employees by June 1985. But even this recruitment was at first just another headache for Vannier who was having to do everything: hire new people, find larger offices and supervise the sale and distribution of Amstrad's machines. She was running so fast that she had no time to stop and admire the extraordinary explosion of sales over which she was presiding.

In the year to June 1984, Amstrad's sales in France totalled 35 million francs (about £3 million). In the following year, thanks to the CPC464, they rang in at 291 million francs (about £24.3 million) – an eightfold increase in twelve months.

*

José Luis Dominguez learned the hard way that Alan Sugar strikes a tough deal. The Spaniard had to agree to two conditions before he was appointed Amstrad's agent in his home territory.

Sugar was so taken with the games given him by Dominguez that he told the Spaniard, 'I'll give you exclusive distribution of Amstrad in Spain, but in return you must give me ten games.'

That was condition number one, and it turned out to be the

easy part of the bargain. Dominguez agreed, but remembers with a smile that those ten games took two years to deliver. Every month Sugar would phone up with the same question: 'What's happened to the new game?'

Condition number two was the difficult part. Sugar refused to give Dominguez any credit; the Spaniard had to pay in advance for all the machines he took, which meant opening a letter of credit four months before he saw the machines, allowing for delivery from Hong Kong.

Dominguez wanted to take about 500 CPC464s initially. But the value of his house at the time was enough to guarantee only about a quarter of the money he needed to finance the purchase, so he trawled all the banks in Madrid for credit to bridge the gap. In the end he put together a credit package from twelve different banks, but not before he started receiving nervous phone calls from Sugar demanding to know what had happened to the letter of credit.

The machines arrived in time for Christmas 1984 and Dominguez placed some adverts in the computer press, promoting the CPC464 as the next step up from the Sinclair and the Commodore. He would have liked to have gone further but, as he explains, 'I had no money to launch a big advertising campaign.'

Even so, the adverts were a success and Dominguez could meet only about a third of the demand that Christmas. Sugar's attitude to the Spanish market began to change. The following summer he invited Dominguez to dine with him while he was holidaying at Los Monteros in Marbella. Over the meal, the pair discussed prospects for the 1985 Christmas season in Spain.

'The credit arrangements are a big limitation on growth in Spain,' Dominguez told Sugar. 'I would like to take 50,000 machines for this Christmas, but I can pay for only 2,000 with my own money.'

Sugar took some convincing, still not sure that Spain had that much potential. But in the end he agreed to alter the credit arrangements and gave Dominguez 90 days to pay for any purchases.

In the early autumn of 1985 Dominguez duly took delivery of

his 50,000 machines, a mixture of the CPC464, CPC6128 and the new PCW8256 word processor. By Christmas they had all been sold. Amstrad's Spanish sales jumped from £4.4 million in the financial year 1984–85 to £32.3 million in 1985–86. Amstrad had arrived in Spain in sensational style.

*

Amstrad was in on the beginning of the first wave of mass personal computing in France and Spain, just as it had been in Britain. On the back of the huge following for the CPC464, the company rapidly became the market leader in volume sales of home personal computers in both countries. The CPC464 sold well in West Germany too, notching up sales of £32.5 million in 1984–85; but it was largely thanks to the efforts of Marion Vannier and José Luis Dominguez that Amstrad's overseas sales soared from just over £10 million in 1983–84 to £72.8 million in 1984–85 and £174.9 million in 1985–86 – a stunning achievement.

France and Spain were by no means identical markets when Amstrad launched the CPC464. In Spain, where personal computing barely existed, the price of the machines was a predominant consideration. By contrast, France had a thriving hobbyist sector populated by techno-freaks who were happy to expend money and time on procuring computer, cassette, plug, screen and add-ons and putting them together.

What both France and Spain lacked was a mass personal computing market in which hundreds of thousands of individuals with no interest in the interior of the machines could buy a personal computer from their local department store, take it home and make it work with the same minimum of fuss they expended on a new television or hi-fi. Amstrad was at the forefront in creating that market in both countries.

Marion Vannier and José Luis Dominguez had contrasting styles in their day-to-day conduct of business – a difference which helps to explain why, in 1989, it was Dominguez who parted company with Amstrad. After Amstrad France took off, Vannier moved into a rigorously functional office block overlooking the single room from which she launched Amstrad France. Sèvres, her base, is a bustling little town whose half-completed office blocks and busy streets are a testament to the prosperity it is drawing from Paris – a workaday setting for Amstrad France, much like that of Amstrad's U.K. headquarters in Brentwood.

When Vannier comes out of her nondescript office to greet her visitors, it is not immediately obvious whether this young woman is the boss or a secretary. Her clothes are elegant but simple – a plain blouse and short skirt. There is no hint of power dressing to impress visitors, either with the wealth she has amassed thanks to her success at Amstrad or with her position as one of the best-known businesswomen in France.

By contrast no one could mistake Dominguez' standing in society, not least because he is followed wherever he goes by a car full of young men in dark glasses with padded suits. In Spain these armed bodyguards are essential to shield the wealthy and famous from kidnapping or terrorist attack. Yet there is a hint in Dominguez' manner that he regards this need for permanent protection as final proof of his rise into the ranks of Spain's super-rich.

Under Dominguez, Amstrad Spain's headquarters were in a fashionable quarter of northern Madrid, not far from the royal palace. There was no chance of mistaking anyone but Dominguez for the boss as he sat in this building in the summer of 1989, shortly before he was effectively forced out of Amstrad. He had a connecting suite of rooms made up of exhibition room, meeting room and a sitting room with a fine view towards the centre of Madrid. Dominguez sat at the far end of this suite in splendid isolation behind a large desk. The Spaniard, aware that this extravagance ran against the Amstrad corporate culture, joked that his offices were more lavish than the company's headquarters in Britain.

Dominguez' success in building up Amstrad Spain made him a star of the Spanish business scene. He was frequently profiled as a leading representative of the more aggressive entrepreneurial spirit which has pervaded the Spanish economy in the 1980s. His views on marketing, a key obsession of modern Spanish business, were particularly canvassed.

Vannier too has been fêted as one of the very few successful female entrepreneurs in France. Named as French businesswoman of the year in 1988, her rise from 21-year-old divorcée with no qualifications to business tycoon has regularly been depicted as a triumph of mythical proportions. With its penchant for English phrases when writing about business, the French press describes Vannier as 'un success story' and 'une star du business'. Portrayed as the symbol of a new wave of female managers in France, she is consulted on any issue linking business and women. In the space of a few weeks in 1989, for example, she turned down not only a request by one of France's biggest advertising agencies to star in a high profile promotional campaign for *Le Monde* newspaper, but also an invitation from Simone Veil's centre party to run as a candidate in the European elections.

Both Vannier and Dominguez were naturally pleased with the fame that success brought them in their native countries. Their work for Amstrad also made them wealthy in the late 1980s. Vannier's fortune came from generous share options, while Dominguez sold his distribution company, Indescomp, to Amstrad when Sugar decided to create subsidiaries in all Amstrad's main spheres of operation. But Vannier gave the impression to visitors of wearing this fame more lightly. There was no suggestion of false modesty in her explanation for her high media profile: 'Journalists here are badly in need of a successful businesswoman.'

Yet these very different personalities gave a common account of the reasons for Amstrad's initial success in the mid-1980s in both countries: total attention to marketing and sales was at the heart of their stories. Both were decisive in persuading the large chains and department stores – groups like Euromarche and Darty in France and Corte Inglés in Spain – to start selling personal computers, partly displacing the specialist outlets in the process.

'I am not a technical person. The technical side is too difficult for me,' explained Dominguez, adding proudly, 'I am a salesman.' His selling instincts helped to make the name Amstrad almost synonymous with low end personal computers in Spain.

Vannier had to delegate responsibility for many of the tasks she was used to doing herself as Amstrad France grew to 125 people by 1989. But marketing and publicity were the two aspects of the

Amstrad business she retained, spending up to 5 per cent of her turnover on advertising. 'To talk straight to the final consumer. That is 90 per cent of my sales effort,' she says.

The marketing approach favoured by both Vannier and Dominguez during the mid-1980s was basically the same as that honed in Britain by Alan Sugar. Vannier was able to translate advertising slogans like 'compatible avec qui-vous-savez' (compatible with you-know-who) – used to sell Amstrad's first I.B.M.-compatible personal computer, the PC1512 – straight from English into French. Her description of Amstrad France could have been taken from the mouth of Alan Sugar: 'We transform elitist products into mass products. We seed new markets.'

The Amstrad emphasis on simple-to-use products, powerfully promoted and priced at a level which most consumers could afford, is a business concept which has travelled well across European boundaries. As Alan Sugar surveyed the take-off of Amstrad sales in France and Spain in the mid-1980s, he was able to reflect that a philosophy forged in the tough world of the low end British audio market was as effective in Paris and Madrid as in London. The question facing Amstrad as it entered the second half of the 1980s was this: would the company be able to build on its international success in France and Spain to forge a genuinely multinational operation?

· 9 ·

The Amstrad Effect

Alan Sugar felt restless as the plane cruised high above Japan en route for Hong Kong. It was July 1984 and only three months since Amstrad had launched its first computer, the CPC464, yet the glimmer of an idea for a new line of computers had been gnawing away at him while he toured his suppliers on one of his regular Far East trips.

He turned to Bob Watkins, sitting next to him. 'Have you got any paper?' he asked. Amstrad's technical director shook his head. 'Well, what's that you're looking at? Give it to me for a second,' said Sugar.

Watkins handed his boss the document he had been reading, a contract between Amstrad and Digital Research. Sugar took out a pen, turned over the paper and sketched away busily for a couple of minutes. 'What do you think of that?' he asked, showing Watkins his handiwork.

Sugar had drawn a computer which took the all-in-one philosophy of the Tower System and the CPC464 to its logical conclusion. He envisaged one box containing monitor, disk drive and printer. The monitor was shaped like an A4 piece of paper, the disk drive was underneath the monitor, while the printer was moulded into the machine on top of the monitor. It was this latter feature – building the printer into the computer itself – that was startlingly novel.

The Amstrad chairman explained his idea to Watkins. A printer normally has its own power supply and its own plug for connection to a computer. Well, why not make the printer part of the computer? That way, it could be driven directly from the computer, which would cut out the need for a power supply in the printer, remove worries about connections between printer and computer (the 'interface', in computer jargon) and deliver a one-plug machine for users.

Watkins grasped the potential for cost-cutting, but what would the machine do? The two of them spent the rest of the journey kicking around two main options. The first was to make the machine a dedicated word processor. That was why Sugar had drawn a screen turned on its side in an A4 shape: it would make the screen as much like a sheet of paper as possible. The second option was to present the machine as an exceptionally compact and cost-effective computer.

The debate flowed back and forth between the two men. Marketing the machine as a computer had advantages. A computer sounded multi-purpose, while a machine sold as a word processor might seem to have limited use. Yet the more they talked, the more they swung towards the notion of a dedicated word processor. If Amstrad could make the machine cheaply enough – to retail at about £400 – it could attack the huge typewriter market. The spread of word processors in Britain's offices had been slow, largely because in the recent past they had cost as much as £10,000. At that price, only the most well-heeled corporations could afford to replace electric typewriters with word processors.

The Amstrad duo also foresaw marketing advantages in presenting the machine as a word processor. Many people were still nervous of buying a 'computer': they were unsure whether they would be able to understand it and what they would use it for. No such techno-fear would be aroused by a word processor – a souped-up typewriter. Indeed, many existing owners of personal computers used them for little more than word processing.

By the end of the five-hour flight, Sugar and Watkins had agreed not only the basic design of their new machine but also how it would be projected. Amstrad was set to build Europe's first low-cost word processor. Not one to hang about, on 20 July 1984 Sugar faxed MEJ Electronics, the small team which had designed Amstrad's first computer, from the company's Hong Kong head-quarters. The fax outlined Sugar's plans for the word processor and attached a sketch of the machine.

'Sorry about spelling, Regards, Alan' was the parting message scrawled in Sugar's hand across the bottom of the fax, which was headed 'Confidential: Re New Projects for 1985.' More pertinent than his spelling was Sugar's ability to set down on one side of a piece of paper the essential features of his plans for the word processor.

Sugar kicked off the fax by telling his designers: 'We are planning to make a promotional priced word processor . . . based on the Amstrad philosophy of all in one unit.' He explained how the price would be kept low:

We have arranged with Orion that will make FDD drive (floppy disk drive) in 1985 and we will not buy from Matsushita. The effect of this will mean we can buy a drive about half the price orig quoted by Hitachi. On the basis of making a major breakthru in price this will open a whole new world for us for the mass market. Orion also have big contacts with printer mechanism makers and they will find us a very cheap method of printer mech. With the facility of cheap FDD and printer mech we can go forward with these new projects to mass market appeal.

Sugar then listed seven points which he wanted his designers to consider, adding that he was doing so 'in my very non-technical way' – a self-denigrating form of wording which at that time was a Sugar catchphrase:

A) We dont need any sound or colour.

B) Consolidate electronics for interfacing printer with com-putor. This means maybe in our existing CPC464 there is some additional electronics needed to make it centronics (one of the most common types of interface between a computer and a printer) and in the centronics printer there is some electronics also. If we can delete this additional electronics we can save money.

C) It is obvious that only one power supply is needed for monitor fdd computor and printer.

D) Although the drawing shows the unit with 2 fdd we only plan 1. The reason is that the actual word processor programme will be in ROM (read only memory) on the main pcb (printed circuit board) and as the unit is only a word processor there will be no need for machine operating ROM like we have in the CPC.

E) On the basis of this unit being a complete intergrated unit you must disregard all industry standards of interface ie centronics etc. This is very important to clear your mind of all these things. It is obvious that as this unit is a complete item there is nothing more to plug on to it.

F) Consider custom ics (integrated circuits) and ula (uncommitted logic arrays or gate arrays) where ever possible.

G) Crt (cathode-ray tube, which illuminates the screen – shorthand for the screen itself). As you can see from our drawing the crt is shown vertically. This is an obvious good idea if the item is to be used as a wp as this configuration is most like a sheet of paper. However as you know we use a TV grade tube with green phosphor. As 80 coloum mode is needed we must consider what kind of tube we need. We cant go for a full high res(olution) tube as they are too expensive. But we can ask maker to make half-way compromise to keep price down.

The Amstrad chairman asked his designers to start thinking about the word processor so that they could discuss it as soon as he returned from the Far East. Or as he put it in the fax: 'I sent you this message so that you can ball park around in your mind what we will discuss on 15 Aug.'

In the event, the precise design which Sugar had sketched on the plane was dropped and the A4 screen was buried in favour of a more conventional shape. It was discovered that moulding the printer into the top of the monitor would have caused the machine to overheat. Some of the assumptions underlying Sugar's fax were also disproved in the longer term: for instance, supplying add-ons to run on the Amstrad word processors has kept a host of little software companies in gainful employment.

Yet Amstrad's word processor remained true to the core vision which excited Sugar high above the East China Sea – that it was possible to run the monitor and printer off a common set of electronics. Mej and Locomotive Software were ideally placed to flesh out this core vision, not only because of their role in the CPC464 but also because they had had plenty of experience of designing word processors (albeit more high cost machines) in their previous work for Data Recall. But it needed Sugar's clarity to prompt these engineers to design a word processor cheap enough to be within the financial reach of almost every small business or self-employed professional in Britain. It was this clarity which shone through his Hong Kong fax, soon dubbed by the Dorking engineers 'the tablets of stone'.

*

Planning the word processor was one of several ways in which Amstrad was drawn more deeply into the computer business during 1984. Back in February, before the launch of the CPC464, Alan Sugar created a new Amstrad division, Amsoft, whose job was to smooth the company's entry into the brave new world of computers. For some time Amsoft lived in an uneasy symbiosis with its parent company, reflecting the adjustment Amstrad needed to make as it became enmeshed in computer culture.

From the start of the CPC464 project, the differences between the computer and audio industries had been impressed on Sugar by Roland Perry and William Poel, the two Ambit employees who acted as project managers for Amstrad's first computer. Companies like Sinclair Research and Acorn had been successful initially because an infrastructure of services had grown up to support users of their machines. Since there would be nothing similar for the CPC464 at first, Amstrad would need to create this infrastructure itself. This meant writing games software and instruction manuals, dealing with the computer press, starting a users' club and publishing an Amstrad users' magazine.

Sugar could see the sense in this, but he also realized how foreign it was to Amstrad's traditions. Amstrad had prospered by shifting boxes to the truck-driver-and-his-wife and then forgetting about them. It seemed poised to enter an era of shipping computers to the journalist-and-his-or-her-partner and then being nice to them.

Hesitating about embracing this cultural shift, Sugar's first thought was to set up the Ambit people in an independent company with an arm's-length relationship to Amstrad. He envisaged the computer boffins working from a rural retreat somewhere off the M11 motorway in Silicon Fen. But he soon realized that this would mean surrendering too much control over their operations and decided instead to make Amsoft a division of Amstrad. Perry, Poel and a handful of other Ambit people left Ambit to form Amsoft in February 1984.

Amsoft wanted to be separate from the rest of Amstrad, a geographical distance which spoke volumes about the cultural gap between the two groups of workers. The Amsoft people refused to move into Amstrad's Tottenham headquarters in the wastelands of North London and Sugar did not try to persuade them. Looking back, Roland Perry believes that Amstrad was half expecting Amsoft to fail: 'They wanted us to be separate from Amstrad, because they were not convinced it was going to be a success. If the whole thing collapsed in a great pile of anarchy and destruction like most computer companies seemed to, they wanted to be able to say, "Oh, that's a load of long-haired weirdos called Amsoft. It's not really anything to do with us."'

Perry and Poel rented an office from Ambit while they looked for a permanent home. Eventually they discovered a nondescript nine-storey office block 100 yards from Brentwood railway station, which was incongruously tacked on to a pub called the Railway Tavern. Its owners, the credit organization run by the Ford motor company, had been trying to lease or sell the building. This had proved an uphill task since the interior looked as though it had survived a nuclear attack and birds flew nonchalantly in and out of the upended filing cabinets and other debris. But Perry and Poel agreed to take the one habitable floor and told Amstrad about their new home.

Sugar pricked up his ears, any lingering desire to keep his distance from Amsoft outweighed by the fact that Amstrad had once more outgrown its premises. He told Amsoft that he would look over this office block in Brentwood, a town in Essex on the north-east fringes of London. One of Amsoft's staff compares what happened next with a scene from *The Godfather*. A line of cars drew up with Alan Sugar in the lead vehicle. He and Amstrad's directors emerged from the cars, all wearing long overcoats; they followed Sugar into the building in single file, up the stairs, round two or three floors and out into the pub next door. Sugar sat in the pub, parcelling out the rooms to the directors; then he returned to Amsoft's offices, picked up the phone and called Ford. After a short discussion, he said, 'I don't care about your bloody lawyers. I want the keys and I want them *now*. If you don't have the keys round by four o'clock this afternoon, the deal's off.' The keys arrived.

Amstrad sold its Tottenham site, moved the warehousing to its Shoeburyness plant and its offices into the Brentwood building, which remained the company's headquarters into the 1990s. Amstrad and Amsoft were after all to be closeted together, but Amstrad insisted on Amsoft having its own floor, receptionist, switchboard and phone number. Amstrad would be responsible for making, marketing and distributing the computers, as well as dealing with retail customers; but it would have nothing to do with individual computer users. Only Amsoft's phone number would be published, because it was Amsoft's job to field calls from end users.

The Amsoft people busied themselves with user support activities. They wrote a leaflet to accompany each computer with a cheery photograph of Alan Sugar welcoming users to the Amstrad family. 'Now you have bought the computer, why don't you join the club?' the leaflet gushed, introducing the company's latest customers to the Amstrad Users' Club. In the early days, William Poel even took computer journalists out to lunch. Spending time and money on the trade press was an activity as far removed from the traditional Amstrad culture as could be imagined: 'Trying to get lunch receipts paid back from the Amstrad exchequer was regarded as almost the most daring thing that anybody in the company had ever tried to do,' recalls Poel, who cannot remember if he succeeded.

Most of Amsoft's activities never took firm root within Amstrad. It soon stopped publishing games software, an activity in which it never distinguished itself. It sold off the users' club and the users' magazine, thus distancing itself from end users. The day came when Alan Sugar decided that Amsoft's workers ought to have Amstrad extensions on their desks. He had tired of having to resort to an outside British Telecom line in order to talk to a group of employees two floors below him. Eventually, the separate Amsoft switchboard was disbanded.

When Poel quit Amstrad late in 1985 to run his own software business, he left with mixed feelings. He believes that Amstrad's chairman understood Amsoft's strategy, but that Sugar was himself too embedded in the Amstrad culture to admit it. Poel explains:

Mr S didn't like to admit to the Amstrad neanderthals around him that he understood what we were trying to do, because it was not quantifiable in pounds, shillings and pence. It was almost like an ethereal concept, the like of which Amstrad had never been party to, which said you can't pin a value on what these people are doing, but it's quite important to the success of the computer. Taking Jack Schofield (computer editor of the *Guardian*) to lunch was something which was alien to the culture, but I think Mr S understood it. . . . He was astute enough to understand these changes. Those around him took a lot longer to assimilate the importance of what was going on.

Amstrad once more gave its undivided attention to what it knew best – ensuring that it was impossible to walk into a store owned by Dixons, Rumbelows and a clutch of other high street chains without tripping over dozens of low-cost Amstrad computers. Shorn of most of Amsoft's activities, Roland Perry reverted to his original brief; he acted as project manager for the development of new Amstrad computers, the day-to-day link between Amstrad and its external design consultants.

Besides its word processor, in late 1984 and early 1985 Amstrad was also working on two new computers within the CPC family. The first, launched as the CPC664 in April 1985, incorporated into the basic design the disk drive unit which came as an optional add-on for the CPC464. In view of its subsequent history, it is unfortunate that inside Amstrad the 664 was codenamed the Idiot (Includes Disk Instead of Tape). The idea was logical enough, but the project was bungled for two reasons. First, the opportunity to provide the 664 with additional memory was missed: 64k of memory was not enough to run serious business programs, the idea behind building in the disk drive. Second, and more importantly, the market for the 664 was destroyed by the announcement in August 1985 of a new and clearly superior CPC computer, the 6128. Codenamed the Big Idiot within Amstrad, the 6128 had 128k of memory, twice that of the 664. It was also cheaper and more elegantly designed.

Customers who had bought the 664 – Amstrad claimed later to have sold 70,000 of the short-lived machine – and dealers stuck with 664 stocks were naturally aggrieved at having been sold a turkey. In retrospect, Amstrad offers a range of reasons for its odd decision to rush out the 6128 just four months after the 664.

Amstrad was under pressure from its agent in the United States to bring out a computer with 128k of memory as soon as possible. A machine with only 64k of memory would not be taken seriously as a computer capable of running business applications in the more sophisticated American market. In the event, the CPC6128 did not sell particularly well in North America, although it became a flagship Amstrad product in Britain and the rest of Europe. The price of memory chips was falling sharply at the time, so Amstrad was able to launch an inexpensive 128k machine more rapidly than it expected. Also, some people within the company were affronted by the cumbersome, inelegant look of the 664, as technical director Bob Watkins recalls:

I just really didn't like it, so I decided I would get our artist to do a rendering of something much smaller. Before the 664 was actually launched, I was designing this other machine on the side. I had a sample of it made up and kept it lying around, so that Alan would understand the error of his ways in being so enthusiastic about the 664. I was careful to make the new machine look a mug's eyeful, nicer and more compact than the 664.

The 6128 was well received. A two-page test in *Personal Computer World* described a micro with 128k of memory, built-in disk drive, the latest version of CP/M and priced from £299 as 'outstanding value for money. . . . As a serious home/small business machine it's great.' The consumer magazine *Which?* named the 6128 its 'best buy' in a feature on home computers as late as November 1987.

But the 664 episode cast a long shadow over the 6128, winning Amstrad few friends. Amstrad would have to wait until after the launch of its new word processor to see its standing in both the business and computer worlds transformed.

*

Chris Hall of Locomotive Software and Mej were summoned to the meeting foreshadowed in the 'tablets of stone' fax at Brentwood in August 1984 to agree the final design plans for the word processor. The machine was codenamed Joyce, after Alan Sugar's secretary of the time. William Poel was later to remark that this was only fitting, since Amstrad's word processor was designed to make Joyce and her kind redundant by inducing executives to type their own memos. The company's first word processor was later to acquire the more formal title of PCW8256 – P(ersonal) C(omputer) W(ordprocessor) with 256k of memory.

Amstrad added little to Sugar's 'tablets of stone' fax other than to say that, like the CPC series, Joyce would use the Z80 processor and 3″ disks. Other options were too expensive: for instance, Amstrad could buy the Z80 for £1 each, whereas the main alternative – a microprocessor from American chip manufacturer Intel – would have cost £10 each at the time. Since the machine would have CP/M as an operating system, it would also be able to run standard business software: but the marketing plan was to push it as a word processor and not a computer.

Designers often wring their hands in frustration at the start of a major project, while their client agonizes over the precise specification. The roles were reversed in the case of Joyce, as Mej explains: 'At the first meeting, Amstrad was actually pressurizing us because we couldn't produce a quotation fast enough. They wanted us to tell them there and then how much it would cost and how long it would take, so that they could give us a contract on the spot to carry out the project.'

The meeting was typically Amstrad – short, sharp and to the point. Looking back, Mej singles out the speed with which Amstrad launched new projects as crucial to the success of the word processor and other products of the mid-1980s: 'One of the things about these projects was how quickly Amstrad made the decision to do them. You would expect any other client who came up with an idea like the word processor still to be talking about it a year later.'

Alan Sugar's commitment to speedy decision-making had been impressed on Mej by an incident earlier in the year. Amstrad's boss refused to commit important documents to the post because of the delays this entailed and badgered Mej to install a fax machine, then a relatively rare adornment of British offices. Mej prevaricated, until one day a van arrived at his office with a fax machine – courtesy of Amstrad. Sugar told him that the fax machine was a loan and he might want it back. Six years later, Sugar had still to reclaim his loan.

On the software side, Chris Hall returned to his partner, Richard Clayton in Dorking, with the barest of specifications. Joyce was to be aimed at the typewriter market and have a 10-page manual. Locomotive Software's main job was to write the word processing program for the Amstrad machine. Bob Watkins had irritated Hall at the Brentwood meeting by emphasizing that Locomotive need not come up with something as good as Wordstar – an ageing word processing program regarded by Locomotive as difficult to use.

Shortly after the meeting, Locomotive Software decided to

clarify its client's unusually short specification. Chris Hall drew up a list of features which could appear in a word processor, classifying them under three headings: basic, useful and advanced. As he had anticipated, Amstrad phoned to say they wanted all of the basic and useful features, but none of the advanced. Amstrad barely interfered with Locomotive's work during the rest of the design phase, asserting its client's prerogatives only on minor details like how the end of a page of text appeared on the screen. The company's interventions were invariably prompted by its anticipation of how customers in a store would react to a particular feature.

Locomotive itself prompted the only major change to Joyce's specification made during the design phase. The original plan was for the word processor to have 128k of memory, but the Locomotive team became convinced that it would be a much better machine if the memory could be doubled to 256k. Chris Hall buttonholed Alan Sugar at an event which the two were attending and explained the case for increasing Joyce's memory. It took Sugar two minutes to agree: the declining price of memory chips reduced the cost implications of the change. 'It was the best two minutes I spent on the project,' Hall says.

In the event Locomotive's word processing program, which it called Locoscript, was welcomed as easy to use by most reviews in the computer press after the launch of the PCW8256. However, the software company repeated the mistake it had made with the CPC464 by not pressing for a royalty payment on the sale of each copy of its software. Instead, it agreed a fixed price of £75,000 for writing Locoscript.

The price envisaged for Joyce was the aspect of Sugar's plans which most astonished Locomotive Software and MEJ Electronics. Joyce was to be a professional business computer, in the sense that it had enough memory to run dedicated word processing and other business programs, yet it would retail at under £400. The contrast with the word processor which the same individuals had helped to design for Data Recall was striking, as Locomotive's Richard Clayton notes: 'It was potentially the same sort of machine we'd been building four or five years before, but it was going to cost £399 rather than £10,000. That was absolutely stunning.'

The low cost was achieved in two main ways. First, by integrating the electronic controls in the way outlined by Sugar in the 'tablets of stone'. People who opened up a Joyce were astounded by how few chips were embedded in its unusually small printed circuit board. The main board contained just 17 chips, including eight 256k memory chips and a large gate array – the densely packed chip which was specially designed to carry out the precise functions of the word processor and which saved money by doing away with the need for dozens of discrete components. Crucially, Joyce's printer ran on the same set of controls as the central computer. Mej describes the design: 'We managed to get almost all the electronics to be inside the gate array, which makes it so much cheaper. We integrated all the controls of the printer into the main board.'

The concentration of functions within the gate array was helped by the freedom which Amstrad allowed its designers. Mej elaborates: 'The great thing about the 8256 was that we didn't have to be compatible with anything. That gave us an immense amount of freedom. It's quite unusual to have that sort of brief from your client: forget about the existing standards.'

Amstrad's technique of ordering parts in very large quantities was the second major way of driving down the cost. Mej was told to think in terms of an initial order for 100,000 Joyces, a volume which he regarded at the time as being too optimistic. He canvassed guide prices from the various parts manufacturers. Alan Sugar and Bob Watkins would then close the deal and Mej was constantly surprised at the amount the Amstrad pair shaved off the guide prices.

Mej explains one of the ways in which Amstrad cut prices to the bone by placing large orders:

In very large volumes, you begin to start talking prices that reflect the real cost of a part. Take gate arrays as an example. Gate arrays often reflect the latest technology, so if you buy in small quantities then the manufacturers try to recover the development costs of that technology in their prices. Amstrad was able to persuade many suppliers to get back their development costs from other people. Amstrad said it was going to give them a very large order and in return it wanted a cost which reflected the materials, not the development cost. The point was Amstrad could place its huge order elsewhere and the manufacturer would still have to recover its development costs.

The instruction manual proved to be the one major feature which was botched during the development work; after the PCW8256's launch, it attracted many user complaints. Alan Sugar blames boffin culture for the manual's faults:

I kept hearing these rumours of people not being able to understand the instruction book. So one day I said, 'Give me the book and I'll have a look at it myself.' Then I realized that it had been written by a bunch of engineers. I looked at it and I thought to myself, 'There's no bloody way a mug like myself would know how to use this.' It assumed that people knew about high density disks and formatting disks and all that cobblers. We had made certain assumptions which we should never do. We had assumed that the engineers knew our philosophy by now. We told them to write the book. And of course they all sat down when the book was finished, the intellects together, and appreciated the excellence of the book. They all thought they were going to get the Nobel prize. From an engineering point of view, the book was fantastic. It had cross references for every single detail of the Z80 processor. But that doesn't tell somebody how to write a quick letter about selling a lawn-mower.

Locomotive Software, which wrote the manual, admits to one basic mistake in the instruction book: 'You have to read it from one end to the other to understand it. Of course, everybody who'd been working on the project had read it from one end to the other. But it was impossible to dip into,' acknowledges Richard Clayton. But Locomotive had also operated within a formidable set of constraints which flowed from Amstrad's cost-cutting ethos. The PCW8256's instruction book was printed in South Korea, because publishing costs were cheaper there. Unfortunately, it takes longer to produce a book than to duplicate the software for the word processor, which meant that the proofs for the instruction book had to be approved before the master codes for the software, in order to have the books and the disks ready at the same time in Korea for shipment to Britain. As a result, parts of the book were written before the feature to which they referred had been finalized. Roland Perry, the PCW's project manager, recalls the problem:

> When the part of the book which described unpacking the computer had to be finished, we hadn't even designed the foam. We didn't know what the packaging was going to look like. Similarly, the software design was in such ferment right to the end that we didn't know which things were going to be included. For example, decimal tabs [a way of lining up figures automatically along a decimal point]: we didn't know whether they were going to be got working in the three days we had left before sending off the master disks.

Amstrad learned the lesson for later products. In future, work continued on the manuals until the boats from the Far East carrying the first batch of computers were a week away from Britain. A local printer would then rush out about 5,000 manuals, which would be placed into the cardboard boxes containing the computers at Amstrad's Shoeburyness facility. The same would occur with disks. Once the initial batch of products had been distributed, the masters of the books and the disks would be despatched to Korea ready for large volume production a month or two after the launch. This procedure involved the company in some extra cost, but it bought invaluable extra development time.

Amstrad initially wanted the design work wrapped up by May 1985, but it was not finally completed until July – a reasonable degree of slippage for such a project. One factor behind the delay was that Locomotive and Mej had been commissioned to design not one but two new computers. Sugar had outlined the second machine on page 2 of the 'tablets of stone' fax, where he described it as 'a full colour computor'.

In one sense, the colour computer was to be an upgrade of the CPC464, because CPC software would run on it: hence its codename of Ant (Arnold Number Two). But it was also intended to be compatible with Joyce. Indeed, Ant could almost be described as the colour version of Joyce. The two were to be launched at the same time and users would decide whether they preferred Ant's jolly colour or the printer which only came with Joyce. The design work on Ant was fairly advanced when the project was suddenly cancelled, Amstrad having concluded that its designers were too stretched to complete both projects in time for the autumn 1985 season. It was also becoming increasingly clear that Joyce was the machine with the potential to turn the computing market upside down.

*

The success of the word processor was perhaps the clearest example in the 1980s of the 'Amstrad effect' – the creation of a whole new market by supporting an innovative, keenly priced product with intelligent well-targeted marketing. The PCW8256 was unveiled with what was becoming typical Amstrad fanfare in August 1985 in a conference centre near the City. Three actresses represented three different types of secretary: a frightfully snooty one would not dream of using anything less than a £10,000 word processor; a tarty secretary swore that a typewriter was good enough for her; while the cool, efficient secretary, of course, preferred the Amstrad word processor.

Alan Sugar was on form at the launch, predicting that his new product 'will blow the lid off the personal computer and word-processing market'. He foresaw wide demand for his machine: 'We have brought computing and word-processing within the reach of every small business, one-man band, home-worker and two-finger typist in the country – not to mention the company chairman who wants one for himself, his secretary and all his managers.'

Amstrad's chairman did not pass up the opportunity to take a swipe at the opposition. Claiming that his word processor was 'four times cheaper than the nearest thing we know', he added, 'The PCW8256 costs less than the average electric typewriter and yet it has features that will make the big transatlantic names wince.'

A few techno-purists sniffed at the machine's 'obsolete' technology – its Z80 processor, 3″ disks, television tube and so on. Sugar reserves a special contempt for techno-snobbery:

> The pundits thought we were bloody mad again. We were using the Z80 processor. When we showed it to the pundits, they all laughed. They looked at us as the poor relation who needed to go to the mental asylum. We had some very funny comments from the snobs in the market about the Z80: 'Doesn't Mr Sugar know there is such a thing as an 8086 or even a 286 processor available for such applications?' What they'd missed is that the people who bought them didn't give a shit whether there was an elastic band or an 8086 or a 286 driving the thing. They wouldn't know what you were talking about. It was bringing computing to people who never even thought they would use a computer.

Most commentators were in fact ecstatic about the PCW8256. It was difficult to be otherwise with a machine which provided 256k of memory, a printer, disk drive and monitor, word-processing software, together with a package of business software – all for £399 plus VAT. Computer journalist Guy Kewney said that the Amstrad machine would spare him much trouble at parties. In the past, he had been obliged to embark on a long disquisition when asked to recommend the best word processor, but in future he would be able to say 'the Amstrad' and then go and have a drink. 'Truly amazing for a computer in this price range,' concluded *Which Computer?* 'Nothing else comes close,' agreed *Popular Computing*. 'Spectacular value for money,' chipped in *Personal Computer World*. One of the most perceptive comments in the specialist press was made by *Electrical Retailer and Trader*, the trade magazine which described the 8256 as 'a grown-up computer that does something people want, packaged and sold in a way that they can easily understand, at a price they'll accept.'

At the word processor's launch in August 1985, Alan Sugar said that 40,000 machines a month would be pouring out of South Korea by October. These arrangements would secure an ample supply of the new computers. He had also been busy ensuring that the machines were greeted with a groundswell of demand when they reached British shores.

Mass advertising through the popular newspapers and television had been central to Amstrad's marketing strategy ever since it had helped make the Tower System so successful. Spending large amounts on advertising generated the volumes which were essential to Amstrad's low price strategy. But the company realized that the nature of its advertising would have to change as it pushed deeper into computers.

Amstrad's computers were not aimed primarily at the truck driver and his wife or the C2, DE market generally – but at the small business person, the professional, the individual who worked from home. A different sales pitch was needed for this AB group of consumers from that evolved by Amstrad for its audio products. Malcolm Miller, Amstrad's marketing director, was instrumental in piloting this change in strategy through the company. 'I felt – and Alan didn't always agree – that with our computers, we needed an advert that talked to business people, not just to the average bloke in the street.'

Amstrad's advertising had been notable for its lack of frills; it told consumers what products were on sale, how much they cost and where they could be bought . . . period. Sugar felt comfortable with this style of advertising, which chimed with his instinctive dislike of anything pretentious or opaque. But Miller argued that Amstrad's new target customers needed a subtler approach; ABs would be bored by the company's traditionally deadpan commercials, so these would have to become more sophisticated, even witty. Not only was quality advertising the way to sell computers, it would also help to bury the cheap and cheerful street-trader image still clinging to Amstrad. In short, it would do wonders for Amstrad's corporate profile.

Eventually persuaded of the sense of this argument, Sugar agreed that Amstrad should find a new advertising agency to promote its computers, leaving audio and other products in the hands of its previous agency, Rupert Lovell Curtis. In late 1984, three agencies were invited to pitch for Amstrad's computer business, including Delaney Fletcher Delaney, a fledgling group which had recently been formed by some high flyers breaking away from larger agencies.

Malcolm Miller briefed Greg Delaney before the presentation, advising him to cut out the detailed analysis of target markets which advertisers typically make when they pitch for business. This flannel would bore Alan Sugar, since no one knew more about the consumer electronics market than the Amstrad chairman. Instead, Delaney should come straight to the point by talking Sugar through sample advertising scripts for Amstrad's computers.

Delaney took Miller's advice, presenting three scripts comfortably within an hour. After he had finished, Sugar tore apart the first script; admitted that the second one was reasonable, but then explained its inadequacies; and said the third was a bit more like it. End of meeting. Delaney was not to know at the time, but this was high praise from the Amstrad chairman, who rarely descends to ad language to describe the efforts of those who work for him. Few things are brilliant, amazing or even good. They are, at best, O.K. This is one of Sugar's ways of keeping people on their toes.

Delaney Fletcher Delaney won Amstrad's computer account, beginning their work with the CPC series. 'Who says business and pleasure don't mix?' was the agency's way of conveying that the CPC6128 straddled the games and business markets. But the first big splash the agency made for Amstrad was over the PCW8256.

Taking its cue from Amstrad's attack on the typewriter market, Greg Delaney shot an ad with dramatic scenes of a truck dumping a pile of typewriters into a scrapyard full of similar dead machines. After describing the PCW8256, the commercial rounded off with the slogan: 'It's more than a word processor for less than a typewriter.' The advert was typical of the aggressive material which Delaney Fletcher Delaney was to prepare regularly for

Amstrad, but the agency had to steer it through two very different groups of people before it could be shown on air.

The first hurdle was the Independent Television Companies Association (I.T.C.A.) which vets all television commercials before they are broadcast. I.T.C.A. at first rejected the advert out of hand, as Delaney recalls: 'They said that you're claiming it's cheaper than a typewriter, when it's not. There are typewriters which are cheaper. You're also showing typewriters being thrown away, and you're not allowed to rubbish the competition – "ash can advertising", as it's called in the business.'

Delaney had to write the advert around these problems. He inserted the word 'most' into the slogan, which eventually read: 'It's more than a word processor for less than most typewriters.' The agency ensured that all the typewriters pictured in the scrapyard commercial were obviously old machines. It then argued that the commercial was designed to persuade white-collar workers to move on to a word processor when they were replacing clapped-out typewriters, and that it did not rubbish manufacturers of new typewriters. This was enough to appease the I.T.C.A.

Amstrad was the second group of people who needed convincing. Sugar wanted to cut down on the moody scrapyard shots in favour of more solid information about the word processor. The film production company working on the commercial was astonished one day when he walked in and asked to see the rushes. Although it is standard practice for the chairman of a company selling consumer goods to take a close interest in the final shape of adverts, no one at the production company or at Delaney Fletcher Delaney had ever heard of a chairman sorting through raw film footage. Sugar wanted to know precisely what film had been taken, so that when it came to editing he would be in full control of decisions about which shots might be added or deleted.

Amstrad's roll-out of a computer product tends to describe a standard trajectory: launch at a computer fair, followed by advertising in the trade and national press, followed three to four months later by a big splurge on television. Invariably spending large amounts on television advertising, the company was the first or second largest spender in its category in 1986, 1987 and 1988, according to the survey of Britain's top 100 advertisers published annually by *Campaign*, advertising's trade magazine. Yet Amstrad does not spray money at a product in random fashion. It closely dovetails the size and timing of its television advertising both with consumer reaction to the initial burst of press advertising and with the flow of machines from its suppliers: 'It's true in a sense that Alan is a risk-taker, but equally he doesn't half cover himself. He makes sure there is a market there. He doesn't just jump in,' notes Greg Delaney.

Sugar was also careful to ensure that the word processor was well received by his customers, the retailers who were the channel between Amstrad and the end users. A few months before the launch of the word processor, he took a prototype to show Stanley Kalms, chairman of Dixons, the high street electrical goods chain. From the start Kalms had a gut feeling that this product would be a winner, but he was also nervous about committing himself to something which had no precedent: 'O.K., it looks good for 400 quid, but who is going to buy the damn thing?' he asked.

Sugar took Kalms through Amstrad's thinking about pricing and target audience and must have been persuasive, because Kalms placed an initial order for 20,000 word processors. But the Dixons chairman – an equally canny negotiator – insisted on a quid pro quo for what was then a very large order for both firms. He asked for Dixons to be given the exclusive right to sell the word processor in the high street for an initial period. 'It was typical of the way we would buy. If we stuck our neck out for 20,000 pieces, we wanted a short competitive edge, a small exclusive window,' Kalms says.

Sugar agreed to grant Dixons exclusivity for four months until the end of 1985. Amstrad would in any case have found it difficult to supply many more machines in addition to Dixons's order before the end of the year, because it would take several months for the supply of word processors to build up to peak volumes, allowing for shipping times from the Far East. But Sugar also knew that the arrangement with Dixons would bring Amstrad many advantages. Having one main outlet for a new product simplified the initial sales message: Amstrad need do no more than tell people to go to a Dixons store. If sales through Dixons went well, other stores would be stung into taking large volumes of the word processor once the Dixons exclusivity ended. Moreover, the arrangement would encourage Dixons to make a big push for the product, as Sugar explains: 'When Dixons have a gut feeling for a product, they get behind it themselves. They will stack it up, pile it high, display it in all the stores, give it prominence, spend a bit of their own advertising on it.'

The reaction of Dixons's customers to the word processor surpassed the highest hopes of Sugar and Kalms, as the Dixons chairman recalls:

> It was one of the great phenomenal take-offs in my experience. Products very rarely take off at the beginning. Usually, they're on the market years before they take off. They're like actors: they can be around for years and one day they become stars. But this was an absolute bombshell. He'd brought a word processor and a computer down to the level of your school-teacher, your local vicar – everybody who was in the business of typing and communicating. Till then, home computers had been just sophisticated toys. Here was the first real professional piece of equipment. So every charity in the country wanted one. Every secretary in every small company went to her boss and said: 'I want one.'

Before the appearance of Amstrad's word processor and its subsequent line of I.B.M.-compatible personal computers, professional computers had been sold almost entirely through specialist dealers. Amstrad and Dixons were the main catalysts in moving sales of professional computers into Britain's high streets. Since the early 1980s Dixons had been trying to add personal computers to its traditional lines such as cameras and hi-fi; it had sold a range of computers made by Japanese companies like Epson, Sanyo and Toshiba, but without much success, as Kalms notes: 'We had been in computers three or four years, making no money, persisting as you often do with a new product group, but waiting for the point of entry. We saw that computers had to be a mass consumer product eventually. And Alan made them a mass consumer product.'

Dixons had been looking for a computer which could be sold without needing specialist advice about peripherals and software. Amstrad filled that gap. 'The dream of a business like ours was that computers should cease to be exclusive, magic products. They would become *consumer* electronics. That was the great break-through. That was the measure of Alan's genius,' Kalms says.

Amstrad's pricing policy was fundamental to this breakthrough, for Sugar believed that the price of his computers should reflect what they cost to make, not what the market would bear. He differentiates this approach from that of the established computer companies:

> The big computer companies were ripping people off for a long, long time. £2,000 was the price of a personal computer and that was it. It bore no relations to the bill of materials, but that's how they made their money. We came along and said it's about time we broadened the market. We looked at a personal computer and we said this is a £399 piece here – though it was a bit tight at £399.

Some retailers tried to persuade Sugar to increase the price: 'People said to us, "You're bloody mad. Absolutely mad. Why don't you sell it for £499 or £599? It doesn't have to be £399."' It was a plea which he resisted.

Thanks to the elegant simplicity of the Amstrad word processor, its unbeatable price and the thoroughness of the company's marketing plans, 1985–86 proved to be an *annus mirabilis* in Amstrad's history. Some inkling of what was to come emerged in February 1986 when Amstrad released figures for the first half of its financial year, the six months to December 1985. The first two sentences of Lex's comment in the *Financial Times* caught the tone:

> The City may have some difficulty understanding anything to do with electronics, but rarely has it misjudged a company so resoundingly as Amstrad. While the stockbroking fraternity was losing its collective sleep on audacious forecasts of a 50 per cent

The Infant Alan Sugar

Alan Sugar playing as a child

Above: Sixteen-year-old Alan Sugar outside the family's flat

Alan and Ann before their marriage

...an making a speech at his wedding in 1968

...an's son Daniel's barmitzvah, l-r: Louise (Alan's daughter); Alan; Ann; Daniel; Fay (Alan's ...other); Nathan (Alan's father); Simon (Alan's son) (photo: Ivan Robin Ltd)

Alan Sugar with Amstrad's first computer, the CPC 464 in 1984

Announcing the acquisition of Sir Clive Sinclair's computer interests in 1986

Rupert Murdoch and Alan Sugar launching Sky Television in 1988 (photo: The Sun)

Appearing on television as part of the Government's 1992 awareness campaign

With Marion Vannier, head of Amstrad France

Shopping the competition in half – the PC 1512 advert

The scrapheap advert for the PCW 8256

Left: Portrait of Alan Sugar by Bryan Organ, commissioned by Amstrad shareholders

Below: 1989 Pro-Am Charity Match, (l-r: Richard Branson, Paul McNamee, Vijay Amritraj, Alan Sugar)

increase in pre-tax performance, Amstrad quietly announced just short of a trebling of interim profits – from £9.5m to £27.5m.

Amstrad's share price had begun to climb steeply in the autumn of 1985, after the well-received launch of the PCW8256 and the release of financial results demonstrating the success of the CPC464. The stock price jumped a further 50p to 342p on the day in February 1986 when the half-year results were announced. In twenty-four hours the value of Sugar's paper fortune increased by £27.5 million to £188 million.

Sugar took the opportunity to add to his real fortune and in May 1986 raised £25.7 million by selling another 5 per cent of Amstrad stock, further reducing his stake in the company to 45.4 per cent. Given Amstrad's performance, there was no problem in placing the 5,000,000 shares at 520p each with institutional investors, some with existing stakes in Amstrad and others new to the company.

Amstrad's chairman issued a formal statement explaining the share sale: 'It seemed to me to be about time that I reduced my holding in Amstrad in order to develop my interests outside the company. But Amstrad will still absorb all my management attention.' The Amstrad chairman gave a more characteristic answer when asked by *Microscope* computer magazine what the money was for: 'It's money for Al. I'm not starting a new company. I'm not building electric cars [the Sinclair electric car fiasco was a recent memory], I'm not funding any new developments. It's my own money.'

Amstrad's surge forward was confirmed in the full year results for 1985–86, issued in October 1986. Profits increased by an astonishing 273 per cent to £75.3 million on sales which were up 123 per cent at £304.1 million. The shares – which had been split in five again in June – reached 136p, valuing Sugar's stake in the company at £340 million. The stock market now reckoned Amstrad to be worth more than Ferranti, a long-standing pillar of the British electronics industry. One brokers' analyst commented that, considering how few assets the company possessed, Sugar was probably the most highly capitalized individual on the London stock market. In both 1985 and 1986, Amstrad was among the top three performing shares on the market.

Amstrad had not neglected its traditional products during its launch into computers. The company re-entered the video recorder market with a machine imported from Japan in 1985, and by June 1986 was claiming 10 per cent of the British market. In January 1986 they broke new ground by embedding a compact disc player in a hi-fi system which cost less than £300. 'We see CD as the future in sound reproduction, but, until now, [it] has been only affordable by the rich,' Sugar said when announcing the move. Philips, the Netherlands-based electronics giant, was stung into revamping its compact disc player strategy a month later. 'If you have Amstrad shares, sell 'em,' quipped Leigh Robinson, Philips's marketing manager in the U.K.

That almost everyone ignored this advice was undoubtedly due to Amstrad's computer activities rather than to anything it was doing in audio or video. Its impact on the word processing market turned out to be as revolutionary as Sugar had predicted. Before the launch of the Amstrad PCW8256, word processor sales in Britain were bumping along at 50,000–75,000 a year. But Amstrad sold 350,000 word processors during its first eight months in the market, attracting a whole new generation of users to computers for the first time.

Amstrad was the most visible beneficiary of this word processing revolution, but its entry into computers caused ripples throughout the microcomputer industry. Take software as an example. Amstrad's word processor, together with the low cost I.B.M.-compatible machine it launched in September 1986, helped to transform the British business software industry. It had been used to supplying high cost, low volume products and a business software package would typically have cost more than the retail price of an Amstrad computer. After Amstrad's entry that no longer made sense, as software entrepreneurs soon realized.

David Goldman, founder and chairman of Sagesoft, first saw Amstrad's PCW8256 when it was launched at a computer show in August 1985. Based in the north-east of England, Sagesoft had been prospering in a modest way since it was founded in 1981.

Goldman immediately recognized the opportunity offered by Amstrad's machine, as he explains: 'It just seemed pretty obvious to me that it was going to make a huge impact on the market.'

Goldman's reaction was to rush back to Newcastle and modify an accounts package which Sagesoft had devised for CP/M and which had been selling for £375. Within a month Sagesoft had a slimmed-down version on sale, suitable for Amstrad's word processor and with a price tag of £100 including VAT. Before the PCW8256 launch, Sagesoft had been selling about 250–300 units of this software a month. By the start of 1986, monthly sales had shot up to 5,000.

Sagesoft was to repeat the trick after the well-trailed launch of Amstrad's I.B.M.-compatible personal computer. Goldman advertised spreadsheet, word processing and other software specially modified for this machine a matter of days after Amstrad's own advertising campaign began. For a couple of years after the launch of the PCW8256, Goldman says, Amstrad was the most important factor spearheading the development of mass market software and therefore the prosperity of companies like his own. His company, by then known as Sage Group, was valued at £21.1 million when it was launched on the stock market in December 1989.

Amstrad prompted a similar upheaval in specialist office equipment retailing. Some specialist computer outlets suffered because they were slow to realize that it was ushering in an era of low-cost, mass market machines, but those who understood the changes prospered. While Amstrad's main sales thrust for its computers was through high street chains, it did not neglect the more specialist outlets, which were exempted from the terms of its exclusivity arrangement with Dixons. Terry Wilding, an East-Ender like Sugar, had launched Wilding Office Equipment in the mid-1960s, and by 1985 it was heavily dependent on the traditional typewriter market. Until then, Wilding's dealings with Sugar had been as a supplier of office equipment to Amstrad.

Before the word processor's launch, Sugar told Terry Wilding that he had a product which might interest him. Wilding recalls that he was impressed with the prototype of the PCW8256, but – seeing no reason to believe it would take off – he took only a few for his shop windows. Customer interest was so intense, however, that he put in a large order. Soon he was selling more than 1,000 PCW8256s a month, significant volumes for what was then a relatively small group.

During the next couple of years, Amstrad played the same catalytic role in Wilding's growth as in Sagesoft's. 'Amstrad helped to take us out of being a traditional office equipment supplier into computers. We did very well out of them,' says Wilding, whose group was valued at over £12 million when floated on the Stock Exchange in November 1986.

Some of the factors underlying Amstrad's performance in 1985–86 were as remarkable as the headline figures such as the near tripling of profits. Amstrad's profit margins increased from 14 to 25 per cent in the year to June 1986, an astounding figure for a manufacturing company battling it out in the cut-throat world of high street consumer electronics. Luck played a part in the achievement of these profit margins, since its launch into computers coincided with a cyclical downturn in the price of memory chips, a notoriously volatile commodity whose supply swings from feast to famine and back again in short order. But Sugar's management of Amstrad's growth also underpinned his ability to squeeze such high profits out of the company. In the financial year 1985–86, when Amstrad's sales grew by 123 per cent, the company increased its work-force by a mere 6 per cent, adding only thirty people to its existing complement of 496. On average, each Amstrad employee generated sales of more than £500,000 in the year – an astonishing ratio.

A tight ship, spiralling sales and little demand for capital investment – it was a recipe for generating cash. As Amstrad grew, it had to finance ever larger orders from its suppliers, which forced the company into substantial borrowings of a temporary nature while waiting for revenues from its sales to flow in. Yet while the scale was bigger, the underlying pattern of its finances had not changed greatly from the 1970s. Over the course of a year, Amstrad was able to fund its activities out of its cash flow and pile up cash in the bank. By the end of 1985–86, it was sitting on a cash pile of about £50 million.

Confident that his entry into computers had been well judged, Sugar felt justified in articulating Amstrad's philosophy for the computer market in his chairman's statements in 1985 and 1986.

Point 1 was on design: 'We are experts in design and engineering – one of our talents is to engineer products with all the specifications and facilities the market demands and delete those unused facilities that are only enjoyed by the minority. In short, we produce what the mass market customer wants and not a boffin's ego trip.'

Point 2 was on manufacturing flexibility: 'Now that the sales volumes are getting larger and the market horizons wider, we are also broadening manufacturing sources. We procure our products and components from [the] U.K., Japan, U.S.A., Korea, Italy, Germany, France, Belgium, Taiwan and Hong Kong. We have the facility to expand our manufacturing capability and at the same time remain flexible, both from a currency exchange and a political point of view.'

Point 3 was on marketing: 'Our marketing skills and understanding of the seasonable nature of our business is one of the main reasons for our success. Having the right inventory at the right time is important, and making sure that our commitment for inventory is continually in line with our regularly updated sales forecasts.'

Sugar rounded off his 1986 statement by telling Amstrad's shareholders to expect more fireworks from the company: 'The year I have just reported has shown excellent growth of sales and profits, once again I would like to say that this is no fluke or flash in the pan. The electronics industry is a fascinating one, inasmuch as there are always new products to develop and markets to explore. . . .'

Shortly before penning the 1986 statement, Sugar gave an interview to *International Management* magazine in which he articulated his philosophy of total product flexibility. 'We're interested in the mass-merchandising of anything,' he told the attendant journalist. 'If there was a market in mass-produced nuclear weapons, we'd market them too.'

· 10 ·

The Boffin and the Entrepreneur

Alan Sugar knew that something big was about to break when he took an unexpected call from Mark Souhami, managing director of Dixons, early in 1986. He was in Hong Kong on one of his regular trips to the Far East, and the last thing he was anticipating was to be contacted by the powers that be at Dixons.

'We heard you were in Hong Kong. There's something we'd like to talk to you about. Why don't you pop over and see us? We're staying at the Mandarin,' Souhami said, explaining that Stanley Kalms, Dixons's chairman, was also there.

Intrigued, Sugar paid the seven-pence fare for the ride across the stretch of water separating Kowloon from Hong Kong Island on the Star Ferry. Idly watching as the ferry weaved in and out of the barges from Communist China heading for the open sea, he turned over in his mind what Dixons might want.

However, the Dixons executives were in no hurry to enlighten Sugar once he had found his way to Souhami's suite in the Mandarin Hotel. They spent a good ten minutes in small talk discussing routine matters which could easily have waited until they were all back in Britain. Sugar's patience, never his strong suit, snapped. 'Come on, what the bloody hell are you driving me mad for? I've come over here on the Star Ferry, sweating hot, because you asked me. Now what do you want me here for?'

The Dixons executives got down to business. They wanted to discuss a deal which could be in the offing with Sir Clive Sinclair.

After leaving the meeting with Dixons, Sugar pondered what he had been told. As he understood it, there was a large stock of Sinclair computers up for sale. Dixons had considered buying them, but the trouble was that Sinclair wanted to sell them as part of a package deal by which someone would take his entire computer business off his hands. Sugar was now left with the question: would Amstrad be interested in buying the Sinclair operation?

Sugar already knew that Sinclair Research, Clive Sinclair's home computer company, had been able to limp through the second half of 1985 only because Dixons had bought 160,000 of its computers and pocket televisions at rock-bottom prices. That £10 million deal had been enough to earn Sinclair a respite from his bankers, Barclays and Citibank, and creditors, led by his main suppliers Timex, Thorn E.M.I. and AB Electronic. However, it was evident to Sugar that this group wanted to sort out the financial problems at Sinclair Research once and for all now that the Christmas season was over.

Sugar explains how he saw the line-up:

Dixons had just finished raping Clive in the Christmas of 85. They were really licking their lips because they had seen all Sinclair's computers flowing through their shops. Clive might be losing his trousers on them, but Dixons were making lots of money from them. Then Dixons heard that the banks and the creditors wanted a solution by the end of March. And there was Dixons saying to itself that this little gravy train was going to end. No way could it allow Sinclair to go down the pan.

The Amstrad boss now believed that Dixons themselves had thought about taking Sinclair over. Looking back at the event, Sugar describes his view of Dixons's position: 'Dixons began to realize in no uncertain terms that this was a very, very, very big can of worms, that involved lots of stock lying around all over the place. Timex, Thorn E.M.I. and AB Electronic – every bloody company in the world was in trouble with Sinclair. So Dixons decided to drop it on me instead.'

Sugar was more than happy to take up the running, because he could smell the potential. Despite its recent troubles, Sinclair was still the dominant force in games computers and accounted for some 40 per cent of the total U.K. home computer market. By acquiring the business, at a stroke Amstrad would become the market leader in games computers, boosting its total computer sales by hundreds of thousands of units a year. It would add another string to Amstrad's bow at the entertainment end of the market, while Sugar pursued his main strategy of pushing further into business computing. Moreover, Sinclair had sold over 5 million computers including more than 1 million Spectrums, its flagship product. Sugar felt he could exploit this huge installed base by selling computer peripherals to Sinclair users.

The Amstrad chairman was confident that he could squeeze a lot more money out of the operation than Clive Sinclair. He would improve the efficiency with which the Sinclair machines were made, eliminate overlapping distribution costs and inject Amstrad zest into selling them. From his point of view, the deal would be all but perfect if he could also win the exclusive right to the Sinclair name, one of the most powerful brands in Britain.

Already excited by the deal's potential, Sugar called a meeting for 9 o'clock the next morning at the Amstrad offices in Kowloon. Bob Watkins was there, as were the people from Dixons. Sugar took charge of the proceedings, wheeling in one of the company's young Chinese designers. Following instructions from Sugar and Watkins, the designer sketched out an improved version of the Spectrum Plus, the latest Sinclair machine, featuring a keyboard with a cassette mechanism tagged on to it.

'Is this the kind of thing you'd want to buy?' Sugar asked Souhami.

'What kind of price could it sell for?' countered the man from Dixons. 'About £159,' Sugar replied. Dixons were more than interested.

Sugar went into overdrive, phoned Amstrad headquarters in Brentwood and told them to have a Sinclair Spectrum delivered from the local Dixons shop immediately. An Amstrad engineer in Brentwood opened up the machine and shouted down the phone to Bob Watkins a list of all the components he found embedded in the printed circuit board; he then faxed through to Hong Kong the Spectrum's circuit diagram. By the next day, Sugar and Watkins had a provisional estimate of how much it would cost Amstrad to make a Spectrum, based on that list of components shouted over the phone.

Sugar explains his thinking: 'We knew how much a cassette mechanism cost and we took a flying guess at a few other parts that were in the Sinclair. And we concluded that if we pressed the button, we could tool up for that product, make 400,000 and have them in the U.K. market and all the other markets of the world in time for Christmas 1986.'

The Amstrad boss knew he could make a tidy profit from the Sinclair business: that much was clear from the favourable Dixons reaction to the price he had quoted for the enhanced Spectrum Plus, and from his calculations as to the cost of making the machine. He was now hooked on the project. Once back in Britain, he called up a supplier in Taiwan to discuss making the Sinclair machines for Amstrad. Amstrad's engineers in Brentwood drafted preliminary sketches of the manufacturing tooling that would be needed to make the Spectrum, and faxed these to the Taiwanese manufacturer. Sugar phoned Taiwan again to confirm his interest: 'There could be a deal cooking, but keep quiet. I can't tell you no names yet. I'll come back to you.'

Sugar had travelled this far without even talking to Sinclair or Sinclair's creditors. With the end-of-March deadline fast approaching, however, a meeting had to be arranged. Both sides agreed that Alan Sugar and Sir Clive Sinclair would kick off the talks by meeting on their own without advisers. As a symbolic half-way house, they chose for their encounter a restaurant in Liverpool Street station, the London railway terminal which served both Sinclair's Cambridge headquarters and Sugar's Brentwood base.

Anyone who saw the two men lunching together that day would have been struck by the contrast. On one side of the table sat the bespectacled Sinclair, whose domed head and quiet, precise manner were perfectly suited to his reputation as Britain's leading boffin. He had projected himself as the ultimate technological guru, a self-image endlessly amplified by Britain's mass media to the point where the *Sun* described him as 'the most prodigious inventor since Leonardo'. At the height of his computer success, his Cambridge headquarters was a monument to high-tech high taste. An atrium featuring a bronze sculpture led off the stainless-steel-clad offices, while one visitor breathlessly recorded, 'Even the bicycle shed was fine art.'

On the other side of the table sat Alan Sugar, a bear of a man who would never knowingly let fine art darken the threshold of Amstrad's offices in Brentwood, a town as nondescript as Cambridge is distinguished. The last title he would ever aspire to was that of boffin, which for him is a term of abuse. Unlike Sinclair, he had no emotional commitment to his products or the technologies that went into them; his unbending commitment was to the bottom line.

Yet both Sinclair and Sugar were seen – at different times and for different reasons – as the great white hopes for a British business revival in the 1980s. The burden of carrying these hopes was on the point of passing from Sinclair to Sugar as the two Thatcherite role models ate their lunch.

Both these electronics tycoons have warm memories of the occasion. Even Sinclair, who might be expected to look back at the events with some regret, says, 'I found Alan Sugar a delightful man to deal with. He tended to say – this is the deal. He never tried to improve his position or deviate from what he said he would do. He was very straightforward and clear-headed. He was very pleasant company, enjoyable to meet – a witty man.'

A misunderstanding had to be cleared out of the way first, however. Sugar was under the impression that he was being asked to buy the whole of Sinclair Research, which would have meant acquiring all Sinclair's various research projects and could have meant taking Clive Sinclair into the Amstrad operation. Luckily, Sinclair put his cards on the table: 'Look, Alan, I'm not going to work for anybody.'

Sugar heaved a sigh of relief. He viewed Sinclair as someone whose reputation had been over-hyped by the media. While admiring Sinclair for having traded on the image the newspapers had woven round him of genius, entrepreneur and scientist *extraordinaire*, admiring a man for having played his hand to good effect was different from wanting to work with him. 'Look, Clive, you can carry on talking in your cultured Etonian accent and fooling everybody into treating you as an undergrad in your lab in Cambridge, but I have your card marked. So let's talk business. What's the bottom line?' Sugar asked.

Sinclair wanted Sugar to buy his computer operations, including the existing stock and the rights to the continuing business, but not Sinclair Research, which would continue as a vehicle for Sinclair's research interests. As the meeting wore on, Sinclair mentioned the figure he had in mind as the purchase price for his computer operations, which was a sum way in excess of anything that Sugar intended to pay.

The deal was heading into a brick wall, as Sugar recalls: 'The bottom line was he sees a way where there could be mutual benefit ... bla-de-bla. Anyway, it was a load of bullshit. He wanted a lot of money. I'm not interested. Goodbye. I literally felt that at the end of that meeting we'd hear no more about it.'

But Sinclair's suppliers and banks were still determined to arrange a deal by Easter which fell at the end of March. The company's position was clearly slipping in the market. With the Christmas sales period behind it, there was the long and unattractive prospect of the dead spring and summer sales months to limp through. The timing was also influenced by a capital gains tax liability which Sinclair Research had. It was so large that it might have tipped the company over into insolvency if ever it were paid in full. If that happened, the creditors and the banks would have had to realize their assets after Sinclair had gone into liquidation. Obviously, in that case they would receive less money than if they could strike a deal while Sinclair was still a going concern. If a deal could be concluded by the end of the tax year, 31 March, then Sinclair could offset losses arising out of the deal against the capital gains tax liability.

A couple of days after his lunch with Sinclair, Sugar took a call from an accountant representing Sinclair, asking if he could come to Brentwood for a meeting. The accountant's opening gambit was to the point: 'Look, we want a deal, what are you prepared to do?'

During the course of this meeting the full scale of the suppliers' inventory holdings emerged. Millions of pounds' worth of Sinclair stock was dotted about the country, both as finished products and as components in various stages of assembly. A hurried round of meetings involving advisers from both sides was arranged. The plan was to hammer out the final deal in a set-piece engagement between Sinclair (together with advisers and creditors) on one side, and Sugar on the other, before the end of March.

The talks with Sinclair's advisers had already forced Sugar to postpone his plans to fly to his holiday home in Florida for an Easter break, and he had no intention of putting off his departure a second time. His ticket for the 7 o'clock Concorde flight that evening was safely tucked into his briefcase as he walked into the headquarters of Barclays Bank in the City to stitch up the Sinclair deal. He was feeling lucky: it was Monday, 24 March 1986, his thirty-ninth birthday.

He recalls the scene vividly: 'There was this bloody great big round table with all these bankers sitting there, grovelling and hovering around. And the bottom line was the banks were in for God knows what and the suppliers had piles and piles and piles of inventory.'

The Amstrad boss opened up by saying that he would throw £5 million in cash into the pot. He would then go off and talk separately to each individual supplier and take all their stock from them. He reckoned there was about £11 million worth of inventory in total. He might be able to strike up some relationship with the manufacturers present, allowing them to continue to make Sinclair machines – but he rather doubted it, because down the years his experience had been that he could not buy anything decent in the U.K. 'British manufacturers are crap because their quality is so awful,' Sugar told the gathering.

Turning to the banker from Barclays who was leading for the other side, Sugar summed up: 'That's the deal I'm offering, but I haven't much time. So if you're interested, fine. If not, it's nice to have met you and I'll say goodbye.'

The bankers and manufacturers across the table were less than impressed by this performance. 'They all started saying at once that this was no good,' Sugar recalls.

Ted Merrette, managing director of AB Electronic, tried to argue with Sugar about quality standards. He told Sugar that British manufacturers like themselves – an electronic component manufacturer based in South Wales – could meet Amstrad's demanding standards because by then they had caught up with the Japanese. The argument was not simply of academic interest to Merrette or the other manufacturers present, because they hoped to continue producing machines for Amstrad: 'Sugar was buying the Sinclair name for something. Presumably he was going to carry on selling the products. My feeling was we could produce them and produce them effectively,' Merrette recalls.

Sugar was in no mood to debate with the manufacturers or to listen to the bankers' protests. 'Look, that's the deal. I'm leaving now. See you,' he told the gathering.

The Sinclair side asked him to wait because they might have an alternative proposition. 'Well, I haven't got much time left because I've got to catch a flight in a couple of hours,' he replied.

The other side then asked him to leave while they considered their options. 'We want you to increase your cash offer to £10 million,' he was told on re-entering the room. Clive Sinclair, who had taken little part in the meeting until then, started talking about the wonders of the technology in his Spectrum machine, but Sugar interrupted him. 'For God's sake, Clive, I don't care if they have rubber bands in them, as long as they work.'

The Amstrad chairman considered for a further micro-second before turning down flat the request for extra money. In the end the Sinclair side accepted; they had little choice. Sitting back in his seat in Concorde, Sugar mulled over a good day's work; the deal appeared to be sewn up. But this assessment proved to be a little premature.

There followed a week of intense activity as the two sides tried to agree on the small print before the end-of-March deadline. The contracts were immensely complicated because so many parties were involved on the Sinclair side. Amstrad's directors – Ken Ashcroft, Bob Watkins, Malcolm Miller and Jim Rice – moved into an office at the City lawyers who were advising the Sinclair team; there they placed a telephone with a loudspeaker unit in the middle of their temporary headquarters, so that they could discuss progress with Sugar in Florida. The Sinclair team occupied another office in the same building. The two sides either negotiated or discussed tactics amongst themselves from 10 am each morning until the early hours of the following morning, every day from Tuesday 25 March and over the Easter weekend to Easter Monday, 31 March.

The fax machine in Sugar's holiday home in Florida worked overtime as he kept in touch with negotiations: 'They were faxing through to me pages and pages and pages of messages. But I was lucky to be in Florida. They were the poor sods having to do the deal,' he says.

Two issues dominated the negotiations. First, Amstrad had to have watertight assurances that it was buying all the technical drawings and other pieces of intellectual property which would give it exclusive ownership of Sinclair's computers. On legal advice, the Amstrad team opened up by demanding to see every notebook ever written within Sinclair Research on the Spectrum project. The Sinclair side countered that this would be an impossible request for any company to fulfil, but was doubly unreasonable to make of one which everyone knew to have had management problems. Forty-eight hours passed in haggling over the assurances on intellectual property ownership which Amstrad really needed.

In the end, everyone agreed that Amstrad's requirements centred on control of the chip design for the Spectrum: 'The heart of the computer was the intellectual property rights held within the gate array custom chip design and the code in the ROM, the operating system. Without that signed, sealed and delivered to us, we'd have bought nothing,' Sugar explains.

A couple of problems on the ownership of the chip design had to be resolved as the end-of-March deadline approached. Ferranti's name appeared on one of the design documents; some time and much nervous energy was expended before Ferranti agreed to waive any claims to ownership. More trickily, a man called John

Grant – who ran a small software house, Nine Tiles Information – had helped to design the Sinclair operating system. Grant was found to have left for an Easter boating holiday on the Grand Union Canal, so a motorcycle courier was hurriedly commissioned to ride up and down the towpath looking for his boat. The dispatch rider kept missing Grant, who was not located until he returned home on Easter Monday. Grant cannily haggled for a day over the price for his waiver, finally signing only on payment of about £25,000 by the Sinclair team.

The second central issue in the negotiations was the mind-numbing task of agreeing the terms governing the payment to each supplier for its pile of inventory. The point of contention was not so much the price Amstrad was offering, but the conditions attached to it: for example, the quality specifications to be laid down for the inventory which the manufacturers would supply to Amstrad and the help Amstrad would give the manufacturers in assembling component parts into finished stock. Depending on how tightly these conditions were drawn, the price Amstrad was offering could be made to appear either fairly generous or impossibly mean.

Negotiations intensified as the deadline approached. The two sides met at 10 am on Easter Monday, 31 March, worked right through Monday night and then right through Tuesday. Tempers frayed and each side formed an increasingly low opinion of the other. The Sinclair team concluded that Amstrad was playing a delaying game in order to force last-minute concessions. At one point, someone on Sinclair's side thought he spotted an attempt by Amstrad to back out of a point already agreed. When the man read out to Sugar his notes of a previous conversation, he was subjected to a barrage of ripe abuse down the telephone wires for his pains.

For his part, Sugar's view of the other side also plummeted as the faxes hummed across the Atlantic: 'I learned then what a bunch of gangsters the banks are. They *really* are gangsters. They thought they were dealing with a boy who had just got bar-mitzvahed, when they were dealing with me. They reckoned I was someone with too much money and didn't know what I was doing.'

The deal nearly collapsed many times as the exchanges on the phone between Florida and London grew increasingly angry. On more than one occasion Sugar told his team of directors, 'Pack your briefcases up. Leave the room and clear off to your wives. We're not buying the thing.'

In the end, terms were agreed at 3 o'clock in the morning of Wednesday, 2 April, technically a couple of days beyond the deadline. 'We were all zombies at the end of it. It's the worst deal I've ever done,' one of Sinclair's bankers recalls.

Amstrad paid Sinclair £5 million for all the rights to his computer products, including the perpetual right to use the Sinclair brand name. The company paid a further £11 million to Sinclair and his sub-contractors for their stock. Self-interest was the glue which held the deal together: the Sinclair side had too much to lose by letting the talks collapse, while Amstrad had much to gain by ensuring the negotiations were successful. The agreement was kept under wraps until Sugar flew home from his holiday.

He landed at Heathrow on Saturday 5 April. Nick Hewer and Andrew Mackay, Amstrad's public relations advisers, spent the weekend worrying over whether the news would leak out. Hewer waited until the Saturday before issuing invitations to a press conference on the following Monday; these baldly stated that Alan Sugar would be making an announcement with major implications for the European computer market. Hewer was careful to leave Sinclair's name off the invitation, knowing that to do otherwise would have given the game away to the Sunday papers.

The first inkling that the assembled newspaper and television journalists had of the deal was when Alan Sugar and Clive Sinclair walked together into the press conference in the Howard Hotel. Sugar allowed himself a quiet moment of self-congratulation as he sat watching the television crew powdering Sinclair's head to dim its reflection in the lights, but he resisted the temptation to gloat: 'The journalists tried to wind me up in the press conference to slag the poor sod off. Why was he so unsuccessful and so on? I wouldn't fall for it. There was no way I was going to run the man down as he was sitting there very dignified. I thought there's no mileage in letting them wind me up.'

Press interest in the news was intense. It was, commented the *International Herald Tribune,* 'the most widely followed $7 million corporate transaction in British history'. Most comment was favourable. 'Amstrad's purchase of Sir Clive Sinclair's home computer brands is so logical it could have been conceived by an electronic brain,' the Lex column concluded in the *Financial Times,* adding that Amstrad would be able to recover the purchase price after just one year of selling the Sinclair machines. The *Daily Telegraph* agreed: 'The man who knew what the technology could do has lost to the man who knew what the customer wanted.'

Amstrad could now claim 60 per cent of the British home computer market – 40 per cent from Sinclair, and the rest from its own share. It had also overtaken Commodore as the biggest volume seller of low cost computers in Europe. *The Times* hailed the deal as 'the end of an era'. The mantle of Britain's foremost electronics entrepreneur had passed from Sir Clive Sinclair to Alan Sugar.

*

The same month that the Sinclair purchase was announced, a Cambridge-educated engineer in his late twenties called Richard Altwasser journeyed to Brentwood for his first day as an Amstrad employee. He looked curiously out of place in the Amstrad headquarters; thin, carefully spoken and with an intellectual demeanour, only his mop of fair hair stopped him from passing as a Clive Sinclair lookalike.

Altwasser had in fact led the small team which designed the Sinclair Spectrum and Sugar was about to benefit from an ideal coincidence: the Spectrum's designer started working for Amstrad at the very moment when the company acquired all the rights to the machine. Yet coincidence – luck, really – was indeed what was involved, for Amstrad had not recruited Altwasser specifically because of his experience with Sinclair Research.

Alan Sugar and Bob Watkins had decided back in 1985 that Amstrad had become so big it needed a well staffed research and development unit. They wanted top-flight engineers to help design Amstrad's new products, especially since they knew that the company's future lay in yet heavier involvement with computers. Watkins began to look for someone to lead the team, turning eventually to head-hunters to complete his search.

The head-hunters recommended Richard Altwasser, who by then was working in the Brussels office of P.A. Technology, a leading group of technology consultants. Altwasser duly made the trek to Brentwood one Saturday in January 1986 for what turned into a rather unusual interview with Bob Watkins.

Watkins kicked off by telling Altwasser that he was not even going to try to probe his technical ability: 'It would be a waste of time because I'm not qualified to do so. What we need is someone with a brain. We intend to develop a huge number of new products, so we want someone who is really good and really understands computers.'

He went on to explain that Amstrad was worried that it was becoming too big to rely totally on the small contractors like MEJ Electronics which had designed its computer products until then. 'They might go down the pan one day and then we're stuck.'

Altwasser was being offered the chance to set up an in-house development team by Amstrad, a company whose track record in taking the home computer market by storm he greatly admired. The Cambridge engineer explained to Watkins the number of people, the floor space and the equipment he would require to create this team. 'You can have whatever you need,' Watkins assured him.

This was an offer that Altwasser could hardly refuse; on returning to Brussels he handed in his notice and prepared to start at Amstrad. During his interview he had told Watkins that he had worked with Sinclair from 1980 to 1982, but at the time this seemed of only passing interest.

By the time Altwasser joined Amstrad in April, just as the deal with Sinclair was being completed, his previous experience could hardly have been more relevant. He was immediately thrown into collecting technical documents and circuit diagrams from people he had worked with in Cambridge. Amstrad drew on Altwasser's intimate knowledge of the Spectrum as it redesigned the Spectrum's cabinet, built a cassette into the machine, improved the sound, devised a new layout for the printed circuit board and modified the basic chip design. The company met its target of getting a Spectrum Plus Two into production by the end of July – time enough to produce the necessary volumes for Christmas 1986.

Sugar set about making the Sinclair computer operations more efficient. 'There was not enough attention paid to quality control, stock control and monitoring of sales,' he said shortly after the acquisition.

He saved money by dropping Sinclair's QL, the computer launched in 1984 which had turned into a quantum leap to nowhere. After placing an initial order with the Timex plant in Dundee, Amstrad also shifted production of the Spectrum to the Far East. Sugar had hinted during the press conference announcing the Sinclair purchase that the days of sourcing the Spectrum in Britain were numbered: 'We would like to manufacture in the United Kingdom, but we're a computer company, not a benevolent society.'

In fact, Sinclair Research had already begun to source some Spectrums from South Korea before Amstrad took over. Looking back, Sinclair thinks the company probably should have switched manufacturing to the Far East earlier. 'Certainly if we had continued to produce a commodity product like the Spectrum, we would have had little choice but to produce in the Far East,' he says in retrospect.

Originally Sugar thought that Amstrad might be able to come up with a radical new design for the Spectrum line; but Amstrad was constrained by one of the very factors which made the acquisition so attractive – the huge installed base of Sinclair machines. Amstrad had to ensure that the libraries of games already held by millions of youngsters could be used by Sinclair machines launched in the future. This need to maintain compatibility severely limited the extent to which they could redesign the Sinclair range.

Instead of working on a fundamental redesign of the Sinclair machines, Amstrad concentrated on improving what it had inherited. Altwasser found that the latest Spectrum embodied a third or fourth revision of the original chip design which he had worked on. The design had evolved haphazardly as logic chips, transistors and other components were added. Amstrad tidied up the interior, thereby reducing the manufacturing cost, and added some features, like a floppy disk version. But it stuck with the basic layout.

In the event it hardly mattered since the Sinclair machine continued to sell well, particularly during the Christmas season, although the computer games market has declined from its peak in the early 1980s. In the second half of 1988, Amstrad was still selling £20 million worth of Sinclair machines, with sales almost equally divided between the U.K. and Spain, where Sinclair has long been a strong brand name.

Sir Clive Sinclair, for one, believes that Sugar has done an excellent job in promoting and selling his old Spectrum range: 'The Spectrum was a commodity product. And I can't think of anyone who would have done as good a job as Alan Sugar did with it. I thought he was an ideal person to take over my Spectrum computer business. He knew what was needed by the customer. He was very, very perceptive. And he knew where to get the product made efficiently.'

Amstrad can cope with the highly seasonal Christmas demand for the Spectrum precisely because it now has plenty of other products which sell all the year round. Alan Sugar explains: 'Sinclair to me is like the suntan lotion that Boots sells. They put it in their windows in July and August and they take it away in the winter. And they can do that because they don't just rely on suntan oil. We can sell Sinclair because we can crank up production and stop it as soon as we want to.'

*

As Richard Altwasser settled into his new job, he came to realize that Amstrad was defined by its laser-like concentration on products. It might be thought that all companies concentrate on their products, but Altwasser's exposure to a host of different concerns in his days as a management consultant had taught him otherwise.

He explains: 'Some companies concentrate on the technology that goes into the product. Some companies concentrate on the management structures of the business: their management gets into all sorts of knots about the administration of the business. It was clear that the thing that gave Alan and Bob a buzz was seeing new products brought out.'

In particular, Altwasser learned to appreciate the difference between the Sugar and the Sinclair ways of working – a difference he summarizes as 'a concentration on products rather than a concentration on technologies'.

At Sinclair, Altwasser says:

There was a great deal of interest in the way in which materials and new technologies can make new components. The Spectrum used Ferranti ULAs [uncommitted logic arrays or gate arrays – a chip which is designed especially to satisfy the needs of particular customers]. These were high tech at the time and were the subject of great fascination to people in the company, Sir Clive included. But the detailed operation of the product, and how the user was going to perceive it, what features it was going to have, were far less interesting. I had a continual struggle to get Clive to sit down with the machine and show him what it could do and how it operated.

At Amstrad, by contrast:

I don't think I've ever discussed with Alan whether a particular chip uses 2 micron or 1½ micron CMOS, or whether it's two-layer metal or one-layer metal, or any of these other wonderful buzzwords. But I spend hours and hours discussing the features and functions, how they're presented and how the machine is going to be perceived by the customer. Alan doesn't get a buzz out of the technologies that go into making up the components. That's not something he finds exciting, but he's very interested in the features of the machine and how the machine operates.

Sugar frequently wanders round the sixth and seventh floors of Amstrad's headquarters where Altwasser and his team of fifteen designers and engineers are based, but he is invariably there to talk about one of three things: features, reliability and cost. He remains totally obsessed with encouraging his designers to use one chip instead of two wherever possible: 'I like to visualize myself walking around with a pair of cutters. And when the engineer says he's got to have this, I look at it and I say, "How much is it?" And he says, "Five quid." So I say, "Cut it out." And he says, "It won't work." So I say, "Well, you have to find a way of making it work for a pound." '

Sinclair would not talk to his engineers in that vein. Indeed, he identifies himself as an engineer and not as a manager: 'I am an engineer, an inventor. I'm looking at very long-term projects – artificial intelligence or electric vehicles or things like that.'

It is easy to exaggerate Sinclair's high-minded remoteness from the market. After all, he presided over the launch and marketing of two products – pocket calculators in the 1970s and home computers in the 1980s – which took the market by storm. His boffin image is partly a marketing tool: it reassured large numbers of technologically ignorant people who were buying such high tech products for the first time.

Even allowing for the myths that were woven around Sinclair in the early 1980s, however, there is an important sense in which he and Alan Sugar are mirror images of each other. Physics journals jostled with books on micro-electronics and inventing on the desks in Sinclair's small offices in the West End of London at the end of the 1980s, reinforcing his image as the boffin par excellence. By contrast, Sugar's desk sat facing a television where he viewed the latest business news, while his office had a flip chart which he used to calculate the margins on his latest product.

Sinclair seemed destined to be an inventor from the time he filled his bedroom with wires and amplifiers as a schoolboy, graduating to write manuals on transistors as a young man. His business roots lay in supplying the enthusiastic amateurs of the hobbyist market, his first commercial ventures involved selling kits to electrical buffs who wanted to assemble their own radios.

Fascinated by the technology, Sinclair tended to neglect the business side of his ventures. Insufficient attention was paid to quality as some of his early products moved from development to production, or while they were being manufactured. It was Sinclair's personal obsessions which drove the direction of his research rather than an appreciation of what consumers wanted. For every success, such as the calculator and the computer, there was a failure, like the mini-television and the electric car. Sinclair tended to become bored with his inventions precisely when they became successful, mass market products. He rapidly ceded his pre-eminent position to others – to the Japanese in the case of calculators, and to Sugar in home computers. 'Personally I don't like controlling a business that makes commodity products,' he acknowledges.

Sugar is almost at the opposite extreme, going out of his way to emphasize his lack of interest in matters technological: 'We aren't here to get national awards for the greatest technology,' he said shortly before the Sinclair acquisition. The Amstrad boss takes great delight in affronting the sensibilities of the boffin class. Soon after the launch of his first word processor, he conceded that purists believed it to be as outdated as a crystal radio set. 'But it isn't. It's what the market wants. We've brought out a machine that operates on an elastic band. But it works,' he said, repeating the typical Sugar exaggeration which he had used in the privacy of Barclays Bank's headquarters during his negotiating sessions with the Sinclair team.

In his heyday Sinclair was often praised by the Thatcher Government and by a gushing press as the very model of the high tech entrepreneur who would spearhead Britain's business revival. Burned by his sudden fall from grace, the opinion formers were wary of heaping the same expectations on Sugar. Yet it is arguable that Sugar, more than Sinclair, embodied precisely the qualities which British business has so notably lacked for much of the twentieth century.

Britain is not short of boffins, clever scientists and technologists who devise new ideas; but it has lacked daring entrepreneurs prepared to translate those ideas into successful products, particularly products to compete in the high street with the offerings of the big battalions from Japan and the United States. There have been too few British businessmen with the determination to keep their eye on the ball, squeezing a product for every last penny of profit once it has become a success. Sugar has the confidence, the determination and the flair to do these things.

At the first business meeting between Sugar and Sinclair in Liverpool Street station, the two men briefly toyed with the idea of joining forces. Sinclair would have invented the products and Sugar sold them. It could have been the perfect partnership, 'the dynamic duo', as Sugar jokingly called it.

'I don't think it would have worked, because we're both too independently minded. I don't think our objectives are the same,' says Sinclair, looking back. He elaborates on this point: 'I think the difference really comes down to this: Alan makes products in order to make money, whereas I make money in order to make products.'

· 11 ·

Sticking to Its Knitting

Alan Sugar was beginning to be noticed by the mid-1980s. After the word processor triumph, newspapers and magazines lined up to profile this rising star of the British business scene. He was talked about as a coming man, a representative of the rejuvenation of the British entrepreneurial spirit.

Unknown to him, the Amstrad chairman was also being watched by one of the giants of the post-war industrial scene, Arnold Weinstock, head of the General Electric Company. Out of a series of brilliant mergers in the 1960s, Lord Weinstock had forged G.E.C. into Britain's biggest manufacturing company. He was a byword for managerial toughness, running G.E.C. through a mixture of rigorous financial controls administered from the centre and a well-developed system for devolving operational responsibility to G.E.C.'s constituent businesses.

By the mid-1980s, Weinstock controlled his empire from Stanhope Gate, a small road off Park Lane and one of the smartest addresses in London. G.E.C.'s head office is a tribute to Weinstock's dislike of corporate extravagance. Its headquarters is a building so small and plain that it could be mistaken for an offshoot of a company a tenth its scale. Inside, Weinstock sits behind a large desk in the corner of a modestly sized room grilling his managers over the phone on the financial ratios of their businesses. The sole concession to luxury is half a dozen paintings of Weinstock's beloved racehorses; the only reading matter on his desk to lighten the wadges of financial data is a racing newspaper offering tips on the latest form.

In the mid-1980s Weinstock came under fire for what appeared to outsiders as creeping stagnation within G.E.C. He seemed content to let the company tick over, sitting on G.E.C.'s cash pile of more than £1 billion. What few people realized at the time, however, was that he was already pushing ahead with the strategy which was to flourish in a string of major deals in the second half of the decade. G.E.C. was to spin off some of its most important subsidiaries into joint ventures with other large companies, keeping either controlling or large minority stakes in the resulting operations.

G.E.C.'s managing director saw de-mergers of his businesses as an alternative to pressure from the City and the media for growth. He had come to the view that the commandment to grow continuously – which is fundamental to the way in which the City polices British business – was incoherent:

> Since the economy cannot grow at anything like the rate the G.E.C. has grown over the last twenty years, how is it possible to expect that we can just get larger and larger? Is that logical? I've always thought that can't be our ultimate fate – just to get larger and larger, and therefore more unmanageable. A more logical way of thinking is that some things become large enough not to be part of us. It's more than ten years since I started thinking about de-mergers.

As Weinstock watched Sugar's progress, he began to think about Amstrad as a possible vehicle for de-merging some G.E.C. businesses. Looking back, he describes why he was drawn to Sugar: 'He has a talent which is not usually found in big electrical companies – his nose for the market. He has courage and nerve. He has commercial flair. He is young and independent. He has built up his business himself. I felt that we could harness that energy and those talents.'

In those days G.E.C. and Amstrad had little in common beyond the fact that they shared Touche Ross as auditors. Weinstock made discreet enquiries through the Touche Ross network about this relative newcomer to the British corporate scene, liked what he heard and so invited Sugar to Stanhope Gate.

G.E.C.'s managing director and Amstrad's chairman hit it off at once. Weinstock, the son of a Jewish immigrant tailor, had begun his career in industry by working in the old Sobell television and radio company, later to merge with G.E.C. He charmed Sugar by reminiscing about the little Polish engineer who used to design television sets for him at Sobell, talking about those times as the good old days by comparison with the present when he was stuck in his office crunching numbers. The chat over, Weinstock got down to business and the two men discussed possible avenues for cooperation between their companies.

After this initial meeting, Sugar phoned Howard Myles in the corporate finance department of his brokers, W. Greenwell. He explained to Myles the drift of his conversation with Weinstock and asked him to draw up a paper outlining options for partnership with G.E.C. Bound by Sugar to strict secrecy, Myles was forbidden to show the paper even to colleagues within Greenwell.

Two main options emerged. The first would have meant G.E.C. spinning off its consumer products businesses into a company run by Amstrad. The second would have entailed G.E.C. taking over the whole of Amstrad and absorbing Sugar into the G.E.C. organization.

It was the first option – a form of joint venture between Amstrad and G.E.C. – which received the more serious consideration. Amstrad would have taken over G.E.C.'s 'white goods' operations, one of the few parts of the company which manufactures products for sale in the high street. They were centred on Hotpoint, consistently one of the U.K. market leaders in products such as washing machines, refrigerators, tumble driers and dishwashers, but also included a number of other businesses. At the time of the talks, G.E.C.'s white goods business had sales of about £300 million – similar to those of Amstrad – but its profits of £30 million were substantially below those of Sugar's company. In return for acquiring a package of G.E.C. assets, Amstrad would have issued new shares to G.E.C., giving it a minority stake in the enlarged

Amstrad operation. Sugar would have run the new business, but he would have drawn on advice and other support from G.E.C.

Weinstock explains how he saw the deal:

Sugar seemed to me a way of de-merging our consumer products business. There was no reason why we should have taken him over unless that made managerial sense. There was more reason for him to run our consumer operations. We would have kept an interest. He could have been a part of G.E.C. but a part separated from the rest. He would have been the boss of what he was doing, but we would have been watching him and helping him.

The joint venture held out other, less tangible benefits for G.E.C. which, unusually for an electronics company of its size, lacked a consumer electronics wing. It had held back from involvement with personal computers, while pulling out of television manufacturing after an unsuccessful collaboration with Hitachi. Weinstock was aware that some of G.E.C.'s main rivals, such as Thomson of France, were immersing themselves more deeply in consumer electronics. Many people believed that new consumer electronics products, like high-definition television, would provide much of the growth in the electronics sector in the 1990s. Partnership with Amstrad would have furnished G.E.C. with a ready-made launching pad into this business.

The discussions about a G.E.C.-Amstrad partnership raised an even more delicate issue – Alan Sugar's standing as a possible successor to Weinstock. There was no obvious heir apparent within G.E.C., and Sugar would have brought a quality many observers believed lacking in Weinstock's empire: marketing flair to complement G.E.C.'s technical, financial and manufacturing strengths.

Both Sugar and Weinstock were later to play down the suggestion that Sugar's suitability for the top G.E.C. post was a significant feature of the talks. Yet a deal between G.E.C. and Amstrad would have been interpreted by the outside world as a sign that Sugar was a candidate to succeed Weinstock. The option of G.E.C. taking over Amstrad would have raised the issue most starkly: Sugar's position within G.E.C. would have had to be clarified. Yet the joint venture option also posed the question of Sugar's role, albeit in more submerged form, since the joint venture would have been seen as a half-way stage. Many outside commentators would have expected Sugar to be drawn further into G.E.C. if he made a success of running the company's white goods operations.

Some of Weinstock's confidants expressed doubts. Within G.E.C.'s most senior councils, Sugar was described as 'strong medicine' – an entrepreneur who was used to running his own company in precisely the way he pleased. Amstrad's boss would have been coming into a large organization with established procedures and would have had to learn the importance of personal relationships in a big company – the necessity to deal tactfully with people who might be manifestly less competent than himself. In short, he would have had to learn patience, a quality which Weinstock himself had acquired only with some difficulty. Indeed, some said that two such strong-willed characters as Sugar and Weinstock would have found it hard to work together: even an organization as large as G.E.C. was big enough for only one of them.

In the end, the Amstrad-G.E.C. talks foundered on more mundane matters. Initially both sides thought there was the making of a joint venture deal. Discussions advanced – though not to the stage of drawing up a draft agreement, because a price could not be agreed. Sugar thought he was being asked to pay too much for acquiring G.E.C.'s white goods operations, although the talks did not get as far as determining precisely which G.E.C. subsidiaries would be included in the package.

As Sugar remembers it, G.E.C. wanted a premium price for its assets, as if it had been selling them in a normal commercial deal. But Sugar did not see it as a normal commercial deal; he was not happy even about basing the price on asset values, as he explains:

> G.E.C. wanted to value Hotpoint not only on the basis of its net asset value, but also as if we were buying it as a proper takeover.

So there would have been a big premium. But I said to them, 'All the Hotpoint plant and equipment is not worth two bob if we stop the production. I might go in there and say that I don't like the way you make motors. I might think I can go to Korea and get motors made at a quarter of the price, which will allow us to bump up Hotpoint's profits. But to do that I've got to shut the motor plant down and then all these so-called assets would be worth nothing.'

Sugar's caution during the G.E.C. talks reflected a deeper reluctance on his part to become involved in corporate deals. He was suspicious of anything that would divert his energies from his prime task of developing Amstrad's products and selling them for all they were worth. In this, Amstrad was untypical of the 1980s. Sugar stayed clear of the City's game of buying and selling companies for ever more inflated prices.

Many corporate stars of the 1980s grew big by gobbling up other companies. Until the stock market crash of October 1987, share prices appeared to be on a gravity-defying upward spiral. In this heady climate, companies were able to launch mega-bids based on paper offers by promising to pay for their victims with new shares issued at bull market prices. It was a game which kept hundreds of advisers in lucrative employment in the City, but it was not a game that Sugar chose to play. For a start, Amstrad's shares rarely traded at inflated prices; indeed, their value often struggled to keep pace with the company's spectacular performance, partly due to the City's perennial nervousness about Amstrad. Moreover, Sugar could have entered the takeover game only on penalty of substantially diluting his controlling stake in Amstrad.

Indeed, Sugar was reluctant to change any aspect of his strategy in order to please the City. In 1984 and 1985, for example, as Amstrad's profits mounted, his financial advisers badgered him to boost the amount of money paid out as dividends to Amstrad's shareholders. True, dividends had gone up, but nowhere nearly as rapidly as profits. W. Greenwell, Amstrad's brokers, thought more generous dividends would reassure the company's critics in the

City. Howard Myles was invited to put Greenwell's case to an Amstrad board meeting. But Sugar argued strongly against allowing cash to seep out of the company in higher dividends, pouring scorn on the idea that City investors would begin to treat Amstrad's shares as a safe haven to be held through good times and bad if dividends were increased. Unsurprisingly, the Amstrad chairman won the day at the board meeting. It was a nice example of Sugar acting against his own narrow self-interest: holding almost 50 per cent of Amstrad's shares, he would have been by far the largest beneficiary of a more generous dividend policy.

Sugar was not averse to acquisitions if they fitted clearly into Amstrad's existing business activities, however. The first such acquisition was of a minnow. In May 1984, just as it was entering the home computer business, Amstrad issued 250,000 shares (then worth about £240,000) to buy Lyons-Turner Enterprises, a wholesaler based near Stoke-on-Trent in the Midlands which specialized in distributing goods to independent electrical retailers. Barely noticed at the time, the acquisition was to bear important fruit in the evolution of Amstrad's computer strategy later in the decade.

Four months later, in September 1984, Amstrad considered buying Fidelity, the hi-fi and television manufacturer. During the 1970s, when the two firms had shared a sub-contractor in L. & N. of Rochester, Fidelity had been the larger company with the more powerful brand name. But it had lost its way in the early 1980s. The Citizen's Band radio episode was symptomatic of the differences in fortunes: while Amstrad was nimbly entering and exiting the market, Fidelity was caught with £700,000 of unsaleable CB stock.

On 4 September 1984, a £13.5 million takeover bid for Fidelity was unveiled by Caparo Industries. Caparo is an industrial holding company run by Swraj Paul, Indian by origin and one-time confidant of Indira Gandhi, India's late premier. Paul has moved easily between the business worlds of Britain and the Indian sub-continent ever since coming to London from Calcutta in the late 1960s. In 1984, he was keen to diversify out of Caparo's base in engineering, steel, tea and property into the higher tech market of consumer electronics.

Sugar was interested in acquiring Fidelity's customer base and possibly also its factory in West London. A week after Caparo's bid, on 10 September, Amstrad announced that it had had informal contact with Fidelity and might launch a rival bid. Behind the scenes, however, Sugar was fully aware that Fidelity had run into problems with its production of televisions and cordless phones. Privately, a large institutional investor in Amstrad contacted Sugar to warn him to be wary: he had heard through the City grapevine that Fidelity was a can of worms. Three days later, on 13 September, Amstrad pulled out of the contest for Fidelity. Sugar explained that the latter's customer base was too similar to his own and that Amstrad's need for extra manufacturing capacity would be met by a further expansion of the Shoeburyness factory.

With Amstrad bowing out, Caparo bought Fidelity later that month by raising its bid to £14.1 million, but Swraj Paul soon came to regret his victory. In July 1985, Caparo Industries issued writs against two former Fidelity directors and Touche Ross, its former auditors. Caparo was seeking damages to cover losses estimated at more than £10 million arising from alleged over-statement of profits and stock values at the time of the acquisition. Swraj Paul spent the following three years in a losing struggle to make a go of Fidelity.

A similar episode occurred – although over an even shorter time-scale – in June 1987 when Thorn E.M.I., the large British conglomerate, sold its Ferguson television subsidiary to Thomson of France for £90 million. In the face of the onslaught from the giant Japanese television manufacturers, Thorn had decided to cut its links with Ferguson, the last substantial British-owned tele-vision maker. At the time of the sale, Ferguson was the largest player in the fragmented British television market, with a share of about 10 per cent. It had made almost 700,000 sets in 1986; it employed over 4,000 people, mainly at two factories in North London and Hampshire; it had a one-third stake in a joint venture with Thomson and Japan's JVC, making around 900,000 video recorders a year in plants in Britain, France and West Germany; and it had sales of about £300 million in the 1986–87 financial year. In short, Ferguson was a substantial force in British consumer electronics.

Thorn's sale of Ferguson to Thomson was announced on Thursday 18 June 1987. Alan Sugar was out of touch with the news for a crucial twenty-four hours and when he heard about the deal late on Friday evening, he was not amused. He immediately phoned the *Financial Times* to vent his displeasure. An *FT* reporter phoned him back, but communication was not at its smoothest because the Amstrad chairman was on a mobile phone which kept cutting out. By dint of repeated re-diallings and ten-second-long snatches of conversation, the reporter pieced together Sugar's concern: he was interested in both Ferguson's market share and its manufacturing plants. Although he had not yet studied the figures in detail, he would consider a counter bid. Amstrad could draw on its own cash pile to match Thomson's £90 million offer, unlike the French company which was having to borrow £40 million from the banks for the purpose. Moreover, Amstrad would try to stop the deal by complaining to the European Commission that it was anti-competitive, because Thomson would totally dominate the European television market with Philips, the Dutch multinational.

Sugar was angry that a British company had not been given the chance to bid for Ferguson. Describing the deal as 'a bit naff,' he told the *FT*, 'I just don't understand why they didn't approach us,' adding that Thorn had committed 'a dead diabolical liberty in not offering its Ferguson to us'.

The Thorn-Thomson deal was in fact too advanced to be unwound. Sugar met Thorn executives the following week, but the company was determined to sell Ferguson to Thomson, its erstwhile partner in the video recorder joint venture 'The time frame just didn't allow for us to interrupt. It was too far down the line,' Amstrad stated when it withdrew from the fray.

Ferguson, Fidelity, Lyons-Turner Enterprises, together with the acquisition of Sinclair's computer business in 1986 – all fitted into a pattern. They were opportunities for Amstrad to build up its existing operations through buying market share, acquiring brands, adding to its manufacturing capacity or developing its distribution capabilities. None remotely followed the mid-1980s fashion for radical diversification.

Amstrad was tempted to abandon this cautious attitude to diversification on only three occasions. The first was during the ultimately abortive negotiations with G.E.C. The second occurred when Sugar looked seriously at refrigerators and washing machines, an interest in white goods which had been sparked off by the G.E.C. talks. By May 1986 he was sufficiently confident to say publicly, 'It is absolutely firm that we will go into white goods – it is only a question of when. We are studying the market very carefully.'

At first sight, white goods such as refrigerators and washing machines were an obvious business for Amstrad to contemplate. Their similarity to traditional Amstrad activities like hi-fi seemed close; both were consumer ranges sold in the high street and many of Amstrad's oldest customers, including Comet and Currys, were important white goods retailers.

However, difficulties emerged as Sugar looked more closely at the white goods industry. One was precisely how Amstrad would enter the business. He had no intention of building his own manufacturing plant, not least because the sector was suffering from considerable over-capacity. The Far East was ruled out as a manufacturing base because it was not economic to ship bulky, low-margin products like fridges half-way round the world. The alternative seemed to be a link-up with an existing European manufacturer and Sugar talked about sub-contracting manufacture to an existing player. He considered buying a small producer in France, Spain or Italy, and in 1986 he had preliminary talks with Thorn E.M.I. about buying its domestic appliance businesses which included the Tricity, Bendix and Parkinson Cowan brands. Nothing gelled.

Devising a marketing strategy for white goods posed an even more fundamental problem. Sugar's initial plan was to make such goods more like consumer electronics. Refrigerators and washing machines are not technology-drive, fashion-conscious items such as stereo sets or home computers; people buy fridges and washing machines out of necessity, not in order to own the latest model.

Sugar intended to change these entrenched buying patterns. 'The trouble is that at the moment nobody buys a fridge until the door falls off. The challenge is to turn it into something desirable, so that when the wife walks down the street she says, "I want that one,"' he said at the time.

The strategy made sense; the difficulty lay in executing it. Amstrad hunted around for features which would transform the humble washing machine or fridge into a product which consumers would change every three years or so – without at the same time boosting prices beyond the reach of its traditional customers. This was to prove a fruitless search, as Sugar explains: 'When we realized that what we were talking about there were very, very bulky products at low margins, we decided we had no interest whatsoever. We could see no way of applying the Amstrad effect – of revolutionizing them, of putting features on them that would put us a cut above the rest of the industry.'

The third time Amstrad was tempted into radical diversification was when it considered launching a hostile bid for Thorn E.M.I. One of the big four of British electronics, along with G.E.C., S.T.C. and Plessey, Thorn had been built up by an émigré businessman, Sir Jules Thorn, with many of the same swashbuckling entrepreneurial qualities as Sugar. But the company had drifted after Thorn's departure, failing to make the transition from his individualistic and proprietorial style of management into a smooth-running, professionally organized multinational. In the first half of the 1980s a new chairman, Peter Laister, had evolved a vision of Thorn as an integrated communications and entertainment business. It would finance films and videos at one end of the production stream, make the televisions and video recorders on which they would appear and then distribute the materials through its own cinemas or shops. Pursuing vertical integration to its logical conclusion, Thorn even moved into chip manufacturing by buying the Inmos semiconductor company. Unfortunately, the grandiose vision was not matched by attention to details and Laister was abruptly removed by a board-room putsch in July 1985 after a sharp drop in the group's profits.

After Laister's departure, Thorn was almost crying out for dismemberment; it had accumulated a ragbag of businesses which would be worth more on their own than as part of the sprawling Thorn empire. With Amstrad's share price riding high in 1986, Sugar cast an eye over the Thorn portfolio, asking his financial advisers to consider a bid. 'The idea at that stage was to break it up and keep the good bits,' he says.

Amstrad's interest in Thorn, which was never publicly announced, did not get past the drawing board. Thorn seemed too big a morsel to swallow: its £3 billion turnover was then ten times that of Amstrad's. 'It was too much of a David and Goliath job,' Sugar says.

In the event, Thorn's new top management began their own piecemeal dismemberment of the group, selling off parts peripheral to its new strategy including the Ferguson television business. With hindsight, Sugar is relieved that Amstrad did not push its interest in Thorn further:

> It would have been a terrible thing, because the problem with Thorn was bad management. And it was really like the pot calling the kettle black because we had no spare managers whatsoever. One of the things about big acquisitions is you've got to have spare brain power. You have to be able to say to your managers, 'Right, we've just acquired that big thing over there. You're in charge of it. Off you go, old boy.' We hadn't really got enough of those people at the time to look after our own business.

Casting an eye over Thorn was one of several symptoms of a period of introspection within Amstrad in 1986 and early 1987. The company had managed a spectacular entry into computers by successfully launching its own products and buying the Sinclair brand. What would it do next? The link-up with G.E.C., the examination of white goods, a bid for Thorn – all reflected Sugar's restless search for the next great leap forward. To introduce order into this process, Amstrad called in the Boston Consulting Group, one of the world's most prestigious firms of management consultants, to advise on future strategy. The kind of action which only a couple of years previously would have cut right across the grain of Amstrad culture, it was one of the first signs that Amstrad was aware of the need to evolve large-company procedures. However, the arrival of the management consultants coincided with the end of the period of uncertainty among their clients.

Sugar cut short the consultants' stay in Brentwood, because they seemed to be echoing what he had already decided. Amstrad would not branch out on to some totally new path. It would stay with what it knew. It would grow organically, from within. It would stick to its knitting.

· 12 ·

Taking on Big Blue

After the successful launch of the word processor in 1985, it became increasingly clear that Amstrad's future lay with computers. In the second half of 1985 Sugar mulled over what product should be introduced to follow the word processor. The options narrowed down to one: Amstrad would attack head-on the largest slice of the personal computer market – that dominated by I.B.M., the world's biggest computer company known throughout the business as 'Big Blue'.

I.B.M. was slow to wake up to the personal computer. During the late 1970s, it watched from the sidelines as Apple and a host of other entrepreneurial companies pioneered the desktop revolution in the United States. Many of Big Blue's most powerful bureaucrats argued that I.B.M. should ignore this upstart industry in favour of what it knew best – selling its huge mainframe computers. By the beginning of the 1980s, however, even highly conservative I.B.M. had realized that personal computers were not a temporary fad. As the computing power which could be stacked onto desktops steadily increased, personal computers would inevitably become central to the computing strategy of all business users.

In July 1980, I.B.M. surrendered to this infant technology by appointing an internal design team, which broke every rule in the I.B.M. book in order to meet its one-year deadline for creating the I.B.M. Personal Computer. Many of the parts for the machine were made by outside contractors rather than in I.B.M.'s own factories; responsibility for the operating system was sub-contracted to Microsoft, a small software company led by a 25-year-old software wizard, Bill Gates. The MS-DOS operating system, written by Microsoft for the I.B.M. PC, was to make Gates a billionaire by the time he was 30. Belying its deepest instincts, I.B.M. gave its PC an 'open architecture'. Instead of keeping details of the circuitry and operating system secret, they were released to the world or, more precisely, to software companies which were encouraged to write business software for it. In that way, business users could be assured that they would find dozens of practical business applications to run on the I.B.M. PC.

The I.B.M. Personal Computer, launched in August 1981, transformed the industry. The machine succeeded not because it was particularly innovative – many computer experts continued to prefer the rival offerings from Apple – but because it came with I.B.M.'s imprimatur. Before the company's entry into the market, many data processing managers would not have been seen dead with a personal computer; the new contraptions were fine for hobbyists, but were despised by the professionals who controlled the computer purchases of large corporations. I.B.M. changed all that. If Big Blue said personal computers were respectable, then they *must* be. The oldest cliché in the industry – that no one was ever fired for ordering I.B.M. – began to weave its magic.

I.B.M. sold 156,000 personal computers in 1982, 455,000 in 1983 and almost two million in 1984, according to market research specialists Dataquest. Four years after the launch of its PC, it was raking in annual revenues of $4 billion from its personal computer division – enough to have ranked the division as the 74th largest corporation in the United States if it had been a free-standing company. This phenomenal take-off exceeded the wildest hopes of the PC's champions within I.B.M. and, crucially, it also helped to introduce order into the personal computer market. The I.B.M. PC, together with its MS-DOS operating system, became the *de facto* standard in the industry. Apple was the only significant computer company to hold out against this encroaching uniformity.

The computer industry seemed to be returning to a *status quo* which it understood: I.B.M. was king again. But this was to reckon without the birth of a new species of computer, the clone. The open architecture of the I.B.M. PC made it easy to copy. Electronic entrepreneurs dotted around the United States began to design computers which were compatible with it but could be made in the Far East for a fraction of I.B.M.'s costs. A new clutch of computer companies was spawned on the back of these clones, which steadily eroded I.B.M.'s market share to the extent that in 1985, sales of I.B.M.-compatibles overtook those of I.B.M.'s own personal computers.

But the early clone wars were mainly fought in North America. I.B.M. did not launch its PC in Europe until early 1983, and at that time most of the successful U.S. clone companies lacked the resources or the expertise to tackle the European market. It was this vacuum in the European market – low-cost I.B.M.-compatibles – which Amstrad set out to fill.

Building an I.B.M.-compatible computer made sense to Amstrad for an additional reason. Soon after the launch of the PCW8256, it became clear that the word processor's overseas sales would not match those in Britain. The PCW8256 was perceived in the United States as a not particularly powerful CP/M-based personal computer, and Amstrad was too small a player there to educate the public into viewing it as a dedicated word processor. A similar fate befell the PCW8256 in West Germany, although there the fault lay partly with Amstrad's agents, Schneider, which promoted the machine as a personal computer and not a word processor, giving it a price tag to match. Unsurprisingly, the word processor did not take off in Germany as it had in Britain.

Whatever the reason for the word processor's relative failure overseas, demands for a new flagship Amstrad product soon began to flood into the company's headquarters from its foreign operations. Sugar recalls: 'We were mainly stimulated by our overseas dealers. They kept saying, "O.K., the CPC is very good, we have the Joyce, but now we want an I.B.M.-compatible." I said to them, "Sell the bloody word processor." And they replied, "No, no, no, we can't sell that. We want an I.B.M.-compatible."'

In the early autumn of 1985 the specification was agreed for

Amstrad's I.B.M.-compatible computer, named the PC1512 – P(ersonal) C(omputer) and 512 after the memory size. Amstrad insiders took to calling the project the Airo (Amstrad's I.B.M. Rip-Off), though it was not a code-name that ever gained the currency which Joyce enjoyed.

In fact, Amstrad went out of its way to ensure that its machine did not copy the I.B.M., since it knew how litigious Big Blue could be; it checked that the PC1512's keyboard layout and keyboard-computer connections differed from those on the I.B.M. MEJ Electronics was given the task of writing the BIOS – the basic input/output system, a key part of the operating system which controls communications between the central processor and peripherals such as disk drives and keyboard. Locomotive Software was originally asked to write the BIOS, but declined because it feared litigation from I.B.M. Mej located the BIOS in ROM (read only memory) – hence its alternative name of ROS (ROM operating system). Slipping easily into boffin language, Alan Sugar later described to *PC User* magazine the steps taken to ensure that Amstrad's ROS did not infringe I.B.M. patents:

> The ROS has been designed and engineered with no reference to the I.B.M. machine. It has been audited by lawyers in the U.S. and the U.K., and the writers of the ROS have been divorced from any I.B.M. ROS, and were just given a specification of what they had to do. We are quite happy that the independent auditors have compared our ROS with [the] I.B.M. [ROS] and that there is no similarity whatsoever. Also our cabinet is totally different.

At the start of the project, Bob Watkins opened up an I.B.M. PC in order to look at the machine which Amstrad was planning to emulate. The technical director was amazed by what he found, as he recalls:

> I looked inside an I.B.M. PC and saw hundreds and hundreds of components. In our previous products, we'd designed our own gate arrays and I just couldn't understand why I.B.M.

hadn't. There were these discrete devices all over the place and not one custom device in the whole bloody thing. It had massive boards stuffed full of chips. So we thought we can save a lot of money here by designing our own gate arrays.

The design was constrained by the need to be compatible with I.B.M. technology. As a result, MEJ Electronics did not achieve quite the same level of integration as it had with the word processor. Nevertheless, it managed to design Amstrad's first I.B.M.-compatible using only three gate arrays, each replacing dozens of components in the I.B.M. computer. Amstrad was keen to repeat the word processor's winning formula of running as many features as possible off the computer's main printed circuit board, so Mej built into the machine many of the features that had to be bought as add-on expansion cards for the I.B.M. PC.

Otherwise, Amstrad kept the cost low by its old tricks. It ordered parts in very large numbers; it priced its machine according to cost, not according to what the market would bear; and it took a cold look at what was really essential to a successful personal computer. Amstrad's computers, for example, were encased in plastic, unlike I.B.M.'s which came in metal. Sugar believes that a machine does not need to be gold-plated if it is designed for the mass market:

There's two ways of designing a product. You either design for the military or you design for the mass market. Now a guy at I.B.M. would not think of using a keyboard with printed legends on the key caps. He wants the legends on the keycaps engraved in by a double moulding process. That means his keyboard is going to be £25, whereas ours will cost three quid. The difference between our keyboard and his is that in n years time the letters on our keyboard may rub off a little bit. But our philosophy is that after three years or so, you can buy another one which will be better and cheaper.

Since Amstrad was entering the I.B.M.-compatible world, it needed standard software to run on the PC1512. It tried to buy a version of MS-DOS from Microsoft, but the American software company wanted to charge an un-Amstrad-like price for its best-selling operating system. So Amstrad turned to Digital Research, whose software had been closely associated with the company's CPC series and its word processor.

Digital Research's Paul Bailey was shown a prototype of the PC1512. He viewed it as the first real opportunity to create a mass market in business software in Europe, as he recalls: 'We were very excited about it. We thought that at the time it was extremely innovative to come in with a sub-£1,000 I.B.M.-compatible. Today, it looks routine, but in 1986 it was pretty revolutionary.'

Bailey agreed to supply Digital Research's DOS-Plus operating system for Amstrad's personal computer. DOS-Plus was a belated attempt to catch up with the lead Microsoft had stolen by supplying MS-DOS to I.B.M. Essentially it was a clone of Microsoft's famous operating system, capable of emulating most – but, crucially, not quite all – of the capabilities of MS-DOS. Digital Research was happy to supply Amstrad with DOS-Plus at an aggressive price, because it saw Amstrad as one of its last chances to become established in the I.B.M.-compatible personal computer operating system market.

Digital Research was also commissioned to adapt its Gem (Graphics Environmental Manager) software for the Amstrad personal computer. Gem allows many of the graphics-based features pioneered by Apple – like windows and icons – to be replicated on other computers. Gem also makes a computer look attractively easy to use when it is running in a shop window, so it was a natural addition to the Amstrad armoury.

Digital Research was convinced that it could piggy-back huge sales of its software on the PC1512 and came out with a range of cheap business software programs adapted for Gem on the Amstrad machine. Bailey recalls that Digital Research was not disappointed: 'It was a big launch for the Gem concept in the U.K. We got behind the Amstrad launch in a very big way. It probably did more for Gem than almost any other initiative in those days.'

Yet Amstrad still hankered after MS-DOS for its computer. Sugar realized that anything less than Microsoft's operating system would be unacceptable to many I.B.M.-compatible users, particularly in North America. Amstrad managed to set alarm bells ringing at Microsoft by convincing the American company that Amstrad's computer really was set to take the European market by storm. This was a sales opportunity which even the mighty Microsoft could not ignore. Shortly before the launch of the PC1512, Microsoft dropped its price and Amstrad was able to announce that its machine would run both operating systems, MS-DOS and DOS-Plus.

In early 1986 it was *the* open secret among computer industry watchers in Britain that Amstrad was working on an I.B.M.-compatible. The September launch took the razzmatazz of Amstrad's previous launches to new heights. A pair of giant red lips spelt out the range's specification on a huge electronic screen in front of 900 journalists, distributors, City folk and other pundits assembled in the Queen Elizabeth Conference Centre in central London. Asked to compute the cost of Amstrad's machine, the lips suggested a figure of £1,700, but added as an afterthought, 'Only one person in the galaxy knows the true price.' Enter Alan Sugar.

Sugar unveiled eight machines in the PC1512 range. The least expensive, at £399 plus VAT, had 512k of memory and a single floppy disk drive. The most expensive, a colour machine with a 20 megabyte hard disk, cost £949 plus VAT. The cheapest I.B.M. personal computer at the time sold to corporate clients in Europe for £1,429, although one computer reviewer argued that the nearest equivalent I.B.M. cost over £4,000.

Amstrad's chairman was in confident mood at the launch and, in a bid to generate momentum for his new computer among retailers and dealers, he released bullish sales forecasts – forecasts which were to return to haunt him. He stated that production of the new machines in the Far East would build up to 70,000 a month almost immediately, and could increase to 100,000 a month early in 1987. He aimed to sell 300,000 by the end of 1986 and 800,000 in a full year, over half outside Britain.

Many specialist commentators contributed to the euphoria.

Computer journalist John Lettice, writing in the *Observer*, said that the Amstrad stood out from the crowd not just because of its price, but also because of what users would get for their money: free software, built-in devices for communicating with printers and other computers, a mouse pointing device and so on. The *Guardian*'s reviewer, noting that Amstrad's Intel 8086 microprocessor made it faster than the I.B.M. PC, concluded, 'While Amstrad is famous for cost cutting, the company has not skimped on the PC1512's performance.' Guy Kewney's five-page bench-test for *Personal Computer World* was ecstatic: 'It goes faster than the I.B.M., it's smaller, has better onscreen colours, and includes functions which have to be added (and paid for) separately on normal I.B.M.-style machines.' *Which?* consumer magazine confirmed these specialist judgements in May 1987 by naming the PC1512 its personal computer best buy.

Amstrad backed the PC1512 with a massive and typically aggressive advertising campaign. 'Compatible with you know who. Priced as only we know how' was the slogan devised by Amstrad and Delaney Fletcher Delaney for the PC1512. The ads showed a whole Amstrad as being equivalent to half an I.B.M., and even less of an Olivetti and Compaq. Fearing trouble from I.T.C.A., the television advertising watchdogs, Peter Horrell – Amstrad account director at the advertising agency – bought I.B.M., Olivetti and Compaq machines and used a laser cutter to slice them in precise ratios according to price. 'That ad took a lot of pre-planning to set up. We had to demonstrate that we were comparing like with like in terms of the machines' specifications. If anything, we were over-generous to the competition,' Horrell recalls.

Yet the PC1512 soon ran into a barrage of bad publicity which dogged the computer for the rest of 1986. The first and most serious allegation was that the PC1512 overheated because it lacked a fan. In mid-October, the *Sunday Times* published an article reporting that chemicals giant I.C.I. had decided against buying the Amstrad computer. The *Sunday Times* attributed this 'decision' to fears that the PC1512 could prove unreliable when used continuously on a computer network. It also quoted Mike Shingler, supposedly an adviser to I.C.I. on computer purchases, as saying that lack of space and ventilation inside the Amstrad cabinet could cause overheating.

The *Sunday Times* report was followed by a deluge of rumours in the computer trade press about overheating and other problems with the PC1512. Part of the difficulty seemed to stem from the fact that, unlike other computer manufacturers, Amstrad had placed its power supply in the monitor, thereby removing any need for a fan in the computer's system unit. Yet the more penetrating computer journalists also detected something amiss with these stories. Guy Kewney described how *PC Dealer* had been bombarded with tips about problems with the Amstrad from hushed informers: a leading distributor had returned its first batch of 1512s because they were all faulty, 'the keyboard will wear out within three months', and so on. On checking, these tips turned out to be bogus. The computer magazine *Microscope* blew the gaffe in late October, when it reported that individual I.B.M. salesmen had been spreading rumours among computer dealers about overheating Amstrads. 'We were told that I.C.I. tested out the Amstrad with a token ring (networking) card and that the casing started to melt,' one I.B.M. dealer told *Microscope*.

Alan Sugar was in understandably angry mood when he flew back from the Far East in the last week of October to confront these rumours. He compared the behaviour of salesmen working for some large personal computer companies unfavourably with his experience at the cut-throat end of the audio market: 'When I was competing against 40 other small-time dealers, similar to myself, who'd kill their grandmothers in order to beat me to a deal . . . these dirty tricks and lies were never thrown at us.'

The Amstrad boss was particularly incensed because the reliability of the CPC range and the PCW8256 had been important to their success: fault rates for the CPC464, Amstrad's first computer, had been notably low in the days when home computer manufacturers were a byword for poor quality. Sugar was affronted at the implication that Amstrad had failed to carry out elementary quality testing of its machines: 'We've been in the business, in hi-fi, for twenty years. We have environmental chambers. We stimulate the worst conditions in the field – drop tests, heating tests, pissing-on-it tests, you name it,' he told *PC Dealer*.

Indeed, the original *Sunday Times* report was quickly shown to be wide of the truth when I.C.I. stated that it was in the middle of lengthy tests of the PC1512, and that the executive quoted in the article had no authority to speak on its behalf on this subject. In January 1987, after completing the tests, I.C.I. wrote an open letter to Amstrad which said: 'During the trials no problems were experienced with overheating when the Amstrad PC was connected to a token ring network. The Amstrad PC1512 has now been approved for purchase by I.C.I. operating units.'

Another charge thrown at Amstrad was that it was almost impossible to buy one of the now famous PC1512s. This complaint was nearer the mark for initial demand exceeded Amstrad's most optimistic projections. Indeed, in late October Amstrad felt confident enough to announce a 12.5 per cent price increase on the PC1512, blaming this on the rising value of the yen – the currency in which many of its supplies were purchased. One dealer told *Microscope* magazine of people placing orders for the Amstrad over the phone without bothering to look at the machine. 'I'd say it's cut demand for the Olivetti by at least 50 per cent. Apart from anything else, the poor bastards who want Olivettis can't get through because the lines are jammed by people calling about the Amstrad,' he said.

Just as important, the pattern of demand differed from Amstrad's expectations. Since its computers were so cheap, many customers ordered the top-of-the-range, hard disk machines. Amstrad had expected hard disk sales to account for up to 10 per cent of demand, but they were running initially at nearer 35 per cent. Sugar made a rapid sweep through Taiwan, Singapore and Japan in the second half of October in a vain bid to find additional supplies of hard disks.

In early November Sugar took the opportunity of an interview with the *Financial Times* to announce how he planned to deal with both the hard disk and the overheating problems. Amstrad would be shifting the mix of its range towards the more expensive, hard disk machines; this shift was possible because it had placed orders for the disks with Tandon and for the control mechanisms with Western Digital, two suppliers based in the United States. Although still vigorously denying that his computers overheated, Sugar had decided to put a fan into all Amstrad's hard disk machines in a bid to kill the overheating rumours. In what was to become his classic statement of the customer-is-always-right principle, the Amstrad chairman told the startled journalist:

> I'm a realistic person and we are a marketing organization, so if it's the difference between people buying the machine or not, I'll stick a bloody fan in it.
>
> And if they say they want bright pink spots on it, I'll do that too.
>
> What is the use of me banging my head against a brick wall and saying, 'You don't need the damn fan, sunshine'?

Shortly after these comments were published, pink spots appeared on computers in the most surprising places, reportedly even in Amstrad's headquarters. The staff of one computer magazine came in to work to find its computers covered in pink spots, together with a little label: 'Congratulations, your computer has been upgraded to Amstrad compatibility.'

Sugar's swift reaction dampened down the rumours, but did not manage to kill them entirely. Questions about the PC1512's reliability continued to appear in print into 1987, and were immediately met by threats of legal action from Amstrad. Libel writs from Amstrad forced several prominent organizations to make humiliating retractions of statements made in their name about Amstrad's computer, including the B.B.C. which apologized unreservedly for an article in its staff magazine which threw doubt on the PC1512's safety.

In the autumn of 1986 some pundits spotted a more fundamental problem in Amstrad's computer strategy, a problem which at first went almost unnoticed amidst all the froth about overheating machines. The PC1512 did not sell to large corporate customers as well as Amstrad had hoped. 'How well are your business sales going?' was later to become a query with which Alan Sugar was routinely confronted by journalists and City analysts. It was a question which irritated him because, as he pointed out, most of Amstrad's PC range was sold to people with VAT registrations – small business people or professionals working from home. Yet his answer could not entirely disguise the fact that Amstrad had expected to sell larger quantities to big corporations.

Some cautious computer buyers in the corporate sector had no doubt been frightened by the overheating publicity, while the more feeble were perhaps put off by Amstrad's lingering image as a low end audio company. The more technically minded pointed to the PC1512's lack of an EGA (Enhanced Graphics Adaptor) capability as a reason for not buying it. Soon after the launch of the PC1512, EGA became the industry-standard system for controlling the colour resolution on a personal computer screen. But the most important reason for Amstrad's difficulties in penetrating the corporate market was undoubtedly the way it actually sold its computers.

Amstrad's personal computers continued to shift in greatest numbers through chains like Dixons or Wilding, which served individual users or small businesses. By contrast, corporate purchasers were accustomed to buying either from specialist computer dealers or direct from a computer manufacturer's own sales force. Like some of its rivals, Amstrad did not have its own direct sales force, relying instead on specialist dealers for sales to professional buyers. Unfortunately, the inevitable corollary of Amstrad's low prices was tight margins for dealers: one estimate suggested that dealers made profits of about 12 per cent selling Amstrad's computers, as compared with approximately 30–40 per cent on rival machines. Crucially, the margins available to dealers on Amstrad computers made it difficult for them to offer corporate customers back-up consulting or repair services. Anticipating this problem, Amstrad arranged for a service company, Dictaphone, to offer maintenance contracts to users of Amstrad computers. Yet the fact remained that a package which was fine for small businesses and individual users – low prices, but minimal service – transferred awkwardly into the large corporate market where spending money for a hassle-free life was the norm. This was an issue which was to assume increasing importance as Amstrad's computers moved up-market.

Amstrad's critics dived for cover in February 1987 when the company announced its results for the six months to the end of December 1986 – reflecting the first burst of PC1512 sales. Profits advanced 159 per cent to £71.3 million, on sales up 112 per cent at £272.5 million. Amstrad shares closed 19p up on the day at 166p, adding £47 million to the value of Sugar's personal stake in the company. A cautious Lex note in the *Financial Times* pointed out that the company had far to fall if its 'prodigious run of marketing triumphs' was to end: only about 15 per cent of the £900 million price tag the City was then putting on Amstrad reflected tangible assets – the rest reflected 'goodwill', essentially the Amstrad brand name and the market's confidence in Sugar. 'The depressing thought is that ever bigger marketing coups are required just to keep up momentum,' Lex commented, before adding in an unusual burst of adulation, 'The less depressing thought is that the company is run by a marketer of genius.'

For the moment, Amstrad was riding high in City eyes. About 50 per cent was added to the company's share price between Christmas 1986 and February 1987, as investors heard the early news about PC1512 sales. Romtec, a microcomputer market research organization, reported that the PC1512 had shot to the top of Britain's personal computer market in December, the first month in which the machines were widely available. Amstrad accounted for 26 per cent of the personal computers sold through dealers in December, as compared with 25 per cent for I.B.M., the traditional market leader. This lead was even more substantial once allowance was made for high street sales, although the higher-priced I.B.M. was still comfortably ahead in terms of sales by value. Romtec confirmed that the PC1512 had achieved the 'Amstrad effect': Amstrad was expanding the overall market rather than eating into its competitors' sales, which in most cases had been largely unaffected. Despite the lower margins, dealers were bowing to the inevitable – selling Amstrads to customers who simply would not have bought a more costly machine.

Yet market reports by independent observers such as Romtec held a double-edged message for Amstrad as 1987 unfolded; they continued to confirm that Amstrad was leading the pack in Britain, but they also suggested that the company would not hit the ambitious sales targets announced by Sugar when launching the PC1512. The story was similar on the Continent: Amstrad was selling large volumes, but not large enough to reach its targets. It began to appear that Amstrad might be selling 'only' about 40,000 PC1512s a month – far short of the minimum of 70,000 a month predicted at the time of the launch.

By all normal standards this was still a phenomenal success, considering that Amstrad was new to the I.B.M.-compatible market. The trouble was that City analysts had based their forecasts on Sugar's launch volumes; they had heard the Amstrad chairman's predictions, estimated the margins, picked up their mobile phones and told their firms to buy Amstrad stock for all they were worth. When the truth began to emerge from Romtec and similar organizations, they hastily downgraded their forecasts, producing a sharp drop in Amstrad's share price. In the first three weeks of June 1987, Amstrad stock fell some 50p, knocking almost £300 million off the company's market value.

Relations between Amstrad and the City reached a new low when Chase Manhattan Securities slashed its profit forecast in early June. Chase had been one of the most bullish followers of Amstrad, talking up its profit forecast despite discreet warnings from Amstrad headquarters that it was becoming too enthusiastic.

Two events prompted Keith Woolcock, a young analyst with a colourful turn of phrase who was then at Chase, to drop his optimistic forecasts for Amstrad. First, a long phone conversation with a senior Amstrad executive convinced him that the company was selling nothing like 70,000 PC1512s a month. Second, he read a report in the *Financial Times* that Amstrad had just launched a new and more powerful personal computer, the PC1640, in the United States at the Comdex computer show in Atlanta, Georgia. The story quoted Alan Sugar as saying that the computer would not be launched in Europe until early in 1988. Woolcock recalls his reaction: 'I thought: "This is a heap of crap. He's lying." I reckoned he was going to launch the PC1640 in Britain too, and the only reason for doing so was because the PC1512 was not selling as well as expected.'

Immediately he read the *FT* article Woolcock changed his mind about Amstrad's prospects. 'I had one of my Pauline experiences. I stood up at our morning meeting and said, without a note, I'm cutting our forecast.'

No company welcomes a profits downgrading from a big City institution, but Woolcock rubbed salt in the wounds by publicly urging Amstrad to come clean with the City. He was quoted in the *Sunday Times* as likening Sugar to a Trappist monk who refuses to talk to anyone except to complain about his critics. On Channel 4 television, the young analyst urged Sugar to emulate the prophet Mohammed by coming down from his mountain to talk to the masses. Now Woolcock muses: 'Being a Jew, that probably didn't go down too well. He'd hit the City pretty hard and I thought he wouldn't mind some similar treatment. Alan Sugar isn't as thick-skinned as you'd think.'

The thickness of Sugar's skin became abundantly clear a week later when a letter arrived from Amstrad's solicitors threatening to sue Woolcock and Chase – a move believed to be without precedent even in the often fraught history of relations between quoted companies and the stockbroking fraternity. The letter accused Woolcock of libel and said that if Chase were to 'lie about Amstrad, or its associate companies, managers, products, perform-ance or sales figures in future, Amstrad will enforce its rights without notice. This is both a threat and a promise.'

More seriously still, Amstrad suggested that Chase had tried to manipulate the Amstrad share price. 'Sugar accused me of acting like a spiv. He said I'd had a profit forecast which was much too high and then cut it, having first squared our market makers book so we could make a tidy profit on it,' explains Woolcock, who insists that on the contrary Chase lost money as a result of his forecasts.

Chase's lawyers wrote back a terse letter rejecting the charges and Amstrad did not press the matter, but diplomatic relations with Chase were ruptured for some months. Woolcock next saw Sugar in November at Amstrad's annual general meeting. Held at the Waldorf hotel in central London, the gathering seemed to the young analyst to be full of private investors who worshipped the ground that Sugar stood on. ('I felt [as if] I was running against the bulls in Pamplona,' Woolcock recalls.) He sat next to a middle-aged woman in a blood-red dress, dripping with jewellery, who told Woolcock that Sugar had changed her life: she had bought her first shares after seeing him on television and now she was an avid stock market follower. Looking around, she said, 'Alan's done the same for a lot of people in this room.' ('Screw British Telecom: this really is popular capitalism,' thought Woolcock.)

When the meeting started, Sugar was asked why Amstrad's dividends had not increased as rapidly as its profits. The chairman leapt at the question as though it were sent from heaven. If he increased the dividend, he said, it would just attract the kind of institutional investors who ran for cover every time they received an ignorant note from some analyst. The private investors cheered, but Woolcock was beginning to feel distinctly nervous: 'I was shitting myself, expecting that any minute Sugar would point to me and say: "And that's the man who's been telling people to sell your shares."'

The year 1987 did nothing to improve Sugar's already low opinion of the City. 'There should be some professional exam for these analysts. Most of the time they talk through their backsides,' he said at the time. The scare stories about the PC1512's performance also reinforced his contempt for much of the specialist computer trade press. A chill descended on relations between them and Amstrad, which at best had been never more than lukewarm. For a time, many journalists were lucky to find anyone at Amstrad prepared to talk to them.

Why should Amstrad care? As far as Sugar was concerned, more reliable measures of his success in introducing the PC1512 could be found in Amstrad's results for the financial year 1986–87, released at the end of September 1987. Profits were up 80 per cent at £135.7 million; sales were up 68 per cent at £511.8 million; and profits as a percentage of sales were at an all-time Amstrad record of 26.5 per cent.

To underline the spread of its interests, Amstrad broke its results into two main groupings: leisure, including audio, video and home computers such as the Sinclair and CPC ranges; and business, including its word processors and I.B.M.-compatibles. Business products accounted for 54 per cent of sales in 1986–87, a sharp increase on the 38 per cent of turnover they had contributed the previous year. Another year and another metamorphosis in Amstrad's many lives: for the first time the company was making most of its money by selling equipment to small businesses and other professional users.

Just three years after launching its first computer, Amstrad had established four broad ranges: Sinclair, CPC, word processor and I.B.M.-compatible. Upgrades could now be slotted into these ranges without any fuss: the PC1640, with better graphics capability, was unveiled in June 1987, followed in November by the PCW9512, with its letter-quality printer and an improved version of the Locoscript word processing program.

After a year of buffeting from the media and the City, Sugar felt justified in a little crowing. The PC1512, he wrote in his chairman's statement,

> ... has revolutionized the so-called computer industry in the U.K. The 'Amstrad effect' of low price high volume production and marketing has taken the wind out of an industry cocooned in a sedate and uncompetitive environment, encapsulated in a hyped-up aura of mystical high technological sophistication. The 'Amstrad effect' of course rocked the boat, the resultant factor being critical comments of the product with which I am sure all and sundry are familiar. I think Pythagoras and Columbus had the same problem when they announced the world was round.

The heralding of yet another phase in Amstrad's history was the most striking feature of Sugar's statement. It was unrealistic, he wrote, to expect Amstrad to continue doubling in size every year.

'Clearly a new strategy is necessary,' he explained. 'The current financial year is going to be one of consolidation and seed planting in formulating our firm plan of growth for the future. A major stepping-stone for Amstrad and one which, I predict, in years to come will be recognized as one of the major strategic milestones in the company's history.'

Alan Sugar was about to usher in another new Amstrad.

· 13 ·

Amstrad Culture

The Amstrad which launched its first I.B.M.-compatible computer in 1986 was still run like a small company. Alan Sugar's style of managing Amstrad was little changed from his early days in the audio market. True, he had needed to delegate more as Amstrad grew, and by 1986 day-to-day relations with even some of the largest customers were handled by his subordinates. But to carry out his wishes, Sugar had gathered round him a group of core workers similar to himself. They were sharp, aggressive, down to earth, pragmatic and convinced that Amstrad deserved to be on top of the pile. Amstrad had none of the diffidence to be found in most British organizations; in this respect, it was more like an American corporation.

If you wanted to work at Amstrad, you had to be ready to take on the world. One visitor to its Brentwood headquarters in Essex in 1986 came away likening the company work-force to a troop of Israeli paratroopers. If Amstrad was an elite force of shock troops, then the identity of the general was never in any doubt. Alan Sugar directed his team from a battered leather armchair in the middle of an open-plan office at the top of the building, on the ninth floor. He might be a multi-millionaire; he might be widely profiled as Britain's new business phenomenon; but that was no reason for him to indulge in the luxury of his own office.

This lack of pretension was a feature of the Brentwood head-quarters. In 1986, Amstrad's products were arranged haphazardly on the shelves in the company's boardroom. Smudged fingerprints competed for attention with sales and production charts on the bare white walls of the offices. Foam rubber poked through the seams of the chairs in a conference room, a journalist from *Time* magazine reported just after the launch of the PC1512.

The Amstrad culture attracted unconventional people and only tough, unconventional people survived. The story of one young man who joined just before the launch of the PC1512 may be extreme, but it gives a representative flavour of what it was like to work there.

In 1986, Thomas Power was a fresh-faced 22-year-old, working in a small advertising agency in Croydon, south London; this was his first job since finishing a course in marketing at a local college. Ambitious and restless, he was looking around for a better opportunity and had begun to read in newspapers and marketing magazines about the exploits of Amstrad, a company by then being described as the marketing success of the decade. In a moment of candour, Power confided in his father that his goal was to work for Amstrad.

In late May, Power noticed an advertisement for a marketing manager at Amstrad, precisely the job he wanted. Unfortunately, it was clear from the advert that Amstrad was looking for someone in their late twenties or early thirties. Undaunted, he persuaded two of his friends to combine their CVs with his and submit a joint application for the job. This unconventional approach must have intrigued Malcolm Miller, because the marketing director called them in for an interview. The three young men put on a presentation, complete with flip charts, explaining to him why they were the triumvirate that Amstrad badly needed.

One of Power's friends dropped out, but he and his remaining partner were interviewed four times over the next five months. At the end of this assault course, Amstrad offered them both jobs, even though Miller was clearly more impressed with Power's friend. The latter then turned Amstrad down, whereupon the job offer to Power was withdrawn. But Power had become obsessed with working for Amstrad and early one morning he travelled to Amstrad's headquarters, buttonholed Miller as he arrived for work and asked for another chance. He handed Miller a letter explaining why he – alone of the three friends who had originally applied for the job – deserved to work for Amstrad. This apparently ruthlessly back-stabbing letter had in fact been drafted by Power and his two friends the night before. Miller looked at the letter and said, 'You've got three months.'

Power floated out of Amstrad's headquarters, having achieved his ambition. The last thing he expected was that the next six months would be, in his words, 'the hardest punishment I've ever been through in my life'.

Amstrad's new marketing manager was in for a shock when he arrived at work bright-eyed and bushy-tailed in a new suit in October 1986, one month after the launch of the PC1512. His first surprise was to realize that Amstrad, then a company turning over more than £300 million a year, had no marketing department. Before his arrival, Sugar and Miller had handled all marketing matters; henceforth Power *was* the marketing department. His second shock was to find everyone too busy to tell him what to do; he was given no training or even introduction to the way Amstrad did business. The only guidance Power had was his job description – a piece of paper with ten points on it, including product management, media buying and advertising.

When Power arrived on Monday morning, Malcolm Miller simply told him to get on with it. Shortly afterwards, Miller introduced the new man to Amstrad's chairman:

Miller: 'Thomas, this is Alan Sugar.'

Power: 'Hallo.'

Sugar: 'What are you doing here?'

Power: 'I've come here to do marketing.'

'Huh,' grunted Sugar walking away, as if to say: *'marketing –* what do you know about marketing?'

Power was given a little table at the far corner of the big open-plan office on the ninth floor – the room dominated by the large desk and battered armchair occupied by Sugar. Grouped around Sugar's desk were some smaller tables at which half-a-dozen old Amstrad hands sat.

When the working day started, Power was in for his third and biggest shock, as he recalls: 'In the middle of this room was this man shouting at the people at all the tables round him. Alan was literally standing in the middle of these tables, barking orders at people. And every now and then he would stare at me out of the corner of his eye as if to say, "What on earth can you contribute to this organization?" And I would stare back and think, "Yes, what *can* I contribute?"'

Once Sugar had given his orders to the men at the tables, they would pick up their phones and shout instructions down the line to Hong Kong, Japan or wherever. Sugar surrounded himself with the people immediately involved in shifting Amstrad's products. They were directing sales processing, exports, shipping and distribution. The managers responsible for manufacturing, finance or product development were elsewhere in the building. Three questions dominated everything on the ninth floor: How many have been sold? How many are in stock? How many are in shipment?

Sales were at the heart of the Amstrad empire and the nearer you approached the flame at its heart, the more likely you were to get burnt. On Amstrad's ninth floor Thomas Power was close to this flame. The ninth floor induced severe cultural shock trauma in the young man. He had left the glitzy world of advertising – one of tasteful furniture, designer carpets and pretty secretaries. And for what? 'I seemed to be working with a bunch of football hooligans who were trading. It didn't matter that they were trading hi-fi and computers. They could just have easily been trading in bananas, orange juice, coffee, bacon – it would have made no odds. We just had to ship this stuff and sell it as fast as possible. The only atmosphere I know that is similar is a dealing room in the City,' Power comments.

The pack turned on Power in the early days when he was referred to derisively as 'the marketing man'. Everyone acted as though he would not last long. During his stint at Amstrad, he saw many young people arrive only to disappear abruptly after two or three weeks. There was no ceremony in their leaving.

But Power survived and carved a job out of what he knew –

advertising, media buying, product launches. Gradually he learned about sales forecasting, the seasonal fluctuations of the products, the distribution channels, differences between overseas markets and so on. He learned also about his powers of endurance. 'You cannot work for Alan Sugar unless you are of sound mind. If you are one of these people who takes things personally, you will have no future with that company. You have to let it slip off your back,' he explains.

Power needed the support of his father, to whom he was unusually close, in order to last his first three months at Amstrad. Every weekend he drove home in order to lift his morale. A standard patter developed between the young man and his father, who had himself been in business.

Father: 'What have those boys in Brentwood tried on you this week?'

Power: 'The guy is out for me. He wants my blood for some reason. He scares me. There's no other word I can use but fear.'

Father: 'Stick it out. He's trying to test you. Stick it out. He must have a breaking point.'

And Sugar did have a breaking point so far as Power was concerned. It came quite unexpectedly about six months after Power had joined Amstrad, in the run-up to the launch of the PC1640 in June 1987. Power spent a weekend showing a prototype of the machine to Alan Fraser, a senior data processing manager for Ciba-Geigy, the Switzerland-based chemicals multinational, who was planning to review Amstrad's new computer in *PC User*. Power treated the Ciba-Geigy man like a king, giving him access to whatever software or technical expertise he needed as he tried out the PC1640. Fraser's review, published soon after, was everything that Amstrad could have wished for: 'I would have no hesitation in recommending the machine in favour of the I.B.M. PS/2 Model 30 (I.B.M.'s latest flagship product) for corporate purchases,' it read.

This ringing endorsement from a data processing professional in a large multinational fitted perfectly into Amstrad's continuing campaign to break into the corporate market. When Power photocopied the review and showed it to Malcolm Miller, the marketing director took one look at it and told him to show it to Sugar.

Sugar had by then bowed to the inevitable and moved into his own office, up a narrow stairway from the ninth floor. Power underlined the Ciba-Geigy quote, walked into Sugar's office, put the review on his desk, said, 'I think you'd better read this' and left.

About 40 seconds later Sugar charged down the stairs, holding the review. He bounded up to Power and said, 'Have you done this? Is this your work? Are you responsible? This is bloody amazing!' Ecstatic, Sugar tried to tell the whole company about the review. He stood by the fax machine sending the review to Amstrad's agents in North America, Germany, Australia, everywhere he could think of.

From that day, Power was accepted; he would never receive so much praise from Amstrad's chairman again, but he was in the club. He went with Sugar to help with Amstrad product launches in the United States. Most important of all, Sugar began to treat him with respect.

Power eventually left Amstrad in December 1987 to set up his own business. Like many others who have survived the Amstrad initiation, he emerged with a respect for Alan Sugar that verges on the embarrassing. 'I love the guy. I walked in there a smug young man of 22. And I had the crap knocked out of me for six months. I became a hard-nosed salesman and a professional. That was due to Alan Sugar. You go into the Alan Sugar school of management and you get the fat worked off you. He has this unbelievable ability to make marketing very simple,' says Power.

In April 1987, at about the time when Power was winning his spurs, Alan Sugar set out his business philosophy in greater detail than ever before. By then Amstrad's chairman was being bombarded with requests to explain in public the secrets of his success. He turned down almost all of them, concerned that speaking engagements would force him to take his eye off Amstrad's day-to-day affairs, but he made an exception when invited to lecture on entrepreneurship at the City University Business School – where he had held occasional discussions with the school's business students.

Few lectures delivered in the world's business schools have ever been like that given by Alan Sugar. It had none of the glib formulae favoured by the management gurus who earn their crust advising other people on how to make a fortune. Amstrad's boss delivered a lecture peppered with jokes, anecdotes and Sugarisms, but it had one overwhelming advantage over the words of wisdom uttered by management pundits: the stamp of authenticity. Sugar had done it. He had made his millions by building up a hugely successful company and he had barely turned 40.

The lecture hall was full of not only the business school's students and staff, but also analysts from London's nearby financial centre. By all accounts, Sugar had his 300-strong audience eating out of his hands. Amstrad's chairman kicked off by giving budding multi-millionaires in his audience a few tips on what to avoid. Rule number one was not to pay too much attention to the City. Rule number two was to shun the press.

'I could spend the whole of my working day talking to journalists, so much so that they have really become a pain in my life. I avoid them like the plague. The priority in life is to keep an eye on the business and not to get lured into the social high life, being exhibited around by the groupie type posers who wish to be seen with the new blue-eyed boy,' Sugar confided.

With that out of his system, he set about the task of defining the essential components of Amstrad's success. 'Amstrad culture is all about realism, swift thinking and decision-making without committees. Rise or fall by your own decisions or get out. A sense of urgency to get to the point.'

Sugar tries to instil this sense of urgency into the people who work for him.

In our company we attract people who either catch on very quickly or they last two minutes. When they catch on, they understand the entrepreneurial flair of the company and see their colleagues using innovative ways and methods to achieve their tasks, not conforming to the standards that are written down in the books, but by cutting corners, taking a few risks, assuming the rest of the team will accept what they are up to when they have finalized their projects, not needing to stop step by step, in their thought pattern to see if the group agrees before they proceed.

Amstrad culture is consciously aggressive. 'We have trained our staff to stand up and be counted. We don't want any corporate wimps. There are so many people in companies who shy away from confrontation, thinking that it will go away just like a bad cold; unfortunately that rarely happens.'

The corporate bureaucrat has no place in Amstrad: 'There are those who are happy to be non-achievers in their life, who get buried in a big corporation and flit from job to job. They will never change their ways and, in a way, you have to admire how they get away with it all their life, without doing a day's work. There are others who are I suppose like me, who never expect anything for nothing and only know how to put one's head down and get on with the job. That is the type we at Amstrad attract.'

Profits are the overwhelming focus of the Amstrad culture: 'Amstrad is active in areas of profit only. We are not interested in producing a range of products just to put on a show.' Anything else would be vanity: 'There is no mileage to be known as the biggest producer in CTV (colour televisions). So what if 75 per cent of the range does not sell or yield profit?'

Focus on profit underpins Amstrad's sales philosophy: 'When we have a hot selling item, you might think that we sit back on our laurels, admire our brainchild, watch it roll in the money for us, and sit around talking to one and all of the marketing success of the century.

'Well, that's wrong! The Amstrad way is to thrash the thing to death. We look at the cost of the item and find ways to reduce this cost, so that we can make even more money while the product is selling. Our suppliers of parts and components of a hot item also think they are made for life and sit back thinking their boat has come in. We wake them up and alert them that all good things come to an end.'

Amstrad has a distinctive attitude to successful and unsuccessful products: 'In most companies, it's normally with a product that doesn't sell that you sit down and find a way to make it cheaper. Not at Amstrad! A product that does not sell simply does not sell, so get out of it as soon as possible and wipe your face.'

Looking coldly at a successful product is a key to making money: 'Another Amstrad move is what the Japanese have termed v.a. It means value analysis. It is a nice way of saying knocking the price down. . . .

'While all the blue-eyed boys in marketing are getting a pat on the back for the product, the v.a. boys are saying, for example, the power cord on that unit costs £1.50 at the moment, we use 50k per month, which is about 600k per year – which means we spend on that one item alone, £900k. Armed with that information, they study to see if they can reduce its specification and at the same time, look for other suppliers, and tell other suppliers that we can offer them, say, half the quantity and . . . what's the price?'

Sugar explained that Amstrad might succeed in cutting the price of the power cord by 25p, yielding savings of £150,000 in a year. The best time to carry out this type of cost cutting is *after* it has launched a winner, because then it can hold out the prospect of large volumes when shopping around between alternative suppliers.

At first, the reduced costs delivered by value analysis feed straight through into extra profits. But later, as a product matures, they can be used to cut the price of a product and thereby extend its life – while still generating the profit margins obtained when the product was first launched: 'For example, when a product was first thought of, we felt that at a retail price of £399 it will sell. If the product turns out to be a hot seller and you did the v.a. work, it is possible then to take the new v.a. cost and apply the original margin criteria and find that now a £299 retail price may be achievable. In doing so you may get some new life out of a product which you think you have already thrashed to death. You can have a whole new re-launch campaign.'

Sugar rammed home the point: 'The moral of this story is that if you have a winner, thrash it to death. Don't get complacent. Don't allow your head to swell. Knock the living daylights out of the thing, as opportunities come very seldom and you must make the most of things when the opportunity allows. I have seen it so many times in our industry that someone gets a hot item and they become untouchable. They feel their boat has come in and nothing can topple them from the cloud-cuckoo-land they are in.'

Amstrad's approach to marketing is equally straightforward: 'For some reason, I have been called a barrow boy. I would take great exception to that if my ambition in life was to be seen daily at Annabel's with Lord and Lady Beseenwith. However, in a way marketing is just like a stall in Petticoat Lane. Frankly, it is no different. The owner of the stall is offering his or her wares. The sales pitch, albeit very rural and loud, is no different than some high cost advertising agency may apply.

'The Amstrad approach to marketing is simple. We work on the philosophy – pile 'em high and sell 'em cheap.

'I suppose there was a big decision made in the early part of Amstrad life. The decision to be in the Bang and Olufsen (a Danish manufacturer of expensive audio and television products) end of the market or be in the Amstrad end of the market.

'The B. & O. end of the market is not for me. Frankly, you spend all your life talking about the quality and performance, trying to hook the up-market yuppy by subtle remarks such as only the great and clever can understand. . . . Unfortunately this high quality hi-tech ramble has to be kept up all your life. You cannot slip back. You cannot be seen to enter the promotion end of the market, whereas it is easier going the other way.'

Simple and direct advertising underpins this straightforward marketing philosophy. 'Philips will tell you they are simply years ahead. Ferguson will employ André Previn to tell you how wonderful the sound is. Toshiba use a misshapen Cockney robot. JVC have dramatic dancing girls. Amstrad show the product, mention the price and tell the punters where to buy it.'

Amstrad's sole interest in launching an advertising campaign is to generate sales and thereby profits. 'It's incredible how other companies are far more interested in being seen to have the most catchy advert that everybody talks about, the advert that wins all the awards at the ad agencies' annual ball. However, they have to ask themselves – did it sell any product?

'I suppose it's an ego trip again. How does this happen? The company loses direction. The marketing manager is left to run riot on his own. The boss – i.e. the non-entrepreneurial boss – will assume his marketing man knows more than he does and allows him to get on with it.

'The Amstrad entrepreneurial method of marketing is a formula built up over the past few years, of trying to get value for your advertising money as soon as possible. We do not take the view that we should just spend a lump sum to promote the brand image. . . . We are happy to spend – and spend we do in big volume – but we want immediate return and at the same time get a branding rub off.'

An Amstrad advertising campaign takes into account three factors: 'One – set the quantity of product, i.e. we plan to sell in the period xxx thousands of units, which will generate xxx thousands of gross margin.

'The second factor is to alert the distribution and to sell in and make sure the goods are in the stores ready for the campaign.

'The third factor is to produce an advert that gets to the bottom line immediately . . .

'This philosophy is a great way to control the marketing people and lock them into results. It keeps your feet on the ground and brings home the reality you have to sell products that generate the profit in order to spend money advertising.'

The Amstrad culture also colours its research and development activities: 'We have taught engineers to think on a commercial basis. This is quite a hard task. . . .

'In Amstrad, when the new custom chip that the engineer has designed comes off the production line, it will be used immediately in the mass production of the product for which it was designed.

'Normally you wait and you test the thing – then you plan

production. As you can see, all this takes time and causes delay. The Amstrad way is to assume that the component is going to work and cut out the delay, but to have a contingency plan if it does not.

'If some outside observers saw the risks that we take in engineering a new product, they would have kittens. But frankly there is no risk. Like all things in science it either works or it does not. If it works, we are months ahead. If it does not work, we are in the same boat as the conventionalists.'

Summing up the Amstrad culture, Sugar took a tongue-in-cheek swipe at the pretentiousness and evasiveness of corporate slogans:

'Pan Am takes good care of you.

'Marks and Spencer loves you.

'I.B.M. says the customer is king. . . .

'At Amstrad – We want your money!'

*

Sugar's City University speech expounded the virtues of the entrepreneur as well as anything written in Britain during the 1980s. A remarkable hymn of praise to the sharp, fast, aggressive values that distinguished the Thatcherite decade, it was also in many ways a quintessentially British performance. Business in Britain has always been marked by a lack of intellectual pretension. Pragmatic, common-sense virtues like those praised by Sugar in his speech appeal to British business people. British executives feel under less pressure than their counterparts in North America or Continental Europe to parade academic qualifications or an intellectual approach to their working lives. Business schools spread later in Britain than in most of its major competitors, notably the United States. Even by the late 1980s, qualifications like the M.B.A. (Master of Business Administration) were much less common in the top echelons of British companies than in corporate America. It is difficult to imagine even self-made entrepreneurs in North America or Continental Europe setting out their business philosophies in the raw style adopted by Sugar.

An instructive contrast can be drawn with the account given by John Sculley of how he pulled Apple Computer back from the brink of financial disaster in the mid-1980s – in the process forcing out Steve Jobs, Apple's visionary founder. Sculley, who had been head of Pepsi-Cola before being lured to Apple by Jobs himself, is painfully concerned to convey his intellectual credentials in the 600-page analysis of his experience at Apple (*Odyssey: Pepsi to Apple*, Fontana/Collins, 1987).

When Jobs first visited his home, Sculley tells the reader, Apple's founder paused to admire Sculley's eclectic collection of books: 'not only on business and management but Zen, philosophy, architecture, art, and astronomy'. Once Sculley had joined Jobs at Apple, the two men would spend a couple of hours each day swapping their thoughts. Jobs told Sculley that he would be a poet in Paris if he did not happen to work in computers. Entering into the spirit, Sculley confided in Jobs that he would undoubtedly have been an artist, if only he had not spent his life elbowing his way to the top of one of America's largest corporations. 'We tended to speak in half sentences and phrases, jumping from subject to subject: our pasts and our futures, marketing and technology, Trotsky and Marx, Coke and I.B.M.,' Sculley gushes.

Much of this might be dismissed as an attempt by Sculley to convince Apple's long-haired computer wizards that he was not a grey man in a suit; but it is evident from his account that PepsiCo – his former home and the epitome of the methodical virtues of corporate America – was as pretentious in its way as Apple. Stonecutters were brought over from Europe to hand-cut the Italian cobblestones in the central courtyard of PepsiCo's 140-acre headquarters in New York state. The grounds are adorned with forty sculptures by some of the world's leading artists, while at the touch of a button on the desk of PepsiCo's chairman fountains shoot 40 feet into the air above a P-shaped, man-made lake.

It is no wonder that the reporter from *Time* was taken aback by the stuffing coming out of Amstrad's chairs. In the cultural vacuum of the United States, business can invest itself with all manner of intellectual and cultural pretension. In Britain, by contrast, business has not developed an intellectual self-image. While it is debatable whether this has been to the disadvantage of British business, Sugar for one has never made any secret of his contempt for the flabbiness he detected at the heart of many large American corporations.

'I have had a bellyfull of Americans who flit from job to job and exist in large empires as statistics – the sales people living in a dream world, asking you to build 50 factories on the basis of their potential customers saying, "Have a nice day." They move around from job to job, usually getting found out for what they are,' he told his City University audience.

Ironically, Sugar delivered his City University speech just as Amstrad was in the process of abandoning crucial ingredients of its ultra-entrepreneurial, small business ethos. Few people realized it at the time, but in many ways the address set the seal on the first twenty years of Amstrad's existence. Indeed, Sugar had already sown some of the seeds which would grow into structures more appropriate for a large company.

The speech contained a clear recognition of the dilemma facing Amstrad:

There is a danger that exists in my company that as we grow, we need to put in place more layers of management, control systems, additional departments and a lot of other paraphernalia which are considered necessary in a big corporation. The problem with this is that the whole machine can lose its speed and direction. . . . All companies, especially in the hi-tech field, must strive to grow – but growing too big too fast makes a bureaucracy and risks the flair and culture stagnating.

In May 1985, Sugar had brought Ken Ashcroft into Amstrad as its new finance director. Then just entering his fifties, Ashcroft came with plenty of experience in the finance functions of large companies, thanks to a career which had included stints at Ford, Philips, Comet, Hepworth and Dixons. He had first caught Sugar's attention through his work at Comet in the early 1970s, when he introduced a computerized planning system for the buyers which gave them precise information about the state of their inventory, orders and cash availability. The quality of information this system generated allowed Comet to be much less volatile than other retailers in its dealings with suppliers like Amstrad.

Ashcroft's speciality was helping companies which had outgrown their existing financial control systems, and that was the job which Sugar wanted him to perform at Amstrad. When he joined, Amstrad's senior managers were not receiving the operating information which is standard in large companies – monthly data about sales, inventories, margins and so on. Instead, Sugar still had sufficiently close oversight of all the company's business to be able to produce an accurate stab at a six-month forecast after spending half an hour with a calculator. However, this situation could not continue much longer. Ashcroft's first priority was to introduce a computer-based reporting system which locked together financial information with data about the physical location of Amstrad's products; this gave the senior managers instant access to information on the company's current financial position, as well as on its immediate prospects.

Introducing these systems required Ashcroft to build up finance and data processing departments at Amstrad, though Sugar's natural instincts were against such developments. 'Why are you spending my bloody money on overheads?' would be Sugar's first reaction. He argued against a proposal and called it stupid, yet he also listened. And if he was convinced, he would agree.

Ashcroft's prodding also prompted Sugar to introduce a professional treasurer to manage the flow of cash through the company. Before Ashcroft arrived, Sugar had been doing this himself. A key part of treasury management in Amstrad, as in most companies with business in more than one country, was to deal with foreign exchange matters. It bought many of its supplies in the Far East in yen or dollars, sold its finished products in Europe and then reported its results in sterling. The Amstrad chairman, with his unrivalled experience of trading in the Far East, proved adept at knowing when it was sensible to borrow in yen and when in sterling. The currency function was never a formal profit centre, as it is in some large companies, but Amstrad did fairly well from it.

Sugar was readily persuaded to relinquish day-to-day currency management to a full-time professional treasurer in 1987, yet he continued to suggest innovative approaches in this area. For example, in the late 1980s he made the unorthodox suggestion that Amstrad should carry out much of its borrowings in yen. Borrowing in strong currencies like the yen carries a substantial risk: as the yen appreciates, the sterling value of the loan mounts correspondingly. But this strategy also has benefits: Amstrad could take advantage of the lower interest rates attached to yen borrowings and Sugar calculated that this interest rate differential was more than enough to offset the risk of currency appreciation.

It was a strategy which gave an orthodox finance director like Ashcroft a few sleepless nights, as he recalls:

I must say that borrowing in a strong currency, taking advantage of lower rates, isn't something that appeals to me as a finance guy. It's very risky. But Alan pointed out that there was such a huge gap in the forward rates that the yen would have had to strengthen a heck of a lot before we needed to take action. And a jolly good strategy it's been, because the yen has oscillated quite violently, so we've found we've been able to buy our requirements in yen when it's been relatively weak against the pound.

Ken Ashcroft joined a team of board members who were Sugar's immediate lieutenants. Malcolm Miller was in charge of sales and marketing. Bob Watkins oversaw the development of new Amstrad products. Jim Rice was in charge of operations such as manufacturing and warehousing. It was a tight team, carrying no passengers and with Sugar the clear leader, as he explained in early 1986: 'Businesses need leaders, spearheads. Some people pad out their boards with right honourables and air marshals and fancy titles like that. But they still need spearheads if they want to succeed. I provide Amstrad with its prime motivation.'

Yet as Amstrad continued to grow in the second half of the 1980s, inevitably it had to take on more and more staff. By the end of the decade, there were about a dozen people working on sales and marketing at Amstrad headquarters under Malcolm Miller.

Bob Watkins and Richard Altwasser, the former Sinclair computer designer, gradually built the firm's in-house research capability into a team of fifteen engineers. Ken Ashcroft's finance and data processing teams grew to about fifty, although many of these were engaged in routine clerical functions.

Even as it grew, Amstrad managed to retain a lack of formality. Ken Ashcroft always impressed on the team of auditors from Touche Ross during their annual visit that they should come straight into his office if ever they had any problems. The accountants were used to more bureaucratic arrangements with their clients: typically, problems would be referred up the line through a client's finance department until eventually they found their way on to the finance director's desk. But at Amstrad Ken Ashcroft's door was always open. Indeed Eric Tracey, the Touche Ross partner in charge of the Amstrad audit, once told Ashcroft half-jokingly that he ought to try closing his door now and again. 'With my chairman, if I closed my door, he would tear it off its hinges,' was Ashcroft's instantaneous reply.

Amstrad was still a lean company if staff numbers were compared with the size of its turnover, yet it was no longer the skeletal organization it had been in the mid-1980s. Malcolm Miller describes the impact in sales and marketing: 'Two or three years ago, it was just me. Me and maybe one other. Over the past three years it's had to change, because the products have become so varied and complex, and the budgets have become so much bigger.'

The inevitable result of this rapid expansion was that Amstrad filled up with new young faces. The company had a clear idea of the type of newcomer it was seeking; Malcolm Miller, who emerged in the 1980s as the most visible person in Amstrad after Sugar, explains: 'We've taken young, bright graduates. But more importantly they have to have the right culture. They have to be entrepreneurial and enterprising. They have to be able to rewrite the rule book, if necessary.'

As Miller's key sales and marketing function expanded, he introduced more structure into the operation, focusing his team on individual products and brands along the lines he had learnt as a young trainee in the Birds Eye division of Unilever: 'Really, I've taken a lot of it from the brand manager position at Unilever, whereby the person is the product. He eats, drinks, sleeps the product from the day it is born to the day it dies. He analyzes the sales trends, the seasonality, the packaging, the pricing, the competition. He's got to know everything. He *is* the product.'

But Miller was careful not to let bureaucracy slip in along with the greater structure:

> If you haven't got a sense of urgency and entrepreneurial flair and you just want to be a bureaucrat pushing people and paper around, it doesn't work here. We will not become like the people who sit on committees all day long, pushing papers around, theorizing about some activity which might increase the brand share by 0.1 per cent to raise at next month's marketing committee. That's not us.

The formal meetings held within the sales and marketing department are tightly circumscribed, as he says:

> Every Monday, we have a sales and marketing management meeting, where we talk about sales on a monthly basis and discuss the problems and opportunities on a weekly basis. Monday for an hour. We have these rules that a meeting shouldn't last longer than an hour. We have another rule that if there's somebody important on the phone, you take that call. You don't say I'm in a meeting, because the call might be more urgent than the meeting you're in.

The influx of newcomers inevitably meant that Amstrad began to employ people with a relatively shallow commitment to the company. Miller describes how new members of staff are inducted into the Amstrad culture:

> We allow them to make important decisions, which they couldn't do in a larger company. We allow them to feel part of

the problems and opportunities, successes and failures we have every day. Certain people like responsibility. They like to feel they can change the face of one of Amstrad's projects – they can do a deal with a big software company on a promotion; they can come up with a new creative idea for an advert; they can find a new retailing opportunity that makes a big difference.

Dealing direct with Amstrad's boss is also an experience that can make or break the young bloods, as Miller explains:

> Now and again, I let Alan loose on them. That experience is always good. They always find it very stimulating. I say to them, 'Let's show Alan this idea of yours.' He'll sit and deliberate and they'll get a chance to argue. Some of them will argue, but if we don't like the idea we say so immediately. Nothing gets hidden here. People are very straight talkers. If you don't like straight talking or you're shocked by being told your idea is crap, then don't come to Amstrad, because we don't pull our punches.

As Amstrad prospered, Alan Sugar hit on a more direct means to encourage the dynamism and loyalty of his staff. Share options are a way of rewarding a company's work-force for the contribution they have made to its success. Typically, a share option scheme introduced on a particular date – call it x – allows the staff to buy shares at a future date, for example x + three years, at the share price which existed at x. If the company has prospered and the share price has risen during the three years, then those covered by the scheme can make substantial capital gains on realizing their options.

Amstrad introduced its first share option scheme on 23 July 1985; it allowed those in the scheme to exercise their options three years later at a price of 13.6p a share (the mid market price on 23 July 1985, after allowing for the subsequent fivefold split of the shares in June 1986). This is a standard format for such schemes. The relatively unusual feature of Amstrad's scheme was the generous treatment it gave to a large number of the company's staff.

In total, 51 directors and employees of Amstrad were included in the company's first share option scheme, about a tenth of the work-force at the time of introduction in 1985. Alan Sugar ensured that all those who had helped him build up Amstrad were in the list, including five Chinese members of the company's Hong Kong staff. Options to buy a total of 11.551 million shares were distributed to these 51 people. On 25 July 1988, the first day on which the options could be realized (allowing for a weekend), Amstrad's share price stood at 215p. The 51 beneficiaries were sitting on a potential capital gain of £23.26 million (11.551 million shares × 215p–13.6p) – almost £500,000 each on average.

This gives only a very general indication of how each of the 51 individuals was affected by the scheme. For a start, the 11.551 million shares were not distributed equally; the options ranged from the 1.176 million allocated to each of the five Amstrad board members in the scheme (Ken Ashcroft, Malcolm Miller, Jim Rice, Marion Vannier and Bob Watkins), to the 73,500 shares allocated to the least senior staff in the scheme. In addition, those covered by the scheme could choose to wait until after 25 July 1988 to sell their shares, which would have brought them either higher or lower gains depending on the share price at the time. In fact, the five board members all made sizeable disposals as soon as they could; they sold between 115,000 and 400,000 shares each on 25 July 1988, yielding capital gains ranging from £230,000 to £805,000.

The five Amstrad board members and two other employees stood to gain over £1 million each as a result of this first Amstrad share option scheme. In other words, seven new Amstrad million-aires had joined Alan Sugar. The most junior staff stood to gain almost £150,000 each. Amstrad also distributed smaller numbers of share options to staff in later years. Alan Sugar was no longer alone in having benefited handsomely from the company's success.

At Amstrad's annual general meeting in 1988, institutional investors questioned Sugar about the share options, which they saw as unnecessarily generous. The chairman would have no truck with these criticisms and defended the policy vigorously, arguing that total dedication by the staff was integral to Amstrad's success and needed to be adequately rewarded.

Amstrad did without much of the rest of the paraphernalia of professional staff relations to be found in more typical companies of its size. Unions, for example, were an anathema, as indeed was the whole bureaucracy of personnel management. One head of an Amstrad subsidiary even had to pretend that its personnel officer did an entirely different job, so fearful was he of the scorn that Sugar would pour on him for carrying such a (in Sugar's eyes) useless post. Sugar also thought that Amstrad could do without a gold-plated pension scheme of the kind typical in most large businesses.

While expecting hard work from its employees, Amstrad does not look for empty demonstrations of devotion. This shows through in its attitude to working hours. Unlike some other high-achieving organizations, no Brownie points are earned at Amstrad simply by burning the midnight oil beyond the official end of the working day. 'Even today, if you stand in front of the exit at a minute to five, you get trodden into the carpet,' one Amstrad insider says.

This attitude flows partly from the top, since Sugar has always made a point of trying to get home to his family at a reasonable hour. His instincts have changed little since 1980 when, at the time of Amstrad's flotation, he told a reporter, 'I take my holidays and I think five days' work is enough. If a job isn't finished on Friday, it can wait until Monday.'

Running the large company which Amstrad has become inevitably increases the demands on Sugar, but efficient time management is his way of cramming an abnormal work-load into a normal working day. Most days he just sits in his office working through whatever is at the top of Amstrad's agenda. He usually skips lunch or, at most, eats a sandwich at his desk. During meetings with staff, he often devotes half his brain to clearing through his paperwork or to completing a few deals on the phone. Most meetings with outsiders are tightly structured, as Paul Bailey – a software supplier to Amstrad – describes:

All Sugar's meetings are very much to the point. They have a fixed agenda and just enough time budgeted to the exercise to get to a closure point. He very rarely passes the time of day in his meetings. Within the first few minutes the objective is clearly established, so each side knows what it is bargaining for. Sugar tends to lay down his terms quite early in a meeting, so it will be up to the other side to say whether they are willing to agree. The other side can move the terms, but usually not by a whole lot. He has an incredibly focused mind.

Perform well or clear out: that is the hard injunction at the centre of Amstrad culture. But its contempt for corporate wimps, bureaucrats and timewasters is not simply macho breast-beating. Amstrad culture has a laser-like concentration on sales and profits: it is focused, like Sugar himself.

· 14 ·

Birth of a Multinational

In 1987 Amstrad set out on a new path which was to propel it far from its small business roots. Breaking with his previous practice, Sugar created a string of overseas subsidiaries – a policy departure which amounted to the re-fashioning of Amstrad into a true multinational corporation.

The impetus for this new strategy came from the policy review which Amstrad had carried out in late 1986 and early 1987, partly with the help of the Boston Consulting Group. Sugar concluded that Amstrad did not need to march into radically new businesses such as white goods. There was still plenty of progress to be made by building on its existing product lines and by extending the geographical spread of its activities, even if growth was bound to be slower than in the heady years of the mid-1980s.

Alan Sugar gave a characteristic account of the new strategy in his chairman's statement accompanying the 1986–87 accounts:

> There is a temptation to follow the experience of other companies which have risen, like Amstrad, to great heights. The phenomenon of meteoric growth followed by the question, 'What do we do for an encore?' The answer is often that the company wanders like a lost lamb with a shopping basket, surveying the shelves of the company lists in desperation, buying profits at a high cost to cloud the ongoing issue.

That would not be Amstrad's way. Instead, Sugar had decided, his company would build up its presence abroad. This required a fundamental re-orientation of its overseas activities, as he explained to the shareholders:

> Amstrad will no longer distribute its products in major overseas markets through agents who, in many cases, also represent other manufacturers. Such arrangements lead to the dilution of the sales and marketing effort. In addition there is no longer any room for a 'middle man's' margin. The group can now offer the resources to overseas subsidiaries, enabling them to penetrate their markets in the way we have done in the U.K. We must control our own destiny and to do so we must control our marketing and advertising effort in each market, as well as product planning.

Mixed experiences overseas lay behind these statements. Before 1987, Amstrad had carried out all its activities abroad through agents except in France – an anomaly explained by the special circumstances of Marion Vannier, boss of Amstrad France – and in Hong Kong, which was a co-ordinating point for the company's interests in the Far East. Yet only in France and Spain had the sale of Amstrad's products begun to match its success in Britain. Every country presented its own problems, but in each case there seemed to be a common solution.

The United States, for instance, is a market which Sugar has consistently approached with great caution. Notoriously, America has been a graveyard for British computer companies. In the first half of the 1980s Acorn, Apricot and Sinclair Research launched into the U.S. with great fanfare. They made initial gains and were then seriously burnt when they found their cheque books too small to take on the giant American personal computer market, particularly when it went through one of its periodic recessions. Learning from their mistakes, Sugar looked for someone else to bear the costs of marketing and distributing Amstrad computers in the U.S., just as he had done in Spain. His aim was to leave Amstrad unexposed if its products did not sell well in North America.

'Everyone in America seems to think that the only way to break into that market is to spend $200 million on a big national ad campaign. That doesn't fit with our first priority – not losing any money there,' Sugar explained.

Amstrad achieved what appeared to be a breakthrough in March 1986, when it signed a marketing agreement with Sears World Trade, the overseas trading arm of Chicago-based Sears, Roebuck – the world's largest retail chain. Sears was bullish at first, telling the *Wall Street Journal* that it expected Amstrad to sell more word processors in North America than in Europe. It seemed set to place an initial order for 100,000 of Amstrad's PCW8256 word processors for sale in the U.S. and it looked as though Sugar had hit the jackpot: a costless route into the North American market on the back of one of the country's most powerful retailers.

In the event, relations between Amstrad and Sears quickly soured. By October 1986, Sears had taken delivery of only 70,000 of the 100,000 word processors which Amstrad was expecting to sell it. Worse, the giant retailer appeared to be doing nothing much with the machines it had. Sears was not selling Amstrad's products in any quantity. Part of the trouble was that the American public insisted on viewing the PCW8256 as a not very powerful CP/M-based computer, rather than as a dedicated word processor. The standards-conscious U.S. market was also disconcerted by Amstrad's non-standard 3″ disk.

While it would probably always have been an uphill struggle to sell many Amstrad word processors in North America, Sugar also became convinced that much of the problem lay with Sears. He aired his feelings six months later in his City University speech:

In the U.S.A., we sold goods to Sears – the mighty Sears, where the left hand does not know what the right hand is doing. They obtained the marketing rights to our word processor, ordered shiploads and stored them in a warehouse in stacks nearly as high as the Sears Tower in Chicago. Someone forgot to organize the marketing.

The machine the *Sunday Times* called the marketing miracle of the decade stayed in stock as the peak selling season came and went. We had been paid for the product but we missed the opportunity of exposing our brand. In short, we went to the wrong people. We went with the buying arm of the world's largest retailer. They were great buyers but they could not sell anything. This is a case of big not being beautiful. The Sears Tower has 100-odd floors and I think they have that many layers of management.

A few months after the word processor deal, Sugar flew on Concorde for a meeting in New York's John F. Kennedy airport to consider U.S. marketing plans for Amstrad's I.B.M.-compatible PC1512 personal computer. Already he was thinking of ditching Sears. Three or four executives came to the meeting from Sears's headquarters in Chicago. A couple of people from the U.S. software company, Digital Research, which supplied much of the initial software for the PC1512, were also there, including its president. Sugar softened up the Sears team by boasting that he had set out for the meeting from Brentwood after they had left Chicago. He then took them through the PC1512 and his sales hopes for the computer in the U.S.

The Sears executives raised doubts about the PC1512's chances in North America: they could not see how a new entry like the PC1512 could hope to make a big inroad into the U.S. which, unlike Europe, had plenty of low-cost I.B.M.-clones in the market-place. As hesitation was heaped upon hesitation, those present could see Sugar grow tense, visibly frustrated with the cautiousness of the Sears response.

After the meeting was over, Sugar drew aside the two men from Digital Research and told them not to worry about the impasse with Sears; he was working on alternative distribution plans for the U.S. Sears's attitude at the J.F.K. meeting had been the last straw, and shortly afterwards Amstrad signed up a new distributor, Vidco, which until then had been a leading U.S. distributor of Commodore computers. Vernon Moore, Vidco's president, severed his links with Commodore and set up as Amstrad's U.S. agent in Dallas, Texas. Amstrad entered 1987 with Vidco handling its North American business, but still with no financial exposure in this tricky market. Vidco paid for all the machines it ordered in advance, and bore all the marketing expenses.

However, it soon became plain that Vidco did not have the financial strength to make much of a dent on the North American market. Amstrad would have to take the reins if it wanted more than negligible U.S. business. In September 1987, Amstrad established its own subsidiary in the U.S. by acquiring Vidco for $7.5 million – $2 million in cash and 2.2 million Amstrad shares.

While Amstrad struggled with Sears during 1986, over in Madrid José Luis Dominguez had been considering his next move. He was wondering how to cash in on his tremendous success in launching the Amstrad brand in Spain. The obvious route was to float his distribution company, Indescomp, on the Spanish stock exchange. Late in 1986, Dominguez phoned Sugar and told him about his plan. The Amstrad chairman was non-committal, so Dominguez began to take the first steps, but in early 1987 Sugar called him over to Amstrad's headquarters. He explained to the Spaniard his plans to strengthen Amstrad's control over its overseas operations, and said that an independent Indescomp would not fit this new strategy. Rather than floating Indescomp in Spain, why not sell it to Amstrad?

Dominguez hesitated about losing his independence, but in the end he conceded, negotiating what turned out to be a more than good price. The deal was announced in September. Amstrad bought Indescomp, renamed it Amstrad España and appointed Dominguez head of its new Spanish subsidiary. It paid £21.65 million for Indescomp – made up of 8.812 million Amstrad shares, worth about £17 million, with the rest in cash. Another Amstrad multi-millionaire had been created.

Sugar also had to develop operations in West Germany, a country where Amstrad had been selling some goods since the early 1980s. An electronics company called Schneider Rundfunkwerke, run by the two Schneider brothers, was the driving force behind the company's entry into West Germany. After noticing Amstrad's equipment at an audio fair in London in 1980, Bernhard Schneider approached Sugar and offered to sell its equipment in West Germany. But at the time Sugar was reluctant to enmesh Amstrad in the expense of tackling the West German market. A deal was therefore agreed by which Schneider bore all the costs and risks of selling Amstrad goods in West Germany. In return, Schneider's name appeared on the products, a decision which Amstrad was to regret.

The first Amstrad product to sell strongly in West Germany was the CPC464 home computer; the West German market contributed £32.5 million to Amstrad's sales in 1984–85, almost a quarter of the company's total turnover. So well regarded was the CPC464 in West Germany that it was paid the compliment of the sincerest form of flattery – imitation. A German outfit thought the ROMs controlling the CPC464's add-on disk drive sufficiently elegant to copy. Roland Perry, Amstrad's technical manager, flew to Munich to testify in the resulting copyright case – the only known example of someone trying to clone an Amstrad design. Amstrad won the case.

But relations with Schneider began to cool when the German company failed to make a success of the PCW8256 word processor. In Sugar's eyes, Schneider committed two cardinal errors. First, it promoted the PCW8256 as a computer rather than as a dedicated word processor. Second, Schneider marked up the price of the PCW8256, pitching the price at what it thought the market would bear and ignoring the Amstrad maxim of creating a mass market by setting a low price based on the costs of production.

Alan Sugar explains the point:

The Germans took the Joyce (PCW8256) too seriously as a computer. That's why it was a failure in Germany. They marketed it as a computer – and put too high a price on it. If they had come into the market with that product at the equivalent of £399 in D-marks and presented it as a word processor, a replacement for a typewriter, they would have had a flaming success. But they entered the market at nearly double the price, thinking they could soak up a lot of profit. But of course the German market said, 'Why should we buy this for £700 when we need spend only another couple of hundred pounds to get an I.B.M.-compatible computer?' It was a wrong attitude to pitch the price near the competition. What we needed in Germany was a blockbuster, something to make people look up and say, 'My God, that's cheap!'

Bernhard Schneider, in charge of Schneider's sales and marketing, disputes this account: 'I'm not really sure why the PCW did not sell so well in Germany,' he says. 'Maybe we in Germany are a little bit more conservative about such things than people in Britain. Perhaps even now the Germans prefer to use a typewriter to a computer. Britain is two years ahead of Germany in that respect.'

Whatever the reason, Amstrad's sales in West Germany stagnated in 1985–86 at £37.5 million, barely up on the previous year. Greater success with the I.B.M.-compatible PC1512 helped Amstrad's German sales to jump to £63.9 million in 1986–87, a 70 per cent increase. With its sales flourishing in other Continental countries, Sugar had become determined to build up Amstrad brand awareness in West Germany: under pressure, Schneider had agreed to put 'Schneider by Amstrad' on its PC1512s. By the time Sugar wrote his chairman's statement in September 1987, however, the days of dealing with Schneider were numbered.

The German company was becoming keen to branch out on its own. Based near the spa town of Bad Woerishofen in rural Bavaria, Schneider is blessed with a touch of Amstrad entrepreneurialism. The Schneider brothers, increasingly uneasy about acting as middle men for Amstrad, wanted to manufacture their own computers. 'Under our old situation, Alan Sugar controlled everything and we had to follow him,' Bernhard Schneider says.

Schneider was chafing under the terms of its deal with Amstrad, which restricted its computer operations to the German-speaking countries, Belgium and the Netherlands. The German company had learned from Amstrad how successful a fleet-footed consumer electronics company could be if it controlled its own design, sourcing and marketing. By the end of the 1980s, after severing relations with Amstrad, the Schneider brothers had built up their firm to annual sales of about DM1 billion (£350 million).

From Amstrad's viewpoint, the break with Schneider came at

an opportune moment, since it was set on the path of creating its own subsidiaries. Head-hunters scoured Germany in 1987 looking for someone to run Amstrad's subsidiary there; Sugar had told them to pick an executive who was number two in an existing computer company and therefore hungry to succeed. The head-hunters recommended Helmut Jost, then Commodore's second-in-command in Germany. He was given the job of setting up from scratch Amstrad's German operation, which became fully operational in 1988.

During 1987, Amstrad formed subsidiaries in two countries where its presence was not as yet strong – Italy and Australia. The ending of the Schneider deal also prompted Amstrad to create companies in Belgium and the Netherlands, where Schneider previously handled sales of its equipment. Within the space of a year, Sugar had formed subsidiaries in seven countries: Australia, Belgium, Italy, the Netherlands, Spain, the United States and West Germany. Amstrad would still make opportunistic sales outside these territories. At one point in 1987, for example, Amstrad's computers accounted for 70 per cent of the air freight between London and Warsaw, as it responded to a surge in Polish demand for personal computers. But Amstrad now had its own operations in place in most of the world's main markets.

While Sugar was busy setting up this marketing network overseas, Amstrad's Hong Kong operation had been going from strength to strength. The numbers employed there by Amstrad grew steadily to a peak of 428 in October 1988. A total of 370 worked in its factory, which was sandwiched into four floors of a large commercial building in Kowloon. The remainder were engineers or administrators working in Amstrad's offices, tucked away in a bustling jewellery quarter. Amstrad still shared its offices with the same textile company which had offered Randall the use of a small room when he opened the Hong Kong operation back in 1981. By the end of the 1980s, however, Amstrad dwarfed the textile company, whose employees could be seen poring over materials in a corner of Amstrad's offices.

By then Amstrad Hong Kong had created a sophisticated system for overseeing the company's sub-contractors dotted around the Far East. Typically, up to five of its Hong Kong engineers would work full-time in a sub-contractor's factory when a new product was being introduced. Amstrad supervised and paid for the installation of new tooling for its products. Once a sub-contractor was bedded down, it maintained pressure on quality through a team of twenty inspectors – based in Hong Kong – who visited its sub-contractors continuously.

Amstrad was loyal to its long-term sub-contractors, like Orion, but it was part of Randall's job in Hong Kong to look out continuously for cheaper sources of supplies – to 'cherry-pick', as Alan Sugar described it, from the best available in the Far East. 'You always have to keep your options open to move your production round the region,' argues Randall.

Amstrad needed to keep an open mind about its suppliers because of the changing fortunes of the different Far East economies. Gradually it reduced the quantities of products and components it sourced from Taiwan as labour costs rose there. It kept a close eye on the rising currency, political instability and labour cost pressures in South Korea, where most of its computers were made. Like many other electronics concerns in the Far East, Amstrad also began to source some goods from China; it had components such as its computer mouse made in factories in Guangdong, the Chinese province next to Hong Kong, tapping China's abundant supplies of cheap, flexible labour.

On one occasion, Randall was impressed by the goods coming out of a Taiwanese factory which Amstrad had not used before. Its Hong Kong engineers took the factory's goods apart, studying the techniques used by their Taiwanese counterparts. Then they worked out a price and quality specification for a large quantity of a particular Amstrad product. 'At that stage, the factory didn't even know we were interested in them,' Randall says.

When Amstrad knew what it wanted and the price it would pay, its team visited the Taiwanese factory and spent four days crawling over its procedures. Satisfied with what they found, they began negotiating an order for tens of thousands of units.

Every month Amstrad's Hong Kong office received bills of materials from its sub-contractors. Its staff examined these, trying to spot components which Amstrad, with its large purchasing muscle, could buy more cheaply. This effort was helped by a central purchasing department at the British headquarters which also monitored prices worldwide.

Amstrad's Hong Kong factory was not just the place where Amstrad made printers, which sold in similar numbers to its computers. It was also used as a testing ground for new production ideas. If these ideas worked, then Amstrad would encourage its sub-contractors to follow suit.

Randall's ability to motivate his young Hong Kong Chinese staff was crucial to his operation, not least because engineers and technicians there are in chronically short supply. He gave his staff responsibility and recognition as early as possible. The best example of this is Callen So, who was promoted from being a secretary to become Amstrad's sales and marketing director in the Far East and then brought to Amstrad's headquarters as special assistant to Alan Sugar, with a desk next to his. Another case was Isaac Ip, a young Chinese man who joined the company as a junior draughtsman. Randall encouraged Ip's early interest in design, with the result that Ip came up with a more efficient mouse for Amstrad's personal computer line. Ip, in turn, was promoted to the number two position in the engineering department in Hong Kong.

Married to a Chinese woman, Randall had little time for the rituals of the expatriate British community; he divided his energies between workaholic devotion to Amstrad and his small sailing boat, moored in the harbour of the fishing village where he lived. He believed that Amstrad's trust in its key Hong Kong staff paid dividends. It not only helped to pick up commercial gossip in the surprisingly small world of Far Eastern electronics sub-contractors, but also came in useful when Randall prepared for negotiations with Japanese suppliers: he went in for role-playing exercises, with his Chinese lieutenants pretending to be his Japanese adversaries.

Alan Sugar typically came to the Far East, usually with technical director Bob Watkins, to handle the main annual negotiations with the company's biggest sub-contractors. Bargaining took place in intensive sessions, unsuitable for anyone weak in mind or body. Once when Callen So went with Sugar and Watkins to see Funai, one of Amstrad's main Japanese suppliers, she had hoped to spend an hour or two looking at the Japanese shops. But no such luck. The Amstrad team was picked up by a Funai car from the hotel lobby each day at 7.30 am and taken to the factory, where they held face-to-face negotiations with about a dozen Japanese managers and engineers right through until 6 pm, without a break for lunch. The two sides argued over the benefits of using a particular component; about whether Funai would shave a few more cents off the price if Amstrad ordered large volumes; and, crucially, over the performance level that could be delivered for a given price.

Yet in the second half of the 1980s, a range of pressures emerged which was to endanger the stability of Amstrad's elaborate system of sub-contractors in the Far East. Labour costs and exchange rates began to rise, notably in Taiwan and South Korea (they had already done so in Japan), throwing into doubt the core cost-cutting reasons for Far East sourcing. A growth of protectionist sentiment within the European Community also threatened Amstrad's network of relationships in the Far East.

This sentiment was channelled into 'anti-dumping' cases by the European Commission against Far Eastern producers. Under international trading rules, anti-dumping duties can be levied against an imported product if it is sold for less than in its home market, or at less than the cost of production plus selling costs and profit. From 1985 onwards, the Commission began to impose swingeing anti-dumping duties on imported Japanese electronics goods, such as electronic typewriters and photocopiers. The Commission's actions set off a furious debate, with many economists and trade experts arguing that Europe was shooting itself in the foot by keeping out low cost goods. The reaction of the Japanese manufacturers was more pragmatic; they began to accelerate plans to build factories in Europe, thereby hoping to avoid Europe's protective barrier. In 1987, Japanese inward investment into Europe almost doubled to $6.78 billion.

Alan Sugar looked askance at what was happening. Most of the anti-dumping complaints in consumer electronics were launched by the few established European giants, notably Philips of the Netherlands and Thomson of France. He believed that they wanted to build a wall around themselves to keep out competition. One result would be that prices to the consumer would remain higher than need be, reflecting the bloated overheads of companies like Philips. It would also be increasingly difficult for anyone to emulate entrepreneurs like himself, for a protective barrier around Europe would put a stranglehold on key electronic components. A budding Alan Sugar would either have to buy from a restricted set of high-cost suppliers or start making components himself – an almost impossible task for an individual entrepreneur, as Sugar explains: 'There's no such thing as a small chip plant or a small TV tube plant. It's either £300 million or nothing.'

Sugar publicized his arguments against the Commission's trade policies whenever he could, but he was too preoccupied to wage a campaign against it as he noted in 1986: 'The legislation designed to protect European industry is actually having the reverse effect. But I'm too busy running the business, and I have not the time, energy, patience or bureaucratic ways to fight the gnomes of Brussels.'

Nevertheless, Amstrad's chairman could see the writing on the wall. He heard that an anti-dumping complaint about imported video recorders, spearheaded by Philips and Thomson, had been lodged with the European Commission in Brussels. Immediately he began to press Funai, the Japanese company which supplied most of Amstrad's VCRs, to set up a plant in Britain. In June 1987, a new VCR factory was opened on Amstrad's Shoeburyness site; breaking new ground for Amstrad, it was a jointly owned operation – Funai had 51 per cent and Amstrad 49 per cent. The initial plan was to make 5,000 recorders a month, building up to a figure of 10,000. Three months later, in September, the European Commission duly launched its anti-dumping investigation of imported video recorders.

Alan Sugar was finally forced to set out on what was, for him, the unusual path of the political lobbyist. A new twist to the anti-dumping saga particularly concerned his company. The European Commission was planning to levy anti-dumping duties on the output of 'screwdriver plants' in Europe – assembly plants set up by Far East manufacturers which imported more than 60 per cent of their parts. Amstrad saw this provision as a threat to its new joint venture factory in Shoeburyness.

In the hope that the British Government would put pressure on Brussels, Sugar lobbied Lord Young, then Trade and Industry Secretary. Amstrad was one of the first British companies directly affected by the Commission's anti-dumping measures. Young was on Amstrad's side, as he recalls:

> I had two or three meetings with him in the Department. And I had tremendous sympathy with him. I did all I could – he may not have thought I did – to help him through those problems. He had – and I know the type because I've been exactly the same way – no damn patience with all the officials, particularly in Brussels. But as a result of his case, I hope we're leaning more and more on Brussels.

But the Government had no choice but to abide by the Euro-rules. In September 1988, the Commission imposed huge anti-dumping duties on five Japanese and South Korean companies. Funai's video recorders were saddled with an 18 per cent levy. Although Amstrad had ceased importing Funai VCRs in July 1988, the Commission, as expected, launched a 'screwdriver' investigation of Funai-Amstrad's Shoeburyness plant which eventually confirmed the 18 per cent duty on its products.

In his frustration, Alan Sugar made the supreme sacrifice: in December 1988 he travelled to Brussels to lobby the Eurocrats. It was not a meeting of minds. Having accused the Commission's officials of acting as the unpaid marketing department of Philips and Thomson, he returned disgusted with the ways of the Commission, describing their anti-dumping policies as '. . . a total sham. There's no logic in their decision. We were taking the markets because we're better marketeers, because we have a product that is good as far as specification is concerned and because we know how to advertise that product correctly.'

The Amstrad chairman called on Mrs Thatcher to intervene: 'If she knew what was going on she would do her nut,' he told B.B.C. television.

The only relief was a cut in the duty on Funai-Amstrad products on appeal to 13 per cent. But this still meant that Amstrad had to charge 13 per cent more for its video recorders than if the Commission had not intervened. Understandably, Sugar believed that such policies threatened the downward spiral in prices and the consequent rapid growth in demand which had been a feature of the VCR market in Europe until then.

The simple Amstrad which Sugar had described in his City University speech was disappearing. Gone were the days when an ultra-lean organization in Britain could source as cheaply as possible in the Far East and then sell at minimum cost via agents throughout the world. But if the new Amstrad had to add to its previously tiny overheads and surrender a part of its old flexibility, Sugar's drive to increase the company's foreign sales also paid dividends.

Britain accounted for only 42.5 per cent of Amstrad's sales in the financial year 1987–88. By building up its overseas sales, the company had correspondingly reduced its vulnerability to a downturn in consumer spending in its home base. Amstrad was clearly stronger in some foreign markets than others, yet its overseas sales were broadly based: 19.4 per cent came from France; 17.3 per cent from Spain; 4.8 per cent from Germany; 4.3 per cent from Italy; 4.9 per cent from other European countries; and 5.4 per cent from North and South America. It was an impressive basis on which to build. Only six years before, in 1982, Amstrad's overseas sales had amounted to £118,000. By 1988, they were running at £359.7 million.

Amstrad's new policy of establishing overseas subsidiaries had a dramatic impact on its once tiny head count. The work-force grew by two-thirds in 1987 and by a similar amount in 1988. By the end of financial year 1988–89, the company was employing over 1,600 people. In the most literal sense, Amstrad was no longer a one-man band.

*

Continuing success in the computer market, particularly with the new top of the range PC1640 personal computer and the PCW9512 word processor, boosted Amstrad once more in the financial year 1987–88. Profits increased 18.2 per cent to £160.4 million on sales up 22.2 per cent at £625.4 million. Sugar's warning in 1987 that Amstrad was facing a year of 'consolidation' while developing its overseas network had not prevented this continuing advance. The share price held up well in 1988 and by August Amstrad's stock was trading at 235p, which valued the company at more than £1 billion. The value of Alan Sugar's own stake increased by £147 million to £430 million over the course of 1988, making him the biggest stock market 'winner' of the year, according to a *Sunday Times* calculation. Amstrad had shrugged off the stock market crash of October 1987 as if it had never happened.

In describing Sugar's immense wealth, newspapers tended to concentrate on the value of his holding in Amstrad, which fluctuated sharply with the Amstrad share price. But this was mainly a paper fortune, since he would never be able to realize it all. In many ways more significant was his real fortune and the opportunities it opened up for him.

By 1986, Sugar had raised more than £34 million through successive sales of tranches of his Amstrad shares. His remaining stake in the company of over 40 per cent yielded large streams of earnings every year: in the financial year 1987–88, for example, his dividends amounted to about £3.5 million. Even if he had adopted the most passive and conservative investment policy imaginable – keeping his money in a building society – capital and dividend earnings on that scale would have generated huge additional income from interest.

However, Sugar did not pursue a passive approach to his wealth. He had the normal spread of investments of the super-rich, with money invested at times in various overseas stock markets such as Tokyo; but he put the bulk of his fortune into commercial property in Britain. It was relatively safe and, just as important, he enjoyed the buzz of managing his growing property portfolio. There were few things that relaxed Amstrad's boss so much as closing a multi-million-pound property deal on the phone. 'The thing is I enjoy deals, and property is a dealing situation,' Sugar notes.

Late in 1989, for example, he was becoming bored with a routine meeting in his office at Amstrad when one of his advisers called to discuss a building that he was on the point of buying: 'Is the architecture O.K? . . . No one's going to pull it down in a couple of weeks? . . . Lease is O.K? . . . Covenant sorted out? . . . Good, get on with it. That's it. Do the deal.'

The person on the other end of the phone hesitated, but Sugar cut him short: 'Look, you're driving me mad. The deal's done, as far as I'm concerned. Get in touch with my solicitors. I want the contracts exchanged in an hour.'

Sugar had bought another £2 million building which he had not seen. He would probably sell it again before seeing it. He employed his brother, Derek, to manage the day-to-day affairs of his property business such as paying the insurance and collecting the rents. 'Everybody has a good laugh at me, because they can't believe the way I go about doing property deals. I buy and sell properties without even going to look at them,' he says.

He has adopted a rule of thumb in his personal property dealings: not to bother with anything worth less than £2 million. 'Some people might spend a week studying a property they're going to buy for £150,000. To them, £150,000 is a lot of money. But I'm used to dealing in millions. It sounds very blasé to friends or associates or even advisers, but for me to spend £2 to £3 million is nothing. It sounds terrible, but it's true.'

By the end of the 1980s, Sugar had also evolved more conventional ways to switch off from Amstrad. He had a circle of friends with whom he could relax, and he had mellowed from his younger days when his conversation had revolved obsessively around the progress of his small business. Often he does not even allude to some deal he has just completed at Amstrad when he meets his friends in the evening; they do not hear about it until they see it reported in the newspapers.

Immediate neighbours, wealthy business people like the Sugars themselves, formed part of their circle. But most were friends they made when they first moved to Chigwell in the early 1970s. Increasingly wary of newcomers, in case they were seeking his company for ulterior purposes, Sugar felt most comfortable with his old gang of friends. 'I think he values his old friends too much to climb the social ladder so as to be out of reach. He doesn't have to be anything other than himself with us,' says Gerry Eriera, his long-standing friend.

Many of the Sugars' friends inevitably inhabit different worlds. Barney and Myrna Lazarus, for instance, live in a small bungalow in Redbridge. A life-long cabbie, Barney has on occasion picked up Sugar or one of his business associates in central London. As Ann Sugar's first cousin, Myrna Lazarus was the link which brought the Sugar and Lazarus families together in the early 1970s.

A meal in a local Italian or Chinese restaurant still ranks as an evening out for the Sugars, and the Lazarus couple admire the fact that their tastes and lifestyle have not radically changed as their wealth has mounted. They also respect Alan Sugar for not patronizing them with his wealth. On special occasions, the Sugars may invite their friends out for a meal, but Sugar does not make people like Barney and Myrna feel uncomfortable by flashing his money around: 'What I like about him is that when it comes to paying the bill, he'll only pay his share. He doesn't try and take over and say, "I'll pay for it all." I admire him for that,' says Barney Lazarus.

Most winters the Sugars visit their holiday home in Florida. A four-bedroomed house with a small patio, a swimming pool and its own tennis court, it backs on to the eleventh hole of a golf course in Boca Raton, the town 35 miles north of Miami where, ironically, I.B.M. built its first personal computer. Some of the Sugars' wealthier friends, like the Erieras, have also bought a villa in the same complex. Others, like the Lazaruses, come over to stay. As a result, a party of Sugar's friends tends to fly over most Christmases, joining the 'snowbirds', the New Yorkers who migrate to Florida for the winter.

Sugar tries to keep his workload down to a minimum during his trips to Florida, spending perhaps an hour a day in his small office there. Otherwise, he plays tennis, jogs, rides his bike and relaxes with his friends. Stories abound about his sense of fun, whether mimicking American accents or impersonating Charles Aznavour from the little balcony overlooking the large living room in his house.

Sugar's time away from work revolves around his family. He has never been tempted into the kind of jet-setting existence which could dilute this fundamental commitment. He is proud that his children – two sons and a daughter – were not spoilt by his great wealth. They were educated at local day schools, mostly in the private sector because Sugar feels that state schools have deteriorated since the days when he attended Brookhouse. Pocket money was limited when they were children, and as young adults they were given modest cars.

Amstrad's chairman hopes that his two sons will follow him in the business, but he insists that they will have to earn promotion. Simon, the elder, did a stint after leaving school working for Dixons in order to understand the viewpoint of Amstrad's customers. Dixons laid on a programme for him, so that he could see different facets of the business, but he was given no special treatment when serving in a Dixons store in the West End of London. Stanley Kalms, Dixons chairman, says: 'He wanted to learn retailing and he did. He is a very quiet, hardworking and modest lad. He was treated just like anyone else – well, just like anyone else who had Alan Sugar for a father. I'm sure he was treated nicer than he should have been, but it wasn't company policy.'

The younger son, Daniel, went to work for Amstrad as an assistant in the marketing department as a 16-year-old straight from school. There was no hint of a 'one day, son, this will be all yours' attitude in the way Sugar treated his son. On the contrary, on Daniel's first day in 1987 Sugar dragged him in to see Thomas Power – Amstrad's marketing manager at the time – and said, 'This is Daniel. This is my son. I want you to teach him all that marketing crap you lot go on about down here. I want you to teach him everything you know. If he gives you any talkback, send him up to me. And if he doesn't do what you tell him, throw him out the door.'

Daniel was used to his father's jokey-aggressive manner. Power found him to be a modest, well-balanced lad, who had coped well with the problem which confronts many children of the successful – living in the parental shadow. Yet Power also detected an entrepreneurial spark in Daniel and says: 'He's got the bolshy, "Oh yeah, I'm a trader, I'm a banana salesman and I'll sell you a satellite dish on the side," attitude. He's got all that. He has a fast mind in the trading, not in the academic, sense.'

As far as Sugar's own parents were concerned, it was an uphill struggle persuading Fay and Nathan to adapt to his great wealth and to let him spend money on them. It took him years to convince them to move out of their flat in Hackney, which was rapidly succumbing to the worst forms of inner city blight. He wanted to buy them a flat in Redbridge, but initially they resisted the move as too extravagant. He paid for them to take holidays in the United States and Israel, but had to tell white lies about the first-class air tickets he bought. Sugar said they had been given to him in the course of business, since without this subterfuge his parents would have worried about the expense.

Sugar's natural competitiveness did spill over into one area of his private life – his tennis – which absorbed more and more of his time after he gave up flying in the early 1980s. The game brought Sugar's business and private worlds together one evening in June 1989, when Amstrad sponsored the pre-Wimbledon pro-celebrity tennis tournament at the Royal Albert Hall. Television personalities, actors and sportsmen like Terry Wogan, Jimmy Tarbuck, Dennis Waterman and Bobby Moore, were among the celebrities who turned out to support the event. Amstrad's business associates joined a large contingent of Sugar's friends, who became more lively as Sugar and his partner – Indian tennis star Vijay Amritraj – progressed through the early rounds. Banners supporting Sugar were unfurled from the balcony of the Royal Albert Hall, while shouts of 'Come on, Alan' echoed round the arena.

The most interesting game was the semi-final which pitched Richard Branson against Alan Sugar. The conduct of two of Britain's best-known entrepreneurs on the tennis court spoke volumes about their contrasting business styles. Virgin's chairman was the perennial public schoolboy, jokily hitting the tennis ball as high into the reaches of the Albert Hall as possible, yet still managing to play well enough to keep Sugar on his toes. Amstrad's boss was the gritty East Ender, focusing on the task of winning the match, though occasionally finding time to flash a sheepish grin at his supporters. Sugar won the day on that occasion and the Sugar-Amritraj duo went on to win the final, giving his friends an excuse to celebrate – not that they seemed to need one.

One of several charitable activities which Sugar undertook in the second half of the 1980s, the tennis evening raised some £170,000 for the Muscular Dystrophy Group. In 1986 Sugar created a personal foundation to distribute money to charity. The Alan Sugar Foundation has given funds to local causes, the largest being a donation of almost £1 million to build a new wing for an old people's home in Ilford. It has also donated to national charities such as the Great Ormond Street children's hospital appeal. Sugar never broadcast these activities and even his close friends did not know about his foundation until some time after it was created.

Amstrad's chairman has worked for Business in the Community (BiC), a group which channels business help towards the inner cities. One day Sugar went with the Prince of Wales, BiC's president, to Hartlepool – an unemployment black spot in the North of England. Hartlepool reminded him a little of the East End of his childhood. It seemed to be full of people like his father, who lacked the confidence to realize they could branch out on their own. Sugar, who was there to talk to a group of unemployed youngsters, told them, 'They could become gardeners, window cleaners, painters and decorators. Perhaps some of them might even be able to employ one or two other people. I suggested they should have the confidence to think of starting up their own business.'

As Sugar became more accustomed to appearing on platforms

and before the television cameras, he revealed an untutored talent for public speaking. Business people are often intensely dull speech-makers, but he has a natural sharpness and sense of humour in public. Jimmy Tarbuck, the Liverpool comedian who has hosted several Amstrad business events, has watched Sugar's confidence in public grow and admires his timing: 'I'd have no complaints about working on a script with him. He'd be very good to bounce off. His delivery is good enough and he'd be all right with a line,' Tarbuck says.

Yet Sugar's facility in public, plus his hard-hitting language, disguises a deep-rooted shyness which surprises people who know only his reputation for bluster. This diffidence helps to explain his indifference to personal publicity. Interest in Sugar and Amstrad exploded after the success of the PCW8256 word processor. Nick Hewer, Sugar's public relations adviser, has regularly to decline forty or so requests a month for interviews, guest appearances and talks by Amstrad's chairman. Sugar has turned down invitations for which many people wait a lifetime – to appear on the Desert Island Discs radio show, or as one of the main commentators on the B.B.C.'s post-Budget programme. Hewer had to struggle hard to persuade him to be profiled or interviewed by some of the world's most prestigious publications like *Time*, *Fortune* and the *Wall Street Journal*. The only way Hewer could secure Sugar's agreement to a profile in *Time* was by showing him the rate for a page advert in the magazine and pointing out how much he would save Amstrad by agreeing to the interview.

Sugar was being drawn – in many ways against his natural inclination – on to a larger stage. In 1988 he was asked by Lord Young, the Trade and Industry Secretary who later became deputy chairman of the Conservative Party, to spearhead the Government's 1992 advertising campaign. Young chose a handful of well-known business leaders to spread awareness in the business world of the European Community's programme to remove internal trade barriers. The Minister wanted people who would be widely recognized on television and on the advertisement hoardings – people like Sugar, Richard Branson, Sir John Harvey-Jones (former head of I.C.I.) and Sir John Egan, who led Jaguar out of public ownership. 'All of them were people who stood out above the crowd. And there's no question that Alan Sugar was the foremost British leader in the computer industry and in electronics goods generally,' says Young.

Disliking the script written for his television commercial by the Government's advisers, Amstrad's chairman phoned Young and said he could do better himself. Young readily agreed: 'I thought that since he knew a thing or two about marketing, I wouldn't worry.'

Sugar's 1992 advert was simplicity itself. It showed him standing in front of Amstrad computers marked for Britain, Germany, France, Spain and Italy. At present, he told the camera, Amstrad's computers have to be adapted for national markets. After 1992, they will all be the same. Research carried out for the Trade and Industry Department showed that this advert was one of the most effective in arousing business people's interest in 1992.

Invitations to lunch with the Queen at Buckingham Palace and to seminars and dinners at No. 10 Downing Street also landed on Sugar's desk. Yet he did not always seem at ease in the great world of politics, at times giving the impression that he would rather be running his business. Lord Young, who first met him at a Downing Street seminar, believes this may reflect the way Sugar's business is developing:

I suppose during the early years of the decade, up to 1986 or 1987, Sugar was riding a tiger which was almost impossible to control. Then, just when it's established and he's worth several hundred million pounds, Amstrad develops some problems. He's got to overcome those. But by the early 1990s, the problems could be behind him and he's got a steady business which is growing fast. It may come to the stage when it's not a 24-hour-a-day job for him to run his business. Then he may look for other things to do. It may be charitable or political activities.

Young also felt that Sugar's unease in governmental circles flowed from his outsider status – his history of having clawed his way up from the East End. 'He's still, I think, got a slight air of insecurity about him. He hasn't shown any sign of wanting to come into the fold. That may happen later on, perhaps when he's Sir Alan Sugar or Lord Sugar of Chigwell, or whatever else happens in their dotage to great industrialists. Who can tell? He may not. He's never struck me as the sort of person who sets great store on being a member of the Establishment.'

· 15 ·

Pennies from Heaven

Once Alan Sugar became a public figure, he was inevitably the target for unwanted attention. Amstrad headquarters began to receive phone calls from cranks, people on the make and those with nothing better to do than call up someone they had read about in the newspapers. Many of these stray callers claimed some long-lost association with Sugar or his family. As Sugar describes the problem:

> The phone does not stop ringing from nine o'clock in the morning to six o'clock at night. That school I went to in Hackney must have had 250 million boys in it, because everybody that phones claims to know me, or went to school with me, or knows a brother who's got an uncle who knows an aunt who knows me. Honestly, I can't talk to everybody who picks up the phone to me every day. So Frances, my secretary, has got this patter of politely saying to people, 'Who are you? Do you really know Mr Sugar?'

One day in May 1988 the routine backfired. Frances, who is politeness personified, came into Sugar's office and said, 'Mr Rupert Murdoch wants to speak to you on the phone.'

Sugar kept his eyes firmly on the pile of papers on his desk. 'Never heard of him. Tell him to piss off, clear off, I'm not interested. I bet he thinks he went to my school.'

Amstrad's chairman explains this surprising reaction:

The problem with me is I'm very bad on names and also I'm very bad at reading the newspapers. I'm very unworldly in the sense that outside the electronics and computer industries, I don't know the names of big-shot businessmen. If you asked me who is the chairman of B.A.T. or Shell or British Telecom, I wouldn't know. There are people who go around name-dropping all the time, saying Sir John This or Sir John That, and you're supposed to know who they're talking about. I really don't. Sometimes people think I'm lying, but I'm not.

Sugar could sense Frances hesitating, so he said, 'Who the bleeding hell is this Murdoch? Go and find out what it's about.'

Frances returned. 'The lady says Mr Murdoch doesn't normally tell people what his business is before speaking to them himself. She rang off, but I have taken their number.'

Sugar lifted one eye from his task. 'Well, who is this bloke Murdoch?'

Frances replied: 'He owns the *Sun*, *The Times*, the *Sunday Times*, the *News of the World* and *Today* newspapers and he's the one who had the big confrontation with the unions.'

'Oh my God,' said Sugar. 'Quick, get him back on the line.'

*

Alan Sugar was one of the first businessmen in Britain to grasp the potential of a new method of delivering television – direct broadcasting by satellite. Technological advances which allowed programmes to be beamed down by satellite, coupled with a political climate in Britain which favoured more competition for the established television channels, combined to usher in this broadcasting revolution.

In 1986 Amstrad's chairman was visiting the headquarters of Granada, the diversified group whose interests include Granada Television and high street rental and retail chains specializing in electrical goods. He was there to discuss Amstrad's business as a supplier to Granada's shops, but the conversation roamed more widely. Granada's executives told him that they were forming a consortium to bid for Britain's first satellite broadcasting franchise. The plan was to provide three new channels and they wanted to know whether Sugar would like to join the consortium. The entry ticket would be an initial £10 million equity stake. Amstrad's role would be to supply a crucial ingredient in the satellite broadcasting mix – the dishes that receive the signals from the satellite.

Sugar liked the proposal. He believed Britain to be seriously under-provided with television channels compared with the United States, where the average American can receive almost fifty stations. He felt there was a healthy appetite for more television among the people who bought Amstrad's audio and video products – the original truck-driver-and-his-wife Amstrad customers who had no qualms about the amount of television they watched, unlike the chattering classes who dominated London's opinion-forming circles. After all, Sugar was happy to admit that he relaxed by watching 'American garbage' on television. 'Satellite broadcasting is good for our type of British consumer,' he was later to tell a meeting of City analysts. 'It may not appeal to you lot, but the *Sun* readership and the *News of the World* readership are going to buy that stuff.'

Sugar agreed to join Granada's consortium, which called itself British Satellite Broadcasting (B.S.B.). It boasted an impressive line-up: Virgin, the music group built up by the ever-youthful Richard Branson; Pearson, the blue-blooded blue chip company whose many interests include the *Financial Times*; and Anglia Television, together with Granada and Amstrad. It appeared to be a well-balanced team, with the television expertise of Granada and Anglia complemented by Pearson's heavyweight respectability and the marketing flair of Amstrad and Virgin. With Amstrad's participation, B.S.B. could point to a credible source of dishes for its satellite service.

The Independent Broadcasting Authority, the television regulatory body, had to judge between the bidders for Britain's first satellite broadcasting franchise. At 3 pm on 11 December 1986, representatives of the five consortia bidding for the franchise were summoned to the I.B.A.'s offices and asked to wait in separate rooms until handed an envelope by Lord Thomson, I.B.A. chairman. When the five opened their envelopes, they found that the I.B.A. had also been impressed by B.S.B.'s mix of expertise. B.S.B.

was the winner and Amstrad seemed to have found itself a new line of business.

But it was not to be. Amstrad quickly began to cool to its new partners. Views differ as to why this happened. A senior B.S.B. executive of the time voices what was a common perception of the reason for Amstrad's disenchantment with B.S.B:

> Amstrad came to realize that it was not going to get a monopoly over the supply of receivers to B.S.B. – which perhaps it had thought it might. Amstrad also perhaps thought that it might get earlier or privileged access to information about things like the specification. But B.S.B. insisted on dealing with Amstrad like any other supplier.

Sugar rejects this version of events: 'There was never any question of us going to get any exclusive rights or any preferential rights, or any privileged knowledge of the receiver.'

Amstrad's chairman explains that he rapidly became uneasy with the B.S.B. operation. Jim Rice, the company's representative at the B.S.B.'s partners meeting, regularly reported back to him on progress, and once or twice Sugar went himself to check out developments. His dissatisfaction mounted during the early months of 1987 as the moment approached when the founding partners would be asked to put up their cash:

> You get a feeling about people and where their priorities lie. When we started listening to them, it seemed their priorities lay in the size of the office suites they had to have and all that kind of stuff. Their own little luxuries came first. I was being asked to entrust my money to a group of people who were going to run this show. And there was no way I felt comfortable in putting my money in the hands of those people. I looked at the extravagance of what they were planning to do there and when it was time to part with the old doshoroney, I said no thank you very much.

B.S.B. looked set to make considerable cash demands on its partners for several years before its service began to operate.

Continuing participation would have cost Amstrad significant amounts with no immediate return. Developing equipment for B.S.B. would be a long and expensive process, because B.S.B. was committed to using a new broadcast transmission system called MAC – eventually it opted for the D-MAC version. D-MAC will ultimately deliver a better picture than the older PAL system currently used in British broadcasting, but its superior picture is at present available on only a relatively small number of new high-tech screens. On the great bulk of sets there is little to choose between the quality of pictures transmitted through the two systems. Backing the development of D-MAC equipment seemed to Sugar a costly irrelevance.

On 15 May 1987 Amstrad quit B.S.B. The news was buried in the simultaneous announcement that B.S.B. had provisionally arranged another £200 million of funding and attracted a batch of new investors. Sugar recalls a conversation with the chairman of Virgin, another B.S.B. partner, at the time: 'I remember Richard Branson said to me, "I hope you're wrong, because I'm staying in." I said, "Well, maybe it's more up your alley than mine." And as we all know, Virgin later got its money out of Bondy and ran for the hills.'

In 1988 Virgin sold its B.S.B. stake to Alan Bond, the Australian businessman. Thus B.S.B. had lost the two people – Branson and Sugar – who gave its initial line-up entrepreneurial fizz.

Amstrad did not entirely lose touch with B.S.B., which in early 1988 was searching for possible suppliers of receiving equipment. As many as a hundred suppliers were considered; a short-list of fifteen, including Amstrad, was announced in early May 1988. Yet Amstrad's heart appeared not to be in it. The company did not ask B.S.B. for the full documentation needed by potential suppliers, which was unusual for such an aggressively competitive firm as Amstrad. Unbeknown to B.S.B., Alan Sugar had received Rupert Murdoch's phone call shortly after B.S.B.'s short-list had been published.

Murdoch's News International had been a member of one of the consortia which failed to win the I.B.A.'s satellite broadcasting franchise, but Murdoch refused to regard this as the end of the story. During 1987, while B.S.B. was making its plans in the full glare of publicity, he was quietly looking for another way into satellite broadcasting. It became apparent that Astra, a private sector satellite service based in Luxembourg, offered a route. Astra was in the business of launching satellites capable of transmitting television from the Ariane space rockets which blast off from French Guiana. The question was: would it make commercial sense for Murdoch to book space on an Astra satellite for a satellite television service of his own?

The small team of executives researching the project for Rupert Murdoch quickly identified the critical factor. Peter Smith, a softly spoken Australian engineer who was later to become Sky Television's director of operations and planning, remembers: 'I'd done some financial projections for Sky and it turned out that what is absolutely crucial is the rate of growth of receivers in the market place. The profitability and survival of the organization is far more sensitive to that than to virtually every other factor put together.'

Murdoch concluded that he would need a supplier who could produce large volumes of receivers at rock-bottom prices. He and his team identified £200 as the magic figure below which receiving equipment might sell in great numbers. Smith, nothing if not methodical, urged on Murdoch the need for market research to see if people would buy receivers at that price. Murdoch disagreed: 'You cannot do effective market research on something that nobody has ever had, because people do not know enough about it to be able to say whether they would buy it.'

Murdoch and Smith were still debating the merits of market research while scouring the Far East for sources of receivers. One of their appointments was with Akio Morita, the legendary Japanese engineer-businessman who built up Sony to become one of the world's great consumer electronics innovators. Murdoch and Morita had met a few times, so they greeted one another fulsomely, took the lift in Sony's Tokyo headquarters to the top floor and waded through the carpet to Morita's office. Following the protocol for meetings between corporate barons in Japan, they drank tea and made speeches praising each other's company.

During the course of this ritual, Morita asked Murdoch, 'Do you ever have trouble with your marketing people?'

Murdoch looked at Smith and replied, 'Yes, as a matter of fact, I do.'

Morita: 'Do they always want you to do market surveys?'

Murdoch: 'Well, yes, why though do you say that?'

Morita: 'I had an idea for my company once. I thought of a new product. I wanted to build a tiny little thing which played cassettes and which people could carry in their pockets while they were jogging or working. But my company told me it would be terribly expensive to build, so I had to do a market survey. But I had a gut feeling that it was going to be right.'

'Gut feeling' is one of the favourite expressions of Rupert Murdoch, who was beginning to enjoy the story immensely.

Morita continued, 'My company then asked me what I wanted to call this machine. I said, "A Walkman." And they told me, "That's a terrible name. We'll have to do a market survey on it."'

The proposal for a market study of satellite broadcasting's potential was not raised again within News International, but Murdoch's trip to the Far East was less fruitful in other respects. He and Peter Smith did the rounds of the great names in Japanese electronics – Sony, Toshiba, Mitsubishi and so on. Even though Japan already had a satellite broadcasting system, none could offer Murdoch what he wanted; the cheapest dish any would promise to produce would have cost £300 – 50 per cent above Murdoch's target price. Also they wanted plenty of time to develop the equipment and precise information from Murdoch about the market – impossible questions to answer since the market did not exist. 'The Japanese manufacturers turned out to be very conservative. They were very European in their approach,' Smith says, looking back.

Murdoch continued to draw up plans for Sky Television, but the lynchpin problem still had not been solved, as he explains: 'I felt the whole thing was contingent on getting a supplier of receiving equipment at a low price. If we waited for the Japanese or the French to come late and expensively, we'd go broke waiting for the market to develop.'

In May 1988, it occurred to Murdoch that he need not look to Japan or the Continent for cheap receiving equipment. The answer lay much nearer to News International's home in the East End of London. In everything he had done, Alan Sugar had shown that he could produce large volumes cheaply. Why not ask him to make Sky's receivers?

By the time Murdoch phoned Sugar, he had already worked out the main parameters of Sky Television: he knew the price he wanted for the equipment, and he thought it sensible to broadcast using PAL rather than D-MAC. But in his first conversation with Sugar, News International's boss wanted to take the measure of the man. So he sounded him out on these issues.

Sugar's answers to Murdoch's questions were to the point:

> The success of a satellite depends on a triangle. The triangle is like this: the satellite, good programmes and receiving equipment. The programmes have got to be good and that means it must have a movie channel. It will be a failure without a movie channel. The equipment's got to be cheap. And we can transmit in PAL, because that's all that's available now. If anyone tells you anything different, it's a load of cobblers because D-MAC does not exist. There are no D-MAC chip sets. All this quality cobblers that B.S.B. is talking about through using D-MAC is also a load of bloody rubbish, because the quality enhancement from a D-MAC transmission will only be realizable when things like high definition television come on the market. In the meantime, there are 22 million televisions out there which can only receive in PAL, and there's nothing which anybody can do to improve the picture. That is a fact of life. If something is transmitted in D-MAC, it's got to come down here, be translated into PAL and be pumped into your television. Otherwise you can't receive it.

So convinced was Sugar of this point that in June 1988, after his link with Murdoch had been made public, he issued a challenge.

Pointing to the television in his office, Sugar said, 'I'll offer £1 million to anyone who can make a better picture than that. D-MAC television sets haven't even been developed yet.'

B.S.B. took up the challenge, showing how a conventional television equipped with a special adaptor could offer a better picture by receiving D-MAC signals. In October, B.S.B. ran full-page advertisements proclaiming, 'Dear Alan, Looks like your PAL just cost you a million.' The adverts asked him to send £1 million to a charity of his choice.

But Sugar would not play ball. He accused B.S.B. of ignoring the terms of his challenge, which applied to the television set in his office – similar to that in 95 per cent of British homes. 'I am ready to stand up and be counted, proved wrong, eat my hat and part with £1 million, if I am wrong,' he said.

The phone call between Murdoch and Sugar showed that they were thinking along the same lines, but Murdoch did not take the conversation further immediately. He wanted to check Sugar out. After all, Amstrad would be able to break Sky if it failed to deliver the receivers. Murdoch telephoned some contacts in the top echelons of British business, including Lord Weinstock, to ask about Sugar. He liked what he heard and called the Amstrad chairman again after a couple of days. This time Murdoch made a proposal: Would Amstrad be able to make very large numbers of receivers to retail at £199 each? Sugar replied he would find out and let him know in a matter of days.

Amstrad's chairman told Bob Watkins, his technical director, that he had a day or two to find out whether Amstrad could make a profit out of receivers selling for £199 in the shops. He briefed Watkins to be flexible: 'There must be some dustbin lid manufacturer who can make the dish for us, or somebody up in the Midlands whose business is waning because the car industry is going down the pan. See if we can do it.'

Bob Watkins has become used to being given tasks like this by Sugar. As a result he has developed an unusual blend of engineering and commercial nous. He often has to decide whether Amstrad can make something for a certain price to a deadline which would give a more conventional engineer nightmares.

Sugar's overriding need for speedy decision-making has demanded it. And Sugar says that Watkins's calculated gambles have proved right within plus or minus 5 per cent 9½ times out of 10.

Watkins gave Sugar the news a couple of days later. Amstrad's technical director was still waiting for a few more quotations to come in, but his gut feeling was that it could be done. This time Sugar phoned Murdoch: 'We'll take a gamble and I'll say, yes, we can do it for £199. But what we will do, is have one model at £199 and, as a contingency plan, another model at £259 with remote control, which gives us a little bit more margin in case we've made a mistake.'

Murdoch agreed to this proposal. Now it was Sugar's turn to make a few demands, as he explains: 'I put my humble hat on and said, "Look, I'm only a little humble lad from Brentwood. I haven't got the multi-mega-millions of your organization. You're not asking me to ponce around making 5,000 pieces; you want me to put hundreds of thousands of receivers out there. So what happens if the bleeding rocket doesn't go up?"'

Sugar would have to start work on the receivers immediately, in May 1988, knowing that two critical dates lay in the future. One would be later in the year when an Ariane rocket would send the Astra satellite into orbit. However, Ariane spaceships had been known to fail to leave the launch-pad or explode on take-off. The other critical date would be in February 1989, when Sky was due to start broadcasting; if Sky pumped out feeble programmes, then Amstrad could be left with large numbers of unwanted dishes.

Alan Sugar and Rupert Murdoch met to hammer out their final agreement. Sugar hit it off with Murdoch, just as he had with Weinstock, recognizing a kindred spirit – someone also used to making swift decisions, taking risks and getting his own way. It did not take the two entrepreneurs long to agree terms.

For his part, Sugar agreed to set the wheels in motion to make a million satellite dishes in a year. He understood from the start that it was a non-exclusive relationship: other suppliers would be free to make receivers for Sky. At this stage, Murdoch did not place an order for a single dish with Sugar. His part of the deal was to agree to repay all Amstrad's costs in one of three cases: either the rocket failed to go up; or the satellite failed to make satisfactory test transmissions; or Sky failed to go on air with four channels. As Sugar recalls,

> He indemnified us that he would go ahead and start with four channels. So we wouldn't go to the trouble of getting a million satellite dishes organized and all he was going to put on the air was some tenth rated Channel 4. Sky would definitely have a sports channel, a movie channel, a light entertainment channel and a news channel. We went on our own gut feeling and the indemnification.

The Murdoch-Sugar link-up, though not its precise terms, was announced on 8 June 1988, barely three weeks after Murdoch's first phone call to Sugar. Amstrad's chairman had been busy on other fronts in this short space of time, and he was able to tell the assembled journalists that Dixons had agreed to take 500,000 dishes from him. The Murdoch-Sugar press conference was as crowded as the Sugar-Sinclair event of two years before; it was before the assembled throng that Murdoch dubbed Sugar 'probably Britain's greatest entrepreneur'.

Sugar busied himself tying up deals with the contractors which would make the various parts of Amstrad's receiving equipment. The order for the convex metal work of the dish was placed with a Birmingham-based metal-basher, as Sugar had anticipated – although the supplier, Concentric, was not known as a dustbin-lid manufacturer and was enjoying booming sales to the European motor industry. The electronics for the receiver, a black box which sits on top of the television, was made in the Far East. This left just one main part for the Amstrad dish: the low-noise block converters (LNBs), which process the signals transmitted by satellites and which stand out from the middle of the metal dishes.

Amstrad was combing the Far East for suppliers of the LNBs when Sugar became aware that Britain's General Electric Company was interested in the work. The interest flowed directly from Lord Weinstock, G.E.C.'s managing director, who had kept in touch with

Sugar since the abortive talks about a joint venture between their two companies. Weinstock had set up a research team to look at ways of generating spin-off consumer products from the company's work in defence electronics, an area where G.E.C. is immensely strong. G.E.C.'s managing director reckoned that its expertise in radar and similar fields could be brought to bear on the LNBs, which Amstrad would need in huge numbers.

Bob Watkins negotiated the outline of a deal with his counterpart at G.E.C. but the talks became stalled over price. It looked as though G.E.C. would lose Amstrad's order to a Japanese rival and Sugar decided to intervene: 'It had to be buttoned up and sometimes there's only one way of sorting things out. So I decided to go straight to Arnold. I told him what was going on and that G.E.C. was about to lose the order,' Sugar says.

After some haggling on the phone, Alan Sugar and Arnold Weinstock closed the deal there and then. Sugar formed the impression that Weinstock enjoyed the deal-making process as much as he did: 'Arnold was excited by it. He liked doing the deal. It reminded him of his early days, because him and me were haggling on the phone over 50 pence, which is probably something he hasn't done for 30 years.'

The collaboration with G.E.C. over the LNBs played an important part in the evolution of Sugar's thinking. The growth of protectionist trade sentiment in the European Commission, coupled with rising wages in the Far East, was forcing him to consider moving more of Amstrad's manufacturing back to Europe. It was a change which he contemplated reluctantly, since his experience of British manufacturing had been largely negative. But G.E.C.'s work on the satellite contract began to give him a new perspective. 'Arnold pulled together a team of people and instructed them to get on with it. And they did. I must give them credit where credit's due. It brought back a lot of my confidence in British electronics when I saw them do that.'

Sugar's relations with Murdoch settled into a groove. The two men tend to talk on the phone every few weeks, not just to sort out any immediate problems but also – once Sky Television was launched – to discuss how the service is faring. Murdoch says he rates Sugar's advice highly because he trusts his understanding of the ordinary British consumer: 'I call him once or twice a month to see how things are going – to keep in touch and get his opinion on the market place,' Murdoch explains.

In the early days, Sugar viewed the newspapermen who ran News International as having strayed into a line of business – consumer electronics – of which they were profoundly ignorant. As a result, he tended to give short shrift to Murdoch's latest query or anxiety, a pattern established at their first meeting in May 1988:

Murdoch: 'What do you think of this B.S.B.? They claim they're going to be on the air in September 1989.'

Sugar: 'No way.'

Murdoch: 'Well, they say they're going to do it.'

Sugar: 'Well, I say they're not.'

Murdoch: 'Why not?'

Sugar: 'Because they haven't got any chips.'

A few months later, after the Sugar-Murdoch deal had been struck, Murdoch warned Amstrad's boss that other manufacturers were now planning to make receivers for Sky.

Murdoch: 'Sinclair is going to make some dishes for us. Toshiba's also coming along and will be delivering dishes.'

Sugar: 'They won't turn up. They won't deliver you any by the date they say, and half of them won't work.'

Sugar began to worry about the view Murdoch was forming of him:

> The kind of impression he must have got of me in the beginning was: this geezer's a bloody great bighead. He knows everything. He says everything quickly. He's so convinced and incisive. But the point is they were trying to tell me about my business, the electronics business. They were unqualified people talking about things they didn't know anything about. They probably thought everything I was saying was just salesman's talk. But it's all come to pass.

Sky and Amstrad had to resolve several problems before Sky's launch, the most serious of which concerned Sky's plans for a movie channel. Originally, Murdoch had intended Sky's movies to be free to all Sky viewers, but he changed his mind during the course of 1988. He realized that he could not buy the rights to many movies in European countries outside the U.K. and Ireland, because they were already owned by various parties who had no intention of selling them. Sky would have to put a scrambler on its system to prevent people on the Continent watching its movie channel in order to avoid actions for breach of copyright. But, Murdoch concluded, in that case why not turn the necessity to scramble into a source of revenue?

Only those viewers in the U.K. and Ireland who paid a monthly subscription would have access to a descrambler to see the movie channel. In this way, Sky would gain an additional stream of cash, which would be particularly valuable while its viewing numbers – and hence attractiveness to advertisers – were building up. Sky would need this revenue badly, since competition between itself and B.S.B. for programming rights pushed up costs sharply during 1988. B.S.B. committed more than $700 million over five years for the rights of five U.S. studios. 'When we came to negotiate for the movies, we found B.S.B. already there spraying literally hundreds of millions of dollars around Hollywood,' Murdoch says.

Sky considered two main descrambling methods. The subscriber could be given a smart card, which would fit into the decoder; or a signal could be transmitted remotely to the decoder. At first Murdoch was set against the smart card, believing it to be an expensive solution. By contrast, Sugar championed this idea to the point of lining up a sub-contractor who could make them for Amstrad. He doubted whether remote descrambling was available except in a form which would be easy for hackers to decode, and mounted a sustained campaign to persuade Sky of his views: 'I sent them lengthy fax messages explaining it to them in baby language,' he recalls.

Sky's technical guru, Peter Smith, also backed the smart card, and Murdoch gave in under the pincer movement from Sugar and Smith. One day he picked up the phone and told Sugar, 'Don't start barking like an old crow and shouting your head off, but basically you were right. We're going with the smart card.'

Sugar naturally hoped to win the contract to make the smart-card descrambling system, but he was thwarted for two reasons. The first – and, Sky insists, most important – was because Peter Smith was not convinced that Amstrad's smart card was secure. The second was a matter of timing: Murdoch wanted the descrambler to be available by April 1989. Sugar sat down with his engineers and decided the deadline was impossible. He told Murdoch that Amstrad could deliver the smart card by September, whereupon Murdoch informed him that Thomson, the French electronics giant, had promised to deliver by June. Murdoch was deluged with more Sugar candour: 'When hair grows in the palm of your hand, then Thomson will deliver in June. Go to Thomson, those great French mega-stars, and you will not scramble until into 1990.'

Thomson got the contract and failed to deliver in June 1989, since the work on the scrambler proved more difficult than either it or Sky had anticipated. As a result, Sky had to postpone the launch of its scrambled movie service until 1990. Moreover, the scrambling discussions held up work on the design and production of Amstrad's dishes in the autumn of 1988, a critical period in the run-up to Sky's launch.

So too did a more technical but related issue. Sky needed to issue a specification of the socket which would allow the decoder to be plugged into the receiver. The difficulty was that this specification had to be suitable for equipment from the twenty or so companies which were thinking of manufacturing receiving equipment for Sky. The latter's starting point in writing the specification was Amstrad, since it would be the first and largest receiver manufacturer. But having determined what Amstrad wanted, Sky then had to ask the views of all the other potential manufacturers. 'It was over a month while they were sodding around making their mind up which way they were going to go,' Sugar recalls.

Sky's planners had a bad moment on 10 December when the Ariane-4 rocket was sitting on its launch-pad in Kourou, French

Guiana, with the Astra satellite on board. Already postponed once from November, the launch was aborted just 26 seconds from lift-off when a faulty valve was discovered. Twenty-four hours later, however, the rocket blasted off perfectly, carrying into the stratosphere Murdoch's and Sugar's hopes.

Preparations were feverish at Sky's new £15 million studios on the western outskirts of London as the February 1989 start-up date approached. Less than a week from launch, visitors found parts of the forecourt still a sea of mud. Meanwhile, Murdoch scaled back his ambitious forecasts for Britain's first satellite television service. In January 1989, Sky told potential advertisers that it was cutting predictions of the minimum number of homes it expected would be receiving Sky after a year from 2.5 million to 1.15 million. One problem becoming obvious to friend and foe alike was that there would be virtually no receivers in the shops at launch date.

When Sky began broadcasting, retailers like Dixons and Currys typically had only one dish in each store which they used for demonstration purposes. Murdoch conceded that most potential Sky customers would have to wait for more equipment to be made by Amstrad's Japanese sub-contractors – 'the night shift in Japan', as he put it – before they would be able to find a receiver. The delays imposed on Amstrad by Sky the previous autumn came home to roost and the build-up to full-volume production of receivers by Amstrad's contractors in the Far East did not occur until a month or so after Sky's launch. Sugar fumed at the suggestion that his company was responsible for the delay; Murdoch, for one, is in no doubt as to where the blame lies: 'It was my fault. That wasn't Amstrad's fault. That was my fault,' he says in retrospect.

Sky's launch went without a hitch, but there was plenty of sniping in that portion of the media not owned by Murdoch about the quality of the programmes on offer. For some unfathomable reason, the show of country singer Dolly Parton was a particular target. Nevertheless, even the most hostile critic had to concede Sky's achievement in simultaneously launching four new television channels – the first time this feat had been attempted in Britain. Sugar was in Japan on the day of the launch, but when he returned the following weekend he switched on Sky at his home, one of the few in the country then sporting an Amstrad dish. 'I'm impressed,' he told a group of City analysts a few days later.

Murdoch's newspapers lost no chance to puff Sky: the *Sun*'s page 3 girl even appeared clutching a satellite dish and little else. This campaign, together with the general publicity surrounding the launch, unleashed a surge of demand for the dishes. Unsurprisingly, greatest interest was found among the skilled working class, the C2s, the bedrock of Amstrad's traditional consumer following. 'People are driving us barmy wanting the dishes,' Sugar said, while Murdoch claimed that retailers had taken deposits from almost 100,000 people.

But there were still not enough receivers. Amstrad considered flying in a batch from the Far East, thereby cutting out their long sea journey, but that would have been an expensive solution for a product on which its profit margins were already tight. Sugar decided that the retailers would have to pay to air-freight the receivers: 'One of us is going to have lower margins, either us or the retailer – and it won't be us,' he said.

Sky managed another early publicity boost by screening the heavyweight title fight between Mike Tyson and Frank Bruno live at the end of February. But the lack of dishes in the shops prevented it from really cashing in on this coup. Daniel, Sugar's younger son, displayed the family's entrepreneurial streak by hiring a hall near the Sugars' Chigwell home. By charging the local populace £30 a head for a meal and a chance to view the fight on a large screen hooked up to Sky, the 18-year old made some useful pocket money.

However, the initial surge in demand for the dishes proved to be short-lived and interest dropped sharply soon after Sky's launch. Sky also had to cope with the embarrassing 'melting dish' story. G.E.C. had made a blue plastic cover for its LNB, but one batch of the covers lacked ultra-violet inhibitors. Unfortunately, Britain was lounging in one of the hottest summers on record and the plastic covers disintegrated in the sun. Amstrad and G.E.C. moved quickly to remedy the defect.

In April, the lack of consumer interest forced Sky to shed half its advertising staff. By June the *Financial Times*'s monthly satellite monitor was reporting that at most 110,000 homes had installed dishes – well under 1 per cent of all British households. Comedians added 'Sky jokes' to their repertoire: 'What's the difference between the Loch Ness monster and Sky Television?' ran one. 'Some people claim to have seen the Loch Ness monster!'

The Sky camp blamed its lack of progress on the hostility of the non-Murdoch media. It was also alarmed by a water-muddying advertising campaign launched by B.S.B. Sky's rival appeared to have successfully confused many people into deferring a decision about whether or not to try out this new satellite phenomenon.

One chink of light for Sky appeared in May, when B.S.B. was forced to postpone its launch into 1990. To its embarrassment, B.S.B. was in the middle of a £20 million advertising campaign telling the British public about its plans to launch in September 1989. But no sooner were the commercials placed than it became clear that if it went on air at this date it would have virtually no dishes for several months. Development work on the chips for B.S.B.'s dishes by I.T.T., the U.S.-based conglomerate, was way behind schedule. Two and a half years after B.S.B. was awarded its franchise, it was still not ready to transmit. Sky, which had launched on target less than a year after announcing its plans, could not resist the temptation to gloat. 'Sky: on air. B.S.B.: hot air,' it proclaimed in newspaper adverts.

Sky would have the market to itself for at least another nine months, including the crucial Christmas period, so Murdoch decided to milk this opportunity for all it was worth. But by this time relations between Sky and the high street retailers had deteriorated. Sky was accusing the retailers of not doing enough to promote the dishes, while the retailers replied that the demand simply did not exist. Sky decided to break the impasse by supplying the dishes direct to customers: 'We went into the business of leasing the dishes ourselves. That was after we'd had big rows with Dixons and all of the multiple chains,' Murdoch explains.

Sky offered customers a promotional deal, by which they would pay £4.49 a week for a package including the installation and maintenance of receivers and a subscription to Sky. Installation companies were appointed around the country to handle the business. Sky also had to buy large numbers of dishes, so Murdoch asked Sugar to call in at his office at News International's Wapping headquarters.

Sugar had to walk through the *Sun* news-room to reach Murdoch's office. 'You are now entering *Sun* country' is emblazoned above the main entrance, while blown-up versions of some of the paper's more infamous front pages are plastered over the walls. Sugar went through another security door – a Wapping feature – past the hexagonal waiting area littered with copies of Murdoch's magazines and into his vast office. Neither Murdoch nor Sugar are slow decision makers. It took less than twenty minutes for Sugar to emerge with an order for about 500,000 dishes to be delivered over the following six months. 'We wanted to back him. We thought we owed it to him. He'd taken great risks. And we still trusted him to give us the most reliable delivery. Everyone else had been talk,' Murdoch notes.

The trade-off for such a large order was a keen price: 'Well, we thought it was a good price. Like a good salesman, Alan tried to convince me that it would only just cover his costs. But I hope he's making something out of it,' Murdoch says benignly.

Sky backed the rental offer with a £21 million advertising campaign. The renewed burst of publicity after it was announced in September also rekindled interest in straight sales of the dishes, an unexpected spin-off which helped smooth a few ruffled feathers among the retailers. By the middle of December take-up of the rental offer was running at 4,000 a day, all of them Amstrad dishes.

As 1989 drew to a close, Sugar turned his mind to selling his dishes into Germany. But first he had to deal with an embarrassing side effect from Astra's German services for Sky's operations in Britain.

Early in December, Astra began transmitting four new German channels which could be received on Amstrad dishes, but due to a technical oversight on Astra's part the Amstrad receivers did not pick up the German sound. As a result, owners of Amstrad dishes throughout Britain were suddenly in the puzzling position of being able to view four new soundless channels. Every satellite television service centre in Britain was flooded with complaints and queries. Once their switchboards became clogged, the viewers began to bombard Sky with calls.

Amstrad and Sky both tried to phone Astra in Luxembourg, but everyone at the satellite company seemed to be out celebrating the successful launch of their German channels. Sugar then called Peter Smith at Sky and they decided they would both send urgent faxes to Astra.

Smith dictated a fax to his secretary who queried it: 'That's a little bit terse, isn't it?' she said. 'No, I think it's O.K., send it,' Smith replied. Sugar then sent his fax to Astra, with a copy to Smith; it was a message of such directness that it took the Australian's breath away, but the two-pronged attack worked: Astra fixed the problem within 24 hours.

Amstrad's chances of selling large quantities of dishes on the Continent vary from country to country, depending on factors such as the broadcasting system and the extent of cable television in each one. But Germany, the Netherlands and Scandinavia should hold out some opportunities. In Britain so far, the satellite story has been mixed.

Clearly sales have not matched the early expectations of either Amstrad or Sky. The weak market has allowed Amstrad's immediate customers – both the retailers and Sky – to drive tough bargains with Amstrad, putting pressure on the profit margins. Yet Amstrad still managed to sell 670,000 dishes in 1989. As both Amstrad and Sky never tire of stressing, the initial take-up of satellite television has been much more rapid than that of previous consumer electronics innovations, such as the video recorder. Moreover, Amstrad had mopped up most of the business that was available: according to Sky, it accounted for 80 per cent of the dishes installed in homes by the end of 1989.

At the end of Sky's first year, Sugar took a ruthlessly realistic view of the future:

What's happening now is you're starting to see the Japanese and other people coming in with reasonably priced equipment.

There will be a lot more choice of satellite equipment soon. Then Amstrad's market share dominance will start to go down, margins will start to erode and we'll say: thank you very much, we're on our BMX bike and we're off, we're out of this market, just like we were out of CB [Citizen Band radio] and 14″ televisions. In two to three years time, the old moss will start growing and Mr Murdoch will not remember me. He won't even know who I am, because there will be 500 different suppliers of satellite receivers out there. But that's life. That's why we had to be realistic. We had to get in and make some money. We have to realize that we haven't got a monopoly. Once we've shown the way to others, everyone will jump on the band-waggon. So don't be upset about it and don't expect any sentiment.

This may in fact turn out to be unduly pessimistic. True, many other players have now launched dishes; but overall sales are likely to expand steadily, assuming that satellite television follows the typical growth path in consumer electronics. Moreover, at least some people at Sky believe that Amstrad will remain in a strong position: 'I don't see their market share falling rapidly. I think they'll maintain a leading role,' says Peter Smith.

The satellite television market will evolve as it becomes more sophisticated, throwing up opportunities for Amstrad to produce new products. An early example is the combined receiver-decoder on which the company was busy working in the first few months of 1990.

Neither does Rupert Murdoch seem likely to forget Alan Sugar as the latter predicts. Murdoch believes that Amstrad's ability to produce large numbers of satellite dishes cheaply, when everyone else was dithering, fully justified his early generous assessment of Sugar: 'He's very entrepreneurial, a tremendous worker. In negotiations, he's a master of detail. I found he came to the point, to the bottom line very quickly. He's been very straight with me – totally. He's kept his word on everything.'

Murdoch was not ruffled by the fact that Amstrad was going through a bad patch in other areas of its business immediately before and after Sky's launch: 'It didn't affect his behaviour towards me at all. Why should it? I had a bad year myself,' says Murdoch.

Indeed, while Murdoch believes that Sugar's share of the dish market is bound to decline, he envisages working with Amstrad on future projects: 'No one knows where electronic communications are leading to. I'm sure there will be lots of other electronic devices, whether they're all built together into one entertainment centre, whether there are printers out of the side of high-definition television. Who knows? But I'd be surprised if there aren't other things we do with him.'

Amstrad participated in one of the most expensive entertainment and consumer electronics projects ever undertaken in Europe without exposing itself to great risk. Sugar ensured that others bore the expense of launching the satellite broadcasting revolution, ducking out of B.S.B. as soon as it became clear that continuing involvement would demand considerable cash with little immediate payback. In the case of Sky, the television company itself shouldered most of the risk. Sky was losing up to £3.5 million a week in 1989, cutting swathes through the profits of News Corporation, Murdoch's Australian holding company. By contrast Amstrad has made money out of satellite broadcasting, even if not on the scale that Sugar had initially hoped.

Meanwhile Sugar watched B.S.B.'s progress with growing incredulity, thankful that he was not still a shareholder. Late in 1989, having already secured £423.6 million from its backers, B.S.B. proposed to raise a further £900 million from a mixture of new shares and loans. Sugar could not understand why the City, which was so alert to every blip in Amstrad's trading performance, could blithely stand by while B.S.B. raised such vast sums for a venture which would take years to make a profit.

The City's treatment of B.S.B. exasperated Sugar. By the end of 1989 it was driving him to the brink of becoming a patron of the arts, as he explains:

If the City allows them to pour all that money into that thing, then how they've got the audacity and cheek to complain about

Amstrad, I don't know. If they pour all that money into B.S.B., that will be the last straw as far as I'm concerned. I'm going to commission a sculptor to produce a great big cement statue of a pair of fingers sticking in the air. And I'm going to hire a contractor to erect the statue in some street right in the middle of the City.

· 16 ·

The Year of Disaster

The thirty City analysts trapped in Liverpool Street station one day in mid-February 1989 were becoming impatient. They had fought through the tunnels and trenches which criss-crossed London's main East-line terminus; they had defied the lack of signposts to find platform 16; but there, in the filthy cavern which passed for a platform, they had to admit defeat. 'No idea,' was the porters' shrugged reply to queries about the whereabouts of a train to Brentwood.

The well-bred complaints mounted as the minutes ticked away. 'Why can't Sugar come to London like everyone else?' the analysts muttered, nervously fingering their portable phones.

For a dreadful moment, it looked as though the City was going to miss its taste of blood. That morning Amstrad had declared the first fall in profits in its history as a public company. Pre-tax profits for the six months to the end of 1988 – the most important half of Amstrad's trading year – were down 16 per cent to £75.3 million on sales almost unchanged at £348.8 million. The analysts who followed Amstrad for their stockbroking firms would have walked to its Brentwood headquarters to hear Alan Sugar's explanation.

Such a drastic remedy proved unnecessary, because British Rail eventually managed to find a train. After the thirty-minute journey, the analysts swept into Amstrad's headquarters, expecting to discover the company flat on its back. They actually found a chastened but chirpy Alan Sugar; Amstrad's chairman was relaxed, funny and remarkably honest when presenting the company's results.

'We can't afford a launch any more,' Sugar replied to a query about plans for new product launches. Unprompted, he told the gathering that he had wanted to call the financial year 1988–89 'the year of disaster', but his advisers had vetoed the idea. Just in case anyone had missed the point, Sugar repeated it: this is Amstrad's year of disaster.

The directors had dissected the factors behind the decline in profits. 'We've been critical of ourselves. We've tried to understand what went wrong, so we can decide what to do,' Malcolm Miller, Amstrad's marketing director, told the analysts.

The essence of the problem was that Amstrad had not been able to make enough of its products in the second half of 1988. This left a pool of demand which the company could not satisfy. Amstrad had worked out the precise gap between the machines it had at its disposal and those it had expected to make, figures which Miller reeled off to the analysts: 90,000 business computers worth £57 million in sales – lost; 45,000 home computers worth £8 million – lost; 22,000 printers worth £3 million – lost; 190,000 audio units worth £22 million – lost; and £24 million worth of video recorders – lost.

In total, Amstrad had lost £114 million in sales because it did not have the machines to meet demand. If those sales had been booked, then half-year profits would have been over £100 million, comfortably sufficient to maintain the company's upwards momentum.

But this explanation, thorough as it was, immediately prompted other questions: Why had Amstrad lost these products? What had gone wrong with Amstrad's famed manufacturing flexibility? Sugar identified two different kinds of reasons when he pointed to 'a chain of events, some outside our control and others the results of our own mistakes'.

Consider, first, the events which were largely outside Amstrad's control. The most important external pressure with which Sugar grappled in 1988 was one of the periodic bouts of shortage in the supply of memory chips.

Memory chips – and especially devices known as DRAMs (dynamic random access memories) – are one of the most important components in a computer. Needed in increasingly large volumes to store the data processed by a computer, memory chips are the work-horses of the semiconductor family. Unfortunately, their supply tends to swing unpredictably from feast to famine and back to feast again with almost biblical savagery.

The memory chip and computer cycles feed off one another in a perpetual loop. Exceptional demand for computers results in strong orders for memory chips; the order books of DRAM manufacturers fill up, delivery times lengthen and the price of the chips rises; escalating chip costs force computer manufacturers to put up their prices, which depresses the demand for computers just as chip manufacturers are churning out DRAMs at maximum volume; the market becomes flooded with memory chips, leading to a cut in DRAM prices; this in turn feeds through into cheaper computers and a resurgence of exceptional demand for computers. And so on, potentially *ad infinitum*.

Towards the end of 1987, the DRAM cycle was exacerbated by political tension between Japan and the United States. In the first half of the 1980s, Japanese companies had identified control of the memory chip market as a key to world leadership in electronics. Huge Japanese investments in memory chip capacity allowed them to offer DRAMs to American and European computer manufacturers at rock-bottom prices, sweeping aside the competition in the process.

The United States Government watched the Japanese assault with growing alarm. Semiconductors are the modern equivalent of steel: they are fundamental to a country's ability to wage successful warfare. No military computer can run without memory chips. Goaded by cries from American semiconductor makers that their Japanese competitors were dumping DRAMs at unfair prices, the United States pressured Japan into signing a semiconductor trade pact in 1986.

The pact forced Japanese chip manufacturers to increase

DRAM prices. They also throttled back their production, cutting the supply of memory chips from Japan. Unfortunately, their drive to dominate the world memory markets had been so successful that few chip makers were left outside Japan to fill the resulting supply gap. The large U.S. semiconductor companies had dropped out of DRAMs one by one: by the end of 1987 there were just two significant American companies selling DRAMs on the open market, Texas Instruments and Micron Technology. Japan had already captured more than 70 per cent of world DRAM supply.

Superimposed on the normal memory chip cycle, the U.S.-Japan semiconductor pact had a dramatic effect. DRAM supplies dried up and prices rose. Alan Sugar told the analysts gathered at Amstrad headquarters that he smelt the first whiff of an impending DRAM crisis in December 1987: 'But I hoped it was going to go away. I'd heard that story before. You get this waffle all day long in the semiconductor industry. I didn't believe it.'

This time, however, it was not waffle. Amstrad was used to paying about $2.50 for a 256k DRAM (a chip capable of storing 256,000 pieces of information). By April 1988, the company was paying $5 as a matter of course. 'In some cases, we were so desperate, we paid $8 or $10 – blackmail prices,' said Sugar.

Between June and October 1988, he spent most of his time on the DRAM problem. He searched the globe for alternative supplies, which meant scouring the Far East and the United States, since Europe was an also-ran in the memory chip race. A type of memory chip from the 256k family, known as a 64k by 4 chip, was vital to the graphics capabilities of Amstrad's computers; yet this chip was in particularly short supply: 'That was the bloodline,' Sugar told the analysts.

Spiralling DRAM prices slashed into Amstrad's profit margins. Each PC1512 personal computer contains 18 256k DRAMs, while each PC1640 contains 30 of the chips. DRAMs at $5 each would gouge $75 from Amstrad's profit on a PC1640, while a $10 DRAM did unthinkable things to the company's bottom line. Sugar reacted by stopping production of the cheaper single disk drive versions of the PC1512 and PC1640 and cutting back on output of home computers, concentrating the company's efforts on the higher priced computers in its ranges. This – together with some price rises on Amstrad's products – helped to stem the erosion of its margins. But overall sales and hence profits were inevitably hit. Sugar reckoned that half the £57 million of lost sales in business computers stemmed from the DRAM shortage.

Of course, Amstrad was not alone in having to face the DRAM crisis. Two weeks before the analysts trekked out to Brentwood, Apple Computer warned that its profits would fall by 29 per cent in the first quarter of 1989 because it had been forced to buy memory chips on the spot market at three times the normal prices. On the very day that Amstrad released its results, star German computer company Nixdorf disclosed that it would be slashing its dividend by 60 per cent to compensate for higher chip costs.

But the fact that others were in the same boat was scant comfort for Sugar who felt the need for a stable solution as DRAM shortages worsened in 1988. All the signs pointed to a prolonged crisis. In July 1988, Dataquest, the respected U.S.-based electronics research organization, estimated that only 20 million 256k DRAMs would be available in Europe in 1988 – 5 million pieces short of the likely demand for these components. Even companies buying in large volumes were having to pay up to $15 for a 256k DRAM on the spot market. By September the memory chip famine was compounding delays of the launch of Amstrad's newest computer range, the PC2000 series.

Sugar decided to reduce Amstrad's vulnerability to this seesawing market by seeking a stable source of memory chips. In October 1988, Amstrad announced that it had paid £45 million for a 9 per cent stake in Micron Technology, then one of the two remaining U.S. producers of memory chips for the open market. The deal gave Amstrad the right to buy up to 9 per cent of the Idaho-based company's output of chips, although it was free to source from elsewhere if it could find cheaper supplies. Amstrad had also signed a one-year contract for DRAM supplies with Samsung, the South Korean electronics giant. 'There is no good done by sitting around, whimpering and hoping that the problem will come right. We had to be decisive and do something,' Sugar said at the time.

Amstrad's stake in Micron was hailed as 'a smart investment' by a U.S. investment analyst in the *Wall Street Journal*, but Sugar was later to regret the decision. Soon after the Amstrad-Micron link was announced, memory chip supply improved. Factories in the Far East began to churn out the new, more powerful one megabit DRAM – capable of storing one million pieces of information. By the end of 1989, the world was flooded with one-megabit DRAMs and memory prices collapsed. Whereas in 1988 one megabit DRAMs had cost as much as $30 each, by August 1989 they were selling in the United States for about $14.50, while by the start of 1990 they were trading for as little as $6.50. Micron's stock price reflected the market for one of its main products. By October 1989, the value of Amstrad's stake in Micron had fallen by about 30 per cent after allowing for currency movements.

Buying the stake in Micron was not 'the greatest deal I've ever done', Sugar acknowledged at the analysts' meeting in February 1989. Yet it did serve to extricate Amstrad from the nightmare of the DRAM shortage. The episode also taught Sugar that Amstrad had become too big to risk similar exposure to the volatile semiconductor market in future: by the end of 1989, he had deals in place with five chip manufacturers – Micron, Samsung, Siemens, Texas Instruments and Toshiba – which secured Amstrad's future supply of memory chips.

The DRAM shortage fed through into fewer sales of Amstrad's computers, which in turn cut demand for the company's printers. Its other product lines were affected by their own problems, again largely outside Amstrad's control. When labour shortages in the feverish Taiwanese economy disrupted the flow of audio products from Amstrad's sub-contractor there, Avnet International, Sugar summoned Avnet's top man from Taiwan to see him in Brentwood and extracted promises that the volumes would improve. But they did not, and Amstrad did not have the number of audio units it wanted for the 1988 Christmas season. The experience reinforced Sugar's growing determination to cut Amstrad's dependence on Taiwan, which was rapidly becoming a high-cost production centre. In Hong Kong, Stan Randall negotiated a supply of low technology audio parts from factories in Communist China, while some of Amstrad's Taiwanese sub-contractors moved their production facilities to Malaysia with its encouragement.

Meanwhile, the Funai-Amstrad joint venture to make video recorders in Shoeburyness was proving 'a disaster', in the words of an Amstrad insider. One view within the company was that the Funai side – which was in charge of running the plant – put less effort into the operation than if it had been a wholly owned subsidiary. Whether or not this was true, the fact was that the factory was slow to build up production. Amstrad hoped to be sourcing all its video recorders from Shoeburyness by the second half of 1988, but as the year progressed it became increasingly apparent that it would not have the volume of video recorders it needed for the Christmas season.

Although Amstrad piled the pressure on Funai, the result was less than happy, as Jim Rice – the Amstrad director with day-to-day oversight of the joint venture – describes:

> The problem was, as always with Amstrad, it was never quick enough. We decided we wanted more product out of the factory, but the Japanese in their normal Japanese way were doing things properly. So along we came and said, 'Sorry, this is not good enough, we need more, and if you can't produce more we will put our own people in to do so.' That's what we did and we began to produce more and more. But then we began to suffer from quality problems, labour problems, all sorts of things – because we were trying to rush it.

The episode confirmed Sugar's distaste for direct involvement in manufacturing. Once the 1988 Christmas season was over, Amstrad's chairman sat down and said to his team, 'I've had enough of Funai-Amstrad. It's chaos. We don't want to be involved with it any longer. Tell Funai they can take over the entire plant.' Amstrad set about selling its 49 per cent share in the joint venture to Funai, although it still planned to take large volumes of video recorders from them.

The DRAM crisis, labour shortages in Taiwan and Funai's delays in building up production – these were factors largely outside Amstrad's control. But two further problems underlay the company's profit dip, for which only Amstrad was to blame.

The first was poor management of the ending of the West German distribution agreement with Schneider. When Amstrad severed its relations with Schneider, it left the German company with large volumes of Amstrad computers badged with the Schneider name, which Schneider proceeded to sell in Germany at discounted prices just as Amstrad was trying to build up its subsidiary there. The Schneider stock undercut Amstrad's own computers, disrupting Amstrad's re-launch in West Germany in 1988. Sugar accepted full responsibility for this uncharacteristic mistake: 'We accept in hindsight that this situation was self-inflicted. We clearly should have taken control of their inventory.'

The second problem – lengthy delays in introducing its new flagship PC2000 computer range – was even more serious. Amstrad had originally hoped to launch the line in February 1988, but Sugar was not able to unveil it until September. Moreover, he then had to disclose that the two most expensive computers in the range – the PC2286 and PC2386 – would not be available in the U.K. until December 1988. Sugar blamed these delays on the memory chip shortage.

The December deadline came and went with still no sign of the PC2286 and PC2386. By then it was apparent that problems within Amstrad were holding up the computers – problems which accounted for the other half of the £57 million of lost business computer revenue. At the mid-February meeting, Malcolm Miller told the analysts that shipping of the PC2386 would begin on that very day, but the PC2286 would not be shipped until March. As a result, the new series would not be fully available in the U.K. until May or June. Faults had been discovered in one of the chips which had been specially designed for the PC2000 range. Repeating its standard trick, Amstrad had tried to cram a large number of functions on to a couple of chips, but the PC2000 range contained more sophisticated technology than anything previously attempted by the company. In retrospect, Sugar concluded that it would have been better to spread the functions around more chips, even if this had added to the cost of the computers. 'It was our own fault. We were being very, very adventurous. We took on more than we could chew,' he admitted to the analysts.

However, Sugar's performance in front of the analysts demonstrated a willingness to recognize mistakes and to tackle them – a quality not always abundantly present in business stars who have faltered. He answered with characteristic frankness the half-dozen or so long-time Amstrad followers whose well-informed questions punctuated the meeting. Yet they were also alarmed by the message that they should not expect any improvement during the second half of financial year 1988–89. Immediately after the meeting the analysts picked up their mobile phones to telephone in downgrades of their profit forecasts. Amstrad's share price plunged 22½p – a 12 per cent fall during the day – before coming to rest at 158½p, wiping £57 million off the value of Sugar's own holding in the company.

The analysts relaxed on the train back to London, preparing themselves for another encounter with Liverpool Street station. One of the youngest of the group, who had sat silent throughout the meeting with Amstrad, turned to his neighbour and asked sotto voce, 'What exactly is a microchip? Where would I buy one if I wanted one?'

*

Worse was to come. When he addressed the City analysts in February 1989, Sugar had hoped that the year of disaster was drawing to a close. But some problems had not even broken. In the next nine months, he was forced by the gathering storm clouds to confront the most serious crisis in his business career. The year of disaster turned into 18 months.

The discovery of technical hitches in the PC2000 series was the most obvious hammer blow. These computers represented a renewed assault on the corporate computer market. The top end of the range – the PC2286 and PC2386 – used the Intel 80286 and 80386 microprocessors, more powerful semiconductors than

Amstrad had designed around before; yet, as one would expect from the company, prices were pitched below the competition.

Even so, the price tickets on the range showed just how far Amstrad had moved beyond the truck-driver-and-his-wife. The PC2086 cost £599 to £1,349; the PC2286 cost £999 to £1,699; and the PC2386 cost £2,649 to £2,999. By Amstrad's previous standards, the top end of the range consisted of big ticket items.

As powerful personal computers aimed squarely at the business market, the PC2000 range had an abundance of features for computer reviewers to crawl over. Inevitably, the reviews were more mixed than in the case of Amstrad's earlier and simpler machines; a reviewer tended to like some features, but not others. Nonetheless, the balance of comment in the main computer magazines was favourable when the series was announced in September 1988.

Personal Computer World, for example, described the range as 'competitive if not breathtaking', adding that 'no corners have been cut in performance to get down to a price'. Reviewing the entry level PC2086 machine, *PC User* commented, 'Amstrads are no longer the cheapest machines on the block – and competition from quality clones has never been tougher.' Yet still it concluded, 'With its distinctive, space age look, good graphics and competitive price, the PC2086 deserves to do well – both among small businesses and among corporates looking for a low-cost intelligent work station.'

In short, the message from the technical reviews was that Amstrad had every chance of success with its PC2000 series. These cautiously optimistic projections were thrown into turmoil – first by the delayed launch of the top end of the range and then by persistent rumours of 15–20 per cent fault rates among the PC2286 and PC2386 once they saw the light of day. Unlike the overheating rumours which had previously beset the PC1512, Amstrad accepted that something was wrong: the problem was in the circuit which controlled the hard disk drive. 'Unfortunately it turned out to be not something that could be fixed with a bit of external tweaking – there was something seriously wrong with the core logic inside the disk controller chip that we had designed,' Sugar said.

In April 1989, Sugar suspended shipments of the PC2286 and PC2386. In a bid to sort out the problem, he called in Western Digital, the U.S. company which is the world's largest supplier of hard disk drives. Western Digital replaced the faulty chip with a standard one of its own; not prepared to take any chances this time, Sugar asked P. & P. – a leading computer distributor – to evaluate its work.

Sugar disclosed the problem and the actions taken to correct it in late July 1989. He ordered the recall of the entire 7,000 hard drive models in stock and signed up Dictaphone, a maintenance company, to replace users' faulty machines. All PC2286 and PC2386 users were given a free one-year on-site maintenance contract with Dictaphone. 'A dramatic gesture is now needed to overcome any suggestion that this company is failing in its duty to supply reliable products,' Sugar stated at the time.

Amstrad won many plaudits for the speed and honesty with which it handled the fault. Sugar estimated the cost of modifying each recalled machine at £75, but added that tumbling memory chip prices more than compensated for the extra cost. He displayed his most confident face after announcing the recall: 'I'm now convinced the machines work perfectly, and we're geared up for the bomb-blast Amstrad effect, creating a mass market as we have done so successfully before.'

Yet worrying questions were raised both within and outside the company by this episode. Why was Amstrad so late in launching the PC2000 series in the first place? And why did it fail to discover the hard disk fault until after it had launched this flagship range? The simple answer is that Amstrad's small design team was overwhelmed by the magnitude of the task.

Once more MEJ Electronics had been asked to design the basic circuitry for the PC2000 series. Adopting the approach which had worked so well with previous Amstrad computer designs, Mej set about embodying many of the computers' features into the gate arrays. One example among many was the cache (a form of sophisticated memory) controller for the PC2386, which Amstrad could have bought off the shelf from Intel, the U.S.-based electronics company; but that would have been expensive, so Mej had to design a cache controller from scratch which could be embodied in a gate array. Looking back, Mej believes it was wrong not to think through more clearly the work entailed by the large number of innovations which were being built into the design: 'We threw a number of ideas into the specification which we thought were good ideas without looking hard at the implications for the development work. It was a mistake for us to put them in without sitting down and investigating how much additional effort they were going to take – and asking Amstrad whether it was worth putting in such a feature or better to stick to the original timescale.'

Mej's company had expanded to about half-a-dozen people by mid-1987, when it began to work on the PC2000, but this was still a tiny team to tackle such a large project. Effectively they were designing two distinct computers, since the PC2286 and PC2386 were based on two different, albeit related microprocessors – the Intel 80286 and 80386. The task was an order of magnitude more complex than the designers' previous work for Amstrad. Mej soon found himself designing a 10,000-gate array; by contrast, the gate array in Amstrad's first computer, the CPC464, had only 1,159 gates. Knee-deep in design work, Mej was unable to keep a sufficiently close eye on the overall project: 'What I should have been doing was overseeing the project and spotting the fact that we were putting additional stuff into the specification. I should then have asked Amstrad whether we should do that and extend the timescales and development costs, or not, as they preferred. It's easy to say with hindsight.'

Mej's team fell badly behind schedule, but still managed to produce innovative, cost-effective designs which worked. MEJ Electronics was not to blame for the fault in the disk drive controller which forced Sugar to recall some of the range, since Amstrad had given the job of designing the controller to another company.

For some time Amstrad had felt that it was unwise for a company of its size to be entirely dependent for its basic circuitry designs on Mej's small outfit. This was one reason for establishing its own research and development team under Richard Altwasser, the former Sinclair designer. But Amstrad decided to go one further with the PC2000 project and parcel the work out to more than one group of hardware design sub-contractors. Mej recognized the logic of Amstrad's decision. Indeed, this was shown to be right in principle by the fact that MEJ Electronics struggled with the remaining workload. There was only one snag: Amstrad was unfortunate in its choice of designers for the hard disk controller.

It was obvious to both Roland Perry, Amstrad's technical manager, and Mej that the hard disk design was inadequate when it was delivered in the summer of 1988. But by then Perry and Mej were engaged in the frantic effort to remove the bugs from the work of Mej's team. In retrospect, Perry believes that radical decisions at that stage might still have avoided the later need for the recall: 'We should have ditched the disk controller round about September 1988 and not tried to debug it. We should have simply recognized that it was in too ropey a state too near to production. We could have bought in a disk controller at that stage.'

MEJ Electronics had shown itself to be a first-rate electronics design team, but by the end of the 1980s it was too small to bear the full strain of Amstrad's demands. Roland Perry had only half-a-dozen engineers working for him in his role as Amstrad's project manager, again probably too few to oversee the development of complex products like the PC2000 range. In addition, by the end of 1989 Amstrad had another 15–20 engineers in its own research and development department under Richard Altwasser – insufficient to cope comfortably with the stream of products that Amstrad was designing in-house such as its home computers, a fax machine, a portable personal computer, modems and combined television-video products. Some outsiders said that the strain on the in-house team showed through in the poor results of some of the projects under its wing. One example was the PC200 games computer, a flop launched in September 1988 which computer journalist Guy Kewney damned in *PC Dealer* as 'Sugar's Christmas turkey'.

The most damaging aspect of the botched PC2000 launch was its impact on Amstrad's standing in the corporate market. The company continued to insist that many purchasers of its computers were 'corporate' in the sense that they were VAT-registered – small businesses and independent professionals. This was undoubtedly true. Many small businesses and other organizations which had been introduced to computing through Amstrad's word processors or earlier personal computer ranges were ready to upgrade to more powerful machines; they were still attracted by the traditional Amstrad value-for-money virtues embodied in the PC2000 series.

Yet there is no doubt that Amstrad intended the PC2000 series to straddle both the small business and large corporate markets. Many large companies used Amstrad's previous top end computer, the PC1640, at least somewhere in their operations, and Amstrad wanted to build on that base. Peter Horrell – the Amstrad account director at advertising agency Delaney, Fletcher, Delaney – directed the PC2000 adverts more squarely at computer professionals: 'The target audience was much more the data processing manager, the chief executive, the senior manager generally – people who would influence purchasing decisions on personal computers in larger companies.'

Amstrad believed that it could use its successful mass market techniques in selling to large companies. Malcolm Miller, company marketing director, explains:

We don't ever want to have the sort of prestige that I.B.M. has and trade simply on that. We're not trying to create this aura round us which others further up the market have. What we want is a good solid image, with excellent features at an attractive price – product you feel secure and familiar with and you can buy from lots of outlets. We are trying to be innovative with designs, techniques and with price; and I think that will always be our philosophy – to bring the price of say the 386 down, add more features, advertise it more aggressively, rather than cloud the product in an exclusive image and put it on a pedestal.

Advertising executive Greg Delaney set out to reflect this strategy in the PC2000 campaign:

> Part of what Amstrad has always done is to educate people as to the advantages of new technology and what it can do for them. As Amstrad sells to corporate buyers and data processing managers, they will get the back-up material and the technical information they need. But our advertising will still try to reduce the impenetrable to the comprehensible. We're in the business of explaining benefits. For example: faster processors – what do they mean? As a philosophy, we have not stuffed our trade press ads full of impenetrable jargon. We may have included more detail, but we haven't allowed it to overwhelm the ad. You see lots of ads in the trade press that are written by boffins. Let's hope that Amstrad never goes down that route, because it would be a disaster. You would land up with boffin talking to boffin. But Amstrad is a mass market company.

Unfortunately, the problems which beset the PC2000 were likely to be particularly offputting to big corporate buyers. These cautious souls, who spend large amounts of other people's money, are the customers most likely to be scared by the PC2000's technical glitches and least likely to focus primarily on price.

As Alan Sugar never tired of pointing out, it is true that Amstrad was not alone in suffering technical problems. Inordinate delays in launching new machines and the discovery of faults necessitating recalls are endemic in the computer world. Tales emerge from within ultra-secretive I.B.M. of printers under development for seven years, while the PCjr – I.B.M.'s only serious attempt to capture the low end of the personal computer market – was a flop of the first order. Launched in November 1983, 350,000 PCjrs were still in stock when I.B.M. stopped making the machine seven months later.

The difference is, of course, that it would take an earthquake to shift I.B.M. from the corporate market, whereas Amstrad was still fighting to establish credibility there. The problems with the PC2000 series threatened to destroy the image which Amstrad had developed thanks to its previous computer triumphs – the image of a producer of machines which were both cost-effective and reliable. People began to remember that by origin Amstrad was a low end audio company.

Some computer commentators resurrected an old chestnut – whether Amstrad's whole approach was unsuited to the big corporate market. One of the biggest clichés in the modern computer industry is that it is smart to be a systems seller, not a box shifter. Most money is made not by simply selling standalone computers to corporate customers, but also by setting up computer networks and supplying the software, training and so on that the networks require. Amstrad was not by inclination an obvious player in the systems game. 'Amstrad is just not the sort of company that can sell systems to corporate users,' said John Lettice, editor of computer magazine *Microscope*, shortly after the PC2000 recall.

This scepticism about Amstrad's chances in the corporate market did not seem to be shared by some of its main rivals. I.B.M. was not alone in cutting the prices of its nearest equivalent machines after the launch of the PC2000 series. Yet the flow of sceptical comment on Amstrad's ambitions in the corporate market continued. This was particularly badly timed for Amstrad, because it came after a period of turbulence in its relationships with other important groups of customers. Many observers believed that its deteriorating customer relations were contributing to Amstrad's problems.

Throughout 1988 complaints had mounted from some computer dealers about the back-up service available from Amstrad. Some alleged that it was next to impossible to get spare parts in good time from the company's service organization, which was then based in Amstrad's Shoeburyness warehousing and factory complex. Looking back Jim Rice, the responsible Amstrad director, accepts the thrust of these criticisms: 'We had a disaster throughout much of 1988 with spare parts. There wasn't enough room given over to it, so there was little spare stock and no systems to make sure we never ran out. We ended up not being able to supply spare parts to our dealer base and getting a really bad reputation because of it.'

Simultaneously, relationships with some of Amstrad's biggest high street customers were becoming fraught. Alan Sugar has always had a view of retailers which is vigorous even by his standards. He sees them simply as conduits passing on Amstrad's goods to the end user:

> Our attitude is that we are doing the retailer a favour, and if one won't buy, we'll find another who will. That means our products must, by definition, be winners and that's how we go about designing them. Then we take a view on our markets and decide how many we can sell. . . . We'll go to a retailer and tell him here it is, it'll be out on such and such a date, there'll only be this many available at the beginning, and it's up to you.

This was said by Sugar in late 1985, at the height of his first word-processor triumph, but it was a view which he changed little over the years. A salesman to his fingertips, he understood the psychological importance of what happens when a customer walks into a shop. His insistence on launching products in ranges flowed from this understanding:

> You get people hooked on computers by leading in with a £399 price. They walk into a store and they ask for the £399 Amstrad computer, and then they see another next to it. So they enquire from the salesman:
>
> > Customer: 'What's that one?'
> > Salesman: 'Ah, that's the one with a hard disk drive and a colour monitor.'
> > Customer: 'Oh. What does that mean?'
> > Salesman: 'Well, a hard disk drive means that it holds more storage. You know, it's got 20 megabytes. You don't have to keep putting floppy disks in it. A colour screen means you can have bar charts on it. Bla-de-bla-de-bla.'
> > Customer: 'Oh. How much is that, then?'
> > Salesman: 'Well, that's a grand.'

He's probably a business customer buying it anyway. For someone in a small business, the difference between £400 and £1,000 is nothing. While everyone thought we were selling a cheap £399 clone, the reality was we sold more high ticket products. That was our marketing ploy. It happened also in the days of our audio equipment. We used to have a £199 Tower Unit with a single cassette deck, and we would only sell it to dealers who would stock both our models – the one with the double deck as well. The idea was to put them side by side, the £199 next to the £260 one. It's absolutely normal for a member of the public to be lured to a shop by Amstrad's advertising of a £199 lead-in price point and to say, 'I want that Amstrad. Oh, what's this next to it?' The salesman Dixonizes them. He jumps on them and says, 'Well, that one is the all-singing, all-dancing, more powerful, double cassette, bla-de-bla.' Nine times out of ten the customer will pay it off on credit, which works out at £1 a month more for the better one. The truth is we advertise the target lead-in price products, knowing that they will often end up being the lower sales.

Sugar grasped the importance of what went on in the shop, yet he also believed there was little which a retailer could do to alter the law of the market: if Amstrad's products are good, they will sell; if not, they won't.

Amstrad's boss drew the implication that he should never expect any favours from a retailer:

If they've got confidence in a product, they will stack it up, pile it high, spend a bit of their own advertising on it. If it starts to sell like wildfire, they'll be on the phone telling me what a wonderful job they're doing for me and how lucky we are to have them as a customer. And if the product drops dead and it doesn't sell, they'll tell me that their warehouses are full of refrigerators and, sorry, they can't book my van in today. They'll tell me not to worry, because they know they gave me an order and they will take the stuff eventually. And then they will renege on the order. That is the life of a retailer.

Indeed, Sugar formed the view that there was no point in trusting a retailer's written order:

> The thing about dealing with a retailer is that their order basically is not worth the paper it is written on – unless you don't ever want to deal with them again. If you need an ongoing relationship with a retailer, there is no way you can start banging your hands on the table and insisting on the letter of the law. If they don't want to take the stuff, they won't take it. The only way you could make them take it is to sue. You'd win in court, but you'd never sell them another thing. It's the law of survival.

Sugar carried this bleakly realistic view into his dealings with his retail customers. As one large retailer says: 'He had a really positive dislike of his customers. He was unsympathetic to the retailers' need. The relationship between the buyers and himself became very strained. He was aggressive to a quite mind-boggling degree. Yet it was all inconsistent with the rather nice guy you would speak to ten minutes later, when the venom had been poured out and gone.'

A more common complaint was that Sugar's staff imitated him. The disadvantage of the tight Amstrad culture was that it encouraged those caught up in it to copy the ways of their leader. But Sugar is inimitable, as one customer explains: 'They imitated his aggressiveness, the worst side of his character, without having the intelligence to know that beneath it was a very perceptive, humorous, intelligent guy.'

William Poel, who worked for Amstrad when the PCW8256 was taking the market by storm, develops this point:

> Amstrad's sales organization forgot some of the basic tenets of salesmanship. Like one day you will find yourself short of customers and you will have to revisit those you told to bugger off six months ago. They failed to operate their position of monopoly in a benign fashion, and were seen as taking a malevolent glee in telling people to get stuffed. In the office,

there was a kind of school-room camaraderie and people tended to get carried away, whereas Mr Sugar knew where to draw the line in dealing with a customer. When he told a customer to stuff himself, there was a twinkle in his eye and the customer knew it was all part of the game. The underlings were unable to apply Sugar's perception and wit and kept blundering through, saying 'bugger off' without a twinkle in their eye. Customers could take any amount of abuse from Mr Sugar, but they couldn't take *any* amount of abuse from the second stringers.

During the second half of the 1980s, Amstrad's most important U.K. customer was Dixons. The market leader in electrical goods, Dixons had spearheaded the introduction of many items which would not have been found in Britain's high streets at the start of the decade – video recorders, telephones, video cameras, Walkmans. The Amstrad-Dixons partnership was crucial in encouraging the rapid take-up of word processing and personal computing by the British public.

In the aftermath of the PCW8256 and PC1512 triumphs, relations between Amstrad and Dixons became very close. Stanley Kalms, Dixons chairman, had demonstrated entrepreneurial flair on a par with Sugar's in forging the world's largest electrical goods retailers out of the modest passport photograph business he inherited from his Polish-born father shortly after the Second World War. In his way, he could be almost as abrasive as Sugar.

Negotiations between the two companies assumed great importance for both sides. Alan Sugar would invariably lead for Amstrad, sitting across the table from Dixons' top executives, Kalms and Mark Souhami, the managing director. The flavour of the occasions is described by a participant:

These were not meetings where you would want to talk unless you had to because you would get ripped apart – by your own side if not by the other. They were fighting over volume and percentage points for hours and hours. It was like playing chess, only more aggressive. Sugar would say, 'You're going to take more than effing 2,000 pieces and you're going to pay more than this effing price.' Kalms and Souhami would come back at him. They're professionals and they can take the verbal. But they weren't as rude as him. I always wondered whether that was part of his act, because he gained a tremendous advantage whenever he broke someone's hard-nosed business exterior. And then he would come up with all the reasons and all the angles why they should take more of his equipment. It was like role playing between Sugar and Kalms. They would slag each other off for a couple of hours, then step outside the room and laugh.

Since Dixons was taking larger volumes than other Amstrad customers, it inevitably squeezed a better deal out of the company. 'Alan had enormous margins. His profitability was quite phenomenal. And if anyone was able to negotiate well, he was. But sure we got better margins,' Stanley Kalms says.

Uniquely among Amstrad customers, Dixons had an arrangement whereby it would pick up and pay for Amstrad's goods in the Far East; it was buying in such large volumes that it could justify hiring its own ships. One person privy to Amstrad's deals with Dixons estimates that the latter was able to cut 5 per cent off Amstrad's prices on the back of this arrangement – more than enough to cover the freight and insurance costs which fell on Dixons through paying for its own shipping: 'Dixons 5 per cent advantage meant a lot. That's a lot. And that was one reason why they managed to rip everyone else apart.'

After the PC1512 was established in 1987, however, both Amstrad and Dixons began to feel uneasy about their mutual dependence. Dixons searched for other personal computer manufacturers so that it could diversify its sources of computers. This caused growing friction between Amstrad and Dixons, which briefly surfaced in March 1988 when the retail chain decided to back a new personal computer from Olivetti, the Italian electronics company. Sugar publicly attacked Olivetti's computer, the PC1, which in the event did not sell well.

For his part, Sugar realized how important Dixons was to Amstrad's success in the U.K. Back in Amstrad headquarters, he would jump on staff he heard criticizing the retail group: 'Don't slag off Dixons. They're our bread and butter in the U.K. Don't you ever forget it,' he would say. Yet he was also aware of the parallel with Amstrad's over-dependence on Comet at the end of the 1970s. If Dixons had a bad year, then Amstrad's British sales would inevitably suffer.

Amstrad began a drive to build up sales through independent computer dealers. Not only would they reduce Amstrad's dependence on Dixons, they also offered a better entry into the corporate market than Dixons. The wisdom of this strategy became apparent in 1989, when Dixons did indeed have a bad year, with profits tumbling in the wake of the slowdown in consumer spending. Some retail analysts argued that Dixons had been slow to adapt to new retailing trends in the second half of the 1980s; the uncertainty hanging over the company was compounded at the end of 1989 when it was the subject of a hostile bid by Kingfisher, the group which owns Woolworth and Comet.

All in all, in 1988 and 1989 Amstrad was faced with the need either to establish or to repair its relationships with at least some customers in three of its important customer groupings – large companies, independent dealers and the high street retailers. This was a challenge as critical as more measurable problems such as the shortage of memory chips.

The final blow which fell on Amstrad in 1989 was the growing realization that matters were badly awry in some of its new overseas subsidiaries. Sugar had been used to running the company's overseas operations on a loose rein, a strategy which in the mid-1980s paid dividends with its success in France and Spain. Occasionally he intervened, as in 1985 when he pressured Marion Vannier (head of Amstrad France) to drop the crocodile mascot which she had placed at the centre of Amstrad's adverts in France. Amstrad's French crocodile was at times a cheeky chappie with a big grin, and on occasion a suave *gentilhomme* in sunglasses. The crocodile had helped Amstrad to achieve wide brand recognition in France – particularly during the successful launch of the CPC464 home computer – much as the petrol company Esso is known in Britain through its tiger mascot. But Sugar became convinced that crocodiles' bad associations were contributing to the relative failure of the PCW8256 word processor in France, so Vannier reluctantly agreed to drop it and copy the anti-typewriter campaign adopted by Amstrad in Britain. French sales of the PCW8256 did not improve, however.

Nevertheless, for the most part Sugar had left Vannier and José Luis Dominguez (Amstrad's agent in Spain) to their own devices. He maintained this policy after 1987 when Amstrad bought Indescomp, Dominguez' company, appointed the Spaniard as head of Amstrad Spain and established subsidiaries in a range of other countries including West Germany and the United States. Sugar believed that if he chose entrepreneurial heads for his overseas subsidiaries, they should be allowed to run their own show. Looking back, he regards this attitude as too lax: 'We allowed people too much of a free ship. We were blinded by the people who claimed to be entrepreneurs in their markets.'

Spain and West Germany were the main problem areas. The number of Amstrad employees and related costs increased rapidly in Spain and, worse still, the Spanish subsidiary failed to sell the large amount of stock it ordered. Inventories mounted in West Germany too, where the new Amstrad subsidiary misread the competitive strengths of Amstrad's computers and pitched its products at the top end of the market.

By the middle of 1989, Sugar realized he would have to step in and remove Dominguez. When the Spaniard resigned as executive head of Amstrad Spain in October, he sold back to Amstrad 4.5 million of its shares – more than half the share element of the original purchase price of Indescomp – for £1 in total. He also paid Amstrad £7 million for Amstrad Spain's headquarters situated in an expensive part of Madrid, while Amstrad Spain moved into a warehouse complex that was being built for it on the outskirts of Madrid.

Sugar removed the head of the West German subsidiary and also of the operation in the United States, where again mounting expenses were not justified by the level of sales. The actions he took were swift and surgical, but they could not prevent the huge increase in stock which emerged as one of the main financial pressures on Amstrad in the second half of 1989.

The problems facing Amstrad combined to make 1989 the worst year in the company's history as a public company. On 20 April, Amstrad issued a warning as the London Stock Exchange opened that delays in introducing the PC2000 series would reduce profits for 1988–89 below market expectations. The market responded by wiping more than 15 per cent off Amstrad's value: its shares plummeted 21½p to 119½p. A string of gloomy circulars from City analysts over the next few months continued to push the share price down and by mid-October – a week before the announcement of the 1988–89 results – Amstrad's stock had fallen to 57p.

The extent of Amstrad's difficulties was revealed later in October when Sugar announced 1988–89 pre-tax profits down 52 per cent to £76.6 million, on sales barely changed at £626.3 million. The accounts highlighted the geographical black spots: in Spain sales were down a quarter to £81 million, while in Germany they had fallen 4 per cent to £28.7 million. But perhaps two figures buried in the small print painted the clearest picture of Amstrad's troubles. The weak control over foreign subsidiaries, coupled with the PC2000 problems, had generated massive inventories: stocks now stood at £325 million, roughly six months' production. This stock mountain, together with the costs of buying the stake in Micron and establishing Amstrad's overseas subsidiaries, had reversed Amstrad's traditionally cash positive position: the company now had borrowings of more than £100 million.

The one aggressive note which Sugar sounded was to warn that he might take Amstrad private again if the City did not improve the rating of its shares. Sugar announced that at the annual general meeting in December Amstrad's board would seek authority to buy its own shares. He pointed out that since the share price valued Amstrad at less than its net asset value, there seemed little point in being a public company: 'If the market does not like us as a company and reflects that in its share price, and if the share price remains low, we will buy it,' he said.

Sugar also declared in his chairman's statement that his immediate priority would be to sort out the inventories and the cash position: 'The short-term objective of getting the company in good shape will focus on securing its existing assets and its good brand name position in the market. It may be a bitter pill to swallow for some investors, since this policy may be at the expense of chasing profits, but [it] will bring back the good liquidity which has been a feature of Amstrad's balance sheet for the last three years.'

This clear warning that higher profits were not on the cards in the short term prompted Amstrad's shares to fall another 4p. Its shares stood at 47p, less than a quarter of the price they had commanded a year previously.

In December, about 200 small shareholders gathered for the A.G.M. at the Tower Hotel down river from the City. The adulation which many seemed to feel for Sugar was still apparent, but it was overlaid by an air of anxiety about what would happen to Amstrad. Sugar was in emollient mood, more or less ruling out the idea of taking Amstrad private in the immediate future. When asked by a shareholder whether he intended to emulate Richard Branson, who had recently re-privatized his company Virgin, he replied, 'I'm not going up in a balloon, if that's what you mean.'

Indeed, Sugar got as close as he had ever done to complimenting the City: 'Contrary to what people think, I and my directors can't complain about being a public company,' he said. 'Rebuilding our image in the stock market means rebuilding our profits. Nothing else.'

· 17 ·

Controlling the Tiger

One common thread ran through almost all the problems which beset Amstrad in 1988 and 1989 – the lack of management control. In the mid-1980s, as Lord Young put it, Alan Sugar had been riding a tiger; the tiger was growth on a scale that few of the world's businesses ever succeed in generating. During the first seven years of the 1980s, the annual increase in Amstrad's sales was never less than 56 per cent and usually substantially more. In 1986 it was already a large company, yet sales grew by an astonishing 123 per cent. Sugar's overwhelming priority had been to feed the tiger, creating the conditions which would continue to fuel this heady expansion. In Amstrad's case, this meant devising innovative new products and marketing them aggressively.

However, there comes a point in the life of every fast-growing business when a change of gear is forced on the founding entrepreneur. A crisis – costs running ahead of sales, an over-optimistic build-up of stocks, a downturn in the market – brings home to the founder what in retrospect appears so obvious: that elementary management controls, the good housekeeping rules of a business, have been neglected during the years of heroic growth. The priority then switches from feeding the tiger to controlling it, and the task is urgent: failure could result in the tiger devouring the business.

The moment when it becomes time to control the tiger varies from business to business and from entrepreneur to entrepreneur.

Some companies never reach this point, because they do not go through a phase of hyper-growth. Other entrepreneurs, by contrast feel themselves losing control almost as soon as their company has pulled itself above the massed ranks of small businesses.

There appears to be some kind of pattern among that tiny handful of businesses which become world-class operations from a standing start. Often they threaten to run out of control when they pass through the $1 billion turnover barrier, and it was at about this point that Amstrad stumbled. This was also the stage, for example, at which Apple Computer lurched into crisis in 1983–84 – a crisis which sent shock waves through the entrepreneurial spawning ground of Silicon Valley. Apple had to confront huge inventories, its first-ever quarterly loss and the unpleasant necessity of dismissing a fifth of its work-force.

The entrepreneur who created the company often turns out to be the wrong person to cope with the crisis. Feeding and controlling the tiger require different skills. The founding entrepreneur is often a charismatic visionary driven by the need to develop one or two brilliant product ideas – a character unsuited to the tedious business of bringing the company under control. The task of dealing with Apple's 1983–84 crisis fell to a method man from corporate America, John Sculley, a former president of Pepsi-Cola. Sculley could not stabilize Apple until he had forced out Apple's co-founder, Steve Jobs, the guru who had fired the company's early growth with his vision of a computer on every desk.

Alan Sugar is not an entrepreneur in the Steve Jobs mould; he has never been driven by the vision of introducing a particular product or set of products. On the contrary, from his first encounters with the City in the late 1970s he made plain his overwhelming priorities: profit and the bottom line. Launching new products is of course essential to Amstrad's ability to turn a profit, and Amstrad's most successful product ideas have flowed from Sugar's brain. But the Tower System, the word processor and the I.B.M.-clone were means to an end – profits. And Sugar is equally obsessed with the other aspects of business which contribute to that end. Sorting through the rushes of Amstrad's latest advert, managing Amstrad's currency requirements, screwing the last few cents out of Japanese sub-contractors, negotiating an order for half-a-million satellite dishes with Rupert Murdoch – he is as ready to turn his mind to these as to thinking about the company's next blockbuster product.

Unlike many entrepreneurs who are driven by one or two product ideas, Amstrad's boss is an unusually complete business man. Yes, he thinks about new Amstrad products, but he then applies his mind to every step which is needed to bring them to market, from component purchasing through to the advertising campaign. In addition he has a quality which is essential for controlling the tiger – a lack of sentiment.

When the crisis struck, one of Sugar's first decisions was to pull Amstrad out of the audio market. By 1989 sales of audio equipment were contributing only £21.4 million to Amstrad's turnover, less than 4 per cent of the total. The crucial factor in prompting his decision was that audio was a low profit margin business compared with Amstrad's other lines. No matter that audio was the business which sustained Amstrad through its first 15 years: abandon it. 'There's no margin left in the product and we're just wasting our time chasing it,' Sugar said when announcing the decision in October 1989.

Pulling out of audio meant closing Amstrad's assembly line in Shoeburyness, with a loss of about 150 jobs. Sugar also closed Amstrad's printer factory in Hong Kong and slashed staff numbers there. By the end of 1989 Amstrad employed 71 people in Hong Kong, down from a peak of 428 a year earlier. He also cut back the numbers of Amstrad employees in other subsidiaries such as Spain and the United States.

Cost-cutting was the way to pare back Amstrad's overheads, but Sugar also needed to shift the large stocks which the company had built up. Amstrad lopped off between £500 and £700 from the price of the PC2286 and PC2386 computers when it announced the recall of faulty machines in July 1989, helping to restore the price competitiveness which had been lost during the delays in introducing the machines. In September, during the run-up to Christmas, Amstrad launched a promotion and price-cutting package which included offering a free portable phone with every Amstrad portable computer. The company boasted at the time: 'You could say this is almost a free portable computer with your mobile phone.'

Amstrad also slashed the price of its camcorder, the video camera which it had launched in May 1988. Although the £499 price tag on this machine was lower than anything else on the market, it had never sold in the volumes Amstrad had hoped. Some observers said this was because Amstrad's low-cost machine did not have enough features and lacked facilities such as zoom; others argued that most British consumers seemed uninterested in the camcorder concept, unlike their counterparts in the United States and Japan. Whatever the reasons, Sugar decided it was time to shift Amstrad's large camcorder stocks, even if it meant disposing of them at or below cost. Dixons sold Amstrad camcorders at £299 each during the Christmas season: 'At this price, it's selling like hot cakes. We're making a good margin. He's not,' stated Stanley Kalms, Dixons' chairman.

These are examples of the immediate measures which Sugar took to pull the company round. Yet securing Amstrad's future also meant changing its operating methods, a point he fully recognized. At the end of 1989 he said:

> There was no financial policing within the organization. There was no proper forecasting of overseas subsidiaries. There was no proper inventory control. There was no real head-count plan. It was a phenomenon brought about by the fact that we had been hot-selling the products. As many as we made, we could sell them. When you're on that kind of gi-normous growth trend, you tend to forget about the instinctive things you used to worry about in a much smaller business – looking after the pennies, making sure you're not spending too much, that your expenses are not running away, that you're not employing too many.

But cutting out unwanted functions had to go hand-in-hand with expanding facets of Amstrad which were under-resourced. 'We've had extravagance in certain areas and we've been stingy in others,' noted Sugar.

Sugar identified senior management as one area for expansion, since the company was too large to be run with its previous ultra-lean organization: 'We have had such phenomenal growth over the past few years that we are still operating with a management team you would expect to be running a company a fraction of our size,' he told the *Sunday Times* in April 1989.

In October Amstrad appointed two new directors-designate to its board: Peter Thoms, who joined the company as group finance director from Gillette; and John Benjamin, who joined as group manufacturing director from the Mars Corporation. Just as important as this influx of resources at top level was the reorganization which it facilitated. Amstrad's top management was given a group responsibility, while a distinct subsidiary to handle day-to-day U.K. operations was created for the first time. Barry Young – previously in charge of Amstrad's distribution to independent retailers – was made U.K. managing director. This structure was belated recognition of the fact that Britain accounted for less than 50 per cent of Amstrad's sales. It also replicated the organization that is standard in many large multinationals: national operating subsidiaries reporting to group headquarters. Simultaneously, Sugar boosted the management in Amstrad's overseas subsidiaries, ensuring that each had a strong financial and a strong marketing manager. 'The flamboyance of the salesman will be balanced by the financial half,' he said.

This structure allowed greater oversight of its overseas subsidiaries by Amstrad's headquarters, which the 1989 crisis had shown to be necessary. Amstrad's top management, including Sugar, devoted one day each week exclusively to a particular foreign subsidiary. They also adopted what they called a 'one month on, one month off' routine: one month, Amstrad's top team would travel to, say, Paris to discuss progress at its French subsidiary; the next month, Amstrad France's senior executives would travel to Brentwood to do likewise. The discussions range widely over sales, stock levels, expenses, advertising, successes, failures, promotions and so on. Thus, when a foreign subsidiary says that it wants to order so many thousand of the PC2000 series, it now has to justify this decision before the group team. Malcolm Miller, group marketing director, describes this as the 'third stage' of Amstrad's evolution:

> The first stage was to get up and run with the product and sell it in great volume. The second stage was becoming more professional, with more marketing skills, more people, more product development. The third stage – now that Amstrad has got so big – is to try to understand our business globally. We need to have a broad global overview of all our products and of how we manage them. We cannot just pick out a single product, run with it and forget everything else any longer.

Hand-in-hand with this more settled structure went a strengthening of financial controls within Amstrad. Ken Ashcroft, who became corporate finance director in the new organization, had predicted at the time when the overseas subsidiaries were established that they would severely affect the company's cash position. This was because Amstrad would not receive payment for its products until much later in their journey to market. For example, when Amstrad's business in Spain was run through the distributor, Indescomp, it was paid for an order as soon as it was placed by Indescomp. But once Amstrad Spain was established, Amstrad was not paid for sales in Spain until payments were received from its customers in Spain, most of whom would expect a period of credit. Therefore Amstrad had to finance its stock while it was on the high seas, in Spanish warehouses and on retailers' shelves.

Although Ashcroft had anticipated the impact of this change on Amstrad's cash flow, no one had anticipated the implication of lax controls over the subsidiaries for its inventory levels. Information on inventory levels existed within Amstrad, but it was neither integrated into a broad picture of worldwide stock positions nor considered an essential tool for top management. When Sugar realized in early 1989 what was amiss in the subsidiaries, he put much greater emphasis on inventory reporting, as Ashcroft describes: 'Alan realized that unless he got stuck in himself and made it clear to everyone in the group that inventory control was the name of the game, we were going to lose all our cash. So he sent out some massive signals to the managing directors, telling them that he was starting to focus on inventory totals. He told them, "We must have cash control. Therefore we must have inventory reporting."'

By the middle of 1989, Ashcroft had put an integrated stock reporting system on to Amstrad's worldwide internal computer network. Management in Hong Kong or Dallas would regularly key its stock position into the computer. This information could then be read in both unit and value terms by Amstrad headquarters. '1989 was the year in which information in the company was really addressed. People have realized that they have to run the company by numbers. Alan's not a paper man; he doesn't like reports. But he now likes inventory reports and he's learned to use them,' says Ashcroft.

To ensure tight control of stock, Amstrad's chairman appointed a group inventory controller, Gordon Marshall. Sugar removed the power to order new products from the operating subsidiaries and invested it in a troika at Amstrad headquarters: Malcolm Miller (marketing), John Benjamin (manufacturing) and Gordon Marshall (inventory). The company also centred its Continental distribution network on two warehouses in Rotterdam and Hamburg, which allowed it to switch goods between countries more flexibly as demand dictated. 'We're centralizing our distribution. We're not having inventory sitting in ten damn countries all over the world,' Sugar said.

He increased the company's research and development staff, placing a special emphasis on testing and checking facilities in a bid to avoid any repeat of the PC2000 problems. 'The difference between our procedures now and what they were is the difference between light and day. We now have a qualification process in place. Every piece of software will be tested thoroughly before it is shipped.'

Sugar stressed that Amstrad was now carrying out 'all the mundane and boring tasks that you have to do in a high technology business. Anyone in the computer industry reading this will say,

"It's boring. It's what all companies should do." Well, we're doing it now.'

Sugar was importing into Amstrad the 'boring' systems which most big multinationals would expect to have as a matter of course, yet the crisis also prompted changes in core areas of the firm's strategy.

One of these concerned manufacturing. Sugar had begun to move some manufacturing requirements from the Far East to Europe when the European Commission tightened the anti-dumping screw in the second half of the 1980s. The Funai-Amstrad joint venture in video recorders at Shoeburyness was a response to this pressure. It was not a stunning success and Sugar contemplated the prospect of moving even more manufacturing to Europe with little enthusiasm. In 1988 he confided in Arnold Weinstock, managing director of the General Electric Company, that he could see little alternative to reducing his dependence on foreign sources of supply. He asked whether G.E.C. would be able to make some of Amstrad's new PC2000 series.

In February 1989 Amstrad announced that up to 20 per cent of Amstrad's PC2000 range – about 10,000 a month – would be made at a Scottish plant in Kirkcaldy, Fife. The deal saved the factory, which employed 700 workers, from closure. At that stage the plant was jointly run by G.E.C. and Plessey, Lord Weinstock having personally intervened with Plessey to ensure that the Amstrad contract went to Kirkcaldy.

Sugar was impressed by the fact that it would cost Amstrad only about £10 more per machine to have his computers made in Scotland than in the Far East. Most of the cost of sophisticated computers like those in the PC2000 range lies in their components, not in the labour used to assemble them, so the traditional cheap labour advantages of the Far East were becoming less relevant. For example, in February 1989 each PC2386 computer contained $720 worth of DRAMs. Moreover, more of the key components for a computer were now available nearer to home. By 1989 Amstrad could buy DRAMs in Europe, because Texas Instruments and Siemens had begun to manufacture them there, which allowed Amstrad to avoid the 18 per cent duty imposed at the time by the

European Commission on chips imported from the United States or the Far East.

The cost advantage of manufacturing sophisticated computers in the Far East was therefore rapidly disappearing, while producing in Europe yielded two inestimable benefits. First, it avoided the risk of anti-dumping actions. Second, it shortened Amstrad's supply lines. Now that Amstrad needed to manufacture in such large volumes, it was a major disadvantage to have huge stocks on the high seas for a couple of months travelling between the Far East and European ports. Such long lines of supply constrained Amstrad's ability to respond flexibly to changes in customer demand – one of the main contributory factors to the increase in stocks in 1989. 'It physically costs us £10 more [to make the computers in Scotland], but in practical terms it costs us a lot less grief and aggravation,' Sugar said.

He followed the G.E.C. deal by announcing in November 1989 that S.T.C., another large British electronics group, would make Amstrad's fax machines at its factory in Northern Ireland. In February 1990, Sugar said that while 25 per cent of Amstrad's goods were now made in the European Community and 75 per cent elsewhere, he envisaged moving rapidly to a ratio of 60:40 in Europe's favour: 'The Far East has no advantage any more in computers, because in the past the most labour-intensive part was the building and testing of the main printed circuit board. Now with automation and modern surface mount technology, that does not require so much labour.'

But Sugar also indicated that British manufacturers would have to be sufficiently flexible to switch their production quickly so as to meet changes in customer demand:

We'll make more and more computers here in the U.K. But I will insist that the manufacturers become more flexible so that they can make the computers in whatever configuration is needed. The configurations are changing so much. One moment there's a mad demand for hard drive versions, then for single drive versions and then for double drive versions. You can never get it right.

Customer relations were the other core aspect of Amstrad's operations to receive attention when the problems emerged in 1988 and 1989. The company's customers had never been left to fend totally for themselves if a fault developed in their machines. Amstrad had a long-standing relationship with Dictaphone, a service organization, by which Dictaphone offered on-site repair contracts to any end user who wanted one. Most large corporate users of Amstrad computers buy their machines from big computer distributors, which typically have their own well-staffed repair and training organizations.

However Jim Rice, the responsible Amstrad director, had been keen throughout 1988 to improve Amstrad's service and spare parts organization. Painfully aware that the existing set-up in Shoeburyness was inadequate, he spent almost a year looking for a separate site for these functions. He finally bought a 111,000 square-ft building in Harlow, Essex. Amstrad occupied the Harlow premises in May 1989 and rapidly built up the work-force. 'There are still lots of things to be done, but we've got more people, more room, better systems and more spares. We don't have the same problems as we did in Shoeburyness, so we're able to give a much better service,' Rice says.

At the end of 1989, Amstrad had about twenty people at Harlow dedicated to answering telephone queries from end users. There were also separate lines for computer dealers, who are more likely to be seeking specific spare parts. Rice acknowledged that the Harlow operation was a departure from Amstrad's box-shifting culture: 'I see it as a very important aspect of our future strategy, and it's going to be developed much more than it currently is,' he stated.

Meanwhile, Amstrad had been taking steps to differentiate its product line. In May 1988 the company paid Swraj Paul's Caparo Industries £3.1 million for the Fidelity name, finally capturing a quarry which Sugar had first stalked in 1984. Since Paul had recently announced the decision to close Fidelity's West London factory, all that was left to acquire was the name, which Amstrad wanted in order to project its products under different brands. Fidelity (or Amstrad Fidelity, initially) would be reserved for the company's leisure products such as video recorders; Sinclair for home computers; and Amstrad for business computers and associated products such as printers. 'It's too much to expect the consumer to differentiate such a wide range of goods under one brand name,' Malcolm Miller said at the time.

Miller was working on a strategy to improve the ability of Amstrad's dealer network to handle the company's most sophisticated computers. In September 1988, Amstrad announced plans to divide the 3,000 computer dealers handling its products into two tiers. The top tier of about 1,000 dealers – to be called Advanced Systems Centres – would concentrate on the PC2000 series; this group would be required to dedicate a section of their showroom to the series and would also have to offer end users installation, testing, delivery and training services, an on-site maintenance contract and a technical hotline.

The appointment of Barry Young in October 1989 to be the managing director of Amstrad's new U.K. subsidiary also signalled a wish on the company's part to improve its customer relations. Young had previously headed Amstrad Distribution Limited (A.D.L.) – an operation designed to service the needs of the independent retailers – which is based in Stoke-on-Trent on the site of Lyons-Turner Enterprises, the wholesaler bought in 1984 when Amstrad made its first acquisition. During the three years he had been running it, Young had built up A.D.L. into a sophisticated and slick operation which supplied a range of services such as display material and training to the independent retailers. He was most proud of A.D.L.'s ability to offer a next-day delivery service for any order, however small, from a dealer anywhere in the U.K. A.D.L. claimed 99.7 per cent reliability for this service, which allowed the small retailers to keep their stock to a minimum. It required careful links between A.D.L.'s computer-based order-taking system and its huge warehouse, which daily despatched a constant stream of lorries to distribution depots all over Britain. In his new post as Amstrad's U.K. boss, Young said, he intended to inject this kind of customer consciousness into all Amstrad's British operations.

The first signs that Sugar's policies to turn Amstrad round were working came in February 1990, when the company announced profits of £30.1 million for the six months to December 1989. These results were way down on the £75.3 million achieved in the corresponding period of 1988, but well above what the City had been expecting. Sales actually increased 7.2 per cent to £373.7 million. Amstrad's revenues could have been even higher, since many of its computer lines were sold out before Christmas, but Sugar had not wanted to tempt fate by stockpiling even more inventory: 'It is evident and very encouraging that our brand image remains untarnished,' he said.

Sugar also reported on the introduction of more management controls into Amstrad: 'We now have in place good systems, and although they still have some way to go before we can claim perfection, I am confident that we are now able to "keep the score" without allowing too much bureaucracy to slow us down,' he wrote in his chairman's statement accompanying the half-year results.

The underlying fundamentals which most concerned the City were also encouraging. Sugar disclosed that borrowings had peaked at £114 million in September 1989, and would be down to zero by the end of February 1990, though this is traditionally a time of the year when the cash demands on Amstrad are not great. Stocks peaked at £335 million in September, and would be down a third by the end of February. The main remaining black spot was the very top end of Amstrad's range, the PC2386, where the company still had two years' worth of stock.

The decision to sell audio equipment, video recorders and camcorders at or below cost over the Christmas season had depressed Amstrad's profit margins. But the business was still making profits, which was more than could be said for many other companies in the computer industry.

The year 1989 was one of tumbling profits for computer companies throughout the world. Shares in Commodore of the U.S. plunged 20 per cent in June when it revealed that it was making losses. Wang Laboratories, another American computer company, was rescued by the banks in August after it had declared fourth-quarter losses of $375 million and stopped payments on some of its debts. In August, the founder and president of Norsk Data, a once high-flying Norwegian computer company, resigned after warning of heavy losses. Zenith of the U.S. disclosed that it was making heavy losses in October, just a few weeks after selling its computer arm to Groupe Bull of France. Also in October, Italy's Olivetti launched a rights issue after profits in its first half plunged 40 per cent. The chairman of Nixdorf of West Germany resigned in November after his company notched up losses of DM 465 million (£277 million) in the first nine months: shortly afterwards, Nixdorf was rescued by Siemens. The same month, shares in Compaq fell 16 per cent after the U.S. computer company issued a profit warning. December saw I.B.M. shed 10,000 jobs in the U.S., bringing the number of jobs lost in the American computer industry during the year to over 40,000. As Christmas approached, Apple Computer warned that its seasonal sales would be below expectations – a warning which was followed by a renewed bout of management restructuring.

In 1988–89, Sugar's 'year of disaster', Amstrad's profit margins fell to 12.2 per cent from the 25 per cent levels they had touched during the preceding years. Nevertheless, 12.2 per cent is a margin that many computer companies would be pleased to make in a *good* year. Over at G.E.C.'s headquarters in Stanhope Gate, Lord Weinstock had been watching Amstrad with interest: 'What's the disaster? He is still making money. Yet he's criticized as a failure. That's hardly fair.'

*

It is impossible to predict what will happen to Amstrad in the 1990s. Anyone who in 1980 had tried to forecast the company's fate over the following decade, including Alan Sugar himself, would have been wildly wrong.

One possibility is that Amstrad will stabilize at its present size and then grow steadily but unspectacularly from that base. It would hardly be a disgrace for one individual to have created a company with annual sales of over £500 million. Yet under this scenario, Amstrad's second decade as a public company would be less notable and exciting than its first.

Whether or not Amstrad resumes more vigorous growth will turn on its ability to recapture its innovative flair in developing new products. Sugar recognized this when presenting his half-year results in February 1990: 'No matter how many systems and controls the company has, it will live or die on its products and the manner in which we sell them.'

By the beginning of the 1990s it was no longer a question – as in the Amstrad of old – of looking simply for the one new blockbuster product. Amstrad was too big and entrenched in too many world markets to think like that any longer. What was required was a steady stream of products which could build on its existing position. The reorganization carried out by Sugar in 1989 was designed partly to channel more resources into product development, and also to allow him to devote more time to thinking about product ideas himself. As Amstrad entered the 1990s, it was working on new products right across its existing lines.

Yet having said that, it remained true that Amstrad would need another breakthrough like the word processor if it was to make a further great leap forward. No one inside or outside the company can possibly know whether this will happen; it is like asking whether Stephen Spielberg will continue to make good films.

Another possibility is that Amstrad will develop closer links with a large British manufacturing group as it gradually moves its manufacturing requirements back to Europe. Sugar is clear that he does not want Amstrad to become a manufacturer by itself: 'We will continue to go down the route of not actually manufacturing much ourselves. We will continue to dream up products, develop them, procure some of the major parts, but then get other people to make them for us. We will not actually have the factories and production lines.'

But if Amstrad sub-contracts more of its work to a handful of British groups, it is possible to envisage the company being drawn into a relationship with one of them – a relationship which could take weaker or stronger forms. G.E.C.'s Lord Weinstock, for one, is thinking along these lines, and says that G.E.C. and Amstrad may deepen their collaboration in future. In particular G.E.C. could provide the manufacturing and technical infrastructure which Amstrad lacks. This in turn could lead to some kind of closer relationship between the two companies: 'You could see a possibility where we together have a factory. He needs technological and production capability. And it's possible that we would provide that for him not as something separate, but as part of his business. It's possible that one of these days, something like that will happen.'

Weinstock sees a development like that as essential for Amstrad: 'If he wants to make the business stable, he will have to acquire assets. He will have to acquire infrastructure, which comes from having a manufacturing and a development capability. He needs more than just good ideas now and again. He knows that. He's learned a lot in the last couple of years.'

But Weinstock believes that any future discussions between G.E.C. and Amstrad would probably take a different form from the talks between the two companies in the mid-1980s: 'It's not impossible that we will come together with him in some way. But I think now, we would be more likely to concentrate on the things he does, so that we help him build up his business, rather than ask him to build up part of ours.'

An Amstrad-G.E.C. collaboration on these lines would provide G.E.C. with a launching pad into personal computers and consumer electronics, areas where it has been absent or weak. Weinstock says: 'He offers a possibility of another go. There are some technical developments coming along, like high-definition television. You can't tell what will happen. But I feel positive about that fellow.'

An Amstrad-G.E.C. joint venture is, of course, just one among many possibilities. Another, in theory, is that Alan Sugar will throw it all up, retire to his Florida holiday home and live on his ample private wealth. Somehow this seems the least likely outcome. Sugar is the type of person who quickly becomes bored stiff sitting by a pool. Even his private property dealing keeps only a small part of his brain engaged. The British business scene has not heard the last of Alan Sugar.

· 18 ·

Electric Warrior

As Amstrad entered the 1990s, Alan Sugar was able to look back on a decade of achievements. First – and dearest to his heart – was the extraordinary series of results reported by Amstrad in the second half of the 1980s.

Sugar had forged a company which regularly topped the league tables of business performance. In both 1987 and 1988, for example, Amstrad beat 250 leading British companies to first place in the *Sunday Times*/P-E Inbucon Business Index to emerge as Britain's most efficient company. The index measured companies against three indicators: profit margins, return on assets and value added. Similarly, a study of the five years to 1988 by James Morrell Associates, an independent research organization, found that Amstrad's productivity increases had outstripped those in 100 other top British companies.

Amstrad also shone when compared with international competitors. *Fortune* magazine reported that in 1987 only Cray Research, a company devoted to the specialist area of supercomputing, had a better return on sales out of the 71 computer and electronics companies in the *Fortune* list of 500 top U.S. corporations. Amstrad's profit margins were double those of Compaq, widely regarded as the most successful manufacturer of I.B.M.-compatible personal computers in the United States.

There is another way of assessing Sugar's achievements. Looking back, it is difficult to remember how few European businesses or households boasted personal computers in 1980; the handful of adventurous souls who had brought these new gadgets from the United States tended to treat them as amusing curiosities, rather than as serious business tools. At the start of the 1990s, by contrast, it was rare for businesses of any size in the more prosperous parts of Europe to lack a computer or word processor.

Sugar was at the forefront of that business and social revolution in large swathes of Europe, particularly in Britain, Spain and France. Amstrad transformed the word processor from a product whose price had been counted in thousands of pounds to one measured in hundreds. Sugar helped to democratize computing power, designing and manufacturing computers which were within the financial reach of every small business, voluntary organization or middle-class family. As a result, by the end of the 1980s in Britain he was on his way to achieving the ambition he had expressed twenty years earlier as a young man – to make Amstrad as famous a brand name as Hoover. Nearly everyone knew what was meant by saying that a document had been written 'on my Amstrad'.

In the process Sugar also made himself immensely rich, but the wealth he created did not flow to him alone. Amstrad left a trail of prosperity in its wake. The creation of the first mass personal computing market stimulated a range of subsidiary activities such as retailing, software writing, peripherals manufacturing and magazine publishing. Countless small businesses, owned by mini-Alan Sugars, prospered on the back of Amstrad.

The company's success might be dismissed as a phenomenon of the frothy economic boom of the years leading up to 1988. With the British economy expanding by almost 5 per cent a year in real terms, faster than any other industrial economy except Japan, how could Amstrad help but succeed?

Like any company which relies on sales in the high street, Amstrad was indeed affected by the economic downturn of the closing years of the 1980s. But to depict it as the creature of the Thatcher boom is to miss a deeper point. Amstrad had ridden out previous periods of economic turbulence, such as the deep recession in the early 1980s, almost unscathed. This is no accident; it reflects one of the defining features of Amstrad's product strategy – its drive to give value-for-money. When times are hard, a small business will not necessarily abandon plans to buy a computer; but it might lower its sights, cutting the amount of money it is prepared to spend and placing greater stress on value-for-money. That is the space occupied by Amstrad.

Sugar's wider relationship to the 1980s – the Thatcher decade – is also more complex than is at first apparent. In one sense, he is the archetypal Thatcherite entrepreneur. A man whose rise from nowhere coincided with the early years of Mrs Thatcher's administration, he embodied the meritocratic, anti-Establishment values which distinguished Mrs Thatcher's Government from its Conservative predecessors. His origins in one of the poorest parts of London fed his distaste for the traditional bastions of privilege. 'There's a new breed of person coming up – the likely lad. You see it in the City and everywhere. It's no longer Mr Heathcote-Smythe's son who's getting the jobs,' he said in 1988 to John Lloyd, the commentator who described Amstrad's chairman as an archetypal representative of a new ruling group, 'the Disestablishment'.

The 'Disestablishment' is marked by a reverence for the creative power of the market, even when its workings threaten traditional power centres. By that measure Sugar belongs firmly within its circle. His open contempt for the City, his reliance on the Far East for his products rather than on British industry, his decision to sell business computers in high street stores like Dixons – Amstrad's history is a tale of Sugar affronting and disrupting one entrenched business interest after another.

Sugar is quick to praise Mrs Thatcher for helping to shake up Britain. Yet he has such a cool view of the changes ushered in by the Conservative administration that it is difficult to brand him simply as a child of the 1980s. He contends that there is nothing to stop an entrepreneur in Britain and never has been. After all, he points out, many people (including Sugar himself) made plenty of money in the 1970s, supposedly the low point in the post-war history of British business: 'There were never any barriers for me. No form of bureaucracy ever held me back.' He adds, 'I never noticed any difference under Labour or Conservative,' thus dismissing one of the standard excuses advanced by British business for its poor performance in the 1970s.

What Sugar asks of government is to be left alone. It was the interfering nature of the European Commission's anti-dumping duties which affronted him as much as anything. In return, he will not bother government: the Funai-Amstrad joint venture in Shoeburyness was one of the very few examples of Japanese inward investment into Britain which did not seek government financial aid.

It made a good story for the media to bracket Sugar with a host of former Thatcherite business stars who had fallen or stumbled by the end of the 1980s: George Davies of Next, Tony Berry of Blue Arrow, the Saatchi brothers, Sir Phil Harris of Harris Queensway, Sir Terence Conran of Storehouse, the group which takes in Habitat . . . and Alan Sugar of Amstrad. Yet there were two major differences between him and many of his supposed companions in grief. First, he was still in full control of his company as the 1990s began. Second, there were signs that the immediate crisis facing Amstrad – the high level of stocks – was responding to treatment.

Indeed, Amstrad never followed many of the fashions which swept British business in the 1980s. It was a notable absentee from the game of expansion by acquisition which had underpinned the success of many of the fallen stars. Sugar was sceptical about the wisdom of radical diversification. Many outsiders were too blinded by the boldness of Amstrad's launches into new product lines to miss this cautious side of Sugar's character. But it also structured his early forays overseas, as well as his approach to the risky enterprise of satellite broadcasting: in both cases, he ensured that others bore the risks.

Sugar is irritated by attempts to define the 1980s as a decade of Thatcher-inspired entrepreneurs which might – literally and metaphorically – have come to an end: 'An entrepreneur, if there's such a thing, is a born schemer and thinker up of things. You can't have a decade of them coming to an end. It's like saying there's a decade of singers or artists coming to an end.'

Relaxed about the prospect of a change of political climate in the 1990s, Amstrad's boss points to the experience of President Mitterrand in France as evidence that a Labour government in Britain could not set the country on a radical new direction:

If you use France as a template, you can see that Mitterrand has recognized that the policies of the right have to be implemented. You can't suddenly tax the rich, or so-called rich, much more heavily, because everybody is basically rich now. There's no such thing as the ordinary British worker any more. Everybody wants their colour TVs, their microwaves and their cars. The Left cannot be as our fathers would remember it in the old days. If the Labour Government comes in, their policies will have to be virtually the same.

Sugar's business strategy was not a creation of the 1980s. Everything distinctive about Amstrad – its flexible approach to manufacturing, its insistence on designing simple products which would appeal to a broad sweep of consumers, its creation of a mass market through undercutting the competition on price – was already present in the Amstrad of the 1970s, the small audio company unknown to most people.

The features which have distinguished Amstrad have remained constant; so too have the criticisms of it as a business phenomenon. Perhaps the most powerful is the charge that Sugar has done little for the British economy because almost all his company's products have been manufactured in the Far East.

An easy response to this would be to point to the copies of the £25 million and £48 million cheques made out from Amstrad to the Inland Revenue which hang in Sugar's office – a fraction of the wealth which has flowed into the Exchequer as a result of his activities. Lord Young, the former Trade and Industry Secretary, puts Sugar's attitude on manufacturing into context: 'Manufacturing wealth is not the be-all and end-all of life. It's wealth creation that counts. That's sometimes done by manufacturing and sometimes done by service sector and other activities. Alan Sugar has enabled the British people to buy goods at better value than they would have otherwise. The more his computers are spread widely, the more they create wealth.'

Critics of Amstrad's manufacturing policy have failed to understand the modern structure of British, and indeed European, industry. The company could not have survived, let alone flourished, if Sugar had tried to meet all its manufacturing needs in Britain. His early experience with the box of components badged by British electronics firms, but made in Japan, brought home to him that many electronic parts were not available at reasonable prices outside the Far East. Although the efficiency of the British components industry improved dramatically in the 1980s, he still had to look elsewhere for key components for his computers. DRAM memory chips, for example, were not made in any quantities in Europe for most of the decade.

By the end of the 1980s, many of the long-established names on the British electronics scene had scaled back their manufacturing in Britain, other than in protected high cost markets such as defence. Thorn E.M.I. had all but abandoned electronics manufacturing. Racal was concentrating on service activities such as communications. ICL relied on Fujitsu of Japan to supply the integrated circuits which lay at the heart of its 'British' computers. Ferranti closed its main civil computer manufacturing plant near Manchester, accelerating the flight of the British computer industry from hardware to software. Apricot sold its computer manufacturing division to Japan's Mitsubishi, leaving it to concentrate on software and services.

Sugar was distinctive in his early recognition of the trend towards global manufacturing. One of the first entrepreneurs in Europe to understand the implications of the manufacturing revolution in the 1960s and 1970s in countries like Japan, he realized that it would be impossible to compete in the low end of markets such as audio unless he manufactured in the Far East. This conviction was reinforced by his admiration for Japanese attention to detail, a quality he prizes highly. 'When the Japanese don't like the colour of something,' he is fond of saying, 'they don't say they want it a little more whitish, as a British company might.

They send you a colour card with 15 shades of white and specify exactly which they want. Then they make sure they get it.'

But, unlike many European executives, he was not blinded by Japanese manufacturing prowess. He detected weaknesses in the Japanese, as he made clear on two separate occasions in 1988: 'The Japanese are a programmed people. If the Japanese ever become flexible, we'd all be dead.' And again: 'The Japanese will not dominate computers the way they dominate hi-fi. . . . They have no flair. All of the originality comes from Britain or America.'

Flexibility and flair: these were the two qualities which helped to give Sugar and Amstrad a competitive edge – even over the Japanese. They were evident in Sugar's innovative approach to the design of Amstrad's products, and to the technology embodied in them.

Many industry experts failed to understand the nature of Amstrad's innovations. They were fixated on the notion that innovation flowed exclusively from fundamental developments in basic components such as microprocessors, rather than from thinking through novel product designs. Underlying this attitude is a prejudice which is contradicted by virtually the entire history of post-war British industry: the prejudice that it is easier to design products which will sell in large volumes than to make fundamentally new scientific or technological breakthroughs.

Amstrad's boss earned the derision of computer buffs because he designed his early computers around a ten-year-old microprocessor. In turn, he poured scorn on the industry's techno-babble by declaring his willingness to design his computers around an elastic band as long as it did the job. And it *was* the job which was so innovative: Sugar made products cheaply enough to create the first European mass market in business computers. Radical innovations in both product design and technology were necessary to deliver these low costs. Sugar's hallmark was cutting out unnecessary functions and using a common set of components for those that remained. An identical design philosophy can be detected in the decisions to run all the elements of the Tower Unit from a common power supply, and to run the word processor from a customized gate array chip.

Also innovative when it came to marketing, Sugar presented his goods as capable of doing the straightforward things which people like himself would want – because that was what they had been designed to do. If that meant selling business computers in the high street, for example, then so be it. In an age of specialization, he had the gift of being able to think simply. In an era of increasing product sophistication, he demystified the markets he entered. In the midst of an upsurge in niche retailing, Sugar catered for the mass market.

In its practice Amstrad anticipated by over a decade some of the theories which kept management gurus and industry pundits in well-paid employment in the late 1980s. They noticed that some of the most efficient companies were sub-contracting many of their activities, leaving only the central management and control functions in-house. A whole theory of 'core' and 'peripheral' business activities was built around this observation, but it was a policy which Amstrad had adopted since the mid-1970s. Sugar saw it as the best means to maintain Amstrad's flexibility – and flexibility is in turn fundamental to the overriding goal of generating profits, as he describes:

We're a very profit-oriented company and the best way to make profits is to be active in an area where no one else is. As soon as you show the way, you create competition and competition means margin erosion. And as soon as margins are eroded, it's time to say 'Sayonara'. We moved out of 14″ colour televisions, car stereos and CB radios years ago. We moved out of audio even though it served us well, because it had come to the point where we could not make money out of the damn thing any more. So it was just a waste of time. You've got to recognize when you're no longer the king of the castle in a certain product area because everyone and his brother has jumped on the band-waggon. When you wake up on a Monday morning, nobody anywhere in the world owes you a living. The minute someone offers a lower price or a better service, you will be dropped like a hot brick. As long as you recognize that and don't expect any kind of loyalty or relationship, you can't go too far wrong.

Flexibility is ingrained in Sugar because from the age of 21 he has been engaged in consumer electronics, one of the most competitive businesses in the world. Its defining features – high volumes and tight margins – force companies into a never-ending race to create new products. A hot seller one year is old news the next. In the computer industry in the 1990s, this competitive dance will be driven by the incredible speed of development of the underlying semiconductor technology. Chip product cycles are down to three years, with each new generation of chips typically an order more powerful than its predecessor. In 1980, for example, the standard memory chip was not capable of storing the information contained on the page of a book. By 1990, the industry was introducing a memory chip capable of storing the whole book and was already laying plans for a new chip 16 times more powerful.

These advances will generate radically improved products in personal computing, telecommunications, fax machines, broadcasting, cameras, video recorders – and no doubt in areas as yet unimagined. But entrepreneurs will have to be flexible and fast moving to take advantage of such dazzling developments.

Alan Sugar has that flexibility and speed of reaction. He learnt it not in a business school or out of a textbook, but in the back streets of London trading a motley assortment of electronic goods as a young man. That experience honed the fighting qualities acquired during his upbringing in the East End. In creating Amstrad, he had to battle against the keepers of conventional wisdom in the City, the media, the European Commission, the established electronics giants and almost any other group which crossed his path. Sugar did not suffer fools at all. When he thought people were wrong he let them know, irrespective of their standing. Many returned the compliment by predicting that he would fall flat on his face. Proving them wrong is one of the main forces driving him forward.

AMSTRAD'S RECORD BEFORE FLOTATION

	1970	1971	1972	1973	1974	1975–76*	1977	1978	1979
Turnover (£000)	99.6	207.5	726	1327	1689	3594	4033	4469	5978
Exports (£000)	—	—	—	142	492	656	381	960	1461
Pre-tax profits (£000)	2	24	99	194	176	354	548	650	908

Key Ratios

	1970	1971	1972	1973	1974	1975–76*	1977	1978	1979
Turnover growth	—	108%	250%	83%	27%	N/A	N/A	11%	34%
Pre-tax profit growth	—	1100%	313%	96%	(9%)	N/A	N/A	19%	52%
Pre-tax profit as a percentage of sales	2%	11.6%	13.6%	14.6%	10.4%	9.8%	13.6%	14.5%	15.2%

* 18 months

AMSTRAD'S RECORD AFTER FLOTATION

	1980	1981	1982	1983	1984	1985	1986	1987	1988	1989
Turnover (£m)	8.8	14.1	28.1	51.8	84.9	136.1	304.1	511.8	625.4	626.3
Exports (£m)	1.3	0.2	0.1	5.3	10.8	72.8	174.9	289.3	359.7	372.9
Pre-tax profit (£m)	1.4	2.4	4.8	8.0	9.1	20.2	75.3	135.7	160.4	76.6
Post-tax profit (£m)	1.1	1.2	2.6	5.3	5.7	14.0	52.0	93.4	105.1	51.1
Dividends pence/share (incl. tax credit)	0.06	0.11	0.14	0.16	0.19	0.27	0.49	0.97	1.87	1.87
Dividend cover (times)	5	3	6	10	8	14	27	24	14	6
Profit retained for the year (£m)	0.8	1.1	2.4	5.1	5.0	12.9	47.2	89.6	93.0	43.1
Earnings pence/ share after tax	0.22	0.26	0.54	1.12	1.17	2.57	9.54	17.13	18.99	9.01
Share capital and reserves (£m)	3.7	4.8	7.2	12.3	29.2	42.2	88.1	179.5	256.2	310.8

Key Ratios

	1980	1981	1982	1983	1984	1985	1986	1987	1988	1989
Turnover growth	56.5%	61.2%	98.6%	84.6%	64.0%	60.2%	123.5%	68.3%	22.2%	0.1%
Pre-tax profit growth	49.9%	74.6%	100.8%	68.6%	13.3%	121.1%	273.5%	80.3%	18.2%	(52.2%)
Pre-tax profit as a percentage of sales	15.5%	16.8%	17.0%	15.5%	10.7%	14.8%	24.8%	26.5%	25.6%	12.2%

Index

A B Electronic 189, 195

Acorn 116, 118, 135, 137, 138, 139, 141, 147, 164; foreign market 148, 261; products 119, 121, 125, 135, 148

A.E.I. 90

Aiwa 102

Alan Sugar Foundation 279

Alexander, Robert, Lord 106

Altwasser, Richard 199–203, 254, 318

Ambit International 115, 117, 122, 128, 130, 164–5

Amritraj, Vijay 278, 279

Amsoft 164–7

Amstrad: *see also* Sugar, Alan
  structure: foundation 40–3; expansion 57–8, 79–83, 96–7, 113, 199, 218–19, 251, 253–6, 331–2; management 8, 65, 83–92, 113, 238–41, 252, 325, 335–7, 342; advertising and marketing 4, 89–90, 96, 103, 177–80, 227–8, 247–8, 319–20; workforce 63–4, 85, 113, 186, 238; r and d 199–201, 318, 337;

Amsoft, Users' Club and servicing 164–5, 232, 316, 339–40; Amstrad Distribution Ltd 341
  business style: value for money 3–4, 69, 124, 127, 159, 165, 172–3, 245–7, 320–1, 347–8; flexibility 58, 101, 111, 187, 339, 350, 353; working methods 128, 238–41, 244–9, 254–6, 258–9; 'Amstrad effect' 4, 81, 175, 184, 185, 233, 316; reputed unreliability 7, 70–2, 228–31; recession periods 93, 96, 137–40
  finance: structure 9, 10, 83, 90, 107–8, 137, 186, 252–3, 336–7, 342; flotation 2, 8–15, 83, 90, 108; sales and profits (1970s) 10, 65, 79, 82, 93, 356; profits and share prices (1980–5) 93, 107–8, 109–10, 112, 137, 139–40, 212–13, 355; (1985–8) 182–4, 186, 218, 232–3, 235–6, 274, 355; (1988–9) 306–7, 314, 329–30, 342, 355; share options 6, 256–8

subsidiaries: France 65, 97, 99, 140–6,151–4, 156–9, 261, 273, 327–8, 335–6; Spain 140, 149–51, 154–9, 202, 261, 264, 273, 328, 335–6; USA 168, 222, 261–4, 273, 328, 335; West Germany 140, 222, 264–7, 273, 301–2, 313, 328; others 267, 273, 302

supply and manufacture: concepts 4, 7, 52, 113–14, 172–3, 224, 261, 312, 350–1, UK operations 62–4, 82, 293–4, 312, 333, 338–41, 98–100, 271–2, *see also* Shoeburyness plant; Japan 58–9, 61, 82, 131–2, 269–70, *see also* Funai; Hong Kong 82, 85, 98–9, 261, 267–70, 333; other Far East countries 61, 82, 100, 131, 177, 191, 268–70, 272, 311–12, 338–9; EC constraints 271–4, 294, 338

retailing: policy 97, 141, 322–4, 327; Comet link 50–3, 65–8, 71, 77–8, 83, 97, 216, 327; Rumbelows 71, 78, 95, 97, 137; Dixons 141, 180–2, 185, 231, 293, 298, 325–7, 334; Currys 33, 78, 95, 97, 216, 298; Wildings 185–6, 231; Woolworths 77, 78, 97; other outlets 97, 167, 231–2, 284–5, 327; Nigerian deal 59–61; BPI case 102–7

joint ventures: Sinclair deal 189–99; G.E.C. 208–13, 344–5; Funai 271, 272–3, 312–13, 338, 349; Micron 310–11; Thorn EMI 217–18; other acquisitions

213–16, 341; diversification 216–19

products: cigarette lighters and intercoms 40–1; audio equipment 44–7, 53–6, 61–2, 64, 69–70, 81–2, 102, 184, 333; Tower System 76–8, 82, 89–90, 96, 100, 124, 332; in-car radio and CB 81–2, 94–6, 100, 115; TV and video 100–1, 127, 184; CPC464 115–34, 140, 150–6, 168, 169, 183, 228, 317, 327; CPC664 168; CPC6128 156, 168–9, 178; PCW8256 (Joyce) and Ant 156, 161–4, 169–78, 183, 185–6, 222, 223, 265, 327–8; Sinclair range 191, 200–2, 203, 340–1; PC1512 159, 223–33, 309, 315; PC1640 234, 236, 242, 274, 309, 319; PCW9512 236, 274; PC200 318; PC2000 range 313–20, 329, 333, 337, 338, 342; software 118–20, 130–1, 133–4, 138, 150–1, 175, 184–5, 224–6; satellite TV 285–7, 290–305; camcorder 334, 342; facsimile machine 318, 339; portable computer 318, 334

Anglia Television 285
Apple, Aaron 21, 29
Apple, John 26–7
Apple Computer 135–6, 147, 220, 221, 225, 249–50, 310, 332, 343
Apricot 141, 261, 351
Argos 95
Ashcroft, Ken 195–6, 251–4, 257, 336–7
Astra 288, 301–2
Atari 134, 136, 147